529 & Education Savings Plans

T0243250

529 & Education Savings Plans

2nd Edition

by Margaret Atkins Munro EA

A Wiley Brand

529 & Education Savings Plans For Dummies®, 2nd Edition

Published by: **John Wiley & Sons, Inc.**, 111 River Street, Hoboken, NJ 07030-5774, www.wiley.com

Copyright © 2023 by John Wiley & Sons, Inc., Hoboken, New Jersey

Media and software compilation copyright © 2023 by John Wiley & Sons, Inc. All rights reserved.

Published simultaneously in Canada

For general information on our other products and services, please contact our Customer Care Department within the U.S. at 877-762-2974, outside the U.S. at 317-572-3993, or fax 317-572-4002. For technical support, please visit https://hub.wiley.com/community/support/dummies.

Wiley publishes in a variety of print and electronic formats and by print-on-demand. Some material included with standard print versions of this book may not be included in e-books or in print-on-demand. If this book refers to media such as a CD or DVD that is not included in the version you purchased, you may download this material at http://booksupport.wiley.com. For more information about Wiley products, visit www.wiley.com.

Library of Congress Control Number: 2023932630

ISBN 978-1-394-16033-4 (pbk); ISBN 978-1-394-16035-8 (ebk); ISBN 978-1-394-16034-1 (ebk)

Contents at a Glance

Table of Contents

Introduction

Welcome to *529 & Education Savings Plans For Dummies*, the practical reference for those who are thinking about and planning for all types of education in the future for themselves or those nearest and dearest to them and who want an explanation of all the options — pro and con — that can help them save for it.

Education. Whether you've had an abundance of it or feel that you're missing a few courses here and there, you've read all the information, looked at the charts and graphs, and know that people with the best educations land better jobs and earn better pay than those who don't. So, of course, because you want the very best for yourself and your family (you do — that's why you're reading this), you want everyone you know, including yourself, to have that opportunity.

That is until you look at the price tag. You're already paying for food, housing, and clothing (not to mention phone, cable, insurance, and everything else under the sun, including dog grooming) and maybe even stashing a little bit into your retirement plan. And then, you sneak a peek at the projected cost of private school or college for the year in which your student expects to begin. And just as you never look at the least wrinkled car in a car crash, your eye automatically drifts to the highest number on that chart of projected costs. And you begin to see stars.

There's no question: Education costs continue to soar, even when the rest of the economy stagnates, and this reality is not likely to change any time soon. Fortunately, everyone, including you, the various governments (federal and state), and the schools themselves, are in on this secret. Everyone can plan well in advance of that eventual first day of school — whether it's kindergarten or graduate school — and plot ways to get that child there and how to help you pay the bills when they come due. Consider this book to be your accomplice.

About This Book

The world of education savings plans is forever changing (or so it seems, as legislative leaders can't seem to resist continuously tweaking the laws). This is another way of saying that it also can be complicated and confusing for everyone, including professionals, financial planners, tax folks, and your local bank or brokerage.

In this one-size-fits-all world, the powers that be have recognized that all people don't save money the same way. Some save more, some save less, some can live with risk, and others can't tolerate any risk. Clearly, no two are alike, but you're all present or potential savers. Numerous options exist that make saving possible and desirable for everyone.

Piling savings option upon savings option has created opportunities for most people. But all the new options have also muddied the waters because choosing between Plan A and Plan B can be downright difficult when they seem so similar. So, many people may choose to opt out, admitting confusion and doing nothing because it's all so confusing, and no one wants to screw up a choice with so much riding on it.

And yet, it doesn't have to be that way. I'm here to tell you that it is possible to understand the costs associated with education, both right now and in the future. It's also possible to find ways to pay for those costs in the most advantageous manner for you, both from a personal and tax perspective. And you can't focus on the personal and ignore the tax implications, nor can you do the reverse. Both are essential components, and the most successful savings program considers both elements.

That's where this book comes in. It's designed to explain the strategies out there to help you save, save, save. There's no doubt that the bill will be large; there's also no question that, with planning, strategy, and purpose, you can achieve your goal and provide the means that will allow you and your family all the benefits of a quality, paid-for education.

529 & Education Savings Plans For Dummies is simply a way to find a reasonable solution to a seemingly unreasonable problem: saving for future education costs in the sanest, least stressful way possible. In keeping with the theme of stress reduction, you can use this book in a variety of ways:

>> **As a reference:** It's all here: the ins, the outs, the do's, and the don'ts. The world of education savings is one of very specific rules, and they're here, in all their glory, and they're all explained.

>> **As an advisor:** It's a case of the very good savings techniques, the merely okay savings techniques, and the truly ugly techniques (which you really want to avoid), and this book highlights them all. Indeed, what works for you may not work for your neighbor, but every savings option involves risks, concerns, and just-plain crystal ball reading. This book explores all the ups and downs and ins and outs.

>> **As a little light reading:** Amazingly enough, the topic of money can be mildly amusing, and education savings is no exception. Read this with an eye toward the absurd, and you won't go far wrong.

Parts of *529 & Education Savings Plans For Dummies* are about very specific situations you will most likely never encounter. Still, this book would be lacking as a complete reference if I didn't include a lot of the minutiae in the text on the chance that someone, somewhere, may need to know what happens to a Section 529 plan in the event of a death of a plan owner, for example.

Also, as a caution, be aware that any projections in the book are just that: projections. I have no special hotline to the powers that determine rates of returns on investments, increases in tuition payments, inflation rates, tax rates, utility rates, or postage increases (which might be really useful). Increases and decreases may be greater or lesser over time — I have no way of really knowing. All the projections should provide you with is a picture of relationships between like numbers; don't read any more into my crystal ball projections than that.

Conventions Used in This Book

To help you navigate through this book, I use the following conventions:

>> Italic is used to emphasize and highlight new words or defined terms.

>> Boldfaced text indicates keywords in bulleted lists or the action part of numbered steps.

>> Monofont is used for Web addresses.

>> Sidebars, which look like text enclosed in a shaded gray box, consist of information that's interesting to know but not necessarily critical to your understanding of the chapter or section topic.

Foolish Assumptions

The world of money and taxes is rife with assumptions, foolish and otherwise. Here are some of the assumptions I've made about you:

>> You're not aware of the variety of ways to save for education available to you, or you're aware but baffled by the number of plans or the way the plans work.

>> You may have some idea of how much sending Junior to college will put you back, but you need more details.

>> If you've been saving for college and now find out that you can pay for private school tuition with your plan, you probably feel as though you're not saving enough.

- » You can't walk into a bookstore or surf the Internet without buying every book you see with a snazzy, eye-catching, strikingly-appealing, jaw-droppin', good-looking, yellow-and-black cover.

- » If you're not yet saving for any form of education, you may feel that you don't have room in your budget for that expense. After paying your monthly living costs, you may have nothing left to save.

If you identify with any of the above, *529 & Education Savings Plans For Dummies* gives you the information you need to start saving or kick your savings into high gear.

How This Book Is Organized

This book takes all the different components of education savings — from its necessity, through all the different sorts of savings plans, and finally to how to augment with grants, loans, and scholarships — and breaks them down into easily digestible chunks (okay, *parts*, if you want to get technical about it). Each part is comprised of a few chapters. The following briefly describes each part:

Part 1: Figuring Out the Cost of Education — and How to Pay It

There's no question; the number is huge, but how huge is it? Sounds like the start of a bad joke, eh? Well, it isn't a joke, but dealing with the big cash question doesn't have to be that bad. After a brief overview of the scope of the book, this part looks at the current and projected future cost of education, including primary and secondary schools, apprenticeships, vocational and trade schools, public and private colleges, two- and four-year institutions, and graduate and professional schools. It focuses on savings techniques, and finally, it lets you know who's available to make contributions to the savings pool.

Part 2: Piecing Together Section 529 Plans

A venerable member of the education savings plan sweepstakes, Section 529 plans offer seemingly unlimited choices and high contribution limits (at least if you listen to the people who are trying to sell you their particular plan). This part dissects these plans, explaining how they work, why they work, and when they work — or don't — as the case may be.

Part 3: Uncovering Coverdell Accounts

Coverdell Education Savings Accounts (formerly known as Education IRAs) have now become real players in the education savings arena, and more and more financial advisors, banks, and brokerages are touting their benefits. This part explores them in full detail, showing their good and bad points and explaining how and when they might (or might not) make sense for you.

Part 4: Filling In the Gaps: More Ways to Save for Education

Saving for education has been around a lot longer than Section 529 plans or Coverdell accounts. So Part 4 examines some of the more traditional ways to save and shows situations where these tried and true methods still may make sense for you. But what happens when all else fails and your savings come up a bit short? This part explains how the world of financial aid works — loans, grants, and scholarships —and how the money you've saved for college may factor into financial aid decisions.

Part 5: The Part of Tens

It's the part you've hopefully come to know and love. The *For Dummies* Part of Tens — this time with an education-savings twist. Do you like easily accessible top-ten lists? Here you go. The whole point of so-called "education savings plans" is first, to save, and second, to pay as little tax on your savings as possible. The chapters in this part give you hints on saving successfully and tell you what you must do to dodge as many taxes as possible. The book includes one final element that's not technically a Part of Tens — it lists *way* more than ten things. But I thought I should let you know about the appendix, which gives you a more detailed look at the various Section 529 plans offered by each of the 50 states and the District of Columbia, plus one private prepaid tuition plan. The appendix gives you an apples-to-apples comparison of what is currently out there so you can make the best decision for your particular situation.

Icons Used in This Book

The icons you come across in this book identify information or words of caution that you may find especially helpful.

REMEMBER

You have a lot to remember when trying to slot your savings into the rules and regulations surrounding many of these education savings plans. This icon alerts you to important information you don't want to forget because it can often make the entire process of saving for education go a lot more smoothly.

TECHNICAL STUFF

If you're the type of person who always needs to know more than the basics, check out the information next to this guy. It points out information that you don't absolutely need to know to save (but you can always use it to impress your friends).

TIP

Life is rarely straightforward, and saving for education may be even less so. When you see this icon, you'll find a strategy to help you get the most out of your savings or make it easier to put money away.

WARNING

This book is littered with ideas of what not to do if you want your education savings plans to succeed. When you find this icon, you've just landed on one of them.

Beyond the Book

If you want to go beyond this book, check out the Cheat Sheet, where I summarize the different college savings plan avenues available to you, from 529 plans, Coverdell accounts, Series EE and Series II savings bonds, and other savings vehicles.

Where to Go from Here

If you want to and have the time, you can read this book from cover to cover. This book gives you a great view of how much, how, and where to save money for education. But if you don't have the time or the interest, you may choose to hop around from topic to topic, skipping those that don't apply to you and paying more careful attention to those that do. That's one of the great things about *For Dummies* books. You can get in and get out wherever and whenever you choose. If the information you need to understand a certain topic is covered elsewhere, the text will direct you, so you don't need to worry that you're missing basic information by skipping over a portion of the book.

1

Figuring Out the Cost of Education — and How to Pay It

IN THIS CHAPTER

» **Figuring out what and how to save**

» **Considering Section 529 plans**

» **Taking a look at Coverdell Education Savings Accounts**

» **Evaluating other savings options**

» **Making the most of your savings**

Chapter **1**

Braving the New World of Education Savings

You may have just found out that you're pregnant. Maybe you're at the point where the college catalogs are beginning to accumulate on your dining room table. Or perhaps your family is somewhere in the middle, with your children out of diapers but not yet into calculus. Wherever your family falls in the age spectrum, one thing is certain: Either in your immediate family or in your extended one, we all want our children to receive the best possible education for them. That might mean public schools all the way, private schools at some point, trade schools, or apprenticeships. The options are endless, but so may be the potential cost.

And therein lies a problem: Although your child can receive a primary and secondary education without incurring significant added expense in your budget (unless you consider things like your local parents' group's fundraisers), there is very little that's free in the way of post-secondary education. For most of us, the privilege of helping your child obtain that degree or learn a trade comes with a hefty price tag. And, while I was convinced when my son was born that he'd receive full scholarships all the way, that is the exception and not the rule (and no, he wasn't one of the exceptions. Darn!). If you've already explored the costs of a post-secondary education, you know that the numbers often are large; if you haven't yet experienced the pleasure, rest assured that the amounts in question will likely take your breath away. So far, we've only spoken about post-secondary education. In this book, we're also going to talk about private schools for grades K–12, apprenticeships, trade schools, and learning opportunities for differently abled children.

In solving any problem, you need to remain calm and focused on the task at hand. That's where this book may help — by making you methodically look at the current state of your education savings, helping you leave your misconceptions about saving at the door, and showing you ways to begin or increase savings. After you convince yourself that you're able to save something and you actually begin to put some money away, you've won a major victory; everything that follows will be easier. Just keep in mind that saving now will create opportunities and open doors for your children in the future.

Doing the Numbers

Up until now, crunching the numbers and figuring out what you think college will cost has usually been where you begin and end your exploration of the topic of how to pay for future educational costs. But after you resolve to start saving and you take the projected costs and create a plan to save for that amount, it's time to take this exercise a bit more seriously.

Figuring up the costs

Depending on the size of your family and your expectations, adding up the cost of a college education can be a fairly straightforward calculation, or it may become quite involved.

TIP

Be realistic about the capabilities and ambitions of your future student and your ability to pay.

Your straight-A student may have to scale back on their dreams of MIT if your budget, including amounts you can add from your current and future earnings, only goes as far as your local state college. (However, they may want to seriously consider applying for some scholarship aid as outlined in Chapter 17.)

Likewise, there's little point in saving for an Ivy League education if your child has plans to open their own auto repair shop. And clearly, the more children you're educating, the thinner your resources may be stretched per child. (Although, depending on how closely spaced your children are in age, this situation may actually work to your advantage if you need to apply for financial aid, as you will learn about in Chapter 18.)

Finding resources to help you save

REMEMBER

No matter how late you may begin saving specifically for future college costs, the entire weight of doing so doesn't necessarily need to rest solely on your shoulders, nor do you need to begin to save from nothing.

Chapter 3 helps you find hidden assets you may have available to augment your education savings. It may also alert you to other resources you haven't even thought of — for example, family, friends, or even the student himself. Just because these are your children, you may not have to come up with the full amount of their education costs from your pockets alone.

Saving efficiently

Too many people equate saving for the future with current deprivation. For most people, living expenses currently equal (or even exceed income), and they may not have money left over in the family budget for saving. Clearly, if you fit into this category, you're not going to be able to save unless you make some changes in your life. Chapter 4 shows you some relatively painless adjustments that will maximize the amount of money you can shave from your current budget while minimizing the effect on your life.

Exploring Section 529 Plans

Most believe that saving money is a good thing, and the federal government is prepared to back up that philosophy with a variety of savings programs that contain built-in tax incentives, some of which you may already be using (tax-deferred retirement plans, anyone?). One of these types of incentive savings plans is the Qualified Tuition Program, or Section 529 plan, which is designed solely to save for college or any other type of qualified education, either tax-exempt or tax-deferred, depending on a number of factors. Like almost everything else the government cooks up, though, Section 529 plans aren't as simple to navigate as everyone selling these plans would have you think. Chapter 5 gives you the tools you need to understand how these accounts work and how you can best make them work for you.

Following the rules

WARNING

Section 529 of the Internal Revenue Code is long, complex, and not for the faint of heart. Still, savings accounts that fall under its regulations can be a fantastic way to save for future educational expenses. However, to make it work, you have to understand its requirements; there's little point in setting up one of these accounts if you don't cross your t's and dot your i's just like the IRS wants. Remember, the IRS doesn't have a category of "close, but no cigar." Either your account will qualify under the regulations for tax deferrals or exemptions, or it won't. And if it doesn't, the consequences may be costly.

Making your money work for you

Creating a successful savings plan involves more than following the rules, although compliance with the rules is a big part. Chapter 6 shows you how to actually begin saving money and then put those savings to work for you.

REMEMBER

You're a big factor in determining whether your savings program flies or falls. Understanding the various ways your savings may earn money and the different investment options available is an important piece of creating the substantial savings you'll need to see your children through college.

Choosing the best options

Even when you understand the rules, manage to regularly save major portions of your income, and discover how to manipulate the investment choices to your best advantage, events in your life may require you to make sudden changes in your Section 529 plan savings accounts. Life happens, whether you're prepared or not, and often the last thing you want to think about when it does is the effect on your investments. Chapter 7 alerts you to some planning opportunities with your Section 529 plan accounts and how to make corrections to your college savings when your life doesn't exactly follow the course you originally laid out.

Checking Out Coverdell Accounts

If the world of tax-deferred/tax-exempt savings accounts were an ice cream parlor, Coverdell Education Savings Accounts (ESAs) might be rum raisin. Rum raisin might not be the most popular flavor, but it might be just what you want on a particular day. Not surprisingly, many people prefer Coverdell accounts when shopping for a place and a way to save money for college. Coverdell accounts provide a wider range of investment options and increased control over the account, and certain expenses qualify for tax exemption under Coverdell rules that aren't under Section 529 requirements. Whatever your reasons, Coverdell ESAs may be just the account flavor you want today.

Understanding the rules and regulations

TECHNICAL STUFF

Internal Revenue Code Section 530, covering Coverdell ESAs, follows hot on the heels of Code Section 529 (those government sorts are sticklers for going in order). In it, you find all the rules, regulations, and other assorted gobbledygook that govern these sorts of accounts.

But you actually don't have to dive into the tortured syntax of the Internal Revenue Code since I've already done that for you. In Chapter 8, you discover what rules you need to know to open an account, save money inside an account once it's been opened, and then make distributions from the account, tax-free or tax-deferred (depending on a number of factors), for qualified educational expenses.

Getting the most from your Coverdell account

You've probably discovered by now that successful savings involve far more than sticking your money in a passbook savings account at your local bank. And, while your investment options are seriously limited inside a Section 529 plan, you have far more latitude in investment decisions when you open a Coverdell ESA. Chapter 9 explores where you can open an account, what information you need to open that account, what sorts of investments you can put into an account, and how to decide what sorts of investments work best for you. Finally, we explain the nuts and bolts of what happens when you begin withdrawing from your student's Coverdell account to pay for qualified educational expenses.

Seeing if Coverdell accounts work for you

Saving now for future educational costs may seem like a no-brainer to you but negotiating the ins and outs of any tax-deferred/tax-exempt savings plan isn't quite so simple. And, not to put too fine a point on it, Coverdell ESAs, while a valuable weapon in the arsenal of college savings accounts, may not be the right choice for you. Chapter 10 gives you some insights into what's involved in effectively managing a Coverdell account for your student and what pitfalls to avoid. Finally, if, despite your best efforts, you unintentionally land in a pile of muck, you find some strategies here to turn lemons into lemonade and perform some damage control.

But Wait! There's More!

REMEMBER

People went to college and private schools long before the Internal Revenue Code, and parents and grandparents saved for those costs even when tax deferrals and/or tax exemptions weren't around. You can save money in many other ways, some even specifically for college. Even though they may not be as tax advantageous as Section 529 plans and Coverdell ESAs, they may make perfect sense in your overall savings plan. And if you're not able to save enough to cover the full cost, all is still not lost: Various scholarships, grants, and loan programs are available to cover any shortfall you may have between what you've saved and the cost of your child's education.

Rediscovering U.S. Savings Bonds

Whether you're able to save only relatively small amounts, you're uncertain about your potential student's future plans, or you love the safety and security found only in U.S. Savings Bonds, you may find that this is an attractive way to save for future college expenses and still take advantage of some tax exemptions on the interest earned on your bonds. Chapter 11 explains how you may be able to use certain U.S. Savings Bonds to pay at least some of your child's post-secondary educational expenses tax-free. It shows you who may invest, how you may invest, and how to allocate and report your taxable and tax-exempt earnings when you redeem your bonds.

Saving for education the old-fashioned way

It may seem strange to even think this, but the trade-off for taking advantage of the income tax breaks available through Section 529 plans and Coverdell ESAs is that you're guaranteeing that you will use that money to pay for qualified educational expenses. If only all of life were so certain and so sure.

REMEMBER

Many of you may be hesitating over how much to save in these plans — or whether to save at all — because of your great uncertainty over your child's future plans. When you save in traditional investment and savings accounts, you eliminate that uncertainty because you're not tied to using your savings in any one way. Of course, in exchange for that freedom to spend your savings as you will, you lose any opportunity to defer or exempt tax on your earnings, but if your world is an uncertain place, you may find that's a small price to pay.

In Chapter 12, you find out about different types of investment accounts, different options of account ownership and their consequences, ways to invest and manage a personal investment account, and, finally, the taxation of investment income.

Putting your faith in a trust fund

For most people, the phrase "trust fund" brings to mind visions of great wealth and privilege; in other words, it has nothing to do with you. And that picture couldn't be further from the truth. If you save money in any form, then you're a potential candidate to create and fund a trust. Chapter 13 explores some different types of trusts and explains why a trust may actually make sense for you as an education savings tool.

Saving in your retirement accounts

Using retirement funds to pay for college usually isn't the best savings strategy to pay for these costs. In certain limited circumstances, however (such as when parents are older or you face unplanned educational expenses), it may make some sense to access funds from a retirement account to pay qualified educational expenses. Chapter 14 explains the tax consequences when you use so-called retirement savings to pay for educational expenses and alerts you to some major considerations you need to consider.

Accessing your home equity

If you (or you and the bank) own your home, you may be sitting on a larger nest egg than you ever considered. A combination of rising home values and shrinking mortgage loan balances has created a large pool of equity for many people, equity that may be made available to fund educational expenses. Chapter 15 illustrates how you may use your house to help put one or more children through college.

Using cash value stashed in your whole life insurance policies

You may have been paying premiums for years on whole-life policies without ever considering the considerable cash value accumulated inside the policy. And, if you took out those policies because you wanted to make sure that the money would be there, in case you weren't, for your children to go to college, this cash value can be used to help your child go to the school of their choice. Chapter 16 will show you how to use this particular tool to provide benefits after your death and as a savings tool during your life.

Identifying sources of free money

TIP

Not every potential student is an academic genius or a future first-round NFL draft pick, but you don't necessarily need to conclude that your child won't qualify for scholarships and grants.

Chapter 17 describes many sources of outright scholarships and grants. Some carry no strings whatsoever for your student (other than actually attending college), and others require some sort of payback, either upfront or after your child completes their education.

Borrowing to fill in the gaps

You're obviously reading this because you don't want to have to resort to borrowing money to pay for your children's college costs. And hopefully, you'll never have to touch the pages of Chapter 18. Still, it's not the end of the world if you do. This chapter explains the types of financial aid available and assesses the costs. It also peeks at some of the benefits and downsides of borrowing money for college.

Maximizing Your Savings, Minimizing Your Tax

This book is, at its heart, about successfully saving and investing money for future education costs on the one hand and minimizing taxes on the other. And if that were the beginning and end of the matter, you'd be looking at a fairly straightforward task, one in which, if you followed all the rules, you'd achieve the desired result at the end of the game.

Unfortunately, you don't live in a vacuum, and many forces impact your ability to save adequately, achieve reasonable investment returns on your savings, and limit the amount of income tax you'll pay on those investment returns. You're operating on a field that is rarely level and that shifts and shimmies through no fault of your own. As a result, you need to be aware of how large and small changes, whether they result from government policy, market forces, or changes in your family's projected college cost needs, will affect your savings programs. And you need to be prepared to move with those changes — to adjust your savings programs to account for these other factors.

At the end of the day, your success will depend not only on how often you make deposits into your education savings plans or how large the deposits are but also on how well that money works for you. Your goal is not to achieve a large balance in one or more college savings accounts. Your goal is to watch your children begin their adult lives with good educations and marketable skills while hopefully reducing or completely eliminating college debt.

Chapter **2**

Checking Out Education Costs

Whether you went to private schools and/or college (and regardless of who paid for your education), the joy of planning and saving for that event for your children, your grandchildren, or even yourself and your spouse has to be tempered somewhat by the uncertainty of the financial costs involved. That uncertainty is the exact amount of the eventual bill because clearly, the cost is going up, up, up, and never down.

And there's the rub: How can you possibly know how much to save if you can't figure out how much that education will cost?

In this chapter, I break down all education costs into their components and compare different types of education. If you know your prospective student plans to attend a prestigious medical school at the end of the rainbow, you need to plan accordingly. If, however, your budding student is fascinated with all things dead and tries to embalm the family pet before burial, you may be looking at a funeral services school, which costs much less than medical school. The point is that you need to be realistic about your expectations and the talents and desires of the prospective student before jumping into your savings program. You want to save enough, but saving far more than you need for education is pointless.

Dissecting the Total Bill

Because tuition is usually the highest cost for both private schools and colleges, many people make the mistake of saving *only* for tuition. But other costs, such as housing (if your student is living away from home), books, and supplies, can account for a large chunk of your child's expenses — a large enough chunk that you should include those costs in your savings plan.

In this section, I explain what costs you should start saving for and give you an idea of how much those costs are.

REMEMBER

Although I cover the major education costs in this section, they aren't the only costs you may encounter as you try to give your child the most suitable education for them. Although I don't suggest you start saving for a beer fund, be prepared to pay for other items, such as parking permits, transportation, health insurance, and a movie ticket or a new pair of jeans.

Tackling tuition

Tuition refers to probably the largest cost for college: the fees for actual instruction. For the academic year 2021–2022, the average tuition costs for a public university averaged $10,740 for an in-state student and more than $27,560 for an out-of-state student. Room and board added almost $12,000 to those numbers. Interestingly enough, the two smallest states by population had the highest and lowest in-state tuition fees: Vermont at $17,747 and Wyoming at $6,097. Clearly, there's a huge difference based on where you live. The numbers for private four-year universities are much direr: average tuition was a lofty $38,070, and average room and board costs totaled $13,620. Just as with state schools, there is an enormous difference between the Harvards, MITs, and CalTechs on the high end as opposed to Brigham Young University on the low end. In 2021-2022, there was a more than $57,000 difference between the highest and lowest private university tuition costs.

Inflation for school tuition isn't capped at whatever the current inflation rate is for the country. Depending on a number of factors, tuitions sometimes outstrip the inflation rate. Other times, such as during the recent COVID pandemic, tuition has actually dropped. Remember, though, that the number of years tuition has dropped is far outweighed by the number of years it has increased, and given that students are now returning to campuses, you can expect tuition rates to start an upward climb once again.

If you want your child to attend private schools for all or some of their primary and secondary years, there are many options. Of course, the cheapest, by far, is public education, which is available to all students regardless of where they live. However, all public educations are not created equal, and if you're not living in a tony suburb of a major city that cherishes education, you may decide that private education is the way to go. Average tuition costs for a private education vary widely. If you can access a parochial school, the tuition will be much lower than if you board your child at a posh academy in leafy New England. Once again, the choice is yours. Average private school tuition in 2021-2022 was $11,146 for the primary grades and $15,762 for the secondary grades. Multiply these numbers to see the total you're looking at for a 13-year private school education — this isn't chump change.

These numbers may seem insurmountable, especially if you're entering the savings game fairly late; however, some relief may be available. Only a small percentage of students (and their families) pay the top-dollar price for college, and even some aid is available for private schools. Many schools and universities offer huge amounts of outright grants and other forms of financial aid (other than loans, although those are available to all), and scholarships and grants for secondary and post-secondary schools from other sources may be available (see Chapters 16 and 17).

TIP

If you're fairly certain your child will attend a public college, you may want to investigate whether your state offers a Section 529 prepaid tuition plan (described in Chapters 5 through 7) to help you pay for those upcoming tuition bills. Even if you can't save for tuition costs in one of these plans, saving money in any Section 529 savings plan or Coverdell Education Savings Account (see Chapters 8 through 10) will allow your college savings to grow faster than conventional savings accounts.

REMEMBER

Up to $10,000 per year is available from 529 plans and Coverdell ESAs to pay private primary or secondary school tuition. This money may only be used for tuition and not for any other ancillary costs of that education, such as room and board, computer equipment, or other fees required. Still, if you have a well-funded plan already set up and you find that the local public school isn't serving your student's best interests, using these plans to pay for qualified tuition at a private school is now an option. In addition, many states now allow up to $10,000 lifetime to repay already existing student loans or pay for apprenticeship programs that were previously excluded from 529 and Coverdell plans' qualifying distributions. Check out this book's appendix for a look at the expenses each state's plans will allow.

Accounting for housing

You may come from a family who assumes that all those going on to higher learning will receive their post-secondary education at the local campuses. And you may fully expect when your student reaches that point, they will live at home.

If so, you can probably skip this part, although you should be stashing some money away for good, reliable transportation, whether that means a car, bus, or subway fare.

If, on the other hand, you suspect that your student won't be satisfied going to the local schools (or if your area is like mine and doesn't really have many post-secondary offerings), you need to add the cost of housing into your savings plan — either college-owned housing or local rental real estate.

College-owned housing

Most colleges provide some sort of room and board options in the form of on-campus or university-owned housing, and they gladly tack those fees onto the tuition bill. Because most university-owned housing is mandatory for all non-commuting students for at least the first year or two, if you plan on sending your child to college, these costs must factor into your savings plan. For 2021-2022, average college-owned housing and a basic board plan cost between $12,000 and $13,500. Where your college falls in this range depends on a few factors, such as the following:

>> **Location:** Generally, city schools tend to have higher housing costs than schools out in the country.

>> **Size:** Generally, larger colleges tend to have higher housing costs than smaller colleges.

>> **Number of students in a room:** If your child insists on having a room all to their lonesome, expect to pay a premium for that privilege. Generally speaking, the more students crammed into a single room, the less you're likely to pay for your student.

TIP

Room and board charges paid directly to an eligible school (the school will be happy to tell you if it's eligible) can be paid by using tax-free distributions from your Section 529 and/or Coverdell plans (see Chapters 5 and 8). Remember, though, if you're paying for room and board for a private secondary school, this is not a qualified expense and, therefore, is not eligible for payment from either a 529 or Coverdell plan. And don't forget; for a low, low overall price, you can turn your long-distance student into a commuter by purchasing a second home for their use close to their school. Chapter 15 gives you the lowdown on how to accomplish this.

Local rental properties

Although colleges and universities attempt to expand their student populations, many fail to increase their own housing to meet the increased number of students, pushing more students into the local housing market. In areas where rental units are being added, this isn't a problem; the rental units increase at a rate equal (hopefully) to the number of students seeking housing. However, many older cities have very limited rental housing, and the increased number of students seeking it has forced prices up sharply. So, if you plan to rent an apartment or house for your student, costs become more variable, making it more difficult to predict how much you may need to save for your student's housing needs.

TIP

If you live close to the college your child attends, the easiest way to check local rental costs is by reading the classified ads and haunting the rental board in the college's housing office. If you're living further away from the action, the Internet can be the way to go. Many newspapers, both big and small, have websites that almost always include the papers' classified ads. Craigslist is also available in most markets. Unfortunately, many apartments are rented long before the ad ever appears in the newspaper, so relying on newspaper ads is probably an exercise in futility. The lag time between the ad appearing in the paper and the website being updated may prevent you from actually locating an apartment this way, but you can get a really great idea of what rental costs are.

REMEMBER

The cost of a rental is only the cost of the rental — it may not include utilities (heat in the northern states and air conditioning in the southern states can both be very expensive), and it certainly doesn't include food. You need to add the cost of any utilities not included, plus money for food or a meal ticket at the university, to accurately compare your costs to the university's room and board plan.

Check the amount of room and board the college considers a "qualified education expense." (You can often find this information buried on its website, or just phone one of the college's financial aid officers.) The money you spend on rent to a non-university landlord can be paid using tax-free distributions from your Section 529 and Coverdell plans (see Chapters 5 and 8). However, if you spend more than the college's estimated amount of room and board on a non-university landlord, you may want to pay the excess some other way. Distributions taken from your Section 529 and Coverdell plans in excess of "qualified expenses" are subject to income tax and a 10 percent penalty.

Factoring in books and supplies

Okay, so you know you've saved enough for tuition and room and board, but the need for money doesn't stop once you unload the SUV on the first day of orientation. After your student is at school, they need to buy books and other supplies and won't know which books and supplies they need until after the first few days of school.

The costs for books and supplies aren't insubstantial. You need to figure on saving at least an additional $1,000 per year for books, plus $500 to $1,000 for other supplies, such as lab coats, protective glasses, notebooks, or even pens and pencils. In comparison to the tuition and room and board fees, this amount may not seem huge, but it's still substantial. Over the course of four years, that bill can be anywhere from $6,000 to $8,000.

TIP

Unlike tuition costs, which the university sets, and housing and food costs, which are set either by the university or by the conditions in the local economy, you can somewhat control how much your student spends on books and supplies. Your student can purchase used copies of most books and then resell them when they're through with them, or they can rent them for the semester or the year, returning the book once the final exam has been taken. Supplies, such as notebooks, don't need to have the university or college crest on them in order to function properly. Finally, the cost of computers has come down considerably since computers became the order of the day. All these costs can be paid for using qualified distributions from either 529 (see Chapter 5) or Coverdell (see Chapter 8) plans, provided you have the receipts to substantiate the distributions.

WARNING

Ignore this category at your peril. There is little point in saving enough money to send your student to the school of their choice and then leaving them in the lurch without the tools to access the education offered.

Looking into the Costs of Various Types of Schools

No matter where your student decides to attend college, you have to pay for the tuition, books, and supplies, and then you have to come up with a solution to the housing question. But because you may need a crystal ball to figure out where your child plans to attend college, the next piece of the puzzle isn't quite as straightforward — estimating the tuition and fees you need to save for. However, after you have an idea of what type of school your student plans to attend — or if your student is either recently or not yet born — you can begin some significant planning for the future by planning for the type of school you *hope* they will attend.

If you plan for your child to attend either a private primary or secondary school (or both), factor in the smaller of the $10,000-per-year or actual tuition fees of the desired school into your savings calculations. Failure to do this could result in you running out of funds before your student completes their education.

To make that planning a little easier — short of a crystal ball — I give you some real numbers to work with in this section for each type of school your child may attend.

Enrolling in career and vocational training schools

Smaller, more specialized schools, such as career and vocational training schools, train students in very specific areas for very specific careers, such as funeral services, dental hygiene, piano tuning, or even bartending. So do apprenticeships. The cost of these programs (which may exist independently of or be attached to community colleges or even four-year colleges) tends to be much smaller than your typical college.

TIP

Do your research before enrolling in any post-secondary school, whether purely vocational, combined vocational and academic, entirely academic, or an apprenticeship. Tuition costs run the spectrum from several thousand to tens of thousands of dollars per year. The education you get from the more expensive option may not be any better than what you can obtain at a less costly institution. Typically, public two-year schools will be less expensive than public four-year schools, and private for-profit schools will cost more than private, not-for-profit schools, but exceptions exist. Keep in mind that if you can commute to school from home, doing so will always be less expensive than moving to another place and adding housing and food costs to your education budget.

Taking community college and continuing education classes

Almost every city of any size has at least one community college, an institution of higher education that gives college-level learning without the college-level price. In addition, many large universities have a continuing education division that provides much the same function as a community college, including the lower cost; just check out the cost comparisons between community colleges throughout the country in Table 2-1.

REMEMBER

Don't assume that because you can't afford an Ivy League college through the normal channels that you also can't afford to take courses in the continuing education division. Tuition at Harvard University in 2022-2023 is $57,261; per-course fees at the Harvard Extension are $$1,980 for most courses that count toward an undergraduate degree. A full-time course load at either school is 4 to 5 courses per semester, which means you can attend Harvard University and pay the higher price, or Harvard Extension at approximately one-third the cost. Both schools award degrees from Harvard University.

Tuition costs for community colleges cover a range. You'll pay the most in the northeast and the mid-Atlantic states and the least in the west. But none of these fees will completely break the bank, especially since you're not required to take a full course load but can take one or two courses a semester if that suits you and your budget.

In addition, 19 states currently provide free tuition to qualifying community college students: Arkansas, California, Connecticut, Delaware, Hawaii, Indiana, Kentucky, Maryland, Massachusetts, Missouri, Montana, New York, Nevada, Oklahoma, Oregon, Rhode Island, Tennessee, Virginia, and Washington State.

While these states don't provide the ancillary costs of education, such as books and computers, room and board, or transportation, if you qualify, this is a very cost-effective way to get the first two years of a four-year degree under your belt, allowing you to use any funds you've specifically saved for education to be used in those last two years. Remember, the name on your degree comes from the college or university you graduate from, even if you only attended that institution for three semesters (usually the shortest amount of time a school will allow you to attend in order to receive your degree from them).

TIP

Funds from all education savings plans can be used to pay either community college or continuing education tuition, provided the school you attend is an eligible institution. However, in order to pay for housing using savings from these plans, you need to be at least a half-time student. Be aware of this and vigilant. A mistake here will cost you income tax on the distribution and a 10 percent penalty.

Going for a four-year public education

Each state has its own public university/college system. Because state universities are larger than colleges and offer much more programming, they tend to be considerably more expensive than state colleges. If your student has a very clear idea of where they're going in life, it will be most cost-effective if you can find that program at a state college rather than a state university, especially for in-state students. Check out Table 2-1 for sample tuition costs for a number of flagship state universities and smaller state universities and colleges.

TABLE 2-1: **Sample Yearly Tuition Costs**

State	Name of Institution	2022-23 In-state Tuition	2022-23 Out-of-state Tuition
Alabama	University of Alabama/Tuscaloosa	$10,780	$30,250
	University of South Alabama	$7,896	$15,792
California	UC Berkeley	$11,442	$41,196
	San Diego State University	$5,742	$17,622
Florida	University of Florida	$4,477	$25,694
	Valencia College	$1,984	$7,933
Massachusetts	University of Massachusetts/Amherst	$17,364	$39,300
	Framingham State University	$11,202	$17,280
Missouri	University of Missouri – St. Louis	$11,328	$29,970
	Missouri State University – Springfield	$6,840	$15,510
Ohio	Ohio State University	$12,485	$36,722
	Kent State University	$6,116	$14,992
Tennessee	University of Tennessee	$13,244	$31,664
	East Tennessee State College	$9,674	$13,484
Vermont	University of Vermont	$16,392	$41,280
	Castleton University	$11,832	$28,800
Virginia	University of Virginia at Charlottesville	$14,878	$50,348
	Virginia State University	$9,654	$21,409

Unlike public elementary and secondary schools, public universities and colleges aren't funded totally by tax dollars (and may actually be funded very little by tax dollars). However, state-run colleges and universities are one of the best bargains around, especially for in-state students. Any state subsidy, no matter how small, is better than no state subsidy for keeping costs down, and this is reflected in the size of tuition bills.

Getting your education in private

Public education may be the cornerstone on which our country is built. However, a vast network of private schools is available at every level for those who can afford to pay. And because no college education is free (unless you look at the

U.S. military academies, where the payment is in kind), all schools that don't rely on public subsidies are referred to as *private*. Private universities can refer to various types of institutions, from Ivy League schools to hundreds of private four-year institutions throughout the country. Each of these colleges and universities offers a unique educational opportunity, as well as a unique price tag. Just check out Table 2-2 for some estimates on private education.

TABLE 2-2:

Sample Yearly Tuition Costs at Private 4-Year Colleges and Universities

State	Name of Institution	2022-23 Tuition
Alabama	Tuskegee University	$19,594
	Birmingham Southern College	$22,750
California	Stanford University	$56,159
	Harvey Mudd College	$62,516
Florida	University of Miami	$58,102
Massachusetts	Tufts University	$65,222
	Northeastern University	$56,500
Missouri	College of the Ozarks	$19,960
	Washington University in St. Louis	$59,420
Ohio	Oberlin College	$57,654
	Case Western Reserve University	$33,780
Tennessee	Vanderbilt University	$58,130
	Rhodes College	$52,000
Vermont	Middlebury College	$62,000
	St Michael's College	$47,640
Virginia	Washington and Lee University	$61,750
	University of Richmond	$60,330

Overall, prices are high — and climbing higher every year — and no relief is in sight. The schools set tuition and room and board fees, and there is no public oversight. Furthermore, college presidents and trustees retain their jobs based on how well their institutions are doing financially — if it takes tuition hikes to keep it that way, that's just too bad.

TIP

If your savings are a bit lacking when the time comes to start forking over tuition payments, the smartest way to look for a private school may be to shop by endowment rather than the tuition ticket price. (An endowment is the amount of money that the school has invested, with the income available for building projects, professors' salaries, and tuition grants.) Schools with large endowments usually devote a large percentage of the earnings from the fund to outright grants, awarded based on need. Some schools with extraordinary endowments now provide free tuition to students from low-income families, and tuition is capped at no more than 10 percent of income for students from families earning $75,000 – $150,000.

Going on to Graduate School

If your student has a burning desire to advance their knowledge for the sake of advancing knowledge, if they absolutely must find a way to cure the common cold in people or beasts, or if the halls of academia beckon them professionally, your student may be on their way to graduate school, which is an additional cost to the four-year degree.

TIP

Being accepted into an academic graduate program is your first step as a professional historian, archaeologist, chemist, or astrophysicist, and as such, they're supposed to be paying you rather than you paying them to further your ambitions. These payments will come in the form of tuition waivers, research assistantships, and teaching assistantships, as well as outright grants and scholarships. If you have been accepted into a graduate program in a purely academic field and the university is not offering you substantial — if not total — aid, you may want to reconsider your professional goals. Offering a position without providing you with a (scant) livelihood is the university's way of saying that they're happy to take your money, but your chances of graduating with the degree of your dreams and with reasonable job prospects in your field are slim. Most universities will decline qualified students if they do not have the funds to support them.

Pushing Forward to Professional Studies

Besides graduate school, professional schools are another alternative for students seeking education beyond a four-year degree. If your student has always dreamed of being a doctor, a lawyer, or even a veterinarian, or if you hope your student will be interested in professional studies, check out Tables 2-3, 2-4, 2-5, and 2-6 to get a better idea of how much extra money you need to start saving to send your student to medical, law, business, or veterinary school.

TABLE 2-3: ## Sample Yearly Tuition Costs for Medical Schools

Name of Institution	2022-23 In-state Tuition	2022-23 Out-of-state Tuition
UCSF School of Medicine	$45,128	$57,373
George Washington University School of Medicine	$66,630	$66,630
Harvard Medical School	$64,984	$64,984
Emory University School of Medicine	$53,184	$53,184
University of Illinois College of Medicine	$51,632	$84,812
Indiana University School of Medicine	$35,000	$60,000
Johns Hopkins University School of Medicine	$59,700	$59,700
Uniformed Services, University of the Health Sciences F. Edward Hebert School of Medicine	—	—
Wayne State University School of Medicine	$39,502	$67,200
Rutgers New Jersey Medical School	$46,806	$70,696
Albany Medical College	$57,723	$57,723
CUNY School of Medicine	$41,600	$69,260
Case Western Reserve University School of Medicine	$68,788	$68,788
Vanderbilt School of Medicine	$64,882	$64,882
University of Washington School of Medicine	$53,480	$94,364

CHECKING OUT IN-STATE VERSUS OUT-OF-STATE TUITION

What makes a university or college public is the fact that, to a greater or lesser extent, funding for it comes from a public source: taxes. Although not every state provides huge amounts of assistance to its state schools, every state provides some subsidy. And because any state subsidy comes from the state's taxpayers, students who live in the state are given not only preference in admissions but also preferential tuition cost. This reflects that they, and their families, are already contributing through their tax dollars.

Even for out-of-state students, tuition at state colleges and universities often provides great value. The vast size of the state systems, their centralized administrations, and the typically lower salaries they offer their employees keep overall costs down. The top tuition price for an out-of-state student, while significantly higher than for an in-state one, is still substantially less than at many private four-year colleges and universities.

Tuition is the only variable between the costs for in-state and out-of-state students. All other expenses, including room and board, books and supplies, and so on, are the same for both.

Historically, the rate of increase in tuition and other fees has been more controlled in the state university systems than in private colleges, especially for in-state students. The annual budget is open to the public for comment, and political futures can rise and fall on the fate of a budget that increases too fast. However, state budget shortfalls can sometimes pressure state legislatures to increase fees at a more draconian rate, hoping that keeping other state services intact (and maybe not raising taxes) will keep the political fallout to a minimum. When states do increase tuition and other fees by a large amount, out-of-state students will typically feel the effects more than in-state students. Remember, in-state students and their parents are voters, and voters unhappy with the rate of tuition increases can effect some powerful changes.

TABLE 2-4:   ## Sample Yearly Tuition Costs for Law Schools

Name of Institution	2022-23 In-state Tuition	2022-23 Out-of-state Tuition
University of Alabama School of Law	$24,080	$44,470
University of California, Berkeley School of Law	$59,237	$67,781
Yale Law School	$71,425	$71,425
University of Georgia School of Law	$18,994	$37,752
University of Chicago Law School	$73,185	$73,185
Tulane University School of Law	$64,868	$64,868
Suffolk University Law School	$55,184	$55,184
University of Michigan Law School	$66,808	$69,808
Columbia Law School	$75,572	$75,572
Duke University School of Law	$71,100	$71,100
University of Oregon School of Law	$44,082	$54,864
Thurgood Marshall School of Law, Texas Southern University	$21,038	$28,261
University of Virginia School of Law	$68,500	$71,500
Marquette University Law School	$49,710	$49,710

TABLE 2-5: ## Sample Yearly Tuition Costs for Business Schools

Name of Institution	2022-23 In-state Tuition	2022-23 Out-of-state Tuition
Pepperdine University, Graziadio School of Business and Management	$54,630	$54,630
Stanford University Graduate School of Business	$74,706	$74,706
University of Hartford, Barney School of Business	$29,304	$29,304
Georgetown University, McDonough School of Business	$54,672	$54,672
University of Hawaii at Hilo, College of Business and Economics	$ 5,868	$13,284
Iowa State University, Ivy College of Business	$18,048	$40,296
University of Chicago, Booth School of Business	$73,440	$73,440
University of Kentucky, Carol Martin Gatton College of Business and Economics	$36,913	$43,439
Bentley University	$43,200	$43,200
Wake Forest University – Schools of Business	$31,990	$31,990
Fordham University – Gabelli School of Business	$53,962	$53,962

TABLE 2-6: ## Sample Yearly Tuition Costs for Veterinary Schools

Name of Institution	2021-22 In-state Tuition	2021-22 Out-of-state Tuition
University of California – Davis	$32,622	$44,867
Cornell University	$58,750	$58,750
Colorado State University	$38,573	$63,420
Tufts University	$63,572	$63,572

Online and Low-residency Learning: The Wave of the Future

Beyond brick-and-mortar colleges, which require your presence on campus for significant periods in order to graduate, there exists the world of online and low-residency programs (see Table 2-7), many offered by schools that also offer a more traditional learning experience to those students who choose to attend classes in person.

TABLE 2-7: **Sample Full-Time Undergraduate Tuition for Online And Low-Residency Learning Options**

Name of Institution	2022-23 In-state Tuition	2022-23 Out-of-state Tuition
Florida Atlantic University	$4,879	$17,324
Eastern New Mexico University	$6,528	$8,568
University of North Carolina at Greensboro	$5,436	$20,595
University of Houston – Downtown	$7,338	$17,196
University of Maryland Global Campus	$9,360	$14,970
Southern New Hampshire University	$9,600	$9,600
Union Institute and University	$4,200	$4,200

These programs are a godsend for adult learners juggling family and work commitments with their degree program. Many online courses provide all your instruction and additional resources you need (such as access to the library) either via the Internet or through the mail. The low-residency options require your presence for one or two weeks each semester or one weekend each month. In either case, in exchange for a manageable amount of time and a great deal of independent study, you receive a full semester's credit each and every semester.

Both low-residency and online programs offer a wide range of degree options, from associate through PhD, although not in all areas. The number of schools offering these programs has mushroomed due to the COVID pandemic, which closed almost all schools to traditional classroom instruction. As with any major change in instruction delivery, distance learning has pros and cons. Because your student does most of their learning through a computer screen, there is very little opportunity to have the full college experience of living in the dorms, eating in the dining hall, and studying in the library. On the other hand, because you're not on the hook for room and board fees, the cost of matriculation is vastly reduced.

Chapter **3**

Realizing All Your Resources

I f you know approximately how much money you need in order to send your children through college (see Chapter 2 for more information on the costs of college), you may be suffering from sticker shock right about now. You may even be reading this while puffing into a paper bag, thinking you'll never save enough money. And you won't, at least not until you pull your head out of your bag and begin to plan how to fund those future college expenses.

While you take a minute to catch your breath, let me ease your mind a bit — you may not be the only resource for your children's education. In this chapter, I introduce a variety of resources you can check out when putting your college savings plan together. You may find that you have more alternatives than you thought, but you may also see that you have some work to do. In either case, read through this chapter carefully, take note of the different resources, and discover which approach works best for your family and your situation.

WARNING

If you feel that you may only be able to save a portion of your child's future education costs and know that you'll be tapping into need-based financial aid programs down the road, be careful of how and where you save that money. Don't contribute your savings to any account that's owned by your child, such as a UGMA (Uniform Gifts to Minors Act) or UTMA (Uniform Transfers to Minors Act). (Chapter 12 covers UGMA and UTMA accounts.) Twenty percent of the account value will be included as part of your expected family contribution under the U.S. Department of Education formula, whereas only 5.6 percent of your assets will be counted. Chapter 18 shows you how to avoid some pitfalls and maximize the amount of need-based financial aid you may qualify for.

Identifying How Parents Can Contribute

No matter how independent your child claims to be and no matter how colleges claim to promote and nurture that independence, the bleak reality remains: the school expects you to pay, and trust me, your student likely does, too.

The financial aid system primarily concerns the parents' ability to pay for college tuition. (See Chapter 18 for more information on how schools determine your financial aid needs.) Like the financial aid system, colleges look to your deep pockets when tuition bills come out because, frankly, they want to get paid. You see, colleges count on two things — that you've been saving for your child's education and that — considering you're well into your prime earning years — you make more money than your child (unless you have a little tyke who is a sitcom darling on national television). In order to live up to those financial expectations, I give you some tips below to evaluate your assets and use your current income for your child's college tuition.

Accessing additional assets

Hopefully, you've been planning for the day your child heads off to school. Hopefully, you've been stashing away every possible penny in traditional savings or brokerage accounts (see Chapter 12), trust accounts (see Chapter 13), the 529 and Coverdell plans (see Chapters 5 through 10), or some combination of those savings vehicles. I discuss all of these savings plans and more throughout this book, but be on the lookout for the following savings opportunities that you may have overlooked, especially if you find that your traditional savings fall short:

>> **Collectibles:** You may be surprised to find yourself with the cost of a college education forgotten amidst the spider webs in a closet or attic. I collected stamps as a kid. On the other hand, my brother had a comic book collection that couldn't be beaten. Others in my family have boxes of original Beatles memorabilia. These collections have the potential to turn into a small fortune. So, check out those remnants of your childhood — they may be very rare and valuable.

>> **Life insurance policies:** If you own life insurance (other than term), you may have a significant amount of cash value in that policy — cash that you can access by taking a loan against the policy's value or by terminating the policy. Many purchase these policies to ensure their children are cared for through college in the event of a tragedy. Because you're still alive and kicking, what better use for the money now than to help pay for those very same college costs? Check out Chapter 16 for more on this option.

>> **Scholarships from your employer:** Many larger employers offer scholarship opportunities to their employees' children. These scholarships are almost always merit-based (your children need to maintain their grades), and they're almost never enough to pay the full amount. Still, some scholarship aid is better than nothing, and you don't have to pay back this aid. See Chapter 17 for more info on scholarships.

>> **Cash value in your home:** After focusing month in and month out on making sure the mortgage, taxes, insurance, and utilities are paid on your house, you may be astounded by the amount of value that's just sitting there in your house. In Chapter 15, I show you how to convert that value to funds you can use to pay college expenses.

TIP

If you've been unable to save enough for your child's education, and the sale of your coin collection won't completely fill the gap, think carefully about how to apportion your savings. Split your savings equally between the number of years you'll be paying tuition bills — if you feel you'll be able to make up the balance each year with current earnings. On the other hand, if you feel you'll have no choice but to borrow money to pay the balance, first spend down your child's savings and then your own as quickly as possible, postponing taking loans as long as you can. By reducing the value of your family's assets, you'll increase the amount of need-based aid your child may be eligible for. Trust me, while you may not go all mushy over the thought of deferred loan interest, when you qualify for subsidized student loans down the road, you'll appreciate you paid attention to this strategy.

Counting on your current income

Oh, if all of life followed fantasy closely, it would be a much simpler world. You would have all the money your child needs, ready to fully cover all the tuition, room, board, and expenses your son or daughter incurs. However, try as you may, when the day comes to start forking over those tuition payments, you may find yourself a little short in the education savings department.

Of course, the whole point of this book is to show you how you can save money for your children's education, but if your savings are falling short of the full bill, your current income could help fill those gaps:

>> **Check out payment plans.** Most private schools and colleges recognize the tuition crunch and offer payment plans. If you know this upfront, you can make arrangements to pay on such a schedule when the tuition bill comes in. Instead of going broke twice a year, you can ease the burden over several months.

>> **Consider diverting some money from other current savings programs to your current tuition needs.** The obvious place to look here is at your retirement plans, where you've presumably been putting away the maximum allowed each year. If you need the money right now to pay college expenses, you may want to explore the possibility of reducing your pension contributions right now and reinstating your full contribution the day after graduation.

REMEMBER

But before you reduce or even eliminate your pension contributions, be certain that you'll be able to make up the difference later. You can borrow for college, but you can't borrow for retirement.

>> **Remember that your child doesn't live at home anymore.** If your child lives away at college, your household expenses decrease when they are at school. With judicious paring and careful budgeting (as shown in Chapter 4), you may find that coming up with the difference between what the private or post-secondary school expects you to contribute and what you're saving is possible.

Accepting Help from Family

Although *your* child is the one you're trying to educate, don't rule out the possibility that other relatives, like your parents or siblings, may be in a position (and may want) to help you out.

WARNING

Families can be strange entities, and the larger the extended family, the more opportunities for really weird behavior. Although your pride shouldn't get in the way of having a family member fund all or part of an education, be aware of any strings that might be attached to the gift. The cost of that assistance could become greater than the value of the gift. Weigh this price tag very carefully before you accept help.

Contributing to established savings plans

You may have already set up a Section 529 plan — see Part II — for your child, or a Coverdell Education Savings Account (ESA) — read all about it in Part III — or even both. If so, nothing in the rules that govern these plans prohibits other people from contributing to those accounts. If grandparents, your siblings, other relatives, or friends want to make donations to these plans, let them. Just be aware of the following:

>> Limits are set on plan contributions in any given year, especially for Coverdell ESAs. These accounts are limited to a set aggregate contribution each year, regardless of the source (see Chapter 8). For example, if you've already contributed the full amount this year, Grandma and Grandpa need to find some other way to save for little Christopher's education this year.

>> Section 529 plans have total plan limits. Each state has its own ceiling on the total size of individual plans, and each state can raise that ceiling at will. Although the limits are very high and calculated to cover a four-year college education at the ritziest school in that state, you need to know where that ceiling is, especially as you approach it (see Chapter 5).

>> All contributions into college savings plans of whatever sort — Section 529 or Coverdell plans, eligible U.S. Savings Bonds, or trust or UTMA/UGMA accounts — are subject to the Gift and/or Generation-Skipping Transfer tax. (See the "Understanding the Tax on Gifts" section later in this chapter).

Promising to pay

Unlike contributions to already existing plans, promises by Grandma and Grandpa (or anyone else) to pay for college are a bit more uncertain; between the time the promise is made and the time to keep the promise, much can, and often does, change.

WARNING

Don't rely on promises. Every baby is adorable, and every grandparent (or other relative) may want to do all they can for that infant. But as time goes on, incomes may drop, health may deteriorate, or relationships may unravel, altering a relative's ability or desire to pay for that child's education. If you've been relying on this promise and not instituting a savings program of your own, you may be out of luck when those tuition bills come due.

Understanding the Tax on Gifts

Whenever you, your child's grandparents, or any other relatives contribute to your child's education, a gift is made to your child. And, because the IRS never leaves any good deed unpunished, that gift becomes subject to the Gift Tax and/or Generation-Skipping Transfer Tax (GSTT). Yep — right when you think you've done something nice for someone, the IRS has to slap some kind of tax on it. However, there is good news. You can find it in the following sections, where I show you how to make the most of your goodwill by explaining the rules surrounding the Gift Tax and the GSTT.

WARNING

If ever a topic defied easy explanations, it's the *transfer tax*, which is the slice the government takes when money is given from one person to another, either in a lifetime gift or an after-death inheritance. There are three component pieces of transfer taxes: gift taxes (for transfers made during your lifetime), estate taxes (for transfers that happen after your death), and generation-skipping transfer tax (for transfers made during your lifetime that bypass the next generation in line and instead go to a subsequent generation, usually a grandchild or greatgrand-child). You can easily go wrong when trying to figure out these taxes, and mistakes are costly to repair. After reading what follows, if you have some gift tax or GSTT questions, please run, don't walk, to a person qualified by the IRS to advise clients on tax issues (a qualified tax advisor, such as an accountant, lawyer, or enrolled agent). The relatively small amount you may spend upfront for advice is peanuts compared to the amount you may have to cough up if you don't play by the IRS rules.

Understanding the gift tax

If you and your extended family and friends are planning and plotting ways to see your child or children through college and beyond, you may begin a gifting program early in your child's life. Every year, every person is entitled to make tax-free gifts to as many other people as they want, up to the *annual exclusion amount.* This amount is adjusted periodically to reflect inflation. (The amount is $17,000 in 2023.) For example, if you have three children, you, your spouse, your parents, and anyone else who has the means and the desire can each transfer $17,000 (or the current exclusion amount) to each of your three children without incurring any gift-tax consequences. Next year, you can do the same thing again.

Now, in its infinite wisdom, the IRS realizes that handing a seven-year-old a check for $17,000 probably isn't a wise move, and this is one time (and maybe the only time) that you probably agree with the IRS. Accordingly, the IRS allows you to make gifts into financial vehicles, such as in trust (see Chapter 13), in UGMA/ UTMA accounts (Chapter 12), in Section 529 Plans (Chapter 5), and in Coverdell

Savings Accounts (Chapter 8), for your children (or grandchildren, or anyone else you want to make gifts to), that hold and maintain that money either for a specific period or purpose. Whether you gift cash, stocks or bonds, jewelry, or anything else, if you give up your interest in the property, the gift qualifies as a completed gift, and you can deduct the annual exclusion amount ($17,000 in 2023) from the total value of the gift. Any amount you've gifted over and above the annual exclusion amount is now subject to the gift tax rules.

For example, if Auntie Elizabeth gives your child $40,000 in 2023, $17,000 is excluded from that gift, and $23,000 is subject to the gift tax. If Auntie Elizabeth and Uncle Bob (who are married to each other) each give your child $20,000, then $34,000 of the combined gift qualifies as annual exclusion gifts (2 x $17,000), and the remaining $6,000 becomes subject to the gift tax.

Splitting gifts

The IRS recognizes that many couples own assets individually rather than jointly and that the asset split between them may not be even. Just as married couples can elect (and most do) to file a joint income tax return, even though one spouse may earn the vast majority of the family income, they can also elect to treat at least part of their lifetime gifting as a joint gift, even if one spouse actually makes the entire gift. If the proper election is made on your gift tax returns, one spouse can give the entire gift and then "split" the gift with their spouse. This is, not surprisingly, called *gift splitting.*

Suppose Auntie Elizabeth (who is still married to Uncle Bob) gives your child $40,000 on her own in 2023, and because Bob is still offended that you forgot he was allergic to nuts and you included them in your award-winning stuffing at Christmas 10 years ago (yes, folks, relatives such as this do really exist!), he gives your child nothing. If they don't take advantage of gift splitting, only $17,000 of the gift is excluded, and $23,000 is subject to the gift tax. On the other hand, if they elect to split the $40,000 gift (thus, each person "gives" $20,000), Auntie Elizabeth can exclude $17,000, and Uncle Bob can exclude $17,000. Then only $6,000 is subject to the gift tax. (Considering his attitude, Uncle Bob almost doesn't deserve to know such a neat trick.)

Getting excited about the applicable credit

The annual exclusion amount seems large, and it is — a great deal of wealth can be transferred without incurring a gift tax over a lifetime. It seems somewhat unfair, however, that if you or someone close to you is in a financial position to gift even larger sums, they should be penalized by paying a tax on the gift. The tax isn't small, either — gift tax rates are bracketed, but the top bracket was

40 percent in 2023. And because most people aren't as wealthy as, say, Bill Gates or Oprah Winfrey, that kind of hit would be hard to take. Ladies and gentlemen, may I introduce the *applicable credit.*

REMEMBER

Although a tax is assessed on every gift made over and above the year's annual exclusion amounts, you don't actually have to pay any gift tax until your lifetime cumulative taxable gifts have exceeded a certain level. The gift taxes assessed are then offset by the applicable credit amount, or an amount that, when applied against the tax assessed, will eliminate or reduce the amount of tax owed. In 2023, the applicable gift credit stands at an amount equal to the tax on cumulative gifts of $12,920,000, not including any of your annual exclusion gifts.

To see how this works, let's go back to Auntie Liz and Uncle Bob, who each gave $20,000 to your child in 2023. Of that amount, $17,000 qualified for the annual exclusion amount. The balance of $3,000 shown on each of their gift tax returns (gift tax returns may only be filed by individuals, not jointly) is subject to the gift tax. Because they've never given a taxable gift before, the gift tax on each $3,000 taxable gift is $600. Instead of writing a check to the U.S. Treasury for that amount, though, they then apply $600 of unified credit against their tax liability. Now they owe no gift tax in 2023, although they now each have only reduced the remainder of their applicable credit to use in future years. Not to worry, though — the applicable credit amount is adjusted annually for inflation, so even though Auntie Elizabeth and Uncle Bob have each used $600 of their applicable credit, in 2024, the total applicable credit will likely increase.

WARNING

The tax code is fickle, and many changes made to it are only temporary. This extremely high amount of excludable wealth from the gift and estate taxes is one of those temporary things. On January 1, 2026, the current law expires, and the law reverts to the prior law, which resets the tax credit to an amount equal to $7,000,000. It's not nothing, but it's a lot less than now. If you've used the full amount of the credit prior to January 1, 2026, no worries — the IRS will let you keep that credit. But if you haven't used the full amount, you'll lose it unless Congress puts a bandage on the problem late in 2025.

Checking out the exceptions

You found this out in grammar class, and the same holds true for the gift tax — for every rule, you can find an exception. In the case of the gift tax, there are two nifty exceptions.

Section 529 plan exception

Section 529 plans are designed to harbor enough money to put a child all the way through college without any other assistance. Consequently, their total balance can be quite large (see Chapter 5 and the Appendix). And, because you may have kids who are creeping up in age and approaching college far more rapidly than you may like, you may want to super-fund your plan, pushing as much money into your Section 529 plan as fast as you can. And you can, without incurring a gift tax or even eating any of your applicable credit.

REMEMBER

An exception to the annual exclusion rules has been made for Section 529 plans. You — or anyone you know — may put up to five years' worth of annual exclusion gifts into a Section 529 plan for the benefit of a specific person *in one year.* That means you can put $85,000 (5 x $16,000) in Junior's Section 529 plan in 2023 without being subject to any kind of gift tax. But wait — it gets even better. Gift-splitting rules still apply, so you can put $170,000 into a Section 529 plan for any beneficiary in 2023 without any gift tax consequences, split the gift with your spouse, and then file gift tax returns for the next five years, allocating one-fifth of the total gift (which equals $17,000 per donor) to each year.

However, any additional gifts made to the same beneficiary during that five-year period are subject to gift tax treatment (remember, you've used up your annual exclusion amounts for five years). It would probably be a good idea if you didn't die during this period either. Any amounts gifted in anticipation of years that haven't happened yet will be pulled back into your estate and become subject to federal estate tax rules.

TIP

If your baby has just been born, and your crystal ball shows ample savings for their college education using normal methods, you probably don't need to worry about super funding a Section 529 account. However, if you've waited until almost the last minute and still want to take maximum advantage of this savings plan, this gives you the opportunity. Likewise, if you have the money available now (perhaps you've just received an inheritance) but wonder if you might squander some or all of it if you wait, super-funding Section 529 plans for your children may make sense.

Qualified education expenses paid exception

Your children may be some of the fortunate ones. Maybe you, your extended family, and/or your friends can afford to just whip out your checkbooks when the time comes and write that check for Harvard, Notre Dame, or your local community college. If you have that luxury, you may be hesitating just a bit now because you suspect there may be gift tax consequences. Think again.

TIP

Tuition for another person, which is paid directly to an educational institution — whether for primary, secondary, or post-secondary education

» *Does not* constitute a taxable gift.

>> *Does not* affect your annual exclusion amounts. (You can still give that lovely, large birthday gift you were planning.)

>> *Does not* cut into your lifetime applicable credit.

WARNING

A word to the wise: If your child is applying for need-based financial aid, tuition payments made on that child's behalf will count as untaxed income to the child on the next year's FAFSA application (see Chapter 18). If Grandma can afford to pay for only one year's tuition and you want to maximize need-based financial aid, ask her to postpone her tuition gift until your child's last year of college.

Figuring out the Generation-Skipping Transfer Tax (GSTT)

The Generation-Skipping Transfer Tax (GSTT) is yet another transfer tax (like the gift tax) that Congress devised to close a particular tax loophole: one generation (the grandparents, for example) bypassing their children in favor of their grandchildren when making a gift. That makes sense for the grandparents involved, as their children may already be set financially, but their grandchildren need help, but to Congress, it meant that they could only collect gift tax once on the value of that property rather than twice — grandparents to children, and then children to grandchildren. The GSTT was instituted to deal with that problem.

Essentially, the GSTT is a tax calculated by figuring out how much the government would have collected had the transferred amounts gone first to your children, subsequently transferred to your children's children, and so on.

The GSTT is designed for the very wealthy; accordingly, you are entitled to a lifetime exclusion of transfers from this tax (over and above annual exclusion amounts, which are the same for the GSTT as they are for the gift tax), totaling $12,920,000 per donor in 2023 and indexed annually for inflation.

For most of us, because of the high GSTT exemption amount and the availability of annual exclusion gifts, the GSTT will remain very far out on the radar. However, if you're one of those grandparents who wants to provide a college education for your grandchildren (and you have more than a few of them) and you've also decided to take advantage of various college savings plans that are now available, you may run up against this tax. You need to contact your legal and tax advisors if you plan to make large gifts into these plans (or into a trust or any other financial vehicle).

WARNING

You should never ignore tax advice, but in this case, missteps in the GSTT can cost you especially dearly — the top gift tax rate in 2023 was 40 percent. Because the GSTT is assessed in addition to any gift tax you may have to pay, the combined gift tax and GSTT on a gift to your grandchild can approach or exceed 50 percent of the total gift!

Seeking Out Student Sources

I know the U.S. has laws against putting children to work these days, but that doesn't mean you can never count on your children to contribute to their own college tuition bill. For most of you, the economics of financing college is a whole-family project, not one dependent only on the pods. Your children can (and often should) take some responsibility for their futures, not only in studying and obtaining good grades but also in trying to ease some of the tuition burdens. Working to earn their own money and keeping their grades up to win awards and scholarships can help defray future college expenses, which means you have to save even less.

TIP

Begin discussions about college tuition with your children early. Obviously, if you're planning on your child attending private schools from kindergarten through the end of their college career, it doesn't make sense to try to have your child contribute in the early years. But begin to raise awareness from the start. Their weekly allowance, which they'd probably rather spend on a new video game or movie tickets, may never add up to an Ivy League education. But discussing the costs of education with your children and encouraging them to save their money gives them a sense of what things cost, including their eventual college education. These early discussions and the encouragement you give your children to save their money may pave their way to future sound financial decisions. As they get older, they may consider stashing a portion of any money that comes their way into savings accounts, hopefully for later college expenses.

Working part-time and summer jobs

You can't send your elementary student to work at the factory after school. As they enter middle and high school, however, their potential to make money to help either pay for their current expenses (freeing you up to contribute more to the education funds) or help defray their college costs increases significantly. So, start encouraging your college hopeful to get off the couch and get a job. Young teens can begin earning their own money with timeless neighborhood jobs such as babysitting, working as a mother's helper, lawn mowing, and snow shoveling. But your child can tap into even greater college money potential by working for an employer who

>> **Provides a tuition-reimbursement program:** One of the most prized fringe benefits today is the tuition reimbursement plan, meaning that your employer essentially pays for some or all of the employee's tuition. Generally, larger employers (including many large retailers and fast-food restaurants) offer these plans. Usually, the plans only cover education expenses that apply to the employee's current job or improve the employee's general job skills.

Other restrictions may also apply, such as limiting participation to full-time employees or employees who have completed a certain service period. However, if your child works for such an employer and meets all the requirements, they may be able to have their employer pay for at least a portion of tuition at a local college or university. Although the number of students who qualify for tuition reimbursement plans is small, if you (or your child) fall into this category, you could offset a significant portion of the eventual cost in this way.

>> **Offers discounts:** Working for discount or retail stores may not sound glamorous, let alone lucrative, but most places offer discounts of some kind. Just think about all of the stuff that college kids need — school supplies, dorm outfittings, those crazy Yaffa blocks that seem to find their way into every college student's room, and so on. When you add up how much you can blow on the small stuff, remember that the money has to come from somewhere. And no matter who's paying the bill, you can reduce it significantly by getting it all at a discount.

>> **Teaches a marketable skill:** I began to work as a bookkeeper the summer I turned 14. My sister worked after school for my uncle, a dentist, and my other sister worked during vacations for a jeweler. Beyond the fast-food restaurants and discount and convenience stores, teens can find summer or part-time jobs that provide them with a marketable skill or with experience in a field they may otherwise not have considered. Even working at jobs like lifeguarding can give teens skills and an experience that lasts much longer than a summer — your teens may have an easier time finding a job at school because of their experience or skill. In addition, if they can keep working while in school, they can further defray incidental and everyday costs that otherwise you or their college savings plans would have to fund.

REMEMBER

Yes, nepotism is a dirty word. Strictly defined, *nepotism* is when a relative is shown favoritism in getting a desirable position. However, I seriously doubt that most people consider hand-drying cars under Uncle Charlie's eagle eye at his car wash a great way to spend a summer. So, when it comes to getting your kids started earning money, it's a who-you-know-not-what-you-know kind of world, and asking your family and friends about any possible openings is a great way for your kids to not only find work but learn how to work.

TIP

After your child begins working, take that time to really emphasize what portion of college expenses you expect your child to contribute — whether it be the cost of books, incidentals, or a computer. Be clear about your expectations. Like most of us, your child is more likely to reach a tangible goal than one with no boundaries.

Going after scholarships, prizes, and awards

The option of scholarships as a way to fund an education may seem so obvious, or it may appear to be unworkable for your student, but local, state, national, and corporate scholarships are available — some based on merit, others on need, and a few are a combination of both. Service groups in your town may offer them, your employer may offer something to children of employees, and the Daughters of the American Revolution is usually good for something at graduation time. In addition, your child's university may also be a source for both merit and need-based grants. (Check out Chapter 17 for more details on scholarships.)

Many achievement awards have checks that accompany them, and no application process is usually involved. Many scholarships and grants, however, are accessed only through an application and/or a test. Encourage your child to apply to as many as they can and take whatever tests are available. What may seem like a hopeless proposition could actually turn out well. For example, I laughed when my mother told me to take the Betty Crocker exam. (I hadn't taken home economics since junior high school.) But I won the prize! For more information about helping pay for your child's education, see *Free $ For College For Dummies* by David Rosen and Caryn Mladen (published by Wiley).

Finding sources of available money and determining what your child may qualify for isn't as tough as it may seem. Check with your child's guidance counselor for lists of what's out there locally. Your child can access the application guidelines for most national scholarship contests via the Internet. Finally, don't be afraid to approach the financial aid office of any school — prior to application, after admission, or while your student is actually attending classes — to see what scholarship award may have your student's name written all over it.

Chapter **4**

Sharpening Your Savings Techniques

At some point early in your children's lives, you need to calculate how much you think you'll need to see your children through school and figure out who will be paying when the time comes. Essentially, you're defining the size of the problem.

Now, your biggest concern is finding a solution. Because, as much as you realize you need to save money, you're not saving money! You're sure you have the will, the desire, and the need — you just seem to be lacking the cash. This chapter dissects your life and your spending habits (just a little bit). It shows you that adding more money to this equation isn't the only way you can ever increase the amount of cash you save. Although finding additional money is always nice, you can use a variety of methods to carve some savings out of what you already have.

Focusing on the Family Budget

REMEMBER

You can call it a budget, a financial plan, microeconomics, or a good excuse to pig out on a pint of ice cream every month. Still, whatever name you give it, the most important part of the family economic dynamic isn't *how much* money you have but rather how you *spend* it. By focusing your attention on budgeting, you can gain control over your family's finances and find that extra money you need to start saving for your children's education.

The mechanics of your family's budget are fairly straightforward — you bring in a certain amount of money through work, entitlement programs such as Social Security or other pensions, or investments. From that income, you need to pay for the basic needs of your family — housing and utility costs, food, clothing, transportation, insurance, and so on. And you also need to pay for the frills your family has come to expect — streaming television services, vacations, and fancy gifts at birthdays and holidays.

While that sounds simple enough, you often find that your family's needs and expectations slightly exceed your monthly income. While you may always intend to push money into your savings, you may sometimes find that you come up short at the end of the month. If you're thinking that saving money for education is impossible, put that pint of ice cream back in the freezer and check out my tips on how to dig for the dollars you need in your monthly budget to jump-start your savings program.

Eliminating most of the fat

Your knee-jerk reaction to trying to tighten your budget may be to cancel all television streaming, clamp down on cell phone service, or start looking for a smaller house or apartment. After all, if the dog can live in a doghouse, why can the youngest kids join him there?

Before adopting tiny house living for the family, take a giant step back and look at the big picture. You need to know how much money you have coming in, how much is going out, and where that money is headed.

Making lists of where you are now

Before you can start making changes to your family's finances, you need to understand what you have right now, at this moment. Sit down and make a list of your monthly income and, if your income tends to be at all seasonal, your yearly income (and then divide that by 12). List all your income from every source. Don't declare this account or that resource as off-limits. Every income item needs to be on the table (no, the IRS isn't looking over your shoulder).

Your next list needs to be those payments that you absolutely, positively, need to make, including the following:

- » Rent or mortgage (plus necessary repairs)
- » Food
- » Utilities (*including Internet but not including cable television or streaming*)
- » Insurance (life, disability, medical, homeowners/renters, and car)
- » Car and other transportation costs
- » Student loan payments
- » Taxes
- » Charitable contributions, including tithing to your faith community
- » Annual clothing costs for your family

Once again, if amounts change seasonally, add up a year's worth of bills and expenses and then divide by 12.

Third, you need to catalog so-called discretionary items — entertainment costs, travel, television, gym memberships, private school tuitions, and so on. Depending on your family, this list can be quite extensive. And while I would never try to dissuade anyone from getting their morning café con leche, you need to include all the small ways that money dribbles out of your wallet or onto your debit or credit card. That morning coffee may seem like it's the nectar of the gods while you're drinking it, but when you add it up as a monthly cost, you may be stunned by how much you're spending on it.

Finally, take a good look at how much you pay each month on outstanding consumer debt (plus the total amount you owe). Make sure you add your credit card payments to your lists of expenditures and any bank fees you may pay on your checking account.

REMEMBER

Try to be as accurate and honest as possible when preparing these lists. It's one thing to lie to your accountant (people do it to me all the time), but lying to yourself really doesn't help here.

After you have all your lists prepared, you'll be able to see where your money goes and how much of it you actually fribble away.

Carving away the truly wasteful

With your income and current spending patterns laid out in front of you, you probably won't have any trouble spotting the expenditure items that are really, really wasteful. Right at the top of the list are bank and finance charges. You may consider these charges to be minimal, but adding those minimal costs up can be another story. Check out the following examples of potential fees you could face, depending on how you manage your money:

>> **Minimum balance penalty:** Some banks assess fees if your checking account carries a balance below the minimum for the month. For example, if my checking account balance drops below $750 in any month (even $749), my bank hits me with a $14 per month fee.

>> **Insufficient funds penalty:** I don't know of any bank that doesn't slap a fee of at least $35, if not more, on bounced checks.

>> **Credit card interest:** Carrying a balance on your credit card can cost you between 10 and 20 percent (or more) per year for the loan of that money in interest alone.

>> **Late-payment fees:** If your payment check doesn't arrive on time, it'll probably cost you at least $20 for the month. (Late payments also decrease creditworthiness and increase the cost of later loans to you.)

Table 4-1 illustrates how these fees can add up for a typical family.

TABLE 4-1   ## Truly Wasteful Spending

What You're Paying	Monthly Amount (Good Credit History)	Annual Amount	Monthly Amount (Slightly Flawed Credit History)	Annual Amount
Bank finance charges	$14	$168	$20	$240
Credit card interest	$25 ($3,000 debt @ 10% a year)	$300	$83.25 ($5,000 debt© 20% a year)	$1000
Late mortgage payment	$80 (5% of $1,600 payment)	$960	$100 (5% of $2,000 payment)	$1,200

TIP

Not only can bank and finance charges waste your money, but consider the following examples:

>> Paying health club dues to a club you haven't attended for over a year

>> Continuing a newspaper subscription that you just haven't gotten around to canceling (and that includes online subscriptions, too)

>> Hitting the coffee shop for a cup o' joe in the morning because you don't get up early enough to make your own

>> Going out for dinner or lunch rather than eating at home

Wasteful spending can be curbed if you take the time to assess your spending. I'm not advocating punishing your family by getting rid of a health club membership, but I am suggesting ridding yourself of expenses that you don't need or put to use. Add up what you "waste" each month. Start getting payments in on time, maintaining the minimum balance in your checking account, making coffee at home, or canceling memberships or subscriptions that you don't use so that you can begin saving that money for college.

Reorganizing what's left

If you've crossed off all the wasteful spending, or if you had no wasteful spending to begin with, you can still lower your total expenses each month. Check out what's left of your expenses and see whether you can take advantage of additional ways to save that I discuss in the following sections.

Lowering your debt

The biggest piece of most budgets is the amount folks pay to their mortgage company, their car finance company, and their credit card companies. Many people are surprised to find that they pay more than they need to in many of these areas. Check out the following ways to reduce your monthly debt:

>> **Consider refinancing your house.** Look at your current housing, car, and credit card payments. You may be able to consolidate all these loans into one mortgage and leave your mortgage closing with one monthly payment that's significantly less than the total of all debt payments you have been making. While this isn't true in every case and is dependent on interest rate fluctuations and the current value of your house, it's certainly worth an afternoon or evening of your time to investigate. Remember, though, that only the mortgage interest that's related to the original purchase price of your house plus the cost of improvements and repairs is deductible, but the ability to drop a credit card interest rate from 20 percent to 5 percent, even without the tax deduction, is well worth it.

>> **Consolidate your student loans.** If you're currently paying off student loans and haven't yet consolidated them, you may find that now is the time. Depending on the amount you owe and current interest rates, you may be able to lower your monthly payment significantly. If you're working in a public sector job, you may even be able to obtain student loan forgiveness — check online with the U.S. Department of Education to see if you're eligible. And depending on what the Supreme Court decides later in 2023, there may be student loan forgiveness of up to $10,000, and up to $20,000 for those who were eligible for federal Pell Grants while in school. Of course, there are always income limits attached to anything that sounds helpful, and here is

no exception. If you earn more than $125,000 ($250,000 for taxpayers who are married and filing joint), your loans won't be forgiven. Sorry.

>> **Liquidate your assets.** Another way to lower debt payments is to liquidate assets that you may have and pay down your debt. For example, if you have shares of stock that aren't increasing in value, it may be well worth selling the stock and paying off your credit cards. Other assets that you might want to consider liquidating are some of the household items you've inherited from Great Auntie Marge — Do you really need that sterling silver flatware set? — or perhaps your comic book collection.

>> **Lower your credit card interest rate.** If you can't retire your credit card debt entirely, negotiate with your credit card companies for lower rates. You'll need a history of timely payments; one late payment will muddy the water considerably; two or more, and they'll probably just laugh. If your current company won't negotiate, go shopping. Many banks are eager for your business, often with introductory rates as low as 0% for three, six, or nine months. Transfer your high-interest balance and pay it off before the introductory rate expires.

>> **Trade down when you trade-in.** Take a close look at your car and the size of your car payments. Consider something less than a Mercedes when getting a new vehicle, even if the dealer says you can afford it. The dealer is trying to put their kids through college, but your responsibility extends only as far as your offspring — not theirs. Alternatively, if you absolutely must have that Mercedes, you might try looking for a used car rather than a new one. Nothing says wasteful spending more than watching the value of your new car shrink as soon as you drive it off the new car lot.

>> **Consider debt consolidation.** If you're *really* burdened by debt and can't find *any* reasonable way out (robbing a bank isn't reasonable), making an appointment with a reputable credit counselor isn't the worst idea. Counselors can often negotiate deals with your creditors that you won't be able to get on your own, and through their services, you may be able to eliminate hundreds of dollars from monthly credit card and other loan bills. If you consider this option, remember that this may damage your creditworthiness. Of course, it may also help: If you're so deeply in debt that you need to consult with one of these services, you're probably also missing payments, making late payments, and otherwise messing up your credit rating. In the long run, your creditors will likely be relieved to see you gaining some control over your finances.

Trimming other costs

Clearly, you need electricity, water, telephone service, heat, and so on. And, for most of you, these costs are not negotiable — the utility companies have cultivated a world of monopolies, and in most cases, no bargains are to be found as far as price per unit goes. However, you may be able to reduce costs within your own household, and these are well worth exploring.

I give you a few ideas in the following list to get you thinking about ways you can reduce other monthly costs:

>> **Ask for a lower rate.** Telephone and heating oil companies are highly competitive. Don't hesitate to shop around and ask your current company to meet, or beat, a competitor's lower price.

>> **Pay for only what you use.** Don't pay for more cable and/or streaming service than you need or can use. Cut back to a place that still provides the programming you want but doesn't give you many extras you rarely use. And don't be afraid to cancel your cable service if the cable company isn't willing to lower the price. The cable companies are so desperate to retain you as a customer that they will slash their monthly rate the minute you say, "Cancel my service."

>> **Practice energy conservation.** Upgrade your house with energy- and water-efficient appliances and improvements. Many of these have small upfront costs (energy-efficient light bulbs and low-flow toilets, for example) but pay off in huge savings over their lifetimes. There are currently new credits and rebates for energy improvements to your home and others for purchasing a plug-in electric car.

>> **Comparison shop for insurance.** Seek out the most competitive price for all your insurance needs — life, disability, homeowners/renters, car, and medical (if you pay for your own.) Just because you've been a loyal customer for years doesn't mean your current company will reward you. In fact, the opposite is usually true, and you can often find comparable, or even better coverage at a lower price from a competitor.

>> Take a hard look at your discretionary spending. You may not believe how much the $2.99 here to play this online game, $14.99 to rent that new movie that just came out, or the multitude of handy-dandy items that come to us in the mail almost every day from online merchants add up. It all seems like chump change while we're spending it, but at the end of the month, those hundreds, or even thousands, of dollars really add up, and it's hard to figure out what you actually purchased.

>> **Trim the grocery bill.** You can reduce your grocery bill by using coupons, store affinity cards, and shopping sales. Also, don't forget that house brands are almost always less expensive than national brands, and the quality remains the same for many items. Just because you've always used a certain brand doesn't mean you have to continue to use it. The manufacturer won't punish you for disloyalty. Remember, fresh fruits and vegetables have a season; when you buy in season, the quality is better, and the price is lower,

too. If you must have out-of-season produce, frozen is a more cost-effective and nutritious option.

REMEMBER

You'll be most successful in your trimming program if you don't slice and dice costs willy-nilly. If you're content with how you're living right now, cutting out the funds to do the things you love will only create a savings ogre that sucks the joy out of your life in exchange for money in the bank.

Changing Your Perspective — Watching Your Savings Grow

Saving for any purpose, whether for education, retirement, a new home, or that dream vacation of a lifetime, isn't a punishment, nor does it need to be a deferral of pleasure. Some people (and you all know someone like this) squeeze every penny until it squeals and never seem to have any fun. Who can forget Ebenezer Scrooge, after all? He began to live only after he stopped clutching his money quite so tightly. And he is, of course, the epitome of the saver — the miser.

Well, he's a fictional character, and plenty of savers out there still know how to have a good time. And maybe they even have a better time because, at the end of the evening, they know they have the money to pay the bill.

REMEMBER

Saving money can and should be neither painful nor pleasurable; it should just be. You should view putting cash into your savings plans and accounts the same way you view paying your other bills. While it doesn't thrill me to pay bills, I do have real satisfaction knowing that all my bills are paid in full and there's still money in the bank.

Paying yourself first

TIP

You've probably heard this advice more than once but never put it into practice: Pay yourself first. As you look at your income, you should carve a portion out and earmark it for savings.

That money needs to be physically segregated from the rest of your income (so you're not tempted to dip into it, even a little, for that extra something you've wanted to buy). Only after you've subtracted it and put it elsewhere should you figure out how much money you have available for all your other expenses, which need to fit into this smaller amount. If, after putting aside your savings amount, you can't pay the rest of your monthly bills, you need to change something — find a cheaper mortgage, eat out less frequently, or buy fewer books. The choice is yours. The only item not on the table for negotiation is your savings amount.

Systematically saving

You can successfully save if you put the same amount of money into some sort of savings account each and every week or month (depending on when your income is paid to you). Even if the periodic amounts may seem small to you, Table 4-2 illustrates how those savings can add up to considerable nest eggs at the end of one, five, ten, or twenty years.

TABLE 4-2   Systematic Savings (at 1.5% Interest, Compounded Daily)

Amount per Week	1 Year of Savings	5 Years of Savings	10 Years of Savings	20 Years of Savings
$10	$534.00	$2,711	$5.623	$12,144
$25	$1,335	$6,788	$14,057	$30,359
$50	$2,671	$13,556	$28,113	$60,718
$100	$5,341	$27.111	$56,227	$121,436

Earmarking certain pieces of income for savings

Most people not only receive their normal income, paid at regular intervals, but they also have periodic injections of additional cash, whether it's in the form of overtime wages, significant salary increases, holiday bonuses, gifts and/or inheritances, or even income tax refunds. (I can't begin to tell you the number of times people have told me they use additional withholdings on their pay to save money.)

If you've been doing your job and dissecting your budget, you've probably already figured out how to live comfortably on what you earn regularly, and you're hopefully saving systematically and regularly.

TIP

So, what should you do when a little extra money comes your way? Of course, from where I'm sitting, the answer is obvious. Save, save, save. You've figured out how to live nicely without it, and you won't miss it, so put it in a safe place and forget about it!

Ah, but I can see ideas of a vacation, a new piece of jewelry, or redoing the kitchen dancing through your head. Obviously, if your household budget hasn't included money for some glaring need (perhaps your roof is leaking) and you've just been waiting for some extra cash to pay for that project, you can divert at least some of that money for that purpose. But if you've managed to pare your spending to a place where you're managing beautifully with what you have, take a big chunk of that extra money and sock it into your savings plans. What's out of sight is also out of mind, and these additional funds may be just the ticket to beef up a somewhat anemic education savings or retirement account.

Educating yourself about investing

There can be no question about it: The world of investing can be a scary place, and the days when stockbrokers did your buying and selling have mostly gone the way of record albums and 8-track cassettes. Investing is now a do-it-yourself operation that can present many pitfalls for the unwary. Before you even think about sticking your big toe in the investing pool, you need to make sure you have a handle on the following.

Know what you're buying

Your success with any investment rests squarely on your understanding of what you're buying. Know what you're paying for, whether it's an individual stock or bond, a mutual fund, or even a certificate of deposit. You wouldn't purchase an orange without first making sure it wasn't rotten; don't assume that every security being sold and touted by the so-called experts is as solid as Fort Knox. Do your own research and make your own decisions.

Understand and be able to live with risk

After you move beyond bank savings accounts, certificates of deposit, and mutual fund money market accounts, you enter the world of ever-increasing risk. Whether you invest in individual securities or in mutual funds (which are nothing more than pools of individual securities), the price of those securities can rise (which you hope for) and also fall (which you dread).

Risk is inherent in the investment world. Whether you buy small pieces of companies (stocks or equities) or lend companies and/or governments money (bonds or debt instruments), your money is only as secure as the company or companies you've tied it to and the general economic conditions in both the United States and around the world.

And then there's digital currency (cryptocurrency or just *crypto*), which is completely unregulated and rises and falls upon the whims of the markets. Of all investment types, digital currency probably carries the highest risk/reward variable, which also means that when it crashes, the effects on your savings will likely be catastrophic.

When it comes to risk, if you can't even contemplate that your savings may be worth less next week, or even next year, than they are today, you may want to reconsider plunging your money into a junk bond fund. (Junk bonds, often referred to as "high yield bonds" are loans to companies Wall Street has serious doubts about, so they're considered risky.) Instead, you may want to consider a mutual fund that purchases nothing but U.S. Treasury bonds and notes (very, very safe).

REMEMBER

If you own an investment that's keeping you awake at night, there's no crime in selling it, whether at a profit or a loss. Even if you don't sell a security at its absolute height, you need never apologize for making a profit. Likewise, if your investment is leaking value, remember that this isn't a sinking ship, and you're not the captain. Jump overboard and live to invest another day.

Balance risk and expectations against future monetary needs

Not every great investment is a great investment for you. If you want to gamble on which company will be the next Microsoft or IBM, you need to have the luxury of time to allow that company to develop and grow. You may need to be patient; many start-up companies struggle initially, and the big payoffs, if they do develop, develop over time.

If you need to make that next tuition payment in the not-so-distant future (within the next five years), you may want to temper your level of risk, keeping a larger portion of your savings in cash and cash equivalents such as money market funds or certificates of deposit. I'm not saying you can't invest your teenager's college savings funds in Wonder Widget, Inc. However, you may want to only invest a small portion of those savings and keep most of your money invested in less risky ventures.

Identify the cost

Just because you invest directly with a mutual fund company or through an Internet brokerage doesn't mean you'll avoid paying anything for the privilege of investing your money. Face it: People aren't in this business for their health; they're in it to make money. And they make a lot of it. And as far as purchasing individual securities, the cost of each transaction is usually right there on your confirmation slip.

Still, identifying exactly what a mutual fund costs you may be difficult because the management costs may be buried deep inside the prospectus. Search for it. A company may charge its fee based on a percentage of the value of the assets within a fund or a percentage of income collected. Know how the fees in your accounts are calculated, and then factor that into the total return for that fund.

REMEMBER

Choose your mutual funds carefully. It's not only price share decreases that can cause you to lose money; excessive fees paid can also eat into your savings Also, be aware that if you're paying someone else to manage your savings, you may be paying fees to more than one player. You could be paying a fee to your financial advisor and a fee to the mutual fund companies in which your advisor invests your money. Every fee takes a slice away from your savings – the more fees you pay, the worse your return will likely be.

Read the fine print about total returns

Every mutual fund company offers literature about how well its fund has performed against other similar funds and about the percentage of increase (or decrease, but those numbers tend to be in much smaller print) the fund has realized over time. The literature probably also touts the expertise of the fund manager (who chooses what to buy and sell within the fund).

REMEMBER

Unless your fund's manager is an expert crystal-ball reader, these numbers are of historical value only. Mutual funds tend to follow the trends of the overall stock and bond markets, and their fortunes rise and fall in concert with the markets. Past performance isn't an indicator of how the fund will do for you, and the bygone wizardry of a fund manager may never be repeated.

Taking advantage of giveaways

You get something for nothing very few times in life, and money-back offers from credit cards and from retailers may or may not qualify as one of those times for you. Still, if you can take advantage of an offer without spending any additional money to do so, well, you would be foolish not to.

Credit card offers

Certain credit cards offer a rebate equaling 1 percent of your total purchases toward a Section 529 plan for you or your child(ren). Sometimes, the rebate is higher for various purchase categories, such as meals at particular restaurants or gas for your car. (See Chapters 5 through 8.) This plan may be in addition to, or instead of, other incentives that credit cards often offer, such as air miles, travel insurance, rental car insurance, and double warranties.

WARNING

You may want to avoid this offer if you don't handle credit cards well. The 1 percent incentive will be more than swallowed up by any interest or other fees the credit card company will charge you.

On the other hand, if you use a credit card anyway, you may want to investigate changing card companies to avail yourself of the offer. Doing so won't put your child through school. However, every dollar someone else puts into your savings plan is one less dollar you need to find.

Upromise and Backer.com

TIP

In a unique twist on the credit card rewards theme, Upromise provides a service that signs up retailers, manufacturers, restaurants, and various sorts of service providers who gift a percentage of your spending into a general account maintained by Upromise. The funds in these accounts can then be invested in a Section 529 plan. For example, a major gasoline company may offer you 1 cent per gallon, an office supply store may give 2 percent of your total purchases, and the return on a new car or home could be in the hundreds.

Granted, these are all small amounts by themselves, but just as your small weekly savings deposits add up over time, so do these. Your savings could be substantial depending on how many of the associated stores and products you use and how much you spend. You can find out all the details on the Upromise website at www.upromise.com.

Backer.com, on the other hand, is a way for a group of people to save together for one or more designated students. If you come from a family that tends to give cash gifts to children for savings as opposed to actual presents, Backer.com provides a platform where all your friends and family can chip in what's comfortable for them when it's convenient and/or important to them. There is a small monthly fee to set up your child's 529 plan through Backer.com, but as you'll find in later chapters, there is an administrator fee for every 529 plan. This one is just a bit more transparent.

Dealing with Debt

Your debt is probably the biggest hindrance when it comes to your plans for saving money for college. You may find it difficult to justify putting money into a college savings account when you feel swamped by debts that need to be paid, and you may feel like you need to pay off all of your debts before you begin saving for your child's college education. Fortunately for you, you don't need to eliminate all debt before you begin to save. To show you how to save for college while drowning in red ink, discover the difference between good debt and bad debt and begin saving right now, regardless of your debt situation.

Understanding good debt and bad debt

The good news: Some types of debt are good, are factored into your monthly budget, and shouldn't hinder you from saving for college. The bad news: Some types of debt are bad and should be paid off as quickly as possible; their presence in your life will effectively stop you from saving for anything, let alone education.

Clearly, you're not planning on paying off your entire mortgage before you start saving for college, at least if you intend for your children to begin college before their hair turns gray. And you probably feel the same about your car payment, which is factored into your budget as a transportation cost, and any student loans that you may still have outstanding.

Even after you finish paying off the loan amounts for your house, vehicle, and education, those items should still have value to you. And from a creditworthiness standpoint, since most credit rating companies expect you to have some form of this debt, the fact that you have these sorts of loans actually makes you more attractive as a potential borrower than having no loans at all (provided that you make your payments on time). This is *good debt:* debt you plan for, budget for, and manage appropriately.

On the other hand, your credit cards (if you carry unpaid balances from month-to-month), your rent-to-own accounts, your layaway accounts, and all your so-called consumer debts are considered bad debt. You should reduce or eliminate them if possible. (See the "Eliminating most of the fat" section earlier in this chapter for ways to reduce and/or eliminate your debt.)

Consumer debt is money you have borrowed to purchase something that is either a consumable (like groceries) or something that has a very limited life (such as last year's clothes that your teenager won't wear this year because they're no longer fashionable). Basically, after you buy things in these categories, they cease to have any monetary value.

Now, I'm not saying you shouldn't buy food, clothing, or even that new television set. You do need to eat, after all, and watching television is still a relatively cheap form of entertainment. What you shouldn't be doing, though, is borrowing money to satisfy these needs. And that is exactly what you do when you carry balances on your credit cards. You're paying interest not only on last night's dinner but also may still be paying for last year's holiday gifts and your wedding dress from ten years ago.

WARNING

However you dig yourself out from under your debt, you also need to break your credit card habit. Stop thinking that just because you still have credit available, you should be free to indulge in anything that crosses your path. If you can't use your cards responsibly and pay them off in full every month, then it's time to make a plastic salad. Sliced and diced credit cards in a glass bowl can make an attractive focal point in a room and also serve as a powerful reminder of spending habits run amok.

Saving while in debt

Being in debt won't preclude you from saving, but it makes doing so more difficult. The following strategies can make saving more manageable even while you start paring down your debt.

» **Understanding the difference between needs and wants:** *Needs* fulfill a necessary function ably but *wants* add other elements — at a price. For instance, you need a new television. The television you need is the one tucked away on the bottom shelf: 32 inches with a flat screen and a remote. But the one you want is on center display: it has every possible bell and whistle available today, and the picture is, well, so sharp that everyone oohs and aahs over it, although, to be honest, with my eyes, I'm not sure I can see the difference in clarity between this one that should be plated in gold and the less expensive model. The first television costs $150; the second setup is a whopping $4,000, and that's before the soundbar, the necessary cables, and the wall mount. Buying the one you need will likely make you just as happy, fulfills your need for a television, and ensures that you don't break the bank or borrow money for it (like using your credit card) and have to pay it off in installments.

As you slice away at your consumer debt and hopefully finally retire it, nurture the habit of looking at every potential purchase and expenditure from a need-versus-want perspective. Although denying yourself everything that you want may, in the end, be self-defeating and make you miserable (you're not a monk, after all, and never took a vow of poverty), constant self-indulgence will prove equally disastrous.

» **Learning to defer gratification until you can afford it:** No matter how badly you want that new television (whether the stripped-down or deluxe version), don't buy it until you've saved enough to pay for it. Most folks see a television as a necessity, but doing without for a period of time won't kill you. You may actually use the extra time you have to rediscover old hobbies, visit with friends, or otherwise spend time pleasurably. When the time comes to plop your hard-saved cash down on the store counter, you'll likely be more pleased with the less expensive TV than you would be with the bells-and-whistles model that you paid for with your charged-to-the-max piece of plastic.

» **Using credit as a tool, not a weapon:** Consumer credit is not, by definition, a bad thing, and used properly, it can be a valuable tool. Paying for purchases using credit cards negates the need to carry large amounts of cash. Also, it allows you to pass unmolested through the checkout line at the grocery store (I'm not keen on giving out all of my personal information to someone I've never met), and at the end of the month or the year, you get an easy way to track your spending habits. Use it improperly, though, and it becomes a weapon that destroys your finances and demolishes good intentions. Be responsible: If you can't pay your credit bill in full every month, destroy your cards and use cash instead. Budgeting cash will allow you to insert a line item for savings.

Saving Throughout the Ages

Saving money for college, beginning the instant you know you have a child on the way, is certainly the most effective approach. However, if you couldn't or didn't save money for your child's education back then, you may be behind in the savings game.

REMEMBER

But it's never too late to begin saving for your child's education. In the following sections, I discuss the best ways to start saving today for your children's education, regardless of their age.

Beginning at, or even before, birth

Saving for future events in your child's life should begin no later than the day they are born, and many people are starting accounts for this purpose during pregnancy or even as they start trying for a baby, but you shouldn't be the only one putting money away for that purpose. Your child eventually can help fund their college accounts, too. Use the occasion of your child's birth to open up one or more college savings plans and an account in your child's name, into which you can deposit any gifts they receive at birth. You can add birthday gifts and other such sums to it regularly until your child is old enough to begin making their own deposits. There's no better way to show your child the benefits of saving than to have a ready-made example with their name on it.

WARNING

Putting small sums of money aside in your child's name (with you as custodian) is great, but you may want to consider depositing larger sums into an account in *your* name (perhaps as trustee for your child but using your Social Security number to open the account) or even using that money to start a Section 529 plan for your child. Teaching your children about money is key if they're to become successful adults. Still, if your child will need any sort of need-based financial aid down the road, the value of the accounts held in their name will be counted more heavily than one in your name. The assumption here is that all the money your child earns and has is available for their education if that child is still your dependent, whereas only a much smaller portion of your assets should be used for your child's education costs since you have many things you need to be saving for, like the education of other children and, of course, your own retirement.

TIP

While your child is still young, you may want to consider investing in high-growth stocks instead of bonds or even money market funds. True, the risk is higher than other sorts of investments, and you may see your value drop periodically. However, time is on your side; traditionally, money invested in the stock market has outperformed other investments. If you have the time (usually anything longer than five years) and a stomach that can handle the risk, your investments will probably appreciate significantly.

Getting in gear during the teen years

If you begin your child's college savings accounts at birth, by the time they are a teenager, you should have a tidy sum inside those accounts. Still, you're edging ever closer to that magic matriculation date, and some of your investments may not have been gold-plated. Plus, you may have been accessing some of these funds for private school education if the public school options in your city or town don't have a stellar reputation. Either way, it's time to start super-funding your Section 529 plan, if possible.

Regarding the money you have saved, it doesn't matter if your investments have done spectacularly or tanked. Now is the time to move at least a portion of the value of your investments into less-volatile areas, such as bond and money market accounts. As each year passes, continue to decrease the amount you have invested in riskier stocks, and increase the amount you maintain in bonds, certificates of deposit, and money market funds. Although the potential for growth in these accounts is limited, so is the potential for loss, and at this stage, you want to know that the money you've saved is secure for your child's education.

TIP

If the writing is on the wall, and you realize your child will need some financial aid, this is also the time to start moving assets away from your child. If you have a Coverdell account for your child, you may want to convert it into a 529 plan at this point. If you choose this option, as Chapter 10 explains, the original Coverdell beneficiary must also be the 529 designated beneficiary. If you decide not to roll over the Coverdell funds into a Section 529 plan, now would be the right time to use the money in the account to buy a computer or pay for extra tutoring. At this point, anything you can do to give your child an academic edge may pay off in the long run. Many scholarships are awarded based on merit rather than need. Money spent now in strengthening academics may pay you back many times over down the road.

TIP

You may have been saving in a 529 plan, but your investments have done so poorly that they're now worth less than the amount you initially put into an account. If you want to keep the option of financial aid open, now may be the time to close that 529 plan that has you listed as the owner. You can then gift the funds over to your parent or another relative and have that person open a 529 plan for your child. Because there are no earnings in the account to tax, the fact that you've just taken a nonqualifying distribution won't matter (no income tax and no 10 percent penalty). If you think this scenario may work for you, check with your tax advisor first.

Finding out it's never too late to start saving

Obviously, if you wait until one year before college to set up a college savings account, you probably won't have as much in it as parents who begin saving the day their child is born. You could let that knowledge defeat you: Why bother saving anything if it's too little, too late? But you can fight back.

Forget a Coverdell account at this point (unless you can roll over an existing one from another child to this one). But a Section 529 plan is still the best bet. While there are few prepaid tuition plans still in existence, where you essentially prepay the cost of your child's college tuition using today's dollars, all 50 states and the District of Columbia have 529 plans, which can be used for a much wider range of education-related expenses. They're all just waiting for you to make that first deposit.

And, although putting money into a tax-deferred or exempt account six months before the first tuition payment is due may not make sense, remember that your child will be attending college for the long haul. That money could earn a considerable amount inside that account before the last tuition payment is due. Consider making your first tuition payments using current income or Stafford or PLUS loans (see Chapter 18) and save money in your child's Section 529 plan for their later college or even graduate-school years.

REMEMBER

No matter when you start or how much you manage to accumulate, saving something is better than saving nothing. That something may mean the difference between your child being able to attend college or not or being faced with massive debt or a smaller, more manageable amount.

2

Piecing Together Section 529 Plans

Chapter **5**

Laying Down the Basics of Section 529 Plans

Even though you probably have come across the terms "Section 529 plan" pretty frequently and "qualified tuition program" (QTP, for short) on occasion, you still may not really know what these terms mean. But, since everyone seems to be selling one, the other, or both, these plans clearly must be the best thing since peanut butter and jelly, right?

In fact, Section 529 refers to a part of the Internal Revenue Code (how's that for sexy?) regarding the rules and regulations concerning qualified tuition programs. And even though the phrases may have become so familiar that the words just drip easily off your tongue, these rules are quite complex and must be followed exactly.

Qualified tuition programs covered under Section 529 of the Internal Revenue Code simply programs that allow you to save money or purchase tuition credits for

>> Future schooling (from kindergarten through apprenticeships, college, and beyond)

>> Expenses for a specific beneficiary in an account that is administered either by the state (yours or any other — some states allow residents of other states to participate in their plans) or by a specific college or university

You may see them called either Section 529 plans or qualified tuition programs — they're one and the same.

In this chapter, you find out what qualified tuition programs under Section 529 of the Internal Revenue Code are, how they work, why they're great, where they could be improved, and how they may be changing in the future.

Discovering the Parts of 529 Plans

REMEMBER

Although you may come across many variations of 529 plans, all have the following component parts:

>> **The plan owner:** The *plan owner* is the person who sets up the plan (and who, presumably, makes contributions into it, although other people can make contributions into a plan that isn't their own). Depending on the plan you're interested in starting, you may need to be a resident of the plan state.

>> **The designated beneficiary:** The *designated beneficiary* is the potential student for whom the plan owner (who doesn't need to be related to the designated beneficiary in any way) intends to provide an education. The plan owner names this person when they set up the account. You can change the designated beneficiary over the account's lifetime, but the account must always have a designated beneficiary. Like the plan owner, and dependent upon the state plan you invest in, the beneficiary may have to be a resident of the plan state to qualify as a designated beneficiary, at least at the time you first open the account. Of course, if you invest in a private plan rather than a state-sponsored plan, there is no residency requirement.

With any luck, the person you name as your designated beneficiary will grow up to also be a *qualified student*. (See the "Making sure your student qualifies" section later in this chapter.)

>> **The plan administrator:** The *plan administrator* is the entity (state, private, or educational) under whose auspices the plan exists. In many cases, especially in prepaid tuition plans, the plan administrator is also the plan manager (see the next item in this list). The plan administrator lays out the rules that are specific to that plan, including how much may be contributed, what sorts of investments are allowed, when contributions may be made, whether plans are open to only resident owners and beneficiaries, or if all may participate.

>> **Plan manager:** Many Section 529 plans (particularly savings plans) are invested in a variety of mutual funds. Because states aren't in the mutual fund business, they farm this work out to mutual fund companies. These companies (and states that actively manage investments) are the *plan managers;* they're responsible for the actual investing of your money.

Figuring Out the Qualifying Criteria

Section 529 plans seem to be wrapped in qualification after qualification, but don't allow these endless lists of criteria to discourage you from using 529 plans. Instead, check out how I break down those lists of qualifications so that you can easily identify whether your plan, your student, and your student's expenses meet the myriad criteria associated with 529 plans.

Making sure your plan qualifies

In order for a Section 529 plan to qualify under the IRS's rules, it must meet the following criteria:

>> Contributions may be made only in cash, including checks, money orders, or payroll deductions, but not in stocks, bonds, or real estate.

>> After a contribution is made into a specific plan, you have limited ability to direct the investments. You may, however, change plans once each year.

>> You may not pledge the account's value as security against any sort of loan.

>> The plan or program you invest in must provide each designated beneficiary a separate accounting.

>> You can't contribute more into an account, or group of accounts, for the benefit of a single designated beneficiary than the beneficiary will use in the payment of qualified education expenses. Sorry, but you have to try to estimate this amount. There's no hard and fast rule about how to make this calculation.

When you contribute to a Section 529 plan, you're not allowed any federal income tax deduction for the amount of your contribution (unlike many sorts of retirement plans, which defer income tax not only on the accrued earnings in the account but also on your contributions). Depending on your state (and if you use its plan), you may get a current state income tax deduction for part or all of your contribution each year, or you may receive a tax credit.

After your money is safely tied up in a Section 529 plan, the interest you earn on it isn't taxed until *distributions* (amounts of money you take out of the plan to pay your student's expenses) are made to your designated beneficiary. And if you use distributions from these plans to pay the qualified education expenses of a student at an eligible educational institution (these are the IRS's words, not mine), accrued earnings generally aren't taxed at all. (See the exceptions outlined in the "Exceptions to tax-free distribution rules" section later in this chapter.)

FUNDING FOR THE PROFESSIONAL STUDENT

You may have already investigated one or more Section 529 plans and discovered the contribution dollar limitation built into each plan. The limits are very high, especially for the Section 529 savings plans (which currently can max out at $550,000, depending on the plan and the state, but with a maximum contribution limit that is regularly adjusted for inflation). But if your designated beneficiary is headed for great things — such as years of graduate or professional education beyond a bachelor's degree — the limits built into a Section 529 plan may not be enough to cover your costs.

If you suspect your child is heading for medical or law school after private primary and secondary schools and then onto college, where nothing but an Ivy League school will do, you have the ability to fund multiple Section 529 plans in more than one state. You can do this even if your total contributions across all plans, regardless of state, equal more than the limit for any single state. Remember, the wording in Section 529 is specifically vague, and the limits are imposed at the state level, not the federal. So long as you do not fund plans in excess of what your designated beneficiary will use during their education from kindergarten through any and all postgraduate degrees, having plans in more than one state is perfectly okay.

DEALING WITH DISABILITIES: FIRING UP AN ABLE 529 PLAN

We all focus on college and getting our students into the best possible position for life. But for many, the hurdles are a little higher, and the challenges greater. It is still possible to use a 529 plan as a vehicle to help your disabled or blind designated beneficiary a leg up on life.

First, you need to understand who these accounts apply to. An eligible beneficiary for an ABLE 529 plan must be a blind or disabled individual diagnosed with a significant disability before they turn 26 years old, with a condition expected to last at least 12 consecutive months. The beneficiary must either be receiving Social Security Disability (SSI) or Supplemental Social Security Disability (SSDI) payments or be able to obtain a doctor's certificate listing the disability.

In an ABLE 529 plan, the designated beneficiary is also the owner of the account.

The account can accumulate up to $300,000; any amount over that must be returned to the contributors. If the account holds more than $100,000 in assets, the designated beneficiary may lose access to Medicaid.

If your beneficiary qualifies under these stringent requirements, you can put up to the annual Gift Tax exclusion amount ($17,000 in 2023) into a 529 ABLE account. These contributions can come from either a new gift or a qualified rollover from an already existing 529 plan.

ABLE 529 plan distributions can be used for all qualified disability expenses, including expenses for improving or maintaining your health, independence, or quality of life. Such expenses can include education, housing, transportation, employment training, assistive technology, and personal support services. This list of what is allowed is quite lengthy, so if you're interested in finding out more about this option, check out IRS Publication 907, Tax Highlights for Persons With Disabilities, located at the IRS website at irs.gov.

Just as with regular 529 plans, many states offer ABLE 529 plans. And just as with regular 529 plans, some states offer tax deductions on your contributions, make the income earned inside the account exempt from state taxation if used for qualifying distributions, or a combination of the two. And some states offer neither. Once again, check out the Appendix at the back of the book for the tax benefits (or not) of your state's ABLE 529 plan.

And one final caveat: if you, the owner, and designated beneficiary, die while you still have an ABLE account, and if you've been receiving Medicaid benefits during your lifetime, any remaining assets in your ABLE 529 plan will be used first to repay Medicaid for your health care benefits before it's available to pass to your heirs.

REMEMBER

In other words, a Section 529 plan allows you to save for education and exempts or defers income tax on the accrued earnings until the designated beneficiary begins taking distributions from the plan.

At this point, you may be thinking that the only educational institutions that these plans are qualified to pay for are colleges and universities. Not true. Qualified institutions include all primary, secondary (up to $10,000 per year per student, and only for tuition), and post-secondary schools that are eligible to participate in U.S. Department of Education financial aid programs, including many vocational and technical schools, community colleges, and even some apprenticeship programs. (Daycare and nursery schools do not qualify, despite their sometimes-exorbitant costs. Eligible institutions don't need to be located in the United States; many foreign colleges and universities qualify. The standard here is that the schools must be eligible. They don't actually have to participate in these financial aid programs. Check with the institutions you or your student are interested in to ensure they qualify. In addition, up to $10,000 of 529 plan qualified distributions may be used toward payments of outstanding federal student loans.

Making sure your student qualifies

Strangely enough, the things you think of when the phrase "qualified student" comes to mind (grades, commitment, drive, and so on) have absolutely nothing to do with the IRS's definition. For Section 529 plans, a qualified student must meet the following criteria:

» They need to be the original designated beneficiary of the plan or, in the case of a tax-free plan rollover to another beneficiary, must be a member of the same family as the original beneficiary in one of these listed relationships:

- Spouse
- Child, grandchild, or great-grandchild (a lineal descendent)
- Stepchild, stepmother, or stepfather (but no step-grandchildren)
- Brother, sister, stepbrother, or stepsister
- Father, mother, or grandparents (a lineal ancestor)
- Niece or nephew
- Brother or sister of your mother or father
- First cousin
- An in-law, either mother, father, sister, brother, son, or daughter
- Husband or wife of any person on this list

» They must actually be an enrolled student at a qualified educational institution.

(See the "Transferring and rolling over plans" section later in this chapter.)

Making sure expenses qualify

When I went to college, a fancy car, a nice apartment, and spring breaks in exotic locations were part of the package for many of my classmates. (My package included public transportation, shoe leather, university housing, and vacations in lovely downtown Baltimore — watching traffic going to the Orioles games was very exciting!) Of course, this was before the days of any qualified tuition plans, let alone Section 529 plans, so the question of what was a qualified expense and what wasn't never entered the discussion. It was more a question of what your parents could afford and were willing to spend.

Things have changed a little in the intervening years. Now, although all the extra perks are still the norm for many students, parents (and other relatives) who fund

Section 529 plans need to be very conscious of what constitutes a qualified higher education expense and what doesn't. (Trips to Cancun, unless part of your child's specific educational program, and a sports car won't make the grade.) Table 5-1 lists qualifying higher education expenses.

TABLE 5-1   **Qualified Education Expenses for 529 Plans**

Type of Fee	Full-Time Student at an Eligible Institution	Part-Time Student at an Eligible Institution
Tuition (for primary and secondary education, this is the only qualified expense, and it's limited to $10,000/year/qualified student)	Yes	Yes
Room and board (paid directly to educational institutions)	Yes	If enrolled half-time or more, yes; otherwise, no
Room and board (paid directly to other landlord and grocery store)	Yes, to the extent allowed by the budget amount set by the school	If enrolled half-time or more, yes, to the extent allowed by the budget amount set by the school
Fees (as required by the institution)	Yes	Yes
Books, supplies, and equipment (including computers)	Yes, to the extent allowed by the school	Yes, to the extent allowed by the budget amount set by the budget amount set by the school otherwise, no
Expenses of a special needs beneficiary necessary for enrollment at an eligible institution	Yes (regulations defining qualifying expenses are still pending)	Yes (regulations defining qualifying expenses are still pending)
Fees (as required by the institution)	Yes	Yes
Books, supplies, and equipment (including computers)	Yes, to the extent allowed by school	Yes, to the extent allowed by the budget amount set by the budget amount set by the school
Expenses of a special-needs beneficiary necessary for enrollment at an eligible institution	Yes (regulations defining qualifying expenses are still pending)	Yes (regulations defining qualifying expenses are still pending)
Up to $10,000 lifetime toward the payment of outstanding federal student loans	N/A	N/A

Distributions from 529 plans that pay for *nonqualifying* expenses *will* qualify for income tax on the earnings portion (not on the amount of your contribution into the plan), but this income will show up on your student's tax return, not yours. Your student will also pay an additional 10 percent tax on the income, otherwise known as a penalty, unless they qualify for an exception. (See the "Exceptions to tax-free distribution rules" section in this chapter.)

All eligible schools are now required to provide you with the price of what you will pay them directly (tuition, fees, and often room and board) and the total cost of what they expect an academic year to cost. This is called the *budget*, or the total cost of attendance, and includes tuition, fees, room and board, books, supplies, insurance, transportation, and miscellaneous items. Remember, even though the total budget amount may be higher, only the expenses in Table 5-1 are qualified for payment from a Section 529 plan.

Qualified expense limitations

The amount of qualified expenses you may be able to use Section 529 plan distributions to pay for are limited if you fall into any of these categories:

>> If your qualifying student receives tax-free educational assistance (outright grants and scholarships), the amount of expenses that would otherwise qualify will be reduced by the amount of the tax-free aid.

>> If your qualifying student is also the beneficiary of a Coverdell Education Savings Account (see Chapters 8 through 10) and receives distributions from that plan, all qualified expenses need to be divided proportionately between the two plans. You can't double dip or take the full amount of qualifying expenses from each plan.

>> If you want to take the American Opportunity Credit and/or Lifetime Learning Credits on your income tax return, you need to use taxable income to pay for at least a portion of your student's qualifying expenses. See Chapter 18 for a discussion of what expenses qualify for these credits, how they work, and how to determine whether it's better to take the credit than to receive the 529 income untaxed.

Exceptions to tax-free distribution rules

Distributions made from Section 529 plans to pay qualifying educational expenses are free from federal income tax (state income tax rules may differ — check with your state). The federal government has found an effective way to provide incentives for sending your children to college and even private primary and secondary schools; however, it has also built in many safeguards to ensure you don't abuse its kindness.

TIP

When taxable distributions do occur, the federal income tax is paid by the designated beneficiary, not by the contributor(s) to the plan (rules regarding state income tax vary by state). Often, the rules aren't clear, even to the IRS, or your situation may be ambiguous. Don't hesitate to seek advice here.

The following are instances where the designated beneficiary may be required to pay a federal income tax on distributions from a Section 529 plan:

» **Using plan distributions to pay nonqualifying expenses:** If the designated beneficiary takes a distribution but doesn't use it to pay qualified expenses, they are basically out of luck. The accrued earnings on that distribution will be taxed at normal income tax rates, plus an additional 10 percent for trying to pull the wool over the government's eyes. The news here is not all bad, though; if only a part of the distribution is used to pay nonqualified expenses, the entire distribution isn't tainted. Only the earnings on the portion that didn't pay qualified expenses will be taxed.

» **Terminating a plan because the designated beneficiary chose not to continue their education or because some money is still left in the plan after completing that education:** When a plan is terminated (rather than rolled over into another plan or beneficiary), the earned income that's distributed, whether to the designated beneficiary or the plan owner, along with the original contribution amounts is taxable. In addition, it's subject to a 10 percent additional penalty. Likewise, if the plan contains more cash than the designated beneficiary will use for qualified higher education expenses, the income portion of that excess distribution is taxable, and the 10 percent additional tax applies.

» **Distributing funds on account of the death of the designated beneficiary:** If you need to distribute funds to a beneficiary's estate or to someone other than the designated beneficiary of the plan because of the death of that beneficiary, the earned income portion of the distribution is taxable; however, no additional 10 percent tax is assessed.

» **Making distributions due to the long-term disability or impending death of the designated beneficiary:** In much the same way as insurance companies can now prepay life insurance policies to terminally ill patients without any adverse tax consequences, the IRS now allows distributions from Section 529 plans to be made to terminally ill beneficiaries and to beneficiaries with a long-term and indefinite disability. The earned income portion of these distributions is taxable, but no 10 percent additional tax is assessed. You do need to provide the IRS with a doctor's note to qualify for this exemption.

» **Using the American Opportunity Credit or Lifetime Learning Credits:** To the extent that you use certain qualified educational expenses to qualify for the American Opportunity Credit and Lifetime Learning Credits (see Chapter 17), those expenses will no longer qualify for tax-free treatment, even if you paid for them from your Section 529. The earnings portion will be taxed with no additional 10 percent tax; again, no double dipping is allowed.

>> **Receiving education benefits that are excludable from gross income:** If you're fortunate enough to receive qualified scholarships, veteran's assistance, free tuition from one of the five U.S. military academies, funds from employer tuition-reimbursement plans, or other tax-free benefits (excluding gifts, bequests, or inheritances), the earnings on Section 529 plan distributions are taxable only if the amount of the 529 plan distribution is less than or equal to the amount of other tax-free educational assistance. There is no 10 percent additional tax. For example, suppose your student's qualified expenses equal $20,000. In that case, they would receive a $20,000 tax-free scholarship, and you would make a $20,000 distribution to them from their Section 529 plan. They will pay income tax on the earnings portion of the 529 plan distribution but with no penalty, even though none of the distribution is being used to pay qualified educational expenses. From the IRS's standpoint, it's enough that it would have been used for that purpose if your student hadn't received the scholarship.

Contributing to a 529 Plan

Contributing to a 529 plan may seem quite simple — you write the check or get the money automatically withdrawn from your checking account, and those funds get deposited into the 529 plan. That much may be true, but you still need to review the restrictions in this section so that you know who can contribute to 529 plans and how much can be contributed so that you avoid — as much as possible — any complications, such as the tax man.

Figuring out whether you can contribute

Anyone can set up a Section 529 plan (whoever creates an account under Section 529 is considered the plan owner). You don't need to be a parent, grandparent, or even a doting aunt or uncle. You don't need to meet any relationship test. You can even set up a plan and name yourself as the designated beneficiary if you plan to return to school.

In fact, the rules regarding who may contribute are so broad that you really need to consider only one major factor before you open a Section 529 plan: Make sure that you have a designated beneficiary (who already must have a Social Security number) in mind and, if they are not a sure thing, one or two beneficiaries in reserve. Section 529 wasn't devised to allow you to save money tax-deferred for any other purpose (you have your retirement accounts for that). Later, if your named beneficiary turns out to be a less-than-sterling student or decides to forgo higher education altogether, you may change your designated beneficiary through a tax-free rollover into a new account. Or you can just change the name of the designated beneficiary on the account. (See "Transferring and rolling over plans" later in this chapter.) The new beneficiary, however, must be related to the original one, as described in the section "Making sure your student qualifies" earlier in this chapter.

TIP

While it's never been possible before, beginning on January 1, 2024, you will now be able to roll over up to $35,000 over the course of your designated beneficiary's lifetime into a Roth IRA in your designated beneficiary's name. Annual Roth IRA contribution limits will apply, and you'll be charged income tax and penalties if the 529 plan you're rolling over from has existed for less than 15 years. So if you misjudged your savings, you now have a way to retrieve the remaining funds, but it's not without its fair share of hoops to jump through.

Estimating how much you can contribute

In establishing Section 529 of the Internal Revenue Code, Congress and the IRS didn't set express limits on how large these plans could be. They had a tacit understanding that higher educational expenses couldn't be accurately gauged and that annual increases bore no relation to the rate of inflation or any other such economic measurement. If they truly wanted to be responsive to the needs of many to be able to sock enough money away, they knew the plans had to be nonrestricting in their contribution limits but not so open-ended that people could stash fortunes away inside these plans.

REMEMBER

The IRS has set no specific dollar limits on the amount of money you may contribute into an individual plan, either annually or over the life of the plan. Instead, it limited the amount you could contribute to the amount of qualified expenses your student will need for higher education. This is where you'll have to do some guessing. Although there is no dollar limit, if you contribute more than your student will eventually spend on qualified educational expenses, the deferred earnings on any amounts you contribute over and above will be taxed when you distribute them. The earnings are also subject to an additional 10 percent tax.

Before you consult your crystal ball regarding how much you think you should contribute, you must consider Gift and Generation-Skipping Transfer Tax issues and individual state contribution limits.

Gift and Generation-Skipping Transfer Tax considerations

Section 529 plans were devised to allow everyone to save very large sums for higher education expenses regardless of their annual income. Because there are no annual contribution limits, you may be tempted to sell the family farm and put all that cash into one or more plans. If this sounds reasonable to you, you need to remember that contributions that you make into a plan for any person (other than yourself or your U.S. resident spouse) are subject to the gift and/or Generation-Skipping Transfer Tax (GSTT) rules (see Chapter 3).

The gift tax regulations include one unique provision, applicable only to Section 529 plans. You may contribute up to five years' worth of annual exclusion gifts $85,000 in 2023, or 5 x $17,000) in one year. If you're married, your spouse can do the same, enabling you to push $170,000 into a plan for one designated beneficiary in a single year (for more info on gift splitting, see Chapter 3). Should you choose this option, you must file gift tax returns for each of the five years, claiming your annual exclusion gifts. Furthermore, any gifts you make to the same beneficiary during those five years are subject to the gift tax and/or GSTT.

WARNING

Gift and Generation-Skipping Transfer Tax returns (Form 709) aren't for the weak of heart. Find a professional with expertise in this area (many pros don't have it, so be sure to check with the pro you're thinking of hiring). Mistakes here are costly; if they're discovered after the donor's death (that's you), they're impossible to fix. Don't take that chance!

Contribution limits imposed by the states

The federal government doesn't impose any specific dollar limitation on the maximum contribution into Section 529 accounts for a specific beneficiary. But the code section is intentionally vague. And most plans are administered by the individual states: They have far more definite ideas as to the actual dollar amounts necessary to see your children through four years of college. And the states are not yet considering that you may also be paying $10,000 per year for private primary or secondary school, even though many states have now amended their tax laws to allow for those primary and secondary school–qualified distributions.

State-imposed contribution limits vary by state, and the state law governing your account will be the state in whose plan(s) you invest, not the state where you live. Thus, you can invest money in a high-limit state, even if you live in a low-limit state. Also, be aware that states can change their limits (and often do), increasing them as tuition costs climb.

REMEMBER

You really need to shop for plans. Every state except Wyoming offers a 529 savings plan, but you are not limited to participation in only your state's plan. Be aware, though, that many states offer current income tax deductions or a tax credit if you are a resident; some states offer other incentives if you're a low-income resident, for example. So, before you go off and buy the plan your cousin Albert suggested, be sure to take a look at what your state offers first. In some states, the income portion of a qualifying distribution may be tax-exempt for primary, secondary, and post-secondary education. Other states limit the income exemption to only qualifying distributions made for post-secondary education. And some states don't give you any tax exemption at all for the income portion of the distribution, whether it's a qualifying distribution or not. The appendix at the back of this book lists state plans at the time of publication. In addition, you can access every plan through the sponsoring state's website or college-saving websites, such as www. savingforcollege.com.

WARNING

Don't rely totally on Web sites for information regarding a specific plan. If you have any questions or see conflicting information, contact that plan manager, who will have the latest information on the plan.

Contribution limits aren't per account but per designated beneficiary by state. Your designated beneficiary may have more than one Section 529 plan set aside for their use; however, the total aggregate account size in all plans in a particular state can't exceed the limit for the state in which the plan resides. States don't share info, though, so if you begin to bump against the ceiling set by one state, you can open a plan in another state. Make sure that all the money in your plans is used to pay qualifying expenses for your student; the income portion of any excess will be taxed and penalized.

Picking Your Plan

I will never forget my high school American history class, where the only lessons I carried away with me were multicausation and that the story of the United States was the ongoing push/pull between the federalists (those who wanted a strong central government) and the states' rights supporters.

Section 529 plans clearly illustrate that the discussion is far from over. The code section is a federal one, the application is almost entirely on the local level, and every state's rules are slightly different. So, this is where things get interesting. You know that, in theory, this type of plan makes sense for you and your family, but you're not quite sure what type of plan you should invest in and where.

Discovering the different plans

Not all Section 529 plans are alike. They all have different contribution limits. Some plans make perfect sense if you're a resident of that state; others might be worthwhile because of the available investment options. You really have to research and understand that this is not a one-size-fits-all scenario for you or your designated beneficiary.

There's an even larger difference in plan types, however. Original 529 plans were all done on the basis of prepaying tuition; many of these plans are now either closed to new investors or have closed down altogether as the rate of tuition rose far faster than the value of the investments. There are still some states that have these plans and that are open to new participants. If you think this may be a good option for you, check the appendix to see if there is a prepaid tuition that makes sense for you.

The more common savings plan (which is what most people think of when they think of 529 plans) is a later addition designed for greater flexibility but perhaps more risk. These are sponsored by all the states and by some private colleges and universities. They are all different, so once again, do your research. Make sure you weigh the benefits of an in-state plan (tax deductibility, matching funds, tax credits, etc.) against the wider investment options that may be available in an out-of-state plan. The $500 tax savings from your in-state plan may be more than offset by the far-better performance of an out-of-state plan.

Prepaid tuition plans administered by the states

As the name suggests, prepaid tuition plans are just that: the purchase of tuition to a particular school or group of schools ahead of when your student will attend. The state or a particular school may administer them (see the next section, "Prepaid tuition plans administered by educational institutions").

In general, prepaid tuition plans, or contracts, allow you to purchase future tuition at current costs. For example, assume that your child (let's call him Alex) will be attending a local state university in 2032, where current tuition is now $15,000 per year, but you expect it will cost $30,000 per year by the time he attends. You have $60,000 available. (Perhaps you just sold one house and didn't plow all the proceeds back into a new one.) You invest that money in a prepaid tuition plan while tuition is still just $15,000 per year. If you purchase the equivalent of four years of tuition at its current cost (4 years x $15,000 = $60,000) when little Alex is ready to attend school, the proceeds from the plan will pay all of his tuition costs (4 years x $30,000 = $120,000). By purchasing $60,000 worth of tuition now, you expect to receive $120,000 worth of tuition down the road.

On the other hand, if Alex chooses to attend a college or university whose tuition costs at the time you invested in the plan were greater than $15,000, the plan will pay a percentage of the higher tuition equal to your original contribution's value against the other school's higher cost. If he attends a school that costs $30,000 at the time the plan was purchased (but that now costs $50,000 per year), the prepaid tuition plan will pay 50 percent of the cost of his tuition at the time he entered the higher-priced school, or $25.000 per year. In this scenario, your initial $60,000 investment in your son's education reaps $100,000 worth of tuition when he actually attends.

With a prepaid tuition plan, your money is guaranteed to buy a certain amount of tuition. You don't need to buy all the tuition at one time — you can buy any part of one or more years — but whatever amount of money you put into this type of account is guaranteed to buy as much tuition in the future as it would on the day that you put it in.

WARNING

Just because you think you're buying a sure tuition payment at the end of the rainbow, don't bank on it. Many states don't absolutely guarantee full tuition payments when your student attends, even if that's what you thought you purchased. And because the entire rationale of prepaying tuition is an assumption that the amount of income earned on your investment will at least equal the increase in college tuition, many states have found their prepaid tuition plans to be a losing proposition. Suppose the value of your investment isn't keeping pace with tuition inflation. In this scenario, most states do provide a state remedy, so you probably won't need to find additional cash to pay for the shortfall between the actual value of your investment when you need to cash it in to pay for tuition and the real cost of tuition. Every plan is different, and plans (and state legislatures) can change funding provisions as the need arises. Stay current, and don't invest in any plan until you have read — and understood — the most recent plan provisions.

REMEMBER

Whether or not your state plan carries a guarantee, Section 529 prepaid tuition plans are trying to ensure a certain payback at a certain time. Because of this, these plans carry several restrictions that Section 529 savings plans don't. Check these restrictions carefully. Among the limitations are the following:

>> Most plans carry restrictions as to who may participate. Usually, either the owner of the account or the designated beneficiary is required to be a state resident at least at the time the account is established.

>> Most plans carry restrictions as to what colleges, universities, and community colleges are covered by the plan. Generally, the state schools are covered; tuition coverage at private colleges and universities within the state is spotty, and out-of-state tuition — while not entirely out of the question —can be

problematic. Before signing up for a particular plan, you need to check which schools are covered.

» Prepaid tuition plans cover only tuition costs. Room, board, and other fees must be paid at the time your student attends, from current income or other savings, like a 529 savings plan.

» Most prepaid tuition plans have a limited enrollment/contribution period each year. If you plan on or are currently investing in a plan, don't miss your window of opportunity.

» If you need to cancel the plan for any reason, be aware that normally fees are charged for terminating the account. In addition, many plans limit the amount that you receive on cancellation to either your contribution amount (less cancellation fees) or your original contribution plus some small percentage of income.

Prepaid tuition plans administered by educational institutions

If you know for certain (and beyond any reasonable doubt) that your child or grandchild is going to attend a certain school in the future (your alma mater, perhaps, because you've already donated the fieldhouse and the science lab?), an institutional prepaid tuition plan may be just the ticket for you.

Since 2003, hundreds of educational institutions have offered a prepaid tuition plan called Private College 529 Plan. This plan is essentially the same as state-run prepaid tuition Section 529 plans, except that it's administered privately, and there are no state tax deductions for contributions.

The rules governing this plan are the same as for the state-run plans. Contribution limits vary from school to school, depending on current tuition costs. You may want to contribute to cover tuition at the highest-cost school to ensure you've covered your bases.

Like all other 529 plans, those administered by an educational institution are transferable. If your designated beneficiary decides to attend a school other than one participating in this plan, you can transfer your account to another plan administrator. (See the "Transferring and rolling over plans" section later in this chapter.) Also, if your designated beneficiary chooses not to attend school at all or receives some sort of free ride, you can make a tax-free rollover and name a new designated beneficiary so long as the new beneficiary falls under the allowed relationship rules. (See the "Making sure your student qualifies" section earlier in this chapter.)

Savings plans

Savings plans are probably what comes to mind when you think of 529 plans. The Section 529 savings plan option broke open the world of college savings, offering truly huge tax advantages to the wealthy and the not-so-wealthy.

A Section 529 savings plan is, in many regards, an investment account. Although states may establish the rules, most of these state-sponsored plans are actually administered by mutual fund companies or fund managers. Having a fund manager in charge of your money has many benefits, including the fact that these companies hire investment professionals, who you hope will wring a better return out of your money than the state will.

That's the theory, anyway, and for several years in the 1990s, when the stock market soared, it was the practice, as well. These funds far outperformed anything the states could do (the states tend to be extremely limited in the investments that they can make with your contributions into a prepaid tuition plan). The fact that you may have had to pay a broker's sales commission to enter the fund and that you were also paying annual management fees to the fund manager made little difference. Your investment was increasing in value. Though your actual contributions to the plan may have been modest in size, visions of college *and* graduate school began dancing in your head.

WARNING

Stock markets don't always soar, and investment markets that are staggering under the weight of years of unsound economics, burgeoning budget deficits, high inflation, and questionable accounting practices tend to affect all mutual funds, including Section 529 funds, negatively. Many investors have watched the value of their savings plans shrink well below their initial contribution amounts. And now, adding insult to injury, the fund managers, who make their money even when the markets are doing poorly, haven't chosen to waive the fees they charge to manage these accounts. Imagine!

TIP

Still, if you envision your son or daughter giving the Latin valedictory address at Harvard at some future date, saving only in a prepaid tuition plan isn't going to fill the bill for you because it only covers tuition. Section 529 savings plans offer some advantages over their prepaid tuition relatives.

>> Distributions from Section 529 savings plans can be used for all qualified higher educational expenses, not just tuition.

>> When planning how much to contribute to your Section 529 plan, you don't need to project costs only for undergraduate school. These plans also can be used to pay for graduate schools. Also, they can make up to $10,000 annual qualified distributions for primary and secondary school tuitions, pay for

apprenticeships and trade schools, and pay off up to $10,000 of already existing federal student loans.

TIP

>> If your savings haven't produced any earnings at all — your plan is worth less than the amount you put into it when you begin to take distributions — you may claim a loss on your income tax return in the year in which you finally fully distribute the plan only if the final distribution from the plan happens in 2026 or later. When the amount you have been able to distribute over the years is less than the total of your contributions (your basis), you may deduct the difference between your cost and the amount distributed as a miscellaneous itemized deduction subject to a 2 percent Adjusted Gross Income limitation on Schedule A of your Form 1040 in tax years beginning after December 31, 2025. This provision adds insult to injury. Not only is the deduction not available for several more years, but when it does become available, your deduction will be reduced by 2 percent of your adjusted gross income in the year you claim the loss.

Guaranteed savings plans

Although all Section 529 plans are created equal under the terms of Section 529 of the Internal Revenue Code, not all savings plans will perform equally well. As a result, many states (but not all) have a guaranteed savings option that functions as somewhat of a hybrid between a 529-qualified tuition plan and a 529-qualified savings plan. These plans are referred to as 529 Guaranteed Savings Plans.

Typically, these plans are limited to designated beneficiaries who are residents of the state sponsoring the plan. The guarantee is not a specified rate of return; instead, it's a rate of return equal to the average annual increase in tuition in that particular state. For example, if you are a resident of Washington State and invest in their Guaranteed Education Tuition (GET) Program, you purchase tuition units. A bachelor's degree at one of Washington State's public universities or colleges requires 800 tuition units, so if you contributed $16,000 before June 30, 2022, you would have purchased 140.339 units of tuition (the purchase price per unit through June 30, 2022, was $114.01). In the same vein, if you wanted to superfund your child's 529 plan, you could put in 5 years of $16,000 contributions ($80,000 total) into the plan and purchase 701.693 units. In year 6 of the plan, to fully fund the Washington State GET program, you would need to purchase 98.307 additional units at whatever the price is in year 6. Once that money is in the Washington State GET plan, you've essentially guaranteed that you have four years of tuition when your student is ready for college.

Only three states currently offer 529 guaranteed savings plans: Pennsylvania, Texas, and Washington State. All require that either the plan owner or the designated beneficiary be a state resident at the time the plan is opened. The Pennsylvania and Texas plans allow you to purchase units at various tiers. That means you could purchase units for a private 4-year or public university. Washington State's plan only allows unit purchases based on the average price of a Washington State public university.

REMEMBER

The guaranteed savings plan is a sane response to burgeoning college costs, assuring your savings' low-risk and reasonable (although not spectacular) growth while not tying you to the more limited contribution amounts of prepaid tuition plans.

Contribution limits in these plans are generally the same as for savings plans administered by those states (except for Washington State, whose plan appears to limit contribution amounts to four-year tuition at an in-state public university — much more in keeping with a prepaid tuition plan limit).

If one is available to you, why would you choose a guaranteed savings plan as opposed to an ordinary 529 savings plan? It's the guarantee. Remember, the stock market fluctuates, and as the past several years have shown, those fluctuations can be significant. The guaranteed savings plan will ensure that the money you think you've stashed away for education expenses is there when you need it. It won't reflect the heights of the stock market when the markets are doing well, but neither will it plummet when it appears the markets are falling off a cliff. If you're looking for an investment in education that will just do its job and be there when you need it without any fireworks and without you losing sleep, this may be just the ticket for you.

Weighing the 529 plan features

Education savings plans are a favorite child of Congress, and they are forever tinkering with what the money in these plans can and cannot be used for. If you open a plan when your eligible student is an infant, I can almost certainly guarantee that the rules will be different by the time you start making distributions. If ever there were a moving target, Section 529 plans would qualify. Still, you should be looking for certain things and getting answers to certain questions before putting any money into any fund.

Checking how your state income tax is affected

TIP

Section 529 plan contributions often are income-tax deductible, either in whole or in part, on your state income tax return. Often that tax deduction is limited to state residents who participate in their home state plans, but some states give a deduction for a contribution to any plan. You need to check.

You also know that distributions to the designated beneficiary of a plan — to the extent it is used for qualifying higher education expenses — are tax-exempt at the federal level. Many states follow the federal rules and offer tax exemption to the earnings on distributions from their own in-state plans. Other states exempt the earnings from any plan. Finally, some states aren't yet on the bandwagon, taxing the earnings from any plan, in-state or out.

You also should be aware that some states (those who don't follow the federal rules) may tax the deferred income earned in accounts when you make a federally tax-free rollover from one state's plan to another's. If you invest in an in-state plan and receive a deduction on your state income tax return(s) for your contributions, and then roll your account over to an out-of-state plan, you may also have to add back, or recapture, your prior deductions and pay income tax on them. If the change of plan is advantageous to you otherwise, you may just have to pay the tax and move on.

Some states lack an income tax altogether. If you live in one of these states, feel free to invest in any state's plan, because your own state doesn't provide any income tax benefit, either on contributions or distributions.

However, some states have a dividends and interest tax that taxes only — you guessed it — dividends and interest. Because the earnings on Section 529 plans consist of primarily dividends and interest, if you make a nonqualifying distribution, the earnings may be liable for this particular tax. Be familiar with the tax law governing your state and the state where your plan is located.

Transferring and rolling over plans

If you find you have more money in an account for one designated beneficiary than they might need (or they won't need at all), you can make a tax-free rollover between accounts for different beneficiaries as often as you'd like.

Transferring between accounts for the same designated beneficiary can only happen once in a twelve-month period. If you make a subsequent rollover to that beneficiary before those twelve months are up, it's considered a taxable distribution, and the penalties will add insult to injury.

Say that you have a 529 savings plan for your daughter. The plan hasn't done as well as you would like, and your daughter is going to a state university in a few years. You decide to transfer your savings plan into your state's Section 529 prepaid tuition plan. You can buy four years' worth of tuition with the amount currently in your savings plan. Because you've kept the same beneficiary on the new plan as was on the old, the transfer is tax-free. Should your student decide that they want to attend college at a neighboring state school, you can transfer your

529 prepaid tuition plan for them to the new state, but you must wait for 12 months before doing so.

Tax-free transfers may be made from any type of Section 529 plan to any other type, between states (so long as residency requirements are respected), and even from Coverdell savings accounts to Section 529 plans.

You may also transfer or rollover an account tax-free to a new beneficiary at any time if you meet the following requirements:

>> You must complete the account transfer or rollover to a new beneficiary within 60 days from when the money leaves the first account (the original distribution date).

>> The new beneficiary must be a member of the same family as the original beneficiary within the permitted relationships.

Finally, even if you don't roll over an account to a new account, you're permitted to change the designated beneficiary on any account at any time without any tax consequence if the new beneficiary is a member of the same family as the original beneficiary.

Opening accounts with funds from a UGMA/UTMA account

From the perspective of a child's well-being, UGMA (Uniform Gift to Minor Act)/ UTMA (Uniform Transfer to Minor Act) accounts may be the worst idea since Al Capone decided not to pay his taxes (see Chapter 12). However, many people set up these accounts for their children and grandchildren when faced with the desire to start gifting away substantial amounts of wealth (especially in the rampant stock market of recent years). At the time, when they were babies, putting securities into these custodial accounts seemed like a great idea. The kids couldn't touch the money (at least not without the custodian's permission), and it would be there, waiting for them, when they reached college age. What a deal — providing college money for the kids and shrinking your personal estate at the same time.

However, now those babies aren't babies anymore; they're getting close to those magic ages when all that money becomes theirs, and they're still incredibly young. For years, they may not know about these custodial accounts, but when they reach ages 18 or 21, they'll definitely find out about them. They'll also discover that everything there is theirs to use wisely or fritter. Unfortunately, your child may be the type to fritter.

Surprise! If you want to add at least a layer of deterrent to your child's ability to squander all, or a portion, of what you've saved in a UGMA or UTMA account, you can transfer the money in a UGMA or UTMA account into a Section 529 plan if you are the UGMA/UTMA custodian. A few different restrictions will be in place, though:

» The funds you contribute aren't really yours — they're funds currently being held in custody for a minor child. Accordingly, although you are the plan owner until the child turns 18, at 18, the plan owner becomes the child. In other words, moving this money into a 529 plan doesn't allow you to regain control over these savings

» You may not choose any designated beneficiary other than the child whose UGMA/UTMA account originally funded the plan, and once the designation is in place, you may not change it.

» When the plan reverts to the child's ownership at age 18, they can take whatever distributions they want, regardless of whether the money will be used for educational expenses. If the money is not used for qualified expenses, however, income tax on the earnings, plus the 10 percent penalty, will be assessed. Unfortunately, most 18-year-olds will do whatever they will with money without regard to the income tax consequences; for them, income taxes are something their parents and grandparents moan about, but it's not a topic even on their radar yet.

Using UGMA/UTMA accounts to fund 529 plans makes money more expensive for a child to access to buy that sports car or take that trip (because of the addition of the 10 percent penalty on top of the income tax owed), but it doesn't make it impossible. Hopefully, the additional cost will make the new account owner think twice before spending the money unwisely.

Opening multiple accounts

As a plan owner, you may open as many Section 529 plans as you want, in as many locations as you can, and that makes sense for you, provided you have enough designated beneficiaries to go around. You may not have more than one designated beneficiary per account; however, a designated beneficiary may have more than one account set up for them. If you're purchasing prepaid tuition but your prepaid tuition plan covers only tuition, also investing in a savings plan often makes sense. When your student finally begins their college career, you'll have money in the savings account to pay all the qualified expenses the prepaid tuition plan won't.

WARNING

Let's say you come from an incredibly generous family. In that case, you may want to be certain that the aggregate amount in all the plans for one designated beneficiary does not exceed the qualified expenses the beneficiary is likely to incur. Excess contributions trigger income tax and a penalty on the income portion of the balance not used for education expenses. However, if you find yourself in this situation, you may want to consider changing the designated beneficiary on one or more accounts. You can even transfer it to yourself and retrain yourself in a new field or pursue a long-held interest.

Assessing the risk

Very few things in life are sure, and most 529 plans belong in the "not sure" category. Anytime you put money into securities other than savings or money market accounts, you put your nest egg at risk. Investments can fall in value as easily as they can rise, as many a dismayed investor has found.

WARNING

The riskiest of all Section 529 plans are the savings plans, although not all savings plans carry the same level of risk. These plans are most closely tied to the stock and bond markets and will enjoy the same bumpy ride. The gains can be spectacular (in a strong market and with a good plan manager); the losses can be devastating. Seeing the value of your savings decrease is never easy. Watching your child's education seeping away is especially difficult.

Both guaranteed savings and prepaid tuition plans are much safer than savings plans because they're usually tied to specific investments that are less volatile. Many prepaid tuition plans may invest only in state obligations (read municipal bonds), which have a fixed rate of return over their lifetime, although bond prices can fluctuate. Although your gains will not be huge, you should do alright if you hold on to your tuition certificates or your guaranteed savings account and redeem these accounts only to pay qualified expenses.

Still, tuition costs often rise higher than the return on the modest investments these accounts are allowed to make. If the earnings in an account don't keep pace with tuition hikes, the state administering the plan may discount the amount of tuition you think you've purchased. You may think you've funded four years of tuition, but you actually have only three.

Most states without a guarantee have provisions to make up for any deficiencies between their plan's earnings and the actual costs. Some states may devote lottery monies, while others may take a percentage of unclaimed property and devote this to the shortfall. Very few states without a guaranteed return on prepaid tuition plans or guaranteed savings plans lack any contingency plan at all. Carefully investigate the plan you're thinking of investing in for these safeguards.

Finally, some states absolutely guarantee that the tuition you think you're pre-paying will be paid, in full, to the extent that you've purchased it. These gold-plated plans often have residency requirements for the plan owner, the plan beneficiary, or both. Check carefully.

Now, because states actually administer so many Section 529 plans, you may be wondering whether the states can liberate money you contribute into any plan and divert it to another function. The answer is an unequivocal no! The money you put into any Section 529 plan is segregated from all the other money that states collect or hold. It is segregated from all tax revenues, and the state (or plan manager) must always account for it. Siphoning money away from a registered account (because that's what these accounts are) is theft, even if the state does it.

Chapter **6**

Applying Section 529 Plans to Your Household

I f you decide that a Section 529 plan makes sense for you and your family (see Chapter 5), the next step is putting theory into action and actually opening and funding a Section 529 plan.

In this chapter, you find all the information you could want on how, exactly, you go about doing that. You figure out how to choose the right plan for your situation (every plan fits someone's life, but not every plan may be right for you) and how to fund it. And after your plan's funded, you find out how closely you should watch your investments and when you may want to consider changing them. Finally, you see what happens when the magic day arrives, and you finally start making distributions from your plan to pay for the qualified educational expenses of your student.

Finding the Best Plan for You

REMEMBER

When you're looking at most things, the cookie-cutter approach almost never works, and that is especially true of financial planning and education savings. No two families are exactly alike, and what works best for your siblings and your friends and their families probably won't be what works best for you and yours. You can make your Section 529 plan(s) a success for your family, but first, you need to consider your needs.

Creating a 529 checklist

Just like shopping for groceries, clothes, or a house, you'll be most efficient in choosing a plan when you know exactly what you need before you ever look at what's being offered. Plans that have features you don't need but lack qualities that you do may work well for some people but not for you.

TIP

Here is a checklist that you should have answers to before you start looking. Keep in mind that your answers today don't necessarily need to be your answers tomorrow; these plans are flexible and can be changed as needed.

>> **Who will be your designated beneficiary?** Your plan choice may vary depending on the age of your student. You may also choose differently for your child who has a lifelong membership in the Future Doctors of America than for your child who lives with his head in a car engine.

>> **Where do you or your beneficiary anticipate attending school?** Obviousy, if your designated beneficiary is an infant or young child, they can't express their college preferences — even if you have taught them every word of your alma mater's fight song. But don't despair — this is where your expectations come into play. You choose; you can always change it later. Don't forget that you may also be living in an area with poor public schools, so adding enough leeway into your plan to afford private school tuition may make sense. On the other hand, you may have a gold-plated public school system, and unless the planets refuse to align properly, you know your student won't be going private.

>> **What do you anticipate the cost will be of that choice at the time your student will be attending, not only for tuition but also for all other expenses?** Now it's time for you to do some homework, checking out all the expenses listed in Chapter 2 and figuring out where your child's choice slots into that equation.

>> **Given your current income and future earning potential, is your student likely to qualify for need-based financial aid when the time comes?** If there's no way you'll ever be able to pay the full amount, looking at how different types of plans are counted in the federal financial aid formula may make one plan preferable to another.

>> **What state do you live in, and does your state give tax benefits either for contributions to its own Section 529 plans or for distributions from its own plans?** Does it give tax benefits to contributions and/or distributions from other states' Section 529 plans?

>> **How much can you put away into a 529 plan regularly without unduly strangling your family budget and dooming you to a life of beans on toast?** You want to save as much as you reasonably can, with the emphasis

here on "reasonably." You still have to live now. If you're happiest when you're squeezing the buffalo on a nickel so hard you can hear it squeal, go for it. But if life without the prospect of an occasional movie or dinner in a nice restaurant (fast food doesn't count here) seems like an endless, dark existence, you may want to save a little less and budget a set amount for current little extras.

>> **Who's your successor-designated beneficiary (see Chapter 5 for the relationship test), and who's your successor owner (see Chapter 7 for instances where that might happen)?** And will your successor beneficiary and owner meet residency restrictions your plan may have?

With the completed checklist in hand, you can select a plan and begin saving.

TIP

If you and your student expect they will attend either a state college or university or a community college, the first place to look is at prepaid tuition options in your state or the state in which your student plans to attend school. But, if you see only private options, out-of-state public universities, or a graduate/professional school career in the future, you may want to look only at the savings plans offered by all states run by mutual fund companies. Or you could take a look at the Private College 529 Plan, which covers tuition at about 300 private universities around the country. Finally, you could look at a combination of the two.

Looking at state-run plans

While there are currently 18 state and private prepaid tuition plans, only 10 are currently accepting new applicants, and 8 of those have residency requirements. In addition to the Private College 529 Plan, the states currently accepting new applicants are Florida, Maryland, Massachusetts, Michigan, Mississippi, Nevada, Pennsylvania, Texas, and Washington. Only the Massachusetts U.Plan (which isn't a 529 plan at all since it predates Section 529 of the Internal Revenue Code) and The Private College 529 Plan are open to residents of all states. All the others carry restrictions limiting initial enrollment to residents of the state offering the plan. Also, because these plans only cover tuition costs (with a few exceptions — read the fine print!), you may want to open a 529 Savings Plan for your beneficiary, so other qualified expenses are covered, such as room and board, books, fees, and other related costs.

TIP

Read the fine print carefully; plans may have restrictions beyond residency. Many limit the age at which you can set up a plan for a specific beneficiary, so you may be out of luck in a particular plan if your student is in high school already and you haven't yet begun. They may also restrict when distributions must start and when you must complete your distribution schedule.

Most plans are backed by the full faith and credit of the state (which means they'll cover any losses, so you're not at risk). Some plans are backed by contingencies written into the statutes governing them, requiring action by state legislatures, the governor, or some other stopgap to plug the holes. But not all plans have backup plans in place. Once again, you need to read the fine print carefully.

Table 6-1 lists the available prepaid tuition and guaranteed savings plans. This is only a place to start. Plans can be added and dropped, and new enrollments and/or new contributions can be suspended at any time. Check with your state or the state whose plan you're considering for up-to-date information when you're ready to enroll your student.

TABLE 6-1   ### Prepaid Tuition (PT) and Guaranteed Savings (GS) Plans, by State

State	Plan Name	Plan	Tuition and Fees	Other Qualified Expenses	2022 Cost of Fully Funded 4-year University Plan for Infant
FL	Stanley G. Tate Florida Prepaid College Plan	PT	Yes	Additional plan available	$28,559
MD	Maryland Senator Edward J. Kasemeyer Prepaid Prepaid College Trust	PT	Yes	No	$47,030
MA	U.Plan	PT	Yes	No	***
MI	Michigan Education Trust	PT	Yes	No	$61,760
MS	Mississippi Prepaid Affordable College Tuition Program (MPACT)	PT	Yes	No	$39,863
NV	Nevada Prepaid Tuition Program	PT	Yes	No	$24,747
PA	Pennsylvania 529 Guaranteed Savings Plan*	GS	Yes	Yes	$511,758
TX	Texas Tuition Promise Fund**	GS	Yes	No	$65,648
WA	Washington Guaranteed Education Tuition (GET)	Both	Yes	No	$91,208
	The Private College 529 Plan**	Units	Yes	No	$317,030

*Guaranteed savings program — contributions up to the allowable amount for all 529 Plans for a particular state
**Current cost of tuition and fees for four years at the highest-cost participating institution

Considering mutual fund plans

Most prepaid tuition plans only cover tuition (and mandatory fees). But for the purpose of what 529 plans are allowed to pay for, education costs only begin with tuition (see Chapter 2). Once your designated beneficiary has left primary and secondary school behind, where only $10,000 per year of tuition may be paid for with a 529 plan distribution, most other college costs can be paid for with the money you've saved in a 529 savings plan.

Almost all states (Wyoming is the only state that doesn't offer any 529 plans, but they have an agreement with Colorado to offer Colorado's plans instead) also offer savings plans that you can purchase directly through the state. These plans are managed by professional money managers located at some of the biggest mutual fund companies in the country. These savings plans allow you to invest in various mutual funds based on your student's current age, a certain percentage of your funds invested in stocks and bonds, or just in a bank deposit program. You choose the type of investments (age-based, static investment options, or bank deposits), and the fund manager for your choice chooses the specific investments within each option. (See the "Considering mutual fund plans" section later in this chapter).

Unlike the savings plans offered directly to you, the purchaser, by the states, there are also numerous plans that must be purchased through a broker. These plans typically carry higher fees since you have to pay that broker/money manager for their expertise. While these plans appear to be sold through a mutual fund company, they are actually sponsored by various states. You'll see these 529 plans marketed as "advisor-sold" plans, which means you can't buy into one of these directly. You'll definitely need a broker.

REMEMBER

The truth is that mutual fund managers are pros, and if there is a way to make money in the stock and bond markets, they're very likely the ones who will figure it out. However, they are not infallible, and many a fund has plunged in value even as the general markets have risen or stayed the same. Those past performance numbers show only how the fund has done in the past — they don't predict how any fund will perform in the future.

No matter how well or poorly a particular manager has done, the fact remains that if you want to invest in a Section 529 savings plan, you're almost definitely going to have to deal with the decisions of at least one mutual fund manager over the lifetime of the account because most states have farmed out their investing to these companies.

Before you jump right into a professionally managed savings account, you need to remember a few things:

>> **Professional money managers don't work for free, nor are they cheap.** Management fees associated with Section 529 savings plans managed by mutual fund companies are notably higher than fees charged by state-managed plans. Fees vary widely. Check carefully and be prepared to pay even when your account isn't gaining in value. The fund companies don't drop their fees out of the goodness of their hearts.

>> **Many mutual fund plans can't be purchased except through a broker or a financial planner.** If the fund you want can only be accessed this way, you need to know that you will spend a substantial amount to join. Not only will you have the fund fees, but you'll also be paying a broker's commission. As you flip through the appendix at the back of the book, any fund that states it's sold only through a financial advisor has this extra fee tacked on.

>> **Mutual fund companies make money on large accounts, not small ones.** Although the amount required to start in any fund varies by state and mutual fund company, many companies require a substantial initial investment. You may find that you need between $1,000 and $3,000 just to open an account. Carefully check the plans you're interested in for minimum opening deposit amounts.

>> **Just because a professional is managing your money doesn't mean you can just sit back and relax.** *You* are ultimately responsible for the well-being of your 529 account, and you need to be ready to make changes when whatever the plan manager is doing is clearly not working.

While a specific state administers them, most mutual-fund managed plans aren't restricted in any way to only state-resident owners or beneficiaries. This lack of restrictions allows you a great deal of latitude when shopping for a plan, especially as more states rework their tax laws to allow tax-exempt distributions from out-of-state plans (most plans don't tax the income portion of qualified distributions from their own plans owned by in-state residents). You need to be careful, though, and make sure that your state not only currently follows these rules but continues to follow these rules. As states struggle to close budget gaps, the untaxed money from 529 distributions may be attractive additional sources of income. If your state changes the rules regarding income taxation of out-of-state plan distributions, you may want to relocate your plan to your home state.

Opening a Plan

After you complete your research and decide what plan you want to invest in, you can obtain an application, complete it, and send it off with a check to open your account (or wire the money directly from your bank through an ACH transfer). Applications for all plans are available on the Internet. States will also snail mail applications for the non-tech savvy among us. If you're investing in a plan that may only be purchased through a financial advisor, obtain the application directly from that person (who'll probably be more than helpful in filling it out, as well). Also, be sure to obtain (and keep) a prospectus for your plan and the plan agreement, which outlines all the rules and regulations governing your plan.

No matter what state's plan you invest in — whether directly with the state or through an advisor — the application process is quite straightforward. As discussed in Chapter 5, you need to provide the information for the plan owner, the designated beneficiary, a successor owner, and parent or guardian information (if the designated beneficiary is a minor child).

Funding a Plan

After you complete your application and send it off, you need to get down to the serious business of making your 529 plan grow. And, although you'd like to think that the stock and bond markets will rocket skyward, multiplying the value of your initial investment so rapidly (and securely, of course) that you'll never have to add any more money to your account, you really do need to be sensible here. Unless you can sock away the full amount your student will likely need when you set up the plan, you have to make additional contributions for this to work. Opening a plan and making an initial investment is only the start of saving enough to send your designated beneficiary to school. Consistent savings is the rest of the equation.

You can add money to a 529 plan in three ways:

>> Periodically send money, either through an ACH (American Clearing House) transfer, writing a check, using a money order, a cashier's check, or even travelers' checks.

>> Schedule automatic withdrawals from your bank account on a weekly, monthly, quarterly, or annual basis.

>> Make contributions through payroll withholdings.

Making an ACH transfer/writing a check

This contribution method may seem like a no-brainer, but for many people, it's the most difficult type of saving to do. Actually, going online and inputting your bank's 9-digit routing number (found on the lower left-hand corner of your check) and your account number, or writing a check and actually depositing it into an account where you won't be able to pull it back out without incurring a penalty takes discipline. I know — I'm guilty of writing many checks only to tear them up months later, knowing that the money I set aside for savings is now long gone and spent elsewhere.

If you are used to writing checks and decide to try the bank transfer instead, please make sure the money is in your account. These transfers happen overnight, so there isn't the usual wait for the post office to deliver your check and for it to be deposited. Overnight! If you don't want to receive that dreaded overdraft notice from your bank, make sure the money is in your account before you initiate the transfer.

However, if you invest in certain prepaid tuition plans (see Chapter 5), you may not have much of a choice. Some plans don't allow contributions except during a specific time window each year. Others, however, are happy to set you up on a payment plan (remember, in a prepaid tuition program, you purchase a set amount of tuition to a specific class of postsecondary schools).

Writing a check may work best for people whose income is variable throughout the year. If you work only in the summer and collect unemployment benefits every winter, you may want to make all your contributions in the summer when the money is rolling in.

Although initiating a transfer or writing a check takes the most discipline, it also gives you the most control.

Automatically scheduling bank withdrawals

You may think of money in very concrete terms. The dollars and cents in your pocket have a certain look and feel, and even checks are tangible. But most money never takes physical form; instead, it whizzes around the world as bits and bytes of computer wizardry. You may already use this technology if you have direct deposits to your bank account or pay bills and fund other savings accounts in this way. Two basic types of transfers are available:

>> **Wire transfers** are made on a one-time-only basis using the Federal Reserve Wire system. You may find that this is the best option for you when opening a Section 529 account. Wire transfers can be made at any time of the banking day.

>> **Automatic fund transfers** are made using the American Clearing House (ACH) system. (No, you aren't entering a sweepstakes, and a celebrity with a six-foot check will not ring your doorbell.) These transfers are generally made periodically (every week, every month, or however you choose) on a specific day of the week or month you choose. The money transfers first thing in the morning before the bank opens.

REMEMBER

When setting up an ACH transfer, be certain the money you're transferring is really in your account. If you get paid via direct deposit on the first of every month, set up your transfer for a few days later (leaving yourself the luxury of a long weekend between receipt of the money and subsequent transfer). Often, money deposited isn't available to you until the next banking day, after the bank is sure that the money isn't going to be yanked back. Also, be aware that if you set up your ACH transfer on a specific day each month, the money transfers on that day, provided it is a day the bank is open. If your day falls on a weekend or legal holiday, the money transfers on the first day *after* (never before) your scheduled day that the bank is open.

In order to set up an ACH transfer, you need to provide your plan administrator with a copy of a check from your account. The face of the check provides all the information necessary to put automatic withdrawals into motion (as you can see in Figure 6-1).

Total qualifying educational expenses	$15,000
SUBTRACT: Scholarship amount	− 2,000
Net qualifying educational expenses	$13,000
Total distribution from Section 529 Plan	$20,000
SUBTRACT: Net qualifying educational expenses	−13,000
Total nonqualifying distribution from Sec. 529 Plan	$7,000
Ratio of nonqualifying to total distribution	$7,000/$20,000 = 35%
Taxable portion of nonqualifying expenses	$3,500 × 35% = $1,225

FIGURE 6-1: Necessary info for automatic fund transfer.

If you're already familiar with automatic fund transfers, you know how easy they are to use and how painless payments are when made in this way. If this is all new to you, you may need a little time to become comfortable with the idea. After an automatic transfer is in place and functioning, you may wonder how you ever managed without it.

Making contributions through payroll withholdings

Contributions through payroll deductions aren't available to everyone, but more companies are offering a payroll deduction for 529 plans. This option works just like all the other payroll deductions that you may be familiar with, such as medical insurance premiums, flexible spending accounts for medical and dependent care expenses, and tax-deferred retirement savings. Payroll withholdings offer several benefits:

>> **Automatic state tax benefits, where applicable:** If you live in a state where contributions into your state plan(s) are tax-deductible, the adjustment for state taxes is made on your paycheck rather than waiting for a refund at the end of the year.

>> **Flexibility:** Most people procrastinate when facing a call to a mutual fund company or a state agency to change amounts being transferred. However, a trip down to your company's personnel office to make a change is easy — and on company time.

>> **Employer matches:** How's this for a novel employee benefit? Nothing in the employer handbook or the Internal Revenue Code says that your employer can't match at least a portion of your contributions into your student's 529 plan. Remember, anyone can contribute to the plan you own. If you're making contributions through a payroll deduction, your employer has an easy way to figure out how much of your contribution to match.

>> **Automatic cessation of fund transfers when employment ends:** No one wants to contemplate losing a job, but it happens. When it does, you may want to consider halting contributions into a Section 529 plan, at least until you've found a new job. If you fund your plan through payroll withholdings, the fund transfers stop when your paychecks stop.

Managing Your Investments

You know, of course, that you're not allowed to direct the investments of a Section 529 plan once your money is safely stowed in a particular plan (see Chapter 5). However, you have choices about where you initially put your money. If your investments aren't doing well, you can move them once in every 12-month period without receiving a penalty for a nonqualified withdrawal.

Selecting an investment strategy that works for you

Section 529 savings plans were created as a response to the perceived inflexibility of the earliest iterations of 529 prepaid tuition plans. Now, instead of guaranteed tuition payments, you have the flexibility to choose the type of investment strategy you want to follow. Of course, as Aunt May always reminds us, with great power comes great responsibility; now that you have choices, you need to understand them to make good decisions for your money and the future education of your designated student.

The element of risk

In the world of investments, nothing is a "sure thing." If you have retirement and other investment accounts that have risen and fallen with the financial markets, this comes as no surprise to you. However, if this is your first serious venture into the wide world of investing, the inherent riskiness may shock you. No investment should ever make your hair stand on end; if it does, you may want to consider changing it.

Mutual funds are made up of equities (stocks), debt instruments (bonds), or a combination of both. When you purchase a stock, you're actually buying a piece of a particular company; when you buy a bond, you're lending money to that company. The income from stocks (which you receive either as a dividend or by receiving more for your stock when you sell than you paid for it) derives from the income from the company. A company that fails to earn more money than it spends rarely issues a dividend. Bond income represents interest payments on the loan you've made to that particular company.

It's all very simple in theory but may be more complicated in practice. The prices of stocks can rise and fall based on rumors rather than solid financial data. Prices are often inflated on hopes and promises rather than on reality. Likewise, a fixed payment on a bond may seem secure, but if the company borrowing the money is on a less-than-sound financial footing, the actual loan amount could be at risk.

TIP

To successfully invest in any mutual fund, whether it's inside a Section 529 plan, a retirement plan, or just as an independent investment, you need to determine what level of risk you're willing to take. If you have trouble sleeping when the stock market is on a roller coaster, you may want to invest more heavily in bond funds (which are generally more stable in price than stock funds but can offer a more moderate rate of return). But, if you can shrug your shoulders even when the stock market is exploring the depths and just continue on with your life, investing in an aggressive stock fund could be just the ticket for you. The higher amount of risk should lead to a higher total return on your investment over time if you have the patience to wait out market downturns.

Short-term versus long-term investing

When you invest in a Section 529 plan, you clearly have an idea that, at a certain time, a certain someone whom you know and probably love will require money for education. That is, after all, why you set up the plan in the first place and put that person's name on the line labeled "designated beneficiary." So, whether that designated beneficiary has just been born or is already in high school, you have some idea of when you might need to access the money you've been saving.

This is where timing issues come into play. One major factor in dealing with risk is allowing yourself enough time to come back from a bad market. If you're in a market downturn, but your designated beneficiary is only just starting public kindergarten, you probably have enough time to sit out this particular market cycle. If you just hang on, your investments should return to where they started and then increase in value again. You do need to be patient, though. Remember, losses are only really losses when you cash out of a plan; until then, they exist only on paper.

As your designated beneficiary closes in on the magic scheduled time of distribution, you may want to think carefully about the level of risk in your current plan and begin to decrease it. Even though a more conservative approach (moving an increasingly large portion of your overall savings into bond funds and money market funds) limits the amount your investments will grow, you want to be sure that, when you need the money in order to make qualified distributions, the money is there.

Age-based management

TIP

If you don't feel that you're a savvy enough investor to make timing decisions on your own or if you don't want to have to keep track of when you should be making changes, many Section 529 savings plans have an age-based management feature that you may opt to use.

Essentially, all this option does is allocate your investment among stocks, bonds, and cash (money market funds, actually, because no money in a mutual fund ever just sits around doing nothing), depending on the current age of your designated beneficiary. When the beneficiary is very young (preschool or younger), your mix may be entirely stocks, where the potential gains should be larger. As they age, the mix slowly moves away from stocks and toward bonds and cash.

Every 529 plan offering an age-based management option allocates among stocks, bonds, and cash a little differently, and the ages at which shifts begin to occur aren't exactly the same either. Investing isn't a precise science.

Management through asset allocation

In addition to age-based management, many plans also offer *static investment options* or access to funds where the asset mixture stays the same over time. You may have a choice of a fund that's 100 percent stocks, one that's 100 percent bonds, or any mixture of the two. In addition, your plan may offer a mutual fund that invests only in foreign investments. Or your plan may offer a mutual fund that works like a money market fund. In a money market fund, your initial investment is protected (it won't decrease in value), but your growth in the fund is limited to the amount of interest currently being earned in money market accounts.

REMEMBER

Choosing to invest through asset allocation can be a double-edged sword. When you invest in this way, you essentially take on the responsibility for shifting from higher-risk funds to lower-risk funds as your student ages. You will need to be the person in charge of timing changes in investment strategy, and if you don't end up with a brilliant result, the fault will be yours. Of course, if your strategy pays off (and you know it will — that's why you're doing this), your market savvy will become the stuff of family legend.

On the other hand, investing through asset allocation makes tremendous sense for people who aren't certain when (or even if) their designated beneficiary will start requiring education funds. If you have doubts about the future plans of your current designated beneficiary, maintaining flexibility through asset allocation allows you to continue with a successful investing strategy long after when age-based management has begun moving your investment mix to a lower-risk, lower-return one. If you find yourself in this position, you may want to continue to manage through asset allocation, at least until your current beneficiary begins to make some concrete plans or you change your beneficiary designation to someone else.

Identifying and changing a strategy that has gone haywire

It's sad to say, but not every child attends college or the college of your choice, not every savings plan works (the road to hell being paved with good intentions), and not every investment strategy miraculously causes your money to grow rapidly and safely. Life is littered with good planning that has failed for one reason or another. The beauty of Section 529 plans is that they do not staple you into one box but rather allow you to make changes, within reason, as your life's circumstances change. (Chapter 7 discusses changes in beneficiary designations and savings shortfalls and overflows in detail.)

Investment strategies that fail to live up to their advanced billing are a big reason why many savings plans fall short of the mark. Investment returns aren't guaranteed, and your investment in a fund will only do approximately as well as the general market. When the markets rise, so will the value of your investment; when they fall, so will your account value.

REMEMBER

Section 529 savings plans don't come with a safety net. There are no state guarantees of your contribution amounts *or* the amounts that may have accumulated from interest and dividends. If you contributed $10,000 last year, it might be worth only $8,000 this year, and it'll buy only $8,000 worth of qualified educational expenses for your designated beneficiary.

Be aware of the performance of your funds over time. You can exchange a fund that isn't living up to your expectations for another fund, either within the same plan or as a rollover of your current plan to a different Section 529 plan of any type. Suppose you find that your investments have lost value and that there is no way that you'll be able to save enough for your designated beneficiary's education at an Ivy League school. In this case, you may opt to roll over all or part of your current savings plan into a prepaid tuition plan that will pay tuition at a state college or university. If any balance remains in the original 529 plan after you purchase all your prepaid tuition contracts, you can distribute it to the designated beneficiary to pay qualified expenses that aren't covered by the prepaid tuition plan.

REMEMBER

If your Section 529 savings plan investments are doing poorly and you choose to make a change, you need to know that you may make a tax-free rollover from one plan to another only once in a 12-month period. If you change plans more frequently, any transfers after the first count as taxable distributions, subject to both income tax on any income and the 10 percent penalty. Of course, if the value of the plan has dropped below the amount you have contributed to it, this may not be a problem, as there won't be any income to tax or penalize. See Chapter 5 to find out the tax consequences of a loss.

TIP

Whatever your risk tolerance, don't stay with an investment that continues to do poorly. Set a limit for how much you're willing to lose from your account (10 percent, 20 percent — it's your money, your limit, and your choice). When your investment starts approaching that lower number, it's time to start researching again and making a decision.

Taking Qualifying Distributions

You've saved, you've invested, and amazingly enough, your investments have grown. Now, your designated beneficiary is ready and raring to head off to college, and you actually have the money you need. What could be better?

In the somewhat odd world of Section 529, where taxability doesn't follow the account ownership, the beneficiary (not the owner) bears all the income tax consequences of distributions made to (or on behalf of) them. Remember, you own the account even if you had to file gift tax returns for giving the money in the account away to the Section 529 plan.

Depending on the state and the type of plan you own, distributions are made directly from the plan to the school (this most likely occurs with a prepaid tuition plan), you, or your designated beneficiary. If checks are being written to you or your beneficiary, make sure you create a good paper trail showing exactly what qualified expenses were paid with the distribution amounts. Remember, it's not enough that you have a qualified student who is actually attending an institution of higher learning; you also need to use the distributions from your 529 plan to pay those expenses.

TIP

Assuming that (a) your designated beneficiary is now a qualified student and (b) that student is now incurring qualified expenses, you now need to figure out just how much of a distribution you should make from your Section 529 plan. In calculating this number, here's what you need to do:

>> **Estimate how much the qualified expenses are likely to be, not only this year but also for the remainder of this student's education.** If you think your savings may be a bit short, spending them all in one or two years may make sense if you need to make up the balance by using your current income. Spread them out over the lifetime of the diploma or degree your designated student is working toward. If you think your student may qualify for need-based financial aid (see Chapter 18), spending down the amount in the 529 plan in the first year or two may be to your advantage down the road.

>> **Explore what other resources are available to make up any gaps in funding.** If you don't have the total cost of all qualified expenses sitting in your Section 529 plan, you'll probably have to pay some portion of qualified expenses from your current earnings. If you also have a Coverdell Education Savings Account for your student, a portion of qualified expenses may also be paid from there (see Chapter 9).

>> **Consider any outright grants and scholarships your student may be entitled to.** To the extent that any sort of scholarship, fellowship, or grant money is available, it always offsets qualified tuition expenses first. The income portion of any 529-distribution amounts not used to pay qualified educational expenses is generally treated as taxable income to the recipient.

>> **If you want to take the American Opportunity Credit or Lifetime Learning Credit, you need to pay at least some qualified expenses using real, taxable income.** This includes wages, taxable interest and dividends, and rental income. You have to admit that this idea makes sense; you really shouldn't get a tax credit for expenses you paid with tax-exempt income.

If you've taken a Section 529 plan distribution that is too large, well, the world as you know it doesn't really end. To the extent that the distribution exceeds the amount of qualified education expenses, the income portion of the overage will be taxed at the designated beneficiary's tax rate, which is usually lower than your own. In addition, unless the excess distribution amount is one of the qualified exceptions outlined in Chapter 5, the student will also pay an additional 10 percent penalty on the income portion only of the nonqualified amount.

REMEMBER

Taking nonqualifying distributions from a Section 529 plan will cost your beneficiary money, but the sky won't fall in. Just don't make a habit of it.

What Does Uncle Sam Have to Say?

Section 529 is a federal code section under the Internal Revenue Code. It's not surprising, then, that the IRS has some input into documentation and reporting requirements. Always remember that the IRS is not in the business of making laws or implementing policies. (Congress is supposed to do that.) Its job is to enforce the laws that are on the books.

Reporting contributions: Income tax versus gift/GST tax

Very little in Section 529 qualifies as easy to understand — but this does. There is no current federal income tax deduction for contributions made into a Section 529 plan. You don't need to disclose to the IRS that you have a Section 529 plan on your income tax return (Form 1040). It doesn't matter how much money you earn; if you have the money to put into a plan, you can contribute it, no matter your income.

Finally, there's no limit to how much you can contribute in a single year or how many plans you can fund. You can put money into one account, six accounts, or a dozen. There is no limit. You can fully fund a plan, any plan, and as many plans as you want. You can fund a plan in one lump sum, up to the stated plan limit in a single year, although you may have gift and/or Generation-Skipping Transfer (GST) tax considerations. (Go back to Chapter 3 to see what this is all about; you can never read about gift and GST tax too many times.)

The rules regarding reporting contributions for gift and GST tax returns are a bit more complex, and you may decide early on to seek professional advice. Smart choice! However, here's a quick overview:

>> If you make gifts of less than $17,000 in 2023 to any one person (including the contribution you make into a Section 529 plan for that person), even if that gift isn't to your child, you don't need to file a Form 709, the U.S. Gift (and Generation-Skipping Transfer) Tax return.

>> If you make contributions into a Section 529 plan of between $17,000 and $85,000 for a single designated beneficiary in 2023, you need to file a Form 709 for this year (and for the next four years if you make any additional gifts in those years). Each year, you show the total amount of the gift and the amount eligible for annual exclusion status. If you give less than $85,000, you will report one-fifth of the total amount each year. You make this election on the tax return itself, which is due at the same time as your income tax return, as extended. You need to make the election only once, in the first year; in the subsequent four years, if you don't make other taxable gifts, you're not required to file a Form 709 for those years. If you're gift splitting with your spouse, both of you need to file a Form 709 in the first year, and both of you need to make the election for spreading the gift over five years.

>> If you make contributions into a Section 529 plan exceeding $85,000 in 2023 for any beneficiary — or $170,000 if you can split the gifts with your spouse (see Chapter 3) — you can still elect to spread $85,000 over five years. However, the balance of the amount over $85,000 is entirely taxable in the year the gift is made. Be certain to make the proper election on your gift tax return to get the five-year treatment.

>> When you contribute an amount exceeding the annual exclusion amounts to a 529 plan for a beneficiary who isn't your child, you need to know where this person fits on the generational scale for Generation-Skipping Transfer Tax (GSTT) purposes. If the person is your relative, this is easy to figure out — your children's children constitute one generation skipped, your niece's child is one generation skipped, and so on. If the designated beneficiary is not related to you, the generations are calculated by using your age as the benchmark as follows:

- For someone born not more than 12 1/2 years after you, they are considered to belong to your generation and is not a skip person.

- For someone born between 12 1/2 and 37 1/2 years after you, they are considered to belong to the same generation as your children and are not a skip person.

- For someone born between 37 1/2 and 62 1/2 years after you, they belong to the same generation as your grandchildren. Gifts made into a Section 529 plan also qualify for GSTT treatment.

GIFTING TUITION OUTRIGHT VERSUS GIFTING INTO A SECTION 529 PLAN

In one of the oddities of the Internal Revenue Code, you can make tax-free gifts of unlimited amounts of qualified tuition (although not room, board, or any of the other expenses qualified under Section 529) to any student without being shackled by annual exclusion amounts.

If you discovered the joys of Section 529 late in your designated beneficiary's secondary school career, you might find that the amount needed to fully fund a Section 529 plan exceeds your annual exclusions, even with the five-year election and gift-splitting. In such a case, pushing all the money needed for qualified educational expenses into a Section 529 plan might trigger a taxable gift. To avoid this, you may choose to put only a smaller amount — the amount your beneficiary might realistically spend for qualified educational expenses other than tuition — into a Section 529 plan. The amount that you'll need to pay tuition alone can be paid — without limitation and any gift tax consequences — directly to the educational institution when the tuition needs to be paid.

Unlimited tuition gifts can be made for tuition at any school, from preschool through graduate school, if you write your check to the school and not to the student (or their parents).

REMEMBER

Whenever you make a gift larger than your annual exclusion amount to anyone more than one generation removed from you, that gift becomes subject to the gift tax *and* the GSTT rules (Chapter 3 has info on these taxes).

Reporting distributions

After you figure out the contribution reporting requirements, you need to know how and where to report both qualifying and nonqualifying distributions for income tax purposes.

When you receive any distribution from a Section 529 plan, the plan manager must furnish a Form 1099-Q to the person receiving the distribution (or the person on whose behalf a distribution is made) by January 31 of the following year. On this form, you'll see the total distribution in Box 1, the earnings portion in Box 2, and your basis (the amount you contributed over the years) in Box 3. Box 2 and Box 3 added together should equal the amount in Box 1.

The good news is that although you or your student will receive this form, you determine what, if any, of your distribution is taxable. If you know the total distribution made to you paid for qualifying educational expenses, then all you need do is keep the 1099-Q safely stored with the rest of your tax information. (If the plan wrote the check directly to your college or university, that's a safe bet.) Doing so ensures that you can defend your position if any questions arise later.

However, if you know that some or all of the distribution was not used for qualifying expenses, then you need to do some calculations and arrive at the amount of taxable income you should include on your Form 1040's "Other Income" line.

For example, say a student received a distribution from his parents' Section 529 plan for $20,000. They also received a $2,000 scholarship. The student's qualifying expenses at their university were $15,000. Box 2 of their 1099-Q shows $3,500, while Box 3 shows $16,500. To arrive at the taxable income from this distribution, the student must make the calculation shown in Table 6-2.

In this example, if the parents have distributed more than the amount of qualified educational expenses to their student, they pay tax on the earnings portion of the nonqualified distribution. Also, the student pays the 10 percent penalty on the earnings included in the nonqualified distribution they would have received if they didn't have the scholarship. (In other words, they're not penalized for someone giving them free money.)

TABLE 6-2: ## Figuring Out Taxable Income from a 529 Distribution

529 Plan distribution	Form 1099-Q Box	Amount
Total distributions	1	20,000.00
Earnings	2	3,500.00
Basis	3	16,500.00
Qualifying education costs		15,000.00
less: Scholarship		(2,000.00)
Total qualifying costs paid from the 529 plan		13,000.00
Total nonqualifying costs paid from the 529 plan		7,000.00
Total taxable portion of 529 Plan distribution		
Total nonqualifying costs paid from the 529 plan divided by the total distribution		$\frac{7,000.00}{20,000.00}$ x 3,500 earnings = ######
Taxable portion of 529 Plan distribution subject to a 10 percent penalty		
Nonqualifying costs before scholarship money are applied Nonqualifying costs after scholarship money are applied		$\frac{5,000.00}{7,000.00}$ x 1225.00 subject to income tax = 875.00 subject to a 10% penalty

Form 1098-T, which your student will receive from their university, will only report tuition, fees, and room and board paid to the university. If your student is living in off-campus housing, the university won't know how much is being spent on rent and food. Don't think qualified education costs are limited by the amount shown on the 1098-T; your student may well have additional costs that also qualify. Just make sure that you keep good records in case the IRS comes calling, wanting proof of the higher amount of expenses you're claiming.

Reporting for purposes of future financial aid awards

Just like no two Section 529 plans are identical, the responses to how these plans affect financial aid awards vary widely and by type of plan.

Currently, distributions from all types of 529 plans are not counted as income in calculating need-based financial aid, whether the plan is owned by a parent or by the child. However, the plan value is treated as a parental asset, even if the child owns the plan. Therefore, it is limited to a reasonably low 5.64 percent inclusion rate when figuring the federal financial aid needs and the expected family contribution (EFC). Unfortunately, not all colleges and universities are satisfied with the Free Application for Federal Student Aid (the dreaded FAFSA). These institutions insist that you also complete a second financial aid application — the CSS/ Financial Aid Profile — used by many schools to provide institutional aid.

The CSS/Financial Aid Profile counts assets differently than the FAFSA. The CSS/ Financial Aid Profile includes some items excluded by the FAFSA, such as

>> The net value of your home (after all mortgages)

>> The value of small family-owned businesses

>> All 529 plans that are for the benefit of the designated student, regardless of who the plan owner is

>> Sibling assets for brothers and sisters under age 19

For FAFSA purposes, a 529 plan owned by Grandma Ida for a grandchild's benefit is not counted as an asset. However, distributions made from the plan are counted as untaxed income to the student. Therefore, they seriously damage federal financial aid eligibility in subsequent years as student income can be counted as much as 50 percent toward the EFC. If Grandma Ida has indeed set up a 529 plan for her grandchild, consider using the funds in that account only in the latter part of the child's education (the last year or 18 months) so that income increase won't appear on the FAFSA.

FAFSA and CSS/Financial Aid Profiles must be submitted for each year of financial aid your student might require. If you think you won't need financial aid or won't qualify for any — even if you do need help — you still need to file these forms. Eligibility for things like work/study jobs is pegged to the FAFSA, as is your student's eligibility for Pell Grants and subsidized and unsubsidized federal student loans.

In a fairly recent change, FAFSA is now filed based on the prior-prior year's income tax returns. This change was established to take the pressure off parents and students to get their prior year's tax returns prepared and filed in time to apply for financial aid. So now, if you are applying for financial aid for the 2023/2024 school year, the tax returns you're going to reference are your 2021 tax returns, not 2022.

Chapter **7**

Weighing the Pros and Cons of Section 529 Plans

I f you discover anything in your research about Section 529 plans, there's probably no such thing as a simple answer and that sometimes these plans won't suit your needs at all. A 529 plan may not be for you if your income is very low and you pay tax at the lowest rates because your student will probably receive full grants, and you may not be able to take advantage of the state tax advantages that might be available. Likewise, if your student is going to give Einstein a run for his money, they may receive a free (or partially assisted) ride to some fabulous institution and won't need the full amount of your savings.

For the rest, though, Section 529 plans — either by themselves or in concert with other education savings devices — may make a great deal of sense. In this chapter, you find out the benefits of having a Section 529 plan. However, because no plan is perfect, I also alert you to some potential problems with these plans and show you how to work around them.

Pondering the Pros of Section 529 Plans

In Voltaire's *Candide*, Dr. Pangloss forever talks about "the best of all possible worlds." Well, in the best of all possible worlds, 529 plans are a wonderful, marvelous creation that can pay all qualified primary, secondary, and post-secondary educational bills (and may even cure the common cold if invested correctly). In any number of scenarios, if you pick the right plan and the right investment strategy for your student, you both win. It's as simple as that.

Higher returns than traditional savings and investment accounts

Saving money is the name of the game, but saving efficiently (and accepting help when offered) is the best way to go about it. Although the federal and most state governments (Colorado, Illinois, and Massachusetts are the exceptions to this rule) won't start a savings account for you or put money into one you've opened, they provide tools to help your savings grow.

REMEMBER

Section 529 plans offer three ways by which your savings can grow faster than they would if you invested them in an ordinary investment account or in your local savings bank:

>> Tax deferrals (postponing when you pay tax)

>> Tax exemptions (not paying any income tax at all on earnings)

>> State income tax deductions and/or credits (sometimes being able to exclude your contributions from your income in the year that you make the contributions or receiving an amount off your taxes based on your contributions into a plan)

Here's how it works. Maryland residents George and Hannah will have their first baby in 2023. They don't have any savings in the bank, only the money they currently earn, so they know paying college costs 18 years down the road might be tough. George and Hannah think it's wise to start planning now.

They do their research and begin implementing their decisions as soon as the baby arrives. First, they decide to open a Section 529 plan, followed by opting for four years of paid tuition in Maryland's prepaid tuition plan, which offers tax-free, qualified distributions and tax-free contributions. They both attended the University of Maryland and received a fine education. It seems like a good choice for their baby.

George and Hannah know the next 18 years will pass quickly and that their son will be heading off to the University of Maryland (or any other college or university, but they're loyal alumni, so Maryland seems the obvious choice) in 2040. By religiously making their payments into the plan, they know they'll have four years' worth of tuition credits when the time comes. They expect their son, who they know will be a motivated student, will complete his degree in four years, graduate, and start his working life with a reasonable job at a reasonable company.

Table 7-1 compares how well George and Hannah will do by investing in Maryland's prepaid tuition plan instead of just saving in the bank for college expenses. The numbers in Table 7-1 show how the numbers work if you save the same amount each month. Several options are included — prepaying the entire amount in a lump sum, using a 17-year payment plan with annual payments, a 5-year payment plan with monthly payments, and a 17-year payment plan with monthly payments. All comparisons assume Congress will keep the tax-free nature of distributions, Maryland will continue to provide tax deductions for contributions (and won't alter the terms of its plan in any way), and college tuition and outside investments will both increase by 5 percent each year.

TABLE 7-1: **Comparing Saving In a Section 529 Prepaid Tuition Plan with Saving In an Ordinary Investment Account, Using Combined 20 Percent Federal and State Income Tax Rates**

Payment option	Payment per period	Total Payments	Value if invested outside of 529 plan, after tax
Lump sum	$47,030.00	$47,030.00	$95,274.15
Annual payments	$4,238.00	$72,046.00	$113,032.67
5-year, monthly payments	$905.00	$54,300.00	$100,238.39
197 monthly payments	$374.00	$73,678.00	$111,077.34

REMEMBER

Although the tuition paid will be the same, whether or not Hannah and George have a Section 529 plan, the amount of money they have to supply will not. Even if they fund a savings account with exactly the same amount of money as they fund an equivalent 529 plan, they'll have to pay federal and state income tax annually on income being earned. In addition, although no federal income tax deduction is allowed for contributions made into a 529 plan, Maryland provides one (as do many other states). In fact, if Hannah and George put their money into a traditional savings or investment account, they may pay between $10,000 and $12,000 more in tax in the years leading up to college than they would have if they'd funded a 529 prepaid tuition plan.

In addition, given that undergraduate tuition at the University of Maryland, College Park was $11,232 for the academic year 2022/2023, if there is a 5 percent yearly tuition increase, the cost of tuition for the four years Hannah and George's child will be attending project out to $116,507.62, or more than any one of the after-tax investment options shown in Table 7-1. And remember, this is for tuition only and doesn't include any other expenses, such as room and board, books, and transportation.

This example uses fairly generous rates of investment return and relatively moderate rates of tuition increase. Real life rarely follows planned examples exactly. If you're not using a Section 529 payment plan, you may need to adjust your budget and your savings accordingly.

Table 7-2 illustrates how your money may grow in a 529 plan and how the same amount of periodic savings (whether you use weekly, monthly, or quarterly deposits) will cost you more if you put it into conventional investments outside of a 529 plan. As in Table 7-1, all numbers assume a 5 percent annual rate of return, and federal and state income taxes are calculated at combined 20 percent. No adjustment is made for state income tax (each state is individual in this regard), and most savings plans don't carry residency restrictions.

Table 7-2 clearly shows that, over time, you'll save much more money if you don't pay tax currently on your earnings. If you live in a state with a state income tax on investment income but follows the Section 529 federal rules, the disparity between Section 529 and ordinary investment funds becomes even greater. Regardless of what your total rate of return is (and no one has any accurate idea what it will be until it's actually earned, although it could be much higher or lower, depending on market conditions and how aggressively you invest), saving money costs you less when you can save in a tax-deferred or tax-exempt account.

Flexibility of funding

Suppose that you're like George and Hannah — settled in one place with no plans to move — and you'd like nothing better than to see your children graduate from one of your state's colleges or universities. In that situation, investing in your state's prepaid tuition plan (if it has one) makes wonderful sense. But you don't have to be like George and Hannah in order to take advantage of a 529 plan because there are not only state-run prepaid tuition plans but also savings plans and college-run prepaid tuition plans. So, if you're saving for the day your child goes to almost any post-secondary school or gets accepted into a private primary or secondary school that will provide them with a better education than their local public school, some 529 plan out there should fit your needs.

TABLE 7-2: Comparing saving in a Section 529 savings plan with an ordinary investment account.

Year	$1,200/year, total contribution = $21,600		$2,400/year, total contribution = $43,200		$6,000/year, total contribution = $108,000		$17,000/year, total contribution = $306,000	
	529 Savings	Investment	529 Savings	Investment	529 Savings	Investment	529 Savings	Investment
2023	$1,200.00	$1,200.00	$2,400.00	$2,400.00	$6,000.00	$6,000.00	$17,000.00	17,000.00
2024	$2,460.00	$2,448.00	$4,920.00	$4,896.00	$12,300.00	$12,240.00	$34,850.00	$34,680.00
2025	$3,783.00	$3,745.92	$7,566.00	$7,491.84	$18,915.00	$18,729.60	$53,592.50	$53,067.20
2026	$5,172.15	$5,095.76	$10,344.30	$10,191.51	$25,860.75	$25,478.78	$73,272.13	$72,189.89
2027	$6,630.76	$6,499.59	$13,261.52	$12,999.17	$33,153.79	$32,497.94	$93,935.73	$92,077.48
2028	$8,162.30	$7,959.57	$16,324.59	$15,919.14	$40,811.48	$39,797.85	$115,632.52	$112,760.58
2029	$9,770.41	$9,477.95	$19,540.82	$18,955.91	$48,852.05	$47,389.77	$138,414.14	$134,271.01
2030	$11,458.93	$11,057.07	$22,917.86	$22,114.14	$57,294.65	$55,285.36	$162,334.85	$156,641.85
2031	$13,231.88	$12,699.35	$26,463.75	$25,398.71	$66,159.39	$63,496.77	$187,451.59	$179,907.52
2032	$15,093.47	$14,407.33	$30,186.94	$28,814.66	$75,467.36	$72,036.64	$213,824.17	$204,103.82
2033	$17,048.14	$16,183.62	$34,096.29	$32,367.24	$85,240.72	$80,918.11	$241,515.38	$229,267.97
2034	$19,100.55	$18,030.97	$38,201.10	$36,061.93	$95,502.76	$90,154.83	$270,591.15	$255,438.69
2035	$21,255.58	$19,952.21	$42,511.16	$39,904.41	$106,277.90	$99,761.03	$301,120.71	$282,656.24
2036	$23,518.36	$21,950.29	$47,036.72	$43,900.59	$117,591.79	$109,751.47	$333,176.74	$310,962.49
2037	$25,894.28	$24,028.31	$51,788.55	$48,056.61	$129,471.38	$120,141.53	$366,835.58	$340,400.99
2038	$28,388.99	$26,189.44	$56,777.98	$52,378.87	$141,944.95	$130,947.19	$402,177.36	$371,017.03
2039	$31,008.44	$28,437.01	$62,016.88	$56,874.03	$155,042.20	$142,185.07	$439,286.23	$402,857.71
2040	$33,758.86	$30,774.50	$67,517.72	$61,548.99	$168,794.31	$153,872.48	$478,250.54	435,972.02

For example, Lisa and Sean have a newborn and a 15-year-old for whom they haven't begun saving. Because they're always on the move from one state to another, they don't think investing in a prepaid tuition plan will work for them because of residency requirements built into so many plans. They also like having very few restrictions on where their children can attend post-secondary school. They decide to invest in a 529 savings plan.

With two children of very different ages to save for, Lisa and Sean can open Section 529 plans for each and fund the plans unequally. They could put more into the older child's account to beef up savings and then super-fund the younger child's account after the older child finishes their education. If any money is left in the older child's account after completing their education, Lisa and Sean can make a tax-free rollover (see Chapter 5) of the remaining balance into the younger child's account.

No taxes to pay (at least for now)

REMEMBER

Saving money is saving money, whether you put cash into a savings account or cut needless expenses. Section 529 plans help you to do both. While you're busy stashing as much away as you can, you're also, at the very least, postponing any income tax reckoning. You may be eliminating it.

When you finally begin making distributions, the accumulated earnings within the plan are tax-exempt, provided the distribution is made to pay qualified education expenses. If the money is being used for something other than qualified education expenses, you will pay tax only on the accumulated earnings portion of the distribution. Also, depending on the circumstances, you might pay an additional 10 percent tax. (To paraphrase Gertrude Stein, this is not a penalty because the IRS hates to call a spade a spade or an additional tax under any other name.)

For example, suppose that you manage to save $2,400 per year for 18 years in a 529 account, and that money invested earns a 5 percent rate of return. If you don't pay any tax, Table 7-2 shows that you'll have $67,518: your contributions of $43,200 and interest and dividends of $24,318 you've earned over the 18 years. If you take a qualifying distribution in the first year of college of one-fourth of the total, your distribution will be $16,880. Of this, $10,800 is your contributions (and therefore not taxed because you've already paid federal income tax on them), and $6,080 represents the income portion of the distribution. If the distribution is made for the benefit of your student for qualifying expenses, no taxes will be owed on the $6,080 of accumulated income.

On the other hand, suppose that same $2,400 was invested each month in a traditional savings or investment account (see Chapter 12), earning 5 percent per year in income. Because the income is taxed each year that it's earned after

18 years, the account value is only \$61,549 (\$5,969 less than the 529 account funded with the same amount of money). Because the total pot of money is smaller, the amounts available to be distributed to the student are also less.

In this instance, if the parent (not the child) owns the account, the income earned in each year is taxed at the parent's rate (usually higher than 10 percent), not the child's. If the child owns the account, much of the income will still be taxed at the parent's highest applicable rate because of the so-called "Kiddie Tax." The Kiddie Tax taxes all but a small portion of investment income at the parent's rate as opposed to the child's rate to deter parents and grandparents from gifting investments to their young children to avoid paying taxes.

This example clearly shows the benefit of tax deferrals, even when the income portion at distribution time isn't tax-exempt. The fact that you've postponed paying tax lets your money grow faster than if you pay tax yearly on your earnings. The tax-deferred account allows larger distributions to your designated beneficiary for exactly the same dollar cost to you.

Working Around the 529 Shortcomings

Tax deferrals, higher investment returns, and funding flexibility are all powerful motivators, and they may be just the enticements you're looking for when shopping for a way to invest your savings for college. But all good things carry a price tag, and Section 529 plans are no exception here.

WARNING

A 529 plan can carry some unexpected, sometimes unavoidable, and often less-than-optimal consequences, such as in the following circumstances:

>> If you save too much or too little

>> If the plan owner or the designated beneficiary dies

>> If your designated beneficiary decides, for whatever reason, not to continue beyond high school

>> If you need to rescue the money you've saved to pay for one of life's surprises that often hit you in the face when you're least expecting it

If you're aware of what can happen ahead of time, however, you may be able to minimize the damage.

Finagling financial aid implications

The impact of owning a Section 529 plan on the amount of financial aid available to your student has been the topic of much discussion over the years. And regardless of whether you were able to save the entire amount you need, you and your student will have to fill out the dreaded U.S. Department of Education's Free Application for Federal Student Aid (FAFSA) form to determine eligibility for federal financial aid (including things like Pell Grants and the federal work/study program) based on the federal methodology. You may also have to complete other aid forms required by individual colleges, which calculate your needs completely differently, using the institutional methodology.

Information you provide on the FAFSA determines how much your family is expected to contribute to your student's education. If the cost of that education is higher than your expected family contribution (EFC), your student is eligible for low-cost loans, possibly need-based grants, and/or scholarships. See Chapter 18 for more info on EFCs and the FAFSA.

REMEMBER

No matter how you slice it, your financial aid award will be affected if you're the owner of a 529 plan and you, your spouse, or your child is the designated beneficiary. The extent to which it's affected depends on several factors:

>> **The amount of the taxable earnings portion of the annual distribution:** To the extent that a distribution has a taxable component that is shown on the student's income tax return, 50 percent of that amount (after being adjusted for the student's income protection allowance) will be included in arriving at the family's expected contribution, regardless of whether the distribution is made from a prepaid tuition plan or a savings plan. Currently, tax-free distributions are not included on the FAFSA. However, no regulations prohibit the U.S. Department of Education from requiring disclosure of even tax-free amounts when determining the need or changing its view on the asset classification of 529s, and it may choose that path in the future.

>> **The value of the plan, whether it's owned by a parent or by the child:** If you own the plan for the benefit of one of your children, the plan's current value needs to be included as part of your net assets on your student's FAFSA, even if the Section 529 plan is not for the benefit of the child applying for aid. Although you don't have to list your assets separately, you may be required to substantiate any number that appears on the FAFSA.

>> **The relationship between the plan owner and the plan beneficiary:** If you're the owner of a savings plan and your child is the beneficiary, a maximum of 5.6 percent of your 529 plan is factored into your student's expected family contribution. If you're the owner and you (or your spouse) are the beneficiary, that percentage remains at 5.6 percent. If you own a plan for

the benefit of a grandchild or a nonrelative, the value of your plan is excluded from any aid calculation. However, distributions made in the year under review for aid will count as untaxed income to the beneficiary. The annual FAFSA, as you may recall, is based on the prior-prior year's income, so if you're filling out the FAFSA for your student for the school year of 2023/2024, the income tax returns you'll use to complete the application will be 2021 (the prior-prior year).

After FAFSA has calculated your student's expected family contribution, if the amount available to you in your Section 529 isn't adequate to meet the contribution amount, you may need to explore other funding sources. These include scholarships (see Chapter 17), federal work-study funds, and student loans (see Chapter 18).

When the plan owner dies

Dying is not something you (or anyone) want to contemplate, especially not before completing the job you've started: educating your children. But it happens to all of us at some point, and sometimes that point is unplanned and downright inconvenient. If you were to die at an inconvenient time, you want to be certain that you've left all your affairs as tidy as possible. And that includes your 529 plan.

WARNING

No surprise here, but different government agencies differ in opinion on who actually owns the assets in a Section 529 plan, and they have conflicting rules. As a result, the death of a plan owner can have some interesting and sometimes unfortunate consequences. Remember, should you fail to plan adequately, the Section 529 plan(s) you own could become part of the residue of your estate and be disposed of following either

>> The terms of your last will (if you were smart and wrote one)

>> According to the laws of *intestacy* (what happens to your stuff if you die without having a valid will) in your state

Should your family members find themselves dealing with the aftermath of your death, you won't be around to help them sort it out. Make sure that your affairs are in order now, and then make certain that they stay that way.

Transferring plan ownership

REMEMBER

All plan applications have a section to designate a successor account owner; many have an additional section to designate an alternate successor account owner. Don't ignore these sections, and remember the names you write in the spaces. If one of your choices for successor owner dies or moves to another state (for states where an owner must be a resident), update your account information with your plan manager. Whoever is deemed the plan owner can change the beneficiary designation at any given time. Be certain that whoever is on your list for successor ownership of your 529 account(s) has the same plans in mind as you did when you established them.

This advice may seem simple and obvious, but many a plan has come to grief through death and divorce. Take, for example, David and Lily. David, a widower, has a daughter from his first marriage, for whom he has set up a Section 529 plan. When he marries Lily, he names her as his successor plan owner. David and Lily go on to have two children of their own. Five years later, David dies suddenly, and Lily becomes the plan owner.

As a result of David's death and Lily assuming ownership of the 529 account, she's now in control of the assets. She and David's daughter have never seen eye-to-eye, and Lily decides to change the beneficiary designation to one of her children. Because Lily's children are half-siblings to David's daughter, this beneficiary change is allowable. The money David saved to send his own daughter to college is now being used to send David and Lily's child to school, and David's daughter needs to fend for herself.

WARNING

Keep your successor owner designations current. Check them at least annually, and never put off until tomorrow what you can do today. If you're part of a blended family with more than one set of parents, make sure the money you've set aside for your beneficiaries is wrapped up in ironclad ties. There's no fixing this mess after it happens, and more than one child whose parent(s) saved money for their education has seen a stepsibling benefit from those funds while they go without.

TECHNICAL STUFF

If you're not sure whom you'd like to name as your successor owner, you can set up a specific trust and name the trust as the successor owner. Provided the trust is a resident in the state where you also live (for Section 529 plans with a residency requirement), it should qualify as a successor owner. You do need to find trustees who will honor your wishes, including successors in case one or more of your named trustees cannot serve, but once you have that all in place, you'll never worry about a successor owner designation again. Consult an attorney to draw up the trust instrument and ensure it follows all the rules and regulations for your particular 529 plan.

Gift/GSTT Consequences

If you've been able to super-fund your Section 529 plan, taking advantage of the five-year election explained in Chapter 5, where you give up to $85,000 per donee in a single year and then plan to spread those gifts out over five years, you need to read this.

Section 529 plans have a unique place in the rules and regulations surrounding Gift and Generation-Skipping Transfer (GST) tax. After you put the money into the plan and designate a beneficiary, it counts as a completed gift. From the perspective of the Gift and GST rules, you've given up "all right, title, and interest" in the money. Except you really haven't. Provided the money you've gifted goes into an account you own, you remain the plan owner and are in control of the assets. You can change the investment strategy (but not the investments themselves) and even change the beneficiary to terminate a plan entirely and take the money back. You will pay a penalty, but you'll have your money back. So much for giving up "all right, title, and interest."

Still, because the IRS considers the gift a completed transfer made while you're alive, you're entitled to use your annual exclusion to gift money into these accounts (see Chapter 3). And, when you die, because you've given the money away previously (even though you really haven't), it's not counted in your estate, even though you are (or were, because you're now dead) the plan owner.

The only piece that may be pulled back into your estate and counted for estate and/or the GST tax is that amount that you super-funded but haven't yet completed the five-year period (see Chapter 3). If you die during the five years that constitute your election period, any amounts for which you haven't filed a gift tax return yet, if you were required to file one, are included in the value of your estate.

For example, Moe set up 529 accounts for his two grandchildren. Moe is a generous guy, and he put $80,000 into each account in 2022 and made the election on his 2022 Form 709 (U.S. Gift and GST Tax Return). He doesn't make any other gifts to the kids in the following years, so he isn't required to file any more gift tax returns. Moe passes away in 2024. Because he was alive during only three of the five years of his election period, his estate tax return must include $64,000 (2 years x $16,000 2022 annual exclusion x 2 grandkids), even though the money is safely tucked away inside the 529 plans. The money for the annual exclusion amounts that would have been made had Moe not died doesn't return to his estate; only the value does to calculate Moe's estate tax.

Estate tax consequences

Except in the situation where the plan owner makes the five-year election but fails to live for the full five years discussed in the previous section, a 529 plan owned by a decedent is not included in their estate for estate tax purposes. Even though you may be considered the plan owner while you're alive, the account carries sufficient restrictions to give the appearance that you lack total control over the account, even before your death. None of the assets appear on your estate tax return, and your estate pays no additional tax due to your ownership of these plans.

Death of a designated beneficiary

Sometimes the unthinkable happens, and the person you've been saving money for all these years dies. In these situations, the rules governing Section 529 non-qualified distributions, rollovers, transfers, and terminations ease, although they don't entirely disappear.

If a distribution was made to the beneficiary or to their estate after their death, and the distribution wasn't entirely used for qualified educational expenses, the income portion of that amount is taxable to the student or their estate on the appropriate income tax return. Because it was clearly not the student's intention to use the money for nonqualified expenses, the 10 percent additional tax (penalty) is waived.

And that is usually the only tax consequence to the designated beneficiary or their estate (assuming they do not have a taxable estate because the distribution becomes part of their estate). Because you remain the plan owner (and, therefore, nominally in control of the plan assets), what happens next with the remaining money in the account is your call.

You now have a plan that has no designated beneficiary (as I explain in Chapter 5, having a designated beneficiary is a requirement of 529 plans), so you need to either name a new one or terminate the plan. As in any change of a designated beneficiary, you can merely change the designation in an existing account, add the funds from the old account to a different existing account for a new beneficiary, or roll over the funds from the old account into a new account.

Even if you've already done a tax-free rollover within the last 12 months or changed your investment strategy in an existing account, any rollover will be tax-free (provided it is completed within 60 days). The 12-month rule is suspended when a designated beneficiary dies. The IRS recognizes that you are not doing this through choice but through necessity.

REMEMBER

Regardless of which direction you choose to go with the account — same account, different account, or new account — the new beneficiary needs to pass the family relationship test, as discussed in Chapter 5.

Finally, should you choose to terminate the account and retrieve your savings, you'll have to pay income tax on the accumulated earnings in the account. Still, the 10 percent additional tax/penalty will be waived.

Making choices if your child skips college

When little Joey grows up, he may no longer want to be a rocket scientist but would rather spend his life surfing. Or maybe Catherine's biggest desire has shifted from studying the law to living in a Katmandu commune. Life and differing expectations sometimes throw curveballs at you, and what may have been your desire doesn't fit into the game plan of your designated student.

When you save in a Section 529 plan, you're not saving for a certain event but one that has a reasonable probability. And sometimes, your reasonable expectations are not realized, and the money you saved specifically for that purpose won't be needed. That's when you can gnash your teeth, rip out your hair, and scream at the heavens because had you known, you would have put all that money into a traditional investment account (see Chapter 12), paid the income tax on an ongoing basis, and never given any thought to how to deal with this unforeseen set of circumstances. Or you could have gone on that round-the-world cruise not just once but twice. Face it, we all have multiple places where we can direct money, but in this instance, you chose to save for future educational costs.

Section 529 offers some flexibility when you face the problem of money in your account but no qualifying student to spend it. Still, the day you first understand that you didn't need to do all this planning for this student is the day you have to begin calculating what to do with the funds you've saved.

Changing beneficiary designations

When you realize that your designated beneficiary isn't going to attend college, your first thought may be to change the designated beneficiary on the account. Good thought. If you have more than one student for whom you bear some financial responsibility, you can do one of three things:

>> Change the beneficiary name on the existing account

>> Open a completely new account for the new beneficiary

>> Roll the value of the old account into an already existing account for the new beneficiary (provided, of course, that the total of the two accounts doesn't exceed the state limit on account size)

So long as you change the designated beneficiary to a new beneficiary who bears a family relationship to your previous designated beneficiary (as explained in Chapter 5), these maneuvers will have no adverse effects on you, your old beneficiary, or your new one.

You can change the designated beneficiary of an already existing Section 529 plan at any time, for any reason, so long as the new beneficiary passes the relationship test in Chapter 5. If you or your spouse can pass the relationship test, you can even choose yourself as the new designated beneficiary (isn't there some degree you've always wanted to pursue?). Unlike tax-free rollovers between plans with the same designated beneficiary, you aren't limited to making a beneficiary change only once in any calendar year.

You may also choose to terminate an existing account (suppose your former beneficiary is a resident in one state, and your new one lives in another) and make a tax-free rollover of the fund balance into a different account, provided the transfer is completed within 60 days. If you can't get the new fund up and running within that 60-day period, you're out of luck. You (not the designated beneficiary) will be taxed on the accumulated income in the fund, and then you can tack on an additional 10 percent penalty.

Whenever you're rolling over a plan, either to an already existing account or a new one, tell your current plan manager that you want to make a "trustee-to-trustee transfer." This prevents a check from being written to you and will keep you well within the 60-day limit. Many a rollover has come to grief because someone forgot to deposit a check in time.

Beware if you initially fund your 529 plan using your child's UGMA/UTMA money (see Chapter 12 for the rules regarding the Uniform Gifts to Minors Act/Uniform Transfer to Minors Act). You can't change the designated beneficiary on such an account, and when they turn the magic age when your custodianship of the money would've ended, it still ends. The no-longer-minor child becomes the plan owner and can make whatever decisions they want concerning this money, including terminating the plan.

Terminating the plan

When your designated student clearly has no desire to continue their education, you may have no other prospective student waiting in the wings. In this case, the obvious choice is to terminate your plan.

Check the rules of your plan very, very carefully. A few prepaid tuition plans don't allow you to receive the money back when you terminate your plan but instead pay it to your designated beneficiary. At the time of termination, the designated beneficiary pays any income tax on the accumulated earnings and may also be hit with the 10 percent penalty for taking the money in a nonqualified distribution.

This whole scenario may work well for you if your designated beneficiary is an absolute wizard who is receiving a full-paid academic scholarship (in which case, the 10 percent penalty doesn't apply; see the next section). However, you may not feel as keen about giving control over a lump sum of money to a child who's not living up to their potential. If your plan will terminate only in favor of the designated beneficiary, you may want to consider making an intermediate tax-free rollover (as described in Chapter 5) to an account that will allow you to terminate in favor of yourself.

WARNING

If you want to terminate a prepaid tuition plan, you may first have to roll it over into a 529 savings plan and then terminate it, depending on how the prepaid plan in your state works. However you choose to terminate — either directly from the prepaid plan or after rolling it over to a savings plan — you'll be subject to income tax on the earnings in the plan plus the 10 percent additional tax (unless you meet one of the exceptions discussed in Chapter 5). And one further caveat: If you received any state tax benefit from contributing to the plan in the first place, you might be liable to pay back any benefit you received either through an income tax deduction or a credit against income tax liability. Ouch!

REMEMBER

The state will not confiscate your money if you choose to terminate a Section 529 plan. However, because the plans are designed for a specific purpose, you'll face the consequences of not achieving that purpose.

Limiting penalties for too much money

Your fondest dreams have been borne out, and your student is headed for a free ride. Or, more realistically, your student received a darn good scholarship and will need only a portion of the money you've saved to pay the difference. You have many options for using this extra money, most of which revolve around your family circumstances and thoughts about money. Here are a few of your options that will minimize the size of Uncle Sam's bite:

>> **You may choose to make distributions to your student equal to or less than the scholarship amount without paying a penalty on the income portion.** Your student is responsible for any income tax on the income portion of the distribution that they're not using to pay for qualified educational expenses, but an additional 10 percent penalty will *not* be tacked on. Remember, lots of incidentals need to be paid for that don't fall under the category of "qualified educational expenses." Chapter 10 shows how this scenario works. If your student has very limited income from other sources, you may find that even though the income portion of the distribution represents income to the student, they may not have enough income overall to trigger any income tax.

>> **You may want to roll over part, or all, of the extra into a Section 529 plan for another child, a grandchild, or yourself.** If you haven't already made a

tax-free rollover in the previous 12 months, you're free to do this and jump-start a new account or supercharge one that's been a bit anemic, as described in the section "Deciding what to do if your child doesn't attend college," earlier in this chapter.

>> **You may want to hold off doing anything, at least for a while.** Many people continue their education beyond a first college degree, and your student could be one of those. Although you may have thought that your ability to pay would stop after college, the fact that your child has received this additional assistance may enable them to consider attending graduate or professional school without taking loans. Remember, there is no age limitation on Section 529 plans — a student may be any age to qualify.

TIP

As always, when you're facing a major financial decision, talk with a professional whom you trust (your accountant, attorney, or financial advisor). This person can help you see all the aspects of your situation and how your decision here may affect it.

Minimizing the blow for retrieving savings to weather hard times

Planning and plotting are part of the human condition, and after you have children, your propensity for doing more than going with the flow increases exponentially. That's why you've been investigating and, I hope, saving in a 529 plan in the first place. But sometimes your life may make a U-turn, and items that you may have thought were sacrosanct now need to be put on the table to deal with immediate family survival. Thinking of the distant future seems hard when the immediate present looks grim.

In these cases, you may need to access the funds you've been so carefully saving in your Section 529 plan. Because 529s are designed for paying for education, you're not really supposed to use that money for something else — that's why the IRS charges you a penalty when you do. Still, the beauty of these plans is that they allow it, with some conditions.

Nonqualified distributions to yourself or your designated beneficiary that trigger an additional tax

Uncertain world economies often lead to unstable family economies, and the last several years have been filled with nothing but uncertainty. Suppose that your income has dropped for any reason (loss of one salary, wage reductions, or investment income decline) or your expenses have increased significantly. You may find that you not only can't continue to fund your 529 plan but also need to liberate some money from an existing plan to pay your current living expenses.

Beating yourself up over a life that is spiraling out of control is a giant waste of energy, and you need to focus all of your energies on what's happening right now and what you need to do to correct the current situation. There's a reason why 529 plans are regarded as the parents' (not the student's) assets when determining a student's financial need, and this is it. You can take a distribution of some (or all) of the money you've saved from a prepaid tuition plan or a savings plan.

That said, it'll cost you. If your investments have appreciated in value, you'll pay the income tax on the accumulated earnings at your income tax rate, plus a 10 percent penalty for a nonqualified distribution. It's not a perfect solution, but if you're in a place where you have to consider making this move, you're in a far-from-perfect situation anyway. Remember, perfection only exists in the imagination, not in real life. Instead of perfection, settling for this month's rent or mortgage may be the best you can hope for.

WARNING

Don't think you get off with only the federal tax and the federal penalty. If your state has an income tax, you also must pay a state income tax. And, if your state gave you an income tax deduction for your contributions into the plan, as you draw that money out, you may need to "recapture" the income that you didn't pay tax on in prior years and pay the tax now.

Nonqualified distributions to or for the benefit of the beneficiary, without penalty

Another benefit of Section 529 is how it separates your unforeseen circumstances from your designated student's. After all, even though you own the plan, you've put the money aside for the student's use and received favorable gift tax treatment on that premise. Accordingly, although you may have to pay a penalty if you take back money from your student's Section 529 plan, if your student needs money and takes a distribution from the plan, it may be subject only to income tax on the earnings (paid at the student's tax rate, not yours), without the 10 percent penalty.

These exceptions, covered in detail in Chapter 5, include the following:

» Distributions that would have been qualified except that your student has received scholarship and/or grant money or other educational benefits from another source.

» Distributions used to pay enough educational expenses to qualify for the American Opportunity Credit or the Lifetime Learning Education Credit.

Remember, in this case, the student needs to claim the credit, so they can't be listed as a dependent on your income tax return, which may limit the value of this technique. Of course, if you (or your spouse) are the beneficiary as well as the owner of a 529 plan, using this becomes much more valuable to you.

>> Distributions that are made on account of a severe disability or because of the impending death of the designated beneficiary.

>> Distributions made to a recipient attending one of the U.S. Military Academies to the extent that the distribution does not exceed what it would actually cost to attend that educational institution if you had to pay for it.

Clearly, nonqualified distributions made that would have been qualified except for the fact that the beneficiary received some other form of educational aid, whether a scholarship or a tax credit, still falls within the rubric of paying for the beneficiary's education. Therefore, it makes sense that the 10 percent additional tax won't apply in these cases.

TIP

In the instance of death or disability, these are also reasons why making non-qualifying distributions make sense and won't be penalized, but the income portion of the distribution is still not entitled to the tax-exempt treatment allowed for qualifying distributions. You won't be penalized by the additional tax in these instances. However, remember that when you use these expenses to pay for medical bills or other expenses incurred solely because your beneficiary is disabled, the expenses you pay might qualify for the medical deduction on Schedule A of your Form 1040 (if you can itemize your deductions) since you are paying income tax on the income portion of the distribution. You should keep good records of all these expenses and talk with your tax professional about which of these expenses can be deducted. Many people are not aware that many items, such as special schools for a child who cannot attend an ordinary school, are tax-deductible expenses.

Having money left over after graduation

Graduation day has come and gone, and your designated beneficiary is now confidently heading out into the workplace, credentials in hand, and with no immediate intention of pursuing an advanced degree, which you may have no intention of paying for anyway. And you're feeling fairly good about yourself, knowing that your good planning and careful attention throughout the process have helped your student reach this point.

Now the only fly in the ointment seems to be that you planned too well, and you still have money left in your Section 529 savings kitty. If you used a prepaid tuition plan, while it's less likely that you'll have anything left, you might still have some unused tuition credits that you need to deal with. Oops!

Actually, good for you! You planned and then carried through. You had no way of knowing how much you would actually need, but you managed to save more than enough. So now on to the next phase — figuring out how to deal with the excess while minimizing (or even eliminating) any tax bite.

Remembering that you own the unused funds

When you funded this account for your prospective student, you may have filed a gift tax return, essentially giving this money to that designated beneficiary for their future education. It would make sense that now that the education is complete, they would get what's left.

Wrong! You've been the account owner from Day 1, and nothing has changed here. The fact that your designated beneficiary has now graduated only means that they no longer need the funds. You remain the plan owner.

WARNING

If you can't decide what to do next, that's okay for a while, but be careful and check your particular plan. Many plans, especially prepaid tuition ones, have very specific time guidelines that you must meet. For example, your plan may require that all distributions are made, and the plan is terminated no later than ten years after your designated beneficiary first begins their post-secondary education. Funds that remain could be either distributed to you at the mandatory distribution time (in which case, you're looking at income tax and penalty on the earnings portion of the distribution) or even sent to the unclaimed property at the state treasurer's office.

Changing beneficiaries

Even if your plan doesn't require that you take action immediately (or within a fixed time), all plans have provisions written in to prevent them from existing forever. Congress, the IRS, and all the state treasuries want to know that you're planning to spend that money on education. Although they'll grant you a bit of leeway in figuring out what to do with your excess, you need to make a decision. And that decision is a fairly basic choice: You need to terminate the account or change the beneficiary designation, either through a simple change of beneficiary on the current account or a tax-free rollover into a new or already existing account for the new designated beneficiary.

If you choose the rollover option, the rules are the same as for any rollover: Your new designated beneficiary must belong to the same family as your original designated beneficiary in the allowed relationships listed in Chapter 5. You can roll the excess into a brand-new 529 plan for the new designated beneficiary (a younger child, perhaps) or an already existing plan. Don't forget that you can also use this opportunity to change your investment strategy. For example, you may not want to be as conservative in your choices with a younger beneficiary as you may have been with the former beneficiary.

TRACKING THE BASIS IN YOUR SECTION 529 PLAN

No matter what type of plan you own and how much it might be growing, you always need to keep track of your *basis*, or how much money you or anyone else has put into the account. Suppose you live in a state that gives you partial or full credit for contributions to a Section 529 plan. If this is the case, you'll need to keep two separate sets of records because your federal contributions will be made after you've already paid income tax on the money, and your contributions for state purposes may be made before state income tax is paid. By knowing your basis, you can calculate just how much of any distribution from the plan represents taxable earnings.

For example, Melinda and Tom, who are Idaho residents, have a Section 529 plan for their son, and they put $2,000 a year into it for 17 years. Because Idaho gives an income tax deduction for up to $6,000 contributions per year for single taxpayers and $12,000 for married and filing joint taxpayers, they've never paid Idaho income tax on their contributions. This means the full amount of their final distribution will be taxed by Idaho (but only the amount of the final distribution). One hundred percent of the qualifying distributions have never been taxed by Idaho and never will be. As for the federal taxation, only the piece of the distribution on which they haven't already paid tax will be taxed now. Since they put $34,000 into the account, and the total value of all distributions is $55,000 ($50,000 of qualified distributions for their son's college costs + $5,000 balance), they will pay federal income tax plus the 10 percent penalty on $1,909 of accumulated income (($55,000 - $34,000 = $21,000)/$55,000 x $5,000 = $1,909.)

Calculating taxes on unused funds

After you see all the members of your family through college and into the great working world beyond, you may finally reach a point where you still have excess funds in the very last Section 529 plan that you own, and no one is left for whom to fund a new account. (Remember, if your children have children of their own at this point, you can always roll over the remainder into new accounts for your grandchildren, as described in Chapter 5.) If you don't have anyone left to fund for, that's okay. You've really done a great job, and your students can stand on their own two feet.

Still, now you really must terminate your last plan and get out of the 529 business. At this time, you need to request a distribution from your plan manager of the entire balance. This is clearly a nonqualified distribution, and your designated beneficiary will have to pay income tax on the earnings portion of the distribution and a 10 percent penalty. But wait, there's one more option you may be able to take advantage of: Provided the final distribution happens after January 1, 2024, you may roll at least a portion of that distribution into a Roth IRA titled in the name of the designated beneficiary. There's still income tax to be paid on the money, and if the money has been in the 529 plan for less than 15 years, you'll also owe the penalty. But this is a way to create something good for your designated beneficiary and jump-start retirement savings for them.

As for any balance, after you've made the maximum contribution into that brand new Roth IRA, taxes and penalties apply to any income portion taxed to the beneficiary. But, when you weigh the total tax being paid on that final distribution, compare it to the huge amount of tax you might have paid over the past decades while the plan was in effect. Focus on all the money you've saved over the years by deferring this tax and all the benefits you and your students have reaped. Approaching the task with this attitude should make paying these final taxes a bit less painful.

3
Uncovering Coverdell Accounts

Chapter **8**

The Changing World of Coverdell Education Savings Accounts

When you're trying to save money for education, there is more in your bag of tricks than Section 529 plans. Coverdell Education Savings Accounts (ESAs), named after the late Senator Paul Coverdell (R-Georgia), who was the chief sponsor of the legislation regulating these accounts, can be a valuable tool in your savings arsenal. As a standalone or together with other education savings accounts such as 529 plans, the Coverdell ESA can provide your student with additional flexibility in paying for their best possible education.

In this chapter, you discover the ins and outs of the Coverdell Education Savings Accounts. You find out why so many people (your banker, your broker, your child's kindergarten teacher) all want you to start investing and investing now. You'll discover many of the benefits, and I'll alert you to red flags and warnings along the way.

TIP

Congress limits who can contribute to Coverdell ESAs based on annual income. If you make more than the phaseout limit allows, you can't contribute to an account. To find out whether your annual income falls within the limits, skip to the "Making Account Contributions" section later in this chapter. If you find that your annual income excludes you from making contributions, don't give up. If Coverdell is the way you want to save, a little careful planning can make it happen for you.

Covering the Basics

Coverdell ESAs are savings plans described in Section 530 of the Internal Revenue Code (IRC). They're accounts that Congress created to allow you to save now for future educational expenses, whether primary, secondary, or post-secondary, of a designated beneficiary.

You can invest money in Coverdell accounts in a variety of ways: stocks, bonds, money market accounts, certificates of deposit, and so on, although you may not invest in life insurance policies. And I really mean that you can invest; under the Coverdell rules (and unlike Section 529 rules), if you designate yourself the one responsible for all decisions on this particular account (also known as the *responsible adult*, who must be the parent or legal guardian of the minor child; see Chapter 9), you keep control of the money and make all the investment decisions for your child's account. Over the years, the investments will hopefully earn significant income through interest, dividends, and capital gains, until the account is closed.

You pay no income tax on the income when it's earned. As distributions are made from these accounts to your designated beneficiary for qualified educational expenses, the income portion of the distribution is not taxed, either to you or to your student.

REMEMBER

A Coverdell ESA must be opened in writing, and you need to designate a beneficiary when you create it; you aren't allowed to take an already existing account and decide that it's now the Coverdell account for your student. Money that you contribute to the account is held by a trustee or custodian, which must be a bank, mutual fund company, or any other entity that's approved by the Internal Revenue Service (IRS).

Understanding Coverdell differences

When these accounts were first introduced in 1997 as Education IRAs, they were limited to a $500 per year aggregate contribution per student, and distributions could be used to cover only post-secondary expenses. If you were thinking of contributing to any plan, you probably would've chosen a Section 529 plan, which had fewer restrictions and allowed you to maintain some contact with your money. Basically, the old Education IRA was a nonstarter for most people because contribution limits were fairly pathetic, and much better ways to save money for college were available.

LOOKING AT THE MAJOR DIFFERENCES BETWEEN COVERDELL ACCOUNTS AND 529 PLANS

On their faces, Coverdell ESAs and Section 529 plans seem to be two peas in a pod: Both are designed to encourage savings for higher education, and both now allow tax-free distributions if they're used to pay for qualified educational expenses.

Still, Sections 529 and 530 (governing Coverdell ESAs) of the Internal Revenue Code are quite different, and the savings plans that they govern contain several crucial differences. Among them are the following:

- Coverdell accounts have strict limits on the amount of income any contributor (except a corporate or charitable one) may earn in a particular year in order to make contributions to the account; Section 529 plans carry no such restriction.

- Coverdell accounts have strict limits on the amount that may be given into any account for a specifically designated beneficiary each year, while Section 529 plans do not (only overall plan maximums). In addition, contributions may not be made after age 18 for the designated beneficiary of a Coverdell account. Section 529 plans have no beneficiary age limit. Accordingly, 529 plans can transfer significant wealth, while Coverdell accounts are much more modestly sized.

- Assets inside a Coverdell account are considered to be owned by the designated beneficiary. Therefore, they are counted as the student's asset when calculating financial aid formulas (see Chapter 18), while asset ownership in a Section 529 plan is counted as the account owner's asset, not the account beneficiary.

- If you live in a state that gives a deduction or credit for Section 529 contributions, no state gives the same benefit for Coverdell ESA contributions. All your contributions will be made "after-tax" for both federal and state purposes.

- While both Section 529 and Coverdell plans allow for distributions to cover K-12 tuition, college and graduate school costs, the Coverdell account also allows qualifying distributions for the ancillary expenses connected with K-12 education, such as room and board, school uniforms, books and supplies, and required transportation costs. The Section 529 plan, by comparison, only allows up to $10,000 per year of tuition for K-12 students. Other mandatory costs during the K-12 years are not allowed as qualifying distributions.

In the current world of Coverdell (same code section, different name), the aggregate contribution limit has been raised to $2,000 per year, the definition of "qualifying student" has been hugely expanded, and you may now contribute to both a Coverdell account and a Section 529 plan for the same beneficiary in the same year. With all these factors, plus an increase in the income phaseout limitations present under Coverdells but not 529 plans, these accounts can become useful savings tools for many families.

Knowing who owns the account

The assets in a Coverdell ESA are counted as belonging to the person who contributed, not the beneficiary. However, because serious income limits exist for contributing to a Coverdell ESA, you may find that you can only fund one by gifting the contribution amount to someone who meets the income requirements rather than funding the account yourself. In that case, the assets will belong to that person, even if it is your student.

You may turn over control of your student's Coverdell ESA when they turn 18. Perhaps your philosophy is to turn your child's finances over to them when they turn 18 to help them establish independence. Or maybe you feel your child at that age is savvier about money and investments than you'll ever be. However, you don't have to relinquish control.

WARNING

If you're inclined to give your child control of their Coverdell ESA account, think carefully before you do. As long as you remain the responsible adult, you make the decisions regarding distribution; your child may have other ideas about what constitutes appropriate use of the money in the account. Even though there are significant penalties for taking nonqualified distributions from a Coverdell ESA, most 18-year-olds aren't known for making decisions based on sound financial reasoning. You must understand that your child may decide to take the money you've saved for their college and run.

Identifying qualifying students

REMEMBER

The designated beneficiary for a Coverdell ESA can be anyone attending (or will attend) any educational institution from kindergarten through graduate school, the same as for designated beneficiaries in Section 529 plans. However, there are some major differences between who is eligible for contributions and distributions in the two types of accounts.

Age limitations at the time of contribution

In general, you have 18 years in which you — or anyone else, for that matter — can fund a Coverdell ESA for your child, from the day they're born until the day before their 18th birthday. After that, you're done. No matter how much or how little you've managed to put away for that student, you can't add any more to the account. Any increases from now until the account is terminated will have to come from the earnings from your good investments.

Age limitations at the time of distribution

Coverdell ESAs must be completely distributed by the time your designated beneficiary hits their 30th birthday. If money is still left in the account on that date, it must be distributed within 30 days. Any earnings on it will be taxed to the beneficiary, plus whacked with a 10 percent penalty.

TIP

If you're fast approaching your beneficiary's 30th birthday and substantial money that you may not want to give as a birthday gift remains in the account, you can change the designated beneficiary on the account to a member of the current beneficiary's family, provided that the new beneficiary is under age 30.

Saving for disabled and special-needs students

While members of Congress have essentially stated that your children should have completed their educations by their 30th birthday, they do also recognize that some students will spend their lives in special schools. Accordingly, if you're the parent or grandparent of a special-needs student, there are no age limitations on contributions or distributions on behalf of these students.

WARNING

Regulations defining who exactly is a special-needs student haven't been released (although we've been waiting for over 20 years, so don't hold your breath), and no one is sure where the line defining a disability will be drawn. The Social Security Administration has issued guidance saying that it's probably safe to assume that if the beneficiary qualifies for Social Security disability benefits or blindness benefits, they will likely also qualify as disabled for the purpose of Coverdell distributions. For instance, total deafness may be included, but a 50-percent hearing loss could fall outside the boundaries. If you feel that your student's disability or special need may not be severe enough to fit a narrow definition and if you're approaching the ordinary deadline for contributions, you may want to err on the side of caution and stop contributing at age 18 until clearer guidelines are available.

Recognizing qualified education expenses

Qualified education expenses under Code Section 530 are those expenses that you're required to pay (or figure out some other way of meeting) if your student is to enroll at an eligible school. As in Section 529, though, many other expenses may be qualified, depending on the school's requirements and the particular program your student may be enrolled in.

First, you need to know what constitutes an "eligible school." For IRC Section 530 and Coverdell ESAs, eligible schools include all public, private, or religious schools that provide either primary or secondary education as determined under their applicable state laws. All post-secondary educational institutions qualified under Section 529 also qualify as eligible schools under Section 530.

Qualified expenses for elementary and secondary education

In addition to tuition and mandatory fees, other elementary and secondary education expenses may be eligible for payment using Coverdell distributions. Some expenses may seem obvious; others may surprise you:

>> **Books, supplies, and equipment related to enrollment:** In these days of shrinking school budgets, parents need to supply their children with more and more of what used to be considered necessary school supplies. Amounts that you spend for pens and pencils, notebooks, erasers, and the like are included here. You may also use a distribution from your Coverdell to pay for textbooks and other required reading material not supplied by the school district.

>> **Academic tutoring related to enrollment:** The math or science tutor (or even a dance instructor if your child is a dancer attending a school for the performing arts) is covered here, but your child's extracurricular piano or dance lessons are not.

>> **Special-needs services for students with special needs or disabilities:** If your student needs a one-on-one aide with them and the school doesn't cover the expense, this service qualifies, as does special equipment necessary to accommodate them. However, when assessing what qualifies here, remember that the regulations regarding special needs haven't been issued yet.

>> **Room and board, but only if a requirement of attending that particular school:** Clearly, if you send your child to a boarding school 300 miles from your home, room and board would be required. However, if you live in the next town, this expense may be questionable.

>> **Uniforms, when required by the school:** The cost of voluntary school uniform programs doesn't constitute a qualified educational expense, nor does the annual cost of buying your child school clothes.

>> **Transportation, when required by the school:** The expense of driving your student to and from school every day doesn't qualify, but the price you're

charged for the mandatory school bus does. As more and more communities begin to charge families for the cost of transportation to and from school, this expense will become an item that more people may choose to pay from their Coverdell accounts.

>> **Supplementary items and services, including extended day programs:** If your child attends an after-school or extended day program at their school, you may choose to pay these costs from your Coverdell account. However, the payment must be made to the school, so those extracurricular piano lessons probably aren't covered here.

>> **Computers, printers, other peripherals, Internet access, software, and so on:** Even if you are the primary user of this equipment, you may pay for it by using a qualified Coverdell distribution, provided you can document that this equipment and software benefits your student's education. Items that aren't used for educational purposes, though, don't count as qualified expenses, so the video games, the joystick you buy for your computer, and any gaming, sports, or hobby software don't qualify.

Qualified expenses for higher education

When your student reaches the halls of higher learning (or any other school after completing high school), the rules change regarding what constitutes a qualified expense for Coverdell distributions. The higher education rules align with Section 529 plans (see Chapter 5), which makes sense.

In general, the following lists constitute qualifying educational expenses for post-secondary education payable by tax-free distributions from Coverdell accounts:

>> **Tuition and mandatory fees at eligible educational institutions:** For a school to qualify, it needs to be able to participate (but doesn't have to if it chooses not to) in federal financial aid programs administered by the Department of Education.

>> **Required books, supplies, and equipment:** The books on the lengthy list that every professor hands out on the first day of class, laboratory equipment, and any required computer equipment (including peripherals) qualify. Your child's cell phone, which you may require for your peace of mind, does not.

>> **Room and board expenses:** These expenses are qualified only if

- They're paid directly to the school itself, and your student is attending class at least half-time, or

- They don't exceed the amount the school budgets for these expenses, provided your designated beneficiary is at least a half-time student.

If the room and board fees you pay directly to the school exceed the amount the school budgets for this expense, that's okay. You can still pay the full amount by using a qualified distribution from a Coverdell plan. It's only for that off-campus housing (including fraternities and sororities) that you need to be careful.

>> **Contributions into Section 529 Plans:** The rules here are fairly straightforward and stringent. If you take a distribution from a Coverdell ESA and contribute it into a 529 plan, the 529 plan needs to be either for the same student or a student who meets the relationship requirements to the original beneficiary outlined in Chapter 5 for 529 plans.

>> **Expenses for special-needs services required for special-needs students:** Once again, the regulations in this area haven't been finalized, so use your common sense. Don't include orthopedic shoes for your flat-footed student or contact lenses. It's a safe bet that these aren't covered under the regulations.

The one apparent rule is that any services paid for using a distribution from a Coverdell ESA need to be required by an eligible educational institution.

Many qualified expenses for elementary or secondary school aren't qualified after your student graduates from high school. When you send your student off to college, don't try to pay for that new computer and peripherals from your Coverdell ESA unless the school requires it as a part of the course. You also won't be able to pay for any after-school programming, transportation, uniforms, or academic tutoring for your post-secondary beneficiary with Coverdell funds unless you also want your student to pay income tax and a penalty on the income portion of the distribution. Qualifying distributions from a Coverdell ESA for post-secondary school expenses are the same as qualifying distributions for post-secondary school expenses from a 529 plan. They are either expenses the school requires you to pay (such as tuition) or expenses that qualify because your student attends the school at least half-time. Other expenses paid with Coverdell funds will be subject to income tax plus the 10 percent additional tax on the income portion of the distribution only.

Following investing rules and regulations

Coverdell ESAs generally follow the same investment rules and regulations as traditional and Roth IRA accounts. Unlike 529 plans, an awful lot is allowed, and not much is prohibited. Still, to keep everything kosher, you need to know what you can't do and ways you can't invest.

>> Your contributions need to be made in cash or cash equivalent.

>> You may not purchase life insurance or anything else that benefits you specifically (like stock in your closely-held corporation, for example, or artwork to hang in your house) with the money in your Coverdell ESA. You're prohibited from buying insurance policies, artwork, household furnishings, antiques, metals, gems, stamps, or certain coins with that money, no matter how fine an investment it may appear to you. Specially minted U.S. gold and silver bullion coins and certain state-issued coins may be permitted. In addition, platinum coins and certain gold, silver, platinum, or palladium bullion are also allowed. If you're interested in investing with Coverdell funds, check Internal Revenue Code Section. 408(m)(3) to make sure that the coins or bullion you have in mind qualify.

>> You may not commingle Coverdell account funds with any other funds. Your Coverdell account needs to be set up and accounted for separately from any other assets. The custodian or trustee, however, can commingle the money in your Coverdell account with money in other Coverdell accounts, creating what's known as a "Common Trust Fund" or a "Common Investment Fund." These funds work to your advantage because they allow the custodian or trustee to buy investments in larger pieces (which are less costly overall) and then split the pieces among all the accounts that contributed to the purchase.

>> You may not pledge the value of a Coverdell ESA as collateral for any sort of loan. Loans to you and your designated beneficiary are prohibited, as are margin or brokerage accounts that allow you to borrow against the value of your stocks to either buy more stocks or take cash out of the account.

>> You may not take a loan from a Coverdell ESA, nor may your designated beneficiary. The money that's in the account stays in the account until it's time to make distributions to your beneficiary. Any money that comes out may only come out as a distribution. After it's removed from the account, it may not be returned or repaid later.

>> You may not pay yourself or anyone else for managing your student's Coverdell ESA by using funds from the account. Only the custodian's or trustee's fees may be charged against the account. If you need to hire an investment advisor to help you select investments, you need to pay their fee out of your funds, not the account's.

>> You may not sell or lease your property or your beneficiary's property to a Coverdell account, nor may you make any other sort of asset exchange. The only thing that goes into the account is cash, and the only thing that should ever come out is cash in the form of distributions to your beneficiary. Any other transaction is prohibited.

The custodian or trustee you choose to manage your Coverdell ESA may have other prohibitions in place. You may not be allowed to invest in real estate, for example, or trade-in anything more complicated than ordinary stocks and bonds (as opposed to options, puts, calls, or the like). The custodian may also limit you to a certain group of mutual funds or their own certificates of deposit. Investigate the custodian's limitations before opening your account, and make sure you can live within those rules.

WARNING

If you goof and make a prohibited transaction under Section 530, you and your beneficiary are out of luck. The entire account will lose its tax exemption or deferral on the day of the prohibited transaction, and your designated beneficiary will be required to report 100 percent of the built-up earnings in the account from inception on their tax return for that year.

Making Account Contributions

You or anyone else in your family or circle of friends, including the student for whom the account has been established, may contribute to a Coverdell ESA, provided that you qualify under the income phaseout rules (see the section "Looking at income phaseouts for contributors," later in this chapter). Even your employer or a charitable organization may contribute (and in these cases, the $2,000 annual limit on contributions for the benefit of a specific beneficiary, which is explained in detail in the section "Spelling out contribution limits," doesn't apply). The income restrictions don't apply to contributions made from a corporation or trust; they only apply to individuals.

REMEMBER

Congress —and, by extension, the IRS — wants you to set up these accounts, and they really want to encourage you to make contributions to save for your students' educational expenses. However, they do not want to turn this program into a giveaway: Contributions into a Coverdell account are not income-tax deductible, either on your federal or state income tax returns.

When contributing to a Coverdell account, keep the following in mind:

>> **Contributions must be made in cash.** Checks, money orders, and so forth are okay, too, but stocks, bonds, life insurance policies, real estate, and trading stamps are not.

>> **Contributions can't be made into an account for the benefit of a beneficiary who's 18 years or older, except if that beneficiary falls under the special-needs category.** After your beneficiary hits that magic age, you must stop putting money into their Coverdell account unless you're absolutely certain that your student will qualify under the special-needs rules, in which case no age cutoff exists.

>> **Contributions for a particular year must be made by the original filing deadline for your tax returns for that year.** Don't plan on making your contribution on October 15 of the following year because your income tax returns are on extension — the original filing deadline means April 15 for calendar year taxpayers. And be certain that you let the account manager know that you're making your contribution for the prior tax year, not the current one. Absent this explicit instruction, the account manager may make an executive decision and assign it to the current tax year, and chances are good you'll lose the ability to contribute for the prior year before you discover the error.

Spelling out contribution limits

Coverdell ESAs have a longish history, and they weren't nearly as attractive in the good old days as they are now. With annual contributions limited to $500 per beneficiary per year, there wasn't a whole lot of savings that could be done inside the plan.

That has all changed through recent years, moving the annual contribution amount per qualified beneficiary to a much more substantial $2,000. But the operative designation is *per qualified beneficiary.* You need to know how much you're putting into any beneficiary's account and how much other people may be putting into that account or other accounts for the same beneficiary.

REMEMBER

As always, the IRS expects you to know or to find out the answers here. Mistakes are your mistakes, and they'll be costly to your student.

Aggregate annual contributions per beneficiary

REMEMBER

Annual contributions into Coverdell ESAs for the benefit of any person may not currently exceed $2,000 per year. This means that you and everyone you know, all together, may not make contributions of more than $2,000 in any year for any beneficiary.

For example, Harvey and Cynthia have one grandchild for whom they've set up a Coverdell ESA. In 2020, they contributed $2,000 to this account. They planned to do the same in 2021, but much to their surprise, they found that their daughter put her $500 birthday gift for her nephew into the account in 2021. (She's a pretty generous aunt.) So, in 2021, Harvey and Cynthia may put only $1,500 into the Coverdell account they established so they don't exceed the maximum contribution *per beneficiary* of $2,000 annually. In fact, Harvey and Cynthia better send around a family letter stating their intention to set up a Coverdell account for this particular beneficiary to find out who else has either set up their own account or has contributed to someone else's account set up for that beneficiary.

As this example shows, your contributions aren't limited to plans you set up; you may make payments into any plan established for a particular beneficiary.

Annual contributions per contributor

REMEMBER

The $2,000 aggregate contribution limit refers only to the amount that may be given *per beneficiary*. Code Section 530 doesn't limit the number of beneficiaries to whose plans you may contribute.

For example, Harvey and Cynthia now have three grandchildren and two great-grandchildren. They may establish Coverdell ESAs for each of their grandchildren and great-grandchildren. Each year they meet the income phaseout requirements, they may contribute up to $2,000 into an account for each of their qualified beneficiaries (as long as their beneficiaries are under age 18), or a total of $10,000 annually ($2000 x 5)). Should any other family member decide to contribute their traditional birthday gifts to the beneficiaries' Coverdell accounts rather than giving the money to them outright, the amount Harvey and Cynthia may contribute will be reduced by the amount of those gifts.

Gift tax and Generation-Skipping Transfer Tax consequences

Unlike gifts in Section 529 plans, which may be quite large and often trigger Gift and Generation-Skipping Transfer Tax (GSTT) consequences on their own, gifts into Coverdell ESAs will never, by themselves, create a situation where you need to fill out a Form 709. The limit on the size of the annual contribution per beneficiary prohibits this, as $2,000 will never begin to approach the $17,000 (in 2023) annual exclusion amount currently available to every donor for every donee.

TIP

However, suppose you use a Coverdell ESA as part of a savings plan and are taking advantage of other ways to push income and assets to your children, grandchildren, or any other friend or relative. In this case, you need to know that a contribution to a Coverdell account constitutes a *completed gift* or a gift over which you've given up all right, title, and interest. As such, if your total contributions into a combination of a Coverdell account, a Section 529 plan or plans, trust account(s), and/or outright gifts to or for the benefit of a single person total more than that specific year's annual exclusion gift amount, then you have to file a Form 709, United States Gift (and Generation-Skipping Transfer) Tax return.

So suppose that Harvey and Cynthia add four additional great-grandchildren into the mix (only one of their grandchildren currently has children, and the other two need to catch up). They can have a Coverdell ESA for each of the beneficiaries under 18, contribute the full $2,000 to each account every year, and never need to file a gift tax return based on the Coverdell contributions alone. However, they also have a Section 529 plan for each child, into which they're putting $16,000 each year per child. Now, their total gift to or for the benefit of each child is $18,000 per year, and a gift tax return is required, as their annual exclusion amount per donee is only $17,000 (in 2023). If they continue to make these annual gifts, the necessity of filing gift tax returns may expire as the annual exclusion gift amount increases to offset inflation. Once that annual exclusion amount is $18,000 or more, no gift tax return is required if Harvey and Cynthia keep their annual gifts the same each year.

REMEMBER

When you consider that gifts may come into any of your beneficiaries' accounts from a variety of sources, remember that for gift-tax purposes, the number you need to focus on is the amount you give to each person in any given year, not the total amount from all sources that is given to each person.

Looking at income phaseouts for contributors

Anyone can contribute to a Section 529 plan, regardless of their income. This isn't the case for Coverdell ESAs; income really matters here. If you earn too much, you may be dumb out of luck in any given year and may have to wait to make contributions to your students' accounts only in the years your income falls below the limits.

The income phaseout range for single taxpayers is $95,000 to $110,000, based on your modified adjusted gross income, described later in this section. The range for married taxpayers is $190,000 to $220,000, or exactly double that of single taxpayers. Here's how the phaseout system works:

>> If you're below the bottom of the phaseout range, you may contribute the full $2,000 per beneficiary.

>> If you're within the phaseout range, your contribution will be limited according to a formula.

>> If you're above the phaseout range, you may not make any contributions in the current year.

To determine whether you may contribute, you need to calculate your *modified adjusted gross income*, which adds the following items to your adjusted gross income from your tax return (from the "Adjusted Gross Income" line):

>> Your foreign-earned income exclusion

>> Your foreign housing exclusion

>> If you're a bona fide resident of American Samoa, your excluded income

>> Any excluded income from Puerto Rico

After you arrive at your modified adjusted gross income, you can determine whether you can contribute at all or if your contribution will be limited. If you fall within the phaseout range, you may calculate your limited contribution using Table 8-1 as an example.

TABLE 8-1: **Worksheet to figure out limited contribution to a Coverdell account from IRS Pub. 970.**

1. Maximum contribution	1. $ 2,000
2. Enter your MAGI for purposes of figuring the contribution limit to a Coverdell ESA (see definition or Worksheet 6-1 in Pub. 970)	2._____
3. Enter $190,000 if married filing jointly; $95,000 for all other filers	3._____
4. Subtract line 3 from line 2. If zero or less, enter -0- on line 4, skip lines 5 through 7, and enter $2,000 on line 8	4._____
5. Enter $30,000 if married filing jointly; $15,000 for all other filers	5._____
Note. If the amount on line 4 is greater than or equal to the amount on line 5, stop here. You aren't allowed to contribute to a Coverdell ESA for 2022.	
6. Divide line 4 by line 5 and enter the result as a decimal (rounded to at least 3 places)	6._____
7. Multiply line 1 by line 6	7._____
8. Subtract line 7 from line 1	8._____

REMEMBER

If you complete the calculation in the worksheet and find that your ability to contribute to a Coverdell account for a given year is limited or not allowed at all, don't despair. Someone else with a lower income may be able to contribute instead of you. If that person doesn't have the spare cash lying around, you can make a gift to that person and trust that they'll then make a reciprocal gift right back to your designated beneficiary in their Coverdell account. Conversely, you may also decide to increase the amount you're putting into your student's Section 529 plan for that particular year.

Getting rid of excess contributions

Because of the limits on contributions, you've probably already deduced that you will have your hand slapped when you give more than the maximum allowed. In fact, it's quite a hand slap — the penalty for making excess contributions is a 6 percent excise tax on the *overage* (contribution amounts plus any earnings attributable to those contributions) for each year that it remains in the account.

Despite your best planning and plotting, excess contributions do happen. You may have put money into your kids' accounts at the beginning of the year and then gone on to earn much more money than you anticipated. Or you could've contributed the maximum amount, unaware that Grandma was also funding an account she had set up for your student. Excess contributions happen for any number of reasons; the important fact is that they can be corrected.

Once your student receives their contribution information from the account custodian or trustee on Form 5498 each year, you can determine whether more than the maximum $2,000 has been contributed in a particular year for that child. If it has been, then you have three ways to deal with the problem:

>> Withdraw the excess cash

>> Pay the 6 percent excise tax

>> Absorb the excess contributions in future years by not making additional contributions

Withdrawing the excess

When you discover that too much money has been put into a Coverdell account or accounts for your child, the easiest solution is to withdraw the excess contribution (plus any earnings that have accrued on that amount) before the due date of the student's tax return. There will be no excise tax on the excess, but the student is responsible for paying the income tax (but no 10 percent penalty) on the income earned for the period of time the extra money stays in their account.

WARNING

Let's say you've made excess contributions and you choose to withdraw money to fix the problem. The distribution you take is taxed to your beneficiary (to the extent of any earnings) and paid to the beneficiary. Depending on the size, this excess could represent a considerable chunk of money you may not want to hand over to a child or teen. Depending on the income and other investment income in that child's account, the additional income could trigger the kiddie tax (where the investment income on the child's return is taxed at the highest applicable rate of their parent). If possible, you want to avoid this at all costs. Adding insult to injury, because this is a type of Individual Retirement Account, any income distributions are treated as ordinary income rather than as qualified dividends, long-term capital gains, or even tax-exempt interest or dividends — all of which qualify for preferential (lower) tax rates.

Paying the excise tax

Suppose that you fail to notice that you've put too much money into your student's account, or you don't manage to correct the problem in time (before your student's tax return filing deadline). As a result, for the year following the year of the excess contribution and for all subsequent years until the problem is resolved, your beneficiary will have to pay an additional 6 percent excise tax on all excess amounts each year that they remain in the account. At any time along the way, you can fix this by withdrawing the overage from the account; in the year the funds are withdrawn, your student will pay the income tax only on the income earned by the excess.

Absorbing excess contributions

Finally, you may find that the problem eventually disappears all by itself. If your designated beneficiary is under age 18, you may stop making contributions to their account. Instead, you could assign up to the maximum $2,000 contribution amount each year (depending on where your income falls in the phaseout rules) from the excess until the excess has disappeared. For example, Aiko's Coverdell ESA currently has $6,000 in excess contributions. Because Aiko is only 8 years old, her parents, whose combined income falls well below the phaseout amounts, choose to assign $2,000 from the excess in each of the following three years instead of making additional contributions into Aiko's account. In the first year, Aiko will pay a 6 percent excise tax on the full $6,000. In year two, she'll pay an excise tax only on $4,000; in year three, $2,000; and in year four, when Aiko is 10 years old, she'll no longer pay any excise tax. Beginning in the following year, provided her parents continue to earn less than the phaseout amount, they may again begin to contribute a maximum of $2,000 per year.

Taking Distributions

The point of having a Coverdell ESA is to enable you to pay for some or all your student's qualified educational expenses with a combination of money you've saved (on which you previously paid income tax) and the earnings on your savings (on which you've paid no tax).

You may not realize that you are not actually the one making the payments for these expenses; your student is using distributions from a Coverdell ESA. When distributions are made from a Coverdell account, the IRS considers them made to the student (even if checks are written directly to an educational institution), and the student bears the financial consequences.

The good news is that your student won't pay any tax if distributions are made for qualified expenses. If a distribution is made for a nonqualified expense (for example, the student used the money to buy a computer for college, even though it wasn't a requirement of their course), then tax must be paid on the income portion only. A 10 percent penalty will probably also be applied for good measure.

WARNING

The amount of qualified educational expenses is always reduced when your student receives any tax-free form of educational assistance, including, but not limited to, tax-free scholarships, veterans' educational assistance, Pell Grants, and employer tuition reimbursement programs. Be aware of these other payments to or on behalf of your student when calculating how big a distribution to take from a Coverdell account; if you're too generous, your student will pay the price.

If your student takes a taxable distribution from a Coverdell account, the 10 percent penalty will be waived under the following circumstances:

>> A taxable distribution is made on account of the designated beneficiary's death, either to the beneficiary or to their estate.

>> A taxable distribution is made when it's used for nonqualified expenses, but the expenses are incurred due to the disability of the designated beneficiary. You must attach a doctor's statement to your beneficiary's tax return, indicating the type of disability and the expected duration or whether it's expected to result in death.

>> A taxable distribution exceeding qualified educational expenses is made because the receipt of nontaxable educational assistance reduced those expenses. For example, Qamar has qualified educational expenses of $10,000, takes a $10,000 distribution from her Coverdell account to pay for those expenses, and then finds that she also is receiving a tax-free scholarship for $5,000 from her school. In this case, only $5,000 of the Coverdell distribution is being used to pay for qualified educational expenses. Because Qamar's qualifying expenses were reduced by the $5,000 scholarship, the income portion of the remaining $5,000 Coverdell distribution is subject only to income tax and not an additional 10 percent penalty.

>> A taxable distribution occurs only because qualified educational expenses were used to enable the taxpayer to take the American Opportunity or Lifetime Learning Credit.

>> A taxable distribution made to a student attending a U.S. military academy, including the U.S. Airforce Academy, the U.S. Coast Guard Academy, the U.S. Merchant Marine Academy, the U.S. Naval Academy, and West Point.

>> A taxable distribution occurs because excess contributions given in the current tax year are returned to the designated beneficiary before filing their tax return for that year.

Transferring Accounts and Changing Account Beneficiaries

As in a Section 529 plan, you save in a Coverdell ESA for a day in the future: the day your child attends an educational institution with some real dollar costs. Of course, this day never arrives for some, and the money languishes in the account until the mandatory magic distribution to the designated beneficiary at age 30. For some, this may not be such a bad thing — you may feel that you saved the money for this particular person, and by the time that person has reached age 30, they are mature enough to manage the funds themself.

If you don't belong to that specific group and the thought of handing over all that money to that particular beneficiary sticks in your craw, you may want to explore whether you can change to a new designated beneficiary, taking the old one right out of the equation.

The designated beneficiary of a Coverdell ESA is the deemed owner of the assets in the account; however, they may not be the person named in the initial account-opening documents as being responsible for making the decisions regarding the account. If you're the named responsible adult, you're in luck, and you can initiate the transfer.

WARNING

You may change the designated beneficiary on the same account as often as you like without incurring any tax or penalty. However, if you choose to roll one account over to another Coverdell account, changing the beneficiary at the same time, you're limited to one such tax-free rollover of the funds in that particular account in any given 12-month period.

Qualifying relationships for successor-designated beneficiaries

In setting up a Coverdell account for your original beneficiary, you transfer all right, title, and interest in the money you gift into the account. Now, as the responsible adult named on the account, you're proposing taking that money away from your beneficiary. If you could do that without restriction, that would mean you retained real control over the money. You don't, so you can't transfer to a new beneficiary without following the rules.

And the rules are quite simple. The new beneficiary must be related to the original beneficiary (not to you) in one of the following ways:

>> A lineal descendent, such as a child, grandchild, or stepchild

>> A lineal ancestor, including the beneficiary's mother, father, grandmother, grandfather, stepmother, or stepfather

>> A brother, sister, stepbrother, or stepsister of the original beneficiary

>> A niece or nephew (but no stepniece or stepnephew)

>> An aunt, uncle, or first cousin of the original beneficiary (but no step-aunts, step-uncles, or step-cousins)

>> A mother-in-law, father-in-law, sister-in-law, brother-in-law, daughter-in-law, or son-in-law

>> The spouse of any of the people listed above or of the original beneficiary

Maximum age of the successor beneficiary

All assets in Coverdell ESAs need to be totally distributed once the designated beneficiary reaches age 30. However, you can transfer the account's balance to a new beneficiary just before that date, keeping the account open and operating well beyond the 30th birthday of the original designated beneficiary. So long as the new beneficiary is under 30 and falls within the acceptable range of family relationship to the original beneficiary, you can affect the transfer. If you choose a new beneficiary who is under age 18, you may even begin to make contributions to the account again.

Here's how it works: You begin funding a Coverdell account for the first designated beneficiary and continue making contributions until you're forced to stop when they reach age 18. Suppose this beneficiary then receives a full-paid scholarship and doesn't need the funds, but you have another child or even grandchild who might benefit from the money you've saved. Instead of waiting and distributing the entire amount to the original designated beneficiary when they're 30, you choose to change beneficiaries and go with the younger child. Until that child reaches 18, you may contribute to the account to the extent allowable by the governing rules.

Additional transfers of this nature can continue to be made using the same account so long as the new beneficiary always is under 30 years old and is related to the original beneficiary in the manner described in the "Qualifying relationships for successor-designated beneficiaries" section earlier in this chapter. Whoever is the beneficiary when the account makes distributions is the person who pays income tax on the earnings if any tax needs to be paid. Whoever is the beneficiary when excess contributions are inside the account is the one who must pay the excise tax on the excess contributions. And whoever is the beneficiary when the account finally terminates is the one who receives the final distribution and pays income tax on whatever income remains inside the account.

Rolling over Coverdell accounts

In addition to changing the designated beneficiary on an account, if you're the responsible adult on an account, you may also choose to move from one Coverdell account to another. You can do this for either the same beneficiary or a new one (but one who fulfills all the requirements listed in the "Qualifying relationships for successor-designated beneficiaries" section earlier in this chapter).

WARNING

You may make an account rollover by withdrawing funds from your current account and then depositing them into a new Coverdell account within 60 days. You need to keep track of the dates; if you wait until the 61st day, you have just made a nonqualified distribution. The designated beneficiary on your first account is responsible for income tax on the earnings plus a 10 percent penalty. In addition (and not to scare you), you're also handing control of that money over to that beneficiary — good luck trying to retrieve it.

Transferring into a Section 529 plan

Although you're limited by beneficiary age within a Coverdell account, Section 529 plans have no age limitations. Accordingly, you may want to make a tax-free transfer from the Coverdell account into a Section 529 plan for the same designated beneficiary before that beneficiary turns age 30. Transferring from a Coverdell account to a Section 529 plan gives rise to some interesting consequences, though, so you want to be careful.

REMEMBER

When you initiate a transfer from a Coverdell account, the account trustee or custodian will write a check to your designated beneficiary, not to the new account. If you choose to have those exact funds go into the Section 529 plan, the 529 plan it goes into needs to have your designated beneficiary listed as the account owner. When you contribute to a Coverdell account, you make a completed gift to your student; you may not take it back.

If giving Baby Alex control over a Section 529 plan gives you the heebie-jeebies, consider contributing directly to a 529 plan instead, using an equivalent amount of your funds rather than the proceeds from the Coverdell account. However, if you want to retain control over the funds, you must deposit your own funds (not the funds from the Coverdell account) within 60 days of withdrawing from the Coverdell account. By funding the 529 plan with your own funds, you maintain control over the 529 plan as the account owner; you've also fulfilled the rollover requirement of completing the transfer within 60 days. The proceeds from the

Coverdell withdrawal now belong to your designated beneficiary (over whose assets you still have control until they reach age 18), and the new 529 assets remain under your control.

REMEMBER

Suppose you choose to fund a Section 529 plan with your own funds, but you're unable to put the full amount that was in the old Coverdell ESA into the new 529 plan. In this event, your designated beneficiary pays income tax and penalties on the income earned on the distribution amount that isn't being rolled over.

Neither scenario is perfect because they allow control over money to pass to your designated beneficiary, either by making them the account owner on a Section 529 plan or by actually handing them the cash. Still, if the amounts are not huge or if your designated beneficiary is incredibly mature for their age, it may work for you.

Transferring due to divorce

When planning for your student's education, you're probably not imagining a time when your designated beneficiary will be old enough to think about any marital issues, especially a marital dissolution. After all, you probably set up this account when your child was young, and the first thought that crosses your mind when you check on them asleep in their bed is not how they will divide their assets after a divorce.

Still, a Coverdell ESA can live on well into adulthood and may still be an asset owned by your designated beneficiary after they marry and even at the time of a divorce. If this happens to your student, there are some things you both should know:

» **Coverdell ESAs aren't counted as community property in community property states.** Funds are gifted directly to the account owner (even if the gifts occur after marriage through a tax-free rollover from a different Coverdell ESA) and are maintained solely for the benefit of the account owner.

» **The account owner may include a Coverdell ESA as part of the divorce or separation agreement, transferring ownership to their spouse or former spouse.** In this case, provided the new owner is under age 30, this is a tax-free transfer, even if another tax-free transfer or rollover occurred within the last 12 months.

Chapter **9**

The Mechanics of Coverdells

lthough Section 529 plans suit many people (or maybe even you), Coverdell Education Savings Accounts (CESAs) are far more flexible in some ways, and they may fill a specific need in your educational funding plans that 529 plans can't. Provided you meet the requirements in order to contribute to an account, you may be able to make this type of savings vehicle really work for you. (Chapter 8 tells you about the rules and regulations surrounding Coverdell accounts, so if you haven't read that chapter, you may want to flip back there first.)

This chapter gets you cooking on the practical stuff: the hows and whats you need to know to get started — and keep going — with a Coverdell ESA.

In this chapter, you find out the nitty-gritty of Coverdell accounts, from how and where you may open an account to what you need to do after that account is open in order to make it a success. You look at what you should and shouldn't do over the account's lifetime and discover pitfalls to avoid as you make your contributions and your student takes their withdrawals. Finally, you see how Coverdell accounts dovetail with Section 529 and other education savings plans, creating a patchwork of savings options that will eventually provide for all your student's needs.

Getting a Handle on What You Want

Before you ever start putting money into a Coverdell account, you need to know your goals and how you'd like to achieve them. You may already have saved some money in a more traditional bank or brokerage account, but it hasn't grown very much in the last several years, or it's actually lost money. Remember, no education savings option is as technically simple a savings technique as opening a bank account and making regular deposits into it. There are consequences to funding any of these accounts, and you need to understand not only what those consequences are but also how they fit into your and your student's future plans.

TIP

You need to be able to supply answers to all the following questions before making your initial deposit:

>> **What are you saving for?** You may already be saving in another education savings plan, such as a Section 529 plan, for the major expenses, such as tuition and room and board. If so, picture your Coverdell account as the place where the funds for some of your student's more personal expenses, such as books and supplies (and their computer, so long as they're still in high school or below, or if your child's college requires it), can come from. Or you may picture your student attending a private or parochial school long before they ever begin college, and you want this account to help pay for that. Have a clear idea of what you plan to use this money for.

>> **Who will be your designated beneficiary, and whom do you have waiting in the wings as a backup?** Saving money in a Coverdell account for the sake of saving money in a Coverdell account just doesn't cut it. You have to be saving for a specific person, and you must have a reasonable expectation that the person you're saving for will need this money to pay for educational expenses at some point before their 30th birthday (or longer, if they're a special-needs student). What if you have any doubts that you won't use up all the money you've saved over the years on that student? In that case, you may want to consider who can step into the shoes vacated by your original beneficiary, either through choice or by necessity, and whether it's another child of yours, a grandchild, or any other allowed relation of your original beneficiary who's included on the list in Chapter 8.

>> **Who is actually going to contribute to your child's plan?** You may not be the obvious choice here. All your good intentions and the practicality of this particular type of account may not amount to a hill of beans if you're prohibited from making contributions because you earn too much money (see Chapter 8). Let's say you'll meet the requirements in some years but not in others. In that event, you may want to line up an alternate contributor who'll meet the income limitation requirements in years that you don't (even if you have to make gifts to that person in order for them to make gifts into the Coverdell account).

>> **What educational costs are you planning to pay with the money in this account?** Coverdell accounts are far more limited in terms of total size than Section 529 plans. (You're just not going to be able to put as much money into an account where the maximum annual contribution is $2,000 as you are in an account that basically has no maximum annual contribution.) However, these plans are much more flexible in the type of expenses you can pay for, especially during primary and secondary school.

You may want to consider just how much of your money you'll need in this account to pay for some of the expenses that your Section 529 isn't able to cover and try to limit the size of your Coverdell ESA to that amount and no more. For example, if you've invested in a Section 529 prepaid tuition plan, you may want to use distributions from your child's Coverdell account to pay for room and board, books, and other supplies. Or your secondary school child may be "sooo close" to achieving that perfect academic record and may need just a little extra tutoring in calculus to make the grade. In this case, paying for tutoring while in high school with Coverdell distributions may actually be a very savvy investment, as that extra edge may now qualify them for lucrative academic scholarships. In Chapter 10, I discuss how Coverdell accounts can complement other savings plans.

After you know for whom and how much you're saving, you're ready to jump in.

Opening a Plan

After you figure out the answers to all the questions in the previous section's list, you need to fill out the forms, write a check, and get this account rolling.

First, though, you need to decide where, exactly, you want to open your account. Unlike Section 529 plans, states don't get involved in Coverdell accounts; accordingly, you have many more options to choose from and need to make many more decisions.

REMEMBER

While you're in the process of choosing a bank, savings and loan company, or other institution, you need to focus on two essential items:

>> The range and variety of investments that the account will offer

>> The cost to you annually, upfront, or both to set up and administer the account

Keep in mind that none of these companies is in the business of paying for your child's education, but they're all in the business of making money. Your account represents nothing more than a moneymaking opportunity for them; make sure that it will also be one for you.

You also need to decide whether to invest in a *self-directed account* (one in which you decide on individual investments, including stocks and bonds, to invest in) or one in which you have a choice of mutual funds, bank certificates of deposit, and/or money market funds. Clearly, in the self-directed account, you bear more of the risk personally because you're making all the investment decisions by yourself (unless you hire, at your own cost, an advisor to select what you should buy and when to buy). If you choose to go the mutual fund route, even if your investments do poorly, you can still lay some of the blame on the fund manager. Still, a bad investment is a bad investment. Your account loses money regardless of who made the decisions of what — and what not — to buy.

TIP

If this is your first venture into the world of investing, you may want to open your account in an institution that limits your investment options or hire someone to make these decisions for you in a self-directed account. If you don't want to go to the expense of hiring an investment advisor, leaving the actual investing of your money in the hands of the mutual fund managers may give you a greater comfort level than choosing your own investments, especially when you're just beginning. A wise approach may be to ease yourself in and make safer (although maybe not as lucrative) choices at first. As you gain confidence in your own abilities, you always have the option to change to other options, such as investing in individual stocks and bonds. On the other hand, if you're making money and happy with your investments, don't think you must keep searching for a better mousetrap. You never need to apologize to anyone for making money, even if you didn't make as much money as you could have.

Shopping for a place to open your account

When you begin shopping for a home for your Coverdell account, you'll find that most banks will offer these accounts if they also offer other types of IRA accounts for retirement. While IRAs are more common and available in more types, a Coverdell ESA is essentially an IRA and follows many of the same rules.

In addition to banks, many nonbank trustees are eligible to hold your Coverdell account. Search for "Approved Nonbank Trustees and Custodians" at `www.irs.gov` to find the most current list. At the top of the page, you'll find a hyperlink to a PDF file that contains the most current list. Here you will find the names and addresses of brokerage houses, investment advisory firms, and the like. You may discover that your employer is approved or that you belong to an affinity group that offers the plans. Do not assume that a likely-looking organization is on the list. There are surprising omissions and equally surprising inclusions. Some life insurance companies and pension funds are included, but many are not. And your investment advisor, brokerage house, or credit union may bypass the list altogether by establishing a partnership with an organization on the list. If this is the case, you want to be certain that you are not paying double fees, one to your investment advisor, for example, and an additional one to the actual trustee of the account.

REMEMBER

The IRS is constantly changing the list, so please check before you open an account with a non-approved trustee. Remember, the person talking to you on the phone may not know their group has fallen off the approved list. If, in your investigations, you find a plan that looks good and that you want to participate in, just make sure you receive a copy of the necessary notice of approval from the IRS before you open an account and hand over your money.

Regardless of whether the plan you choose is sponsored by a bank or institution listed on the IRS' most current list of nonbank trustees, your custodian or trustee must provide you with a copy of the trust or custody agreement governing your account before you ever open it. Very frequently, it's attached to the actual application; keep this agreement as part of your permanent records.

WARNING

Just because your current bank, savings and loan company, or favorite mutual fund company offers these accounts doesn't mean that's the best place to park your account. Although your bank may seem like the obvious place to open this account, it may allow you to invest your money only in certificates of deposit or money market funds, neither of which will generate much income from earnings. Likewise, mutual fund companies may limit investments in Coverdell accounts to only certain mutual funds. Shop around for something that best suits your needs.

Meeting the initial requirements (besides money)

After deciding where to open your Coverdell account, you must complete the necessary paperwork. And there should be no surprise here — nothing is ever as simple as filling out and signing a signature card anymore. You'll most likely have to complete an account setup form (which is often the same form you use to open a traditional IRA or a Roth IRA account — make sure to check the correct box). You'll also need to complete a Form W-9, which certifies the Social Security number for both the account owner and the designated beneficiary, which prevents backup income tax withholding. You may also have to fill out a separate form to choose your investments or a form that certifies that your designated beneficiary falls under the "special-needs student" category. Some applications will also ask that you complete the information for a designated death beneficiary if your designated beneficiary dies before the account has been emptied.

Due to The USA Patriot Act of 2001, the amount of information you must provide to open any account is fairly extensive, and banks and other financial institutions no longer allow you to leave blanks in their paperwork to fill in later. If you can't provide this information when you want to open the account, the account won't be opened until you can.

The IRS has provided a sample application that includes all the required information in Form 5305-EA, which you can obtain directly from the IRS website at irs.gov. Amazingly enough, Form 5305-EA is a straightforward and reasonably short form (only 2 pages), and most of that is the trust agreement that must accompany any Coverdell account opening documents. In it are laid out all the requirements for the account.

Of course, if everything financial were as concise as Form 5305-EA, most people in the financial services industries would be out of work. Accordingly, it's unlikely that the forms you must complete to open an account will be this short. In addition to the information required by the IRS, every bank and nonbank trustee will likely require additional information (because that's what banks and nonbank trustees do).

Some of the additional information they will ask for may include the following:

>> **For the responsible individual:** You may also be required to provide proof of citizenship and proof of residence, and, if a non-U.S. citizen, proof of resident alien or valid visa information. Be prepared with photocopies of birth certificates, Social Security cards, passports, green cards, and the like.

>> **For the designated beneficiary:** Whatever information the custodian asks to see for the responsible individual, it's safe to assume they will want to see the same documentation for the designated beneficiary.

>> **Name, address, date of birth, and Social Security number for all contingent or death beneficiaries.** Once again, you'd be wise to make sure all the required documentation is in your hands prior to opening the account. Not having it may delay the process.

Form 5305-EA allows you to retain control of the account after the beneficiary reaches age 18 only if you check the box in Article V of the agreement. If you want to retain the ability to roll this account over to a different designated beneficiary (trust me, you do), you make that election in Article VI.

Don't forget, if someone other than yourself is contributing the initial funds to open the account, you must disclose that on Form 5305-EA. And, as stated earlier, the initial funds to open the account don't necessarily need to come from an individual — a corporation, trust, or charitable organization can provide them.

Finally, although not all account setups require this information, many will require you to provide the name of someone to succeed you as the responsible individual should you no longer be able to act in that capacity. It's not a bad idea, but please talk it over with the person you are appointing to that job and make sure you agree on how and when you want the funds to be distributed for the benefit of the beneficiary.

TIP

Save yourself some trouble by lining up all the information you need to open a Coverdell account ahead of time.

Devising an Effective Investment Strategy

After your account is open and you've actually placed money into it, you need to create an investment strategy you feel comfortable with. If your student is very young, you may choose to begin aggressively, putting most of your money into stocks or cybersecurities rather than bonds, certificates of deposit, or money market funds. If your student is older and closer to needing the money in the account, you may select a less risky approach, leaving only a small amount of money in the stock market and placing most of your funds into safer investments. Limiting your risk also limits the amount of money you're likely to make; however, the trade-off is in knowing how much money will be in the account when you need it.

You also need to create a set of rules under which you feel comfortable operating. Maybe you're the type of person who begins to sweat when your investment appreciates by 20 percent. Or perhaps you won't be satisfied until it approaches 50 percent or 100 percent appreciation. And when will you sell if an investment doesn't perform the way you thought it would? Do you begin to bite your nails once it drops 10 percent below its purchase price and proceed to chew on your knuckles, elbows, and toes as it continues to decline by 20 percent, or more, below the amount that you bought it for? Maybe your blood pressure can only survive a drop of 20 percent below its absolute high point, and that next penny of loss has you reaching for the telephone at the same moment that you eat a bottle of antacid tablets. Just like in most other areas of life, establishing guidelines in investing gives you a structure within which to work.

REMEMBER

Rules and guidelines are meant to be broken and changed. After you devise a strategy, don't set it in stone. These are your guidelines, not actual laws or regulations that must be followed. As your student ages, you'll need to reassess your actual investments and investment strategy periodically. They'll need the money soon, and you may want to preserve at least some of the money you've managed to accumulate to date in a more conservative, safer investment while leaving the remainder to hopefully grow more rapidly.

TIP

Creating a set of investing guidelines gives you a valuable tool when determining what's going right and what's going wrong inside your student's account. If you have no specific strategy, you'll have a hard time knowing what to change if you're not achieving your hoped-for results. With guidelines in place, you can better understand what's not working quite the way you want and then change it.

Understanding your investments

You've heard all the cautionary tales since you were a kid: Look before you leap, test the waters with your big toe before you stick your whole foot in, read the fine print, and don't let yourself be blindsided. So, why do most people faced with an investment decision close their eyes and buy whatever Great-Uncle Al or their next-door neighbor's nephew tells them to buy?

REMEMBER

If you're going to have any success at all in investing, you need to understand what you're buying, and you need to be comfortable with that knowledge. You gain absolutely nothing by being able to explain how a covered option works if the idea of putting your hard-earned money to work for you in that manner makes you sweat.

Understanding your investments and how they work makes devising an appropriate investment strategy easier for you. Terms such as risk, high-growth, low-yield, and so on, which trip effortlessly off your financial advisor's tongue, may be meaningless to you. And your financial advisor is pretty much counting on that fact (they look good, you feel not-so-smart, and they can then peddle their expertise to you). Understanding investment terminology helps you to figure out where your comfort level lies and allows you to stay there.

Your goal is to create a balanced portfolio in which the risk level is tolerable to you and includes various investments. This approach is also the most effective long-term way to invest. Any portfolio that relies too much on one particular investment or one sort of investment adds unnecessary risk. Spread your money over as wide a range as possible to maximize your opportunities while minimizing your risk.

REMEMBER

Although what follows focuses on stocks and bonds (because that's where most people need the most help), remember to keep all money invested at all times. Every Coverdell ESA has some sort of money market option; make sure that any cash sitting in your account is swept daily into the money market funds. Even though the interest you earn on this money won't pay for much on its own, over time, it will help to improve your overall investment result.

Regarding risk

Whether you're investing in *stocks* (shares in companies that you own) or *bonds* (loans that you make to companies in exchange for interest payments), an element of risk is involved. It's up to you to determine how big an element of risk you're talking about and how much risk you're willing to assume. Here are some points to keep in mind when pondering the level of risk to take:

>> **Never put all your eggs in one basket.** No matter how confident you are that something will take off, invest part of your money in other ventures just in case. There is no denying that the opportunity exists for you to make a killing in the market. Just look at the run-up in the stock markets since the 2007-2009 financial market meltdown. But the opportunity to lose it all is just as great (if not greater), as evidenced by the COVID crash, followed by the bear market of 2022.

>> **Most people assume that buying stocks is riskier than buying bonds, and to some degree, that's true.** In a worst-case scenario, where a company goes bankrupt, a bondholder has some opportunity to recoup their investment because they're a company creditor. However, a shareholder in that bankrupt company knows to kiss the value of their investment goodbye. As a partial owner of the company, they'll receive money only after all creditors have been paid in full, and the reason the company is bankrupt is that not all the creditors can be paid in full.

However, understand that some companies' financial situations are so solid as to represent an almost sure thing, not insofar as the variations in its stock price go, but as to whether they're still going to be around tomorrow or next year. In this regard, they may represent a less risky investment than investing in *junk* or *high-yield* bonds — bonds rated lower than investment grade by bond rating companies such as Moody's or Standard & Poor's (S&P). Junk bonds (which is anything that Moody's grades as Ba or lower and that S&P rates as BB or lower) present the potential of a very high-interest rate on your money. The bond ratings companies also recognize that the companies issuing these bonds have a higher-than-average chance of defaulting on their loans. Once again, risk raises its head — you've invested in something that has the very real potential of significantly raising the value of your investment account. Still, it also carries the possibility of sucking that amount of value — and more — out.

>> **Doing some research helps you assess a particular investment's risk. Check the history of a stock price.** If you see wild fluctuations and you don't have a strong stomach, you may want to pass on that particular issue. Look to see whether dividends have been paid and whether they've been paid regularly and over a long period of time. A company's ability to pay dividends to its shareholders shows a tendency for financial health, although it's not a sure indicator. And look at a company's balance sheet before you ever hand over a single dollar into its care. The balance sheets of all publicly owned companies are matters of public record and are available either from the company itself or on the Internet.

Bonds and mutual funds carry creditworthiness ratings; check the ratings. Moody's Investors Service and Standard & Poor's are the best-known bond rating organizations. They judge bonds from the highest quality (S&P = AAA, Moody's = Aaa) to those in default, with recovery unlikely (S&P = D, Moody's = C). The higher the bond quality, the lower the stated interest rate is likely to be, but the higher your chance of actually collecting that interest. Generally, any bond rated B and below is increasingly speculative. However, some may represent the debt of genuinely solid companies, so you need to begin researching a bit more carefully to identify these gems.

WARNING

A word of caution regarding bond and mutual fund ratings: the companies assigning creditworthiness scores are funded by the bond issuers and mutual fund companies. It's definitely a case of the fox guarding the hen house here, but unfortunately, it's what's currently available.

REMEMBER

>> **No investment is absolutely risk-free.** Your bank may go belly up (although your bank deposits, but not your investment accounts, are protected by deposit insurance up to $250,000 per depositor per bank, not per account). The United States Treasury may start defaulting on its loans (and in several recent instances, has threatened to due to Congress treating the federal debt ceiling as a political football, which could be a much larger problem than the fact that the U.S. Treasury has just stopped paying its bills). Your house may float away, taking all the savings you've stitched into the mattress down the river with it. There is no such thing as a sure thing.

Choosing growth stocks versus value stocks

Any discussion about stocks and the stock market inevitably includes the terms "growth" and "value." Here's what those terms mean.

>> **Growth stocks:** Very simply, *growth stocks* are shares in companies that still are experiencing — or anticipate experiencing — significant earnings growth. They may be pharmaceutical, high-tech, green energy, or biotech companies — all busy inventing the next great magic pill, miracle cure, or computer application that will completely change your life. And it may, but not in the way they think. There is great potential for a significant increase in the value of your investment when you put some of your money in a growth company.

>> **Value stocks:** On the other hand, *value stocks* are shares in companies that already have an established product line or service, a product or service that generates steady income for the company. Usually, the company's current share price is well below the company's actual value if it were sold or otherwise liquidated.

Value companies often include banking, energy, retail, and utility companies (but not the telecom companies, which are generally seen as more high-tech, although many do pay a very good dividend). Somehow, even though a breakfast cereal company may seem to constantly be bringing new cereals on to the market, it's still making breakfast cereal and generating roughly the same amount of net income from that cereal.

TIP

Value stocks are often viewed as stodgy, but the stodginess that makes you money can be beautiful. Because of their low valuations against share price, their prices often creep up, increasing the worth of your investment. At the same time, you're still receiving those quarterly dividends. It's a win-win situation, especially when the overall stock market tends to be in the doldrums. Historically, value stocks have outperformed the overall market during market downturns. For more about value stocks, check out *Value Investing For Dummies*, by Peter Sander and Janet Haley (published by Wiley).

Comparing mega-cap to nano-cap companies, and everything in between

This section is not a comparison of top hats, stocking caps, and flat caps. It refers to the size, or market capitalization, of a company selling shares in itself. *Market capitalization* is the value the market has put on a company (as opposed to the company's actual value, as determined by its assets and balance sheet).

For example, if a company has 1 million shares issued and outstanding and the shares sell for $10 per share, the company's market capitalization is $10 million. But because this company may only be worth the value of one bright employee's new idea (which is still being developed and so hasn't earned the company a red cent yet), the market clearly values the company far higher than the total value of the underlying assets. And maybe the market is right; the new idea may just pay off, and those who gambled $10 per share when it was nothing more than an idea will turn around in a few years and sell those shares for $100. Such is the magic of the stock market.

As valuations of some companies have soared into the stratosphere at the same time as ever more start-up companies leap into the publicly traded stock markets, the market cap designations have evolved. Whereas there were once only large-cap, mid-cap, and small-cap companies, there are now mega-cap, micro-cap, and last and certainly least, nano-cap in addition to the traditional categories. They break down as follows:

>> Mega-cap corporations have a market value range of greater than $200 billion. There are currently 29 mega-cap stocks, and I'm not going to list them because you can probably name most of them without my help.

>> Generally, large-cap companies have market capitalization ranges from $10 billion to $200 billion.

>> Mid-caps cover those companies with market capitalization between $2 billion and $10 billion.

>> Small-cap companies' market valuations range from $300 million - $2 billion.

>> Micro-caps are those companies with market valuations between $50 million and $300 million.

>> Finally, the lowly nano-cap companies have market valuations of less than $50 million.

While there are no hard and fast rules here, generally speaking, the larger the market capitalization (including all 30 stocks on the Dow Jones Industrial Average but also a great number of stocks listed on the S&P 500 or the NASDAQ exchanges), the more stable the company. Just as a semitrailer takes a while to get up to speed after starting up when the traffic signal turns green, a mega-cap corporation is a behemoth that isn't going to do anything quickly. Share prices can rise and fall, but you won't often see spectacular leaps or plummets. Instead, the price changes tend to be slow and gradual (although you should never forget the lessons of Enron, Tyco, and WorldCom, to name a few large-cap corporations that hit the skids and failed spectacularly).

Overall, mega and large caps tend to hit lower on the risk scale than mid-caps or small caps, and nano-caps will be the riskiest of them all. As market capitalization decreases, risk, with both its upside and its downside, generally increases.

Looking at your bond options

Bonds are loans that you make to government entities or corporations. In exchange for using your money, whoever you've lent the money to is supposed to pay you interest. You'll receive interest payments during the bond's lifetime, probably twice each year. When the bond matures, or the issuing body chooses to pay it off early, you receive back the full-face amount of the bond, plus any interest still owed to you. When interest rates are falling overall, the borrowers may call in loans with higher interest rates and immediately turn around and borrow at a lower rate. However, as rates rise, you won't find anyone volunteering to surrender their low-interest loans in order to refinance. In theory, bond investing is fairly simple. Overall, it seems like a reasonably safe, essentially unexciting sort of investment. Here are your options when it comes to bonds:

>> **U.S. Treasuries:** There may be nothing duller than U. S. Treasury bills (which exist for no more than one year), notes (the period from issue to maturity from one year and a day to ten years after issue), and bonds (maturities begin more than ten years after their issue). These debt instruments represent pieces of the *national debt* — the cumulative amount of money the U.S. government has spent in excess of the total tax revenues collected since the beginning of the U.S. government. And because the U.S. government needs to be able to finance its debt at the lowest-possible interest rate it can afford, U.S. Treasury bills, notes, and bonds are guaranteed by the full faith and credit of the United States. In other words, they're about as safe and risk-free as you can get, probably even beating the money-under-the-mattress scenario. To make them even more attractive, interest from U.S. Treasuries is income-tax-free in all states. U.S. Treasury obligations may be purchased through banks, brokers, and dealers or directly from the U.S. Treasury through treasurydirect.gov

>> **Government bonds and certificates:** Moving up the risk and excitement scale for bonds, you next reach so-called government bonds and certificates, such as those issued by the Government National Mortgage Association (GNMAs, or Ginnie Mae) and the Federal National Mortgage Association (FNMAs or Fanny Mae), to name two. These are very similar to Treasuries in that the federal government and its agencies issue them, but they're not exactly Treasury-like, either in risk or state income tax treatment. There's no "full faith and credit of the U.S. government" standing behind these investments. Still, it's highly unlikely that any federal agency will go belly up and stop its debt repayment. Because these investments are marginally riskier than U.S. Treasury issues, they do pay slightly higher interest rates. Unlike U.S. Treasuries, government bonds and certificates may not be purchased directly from the U.S. government but only from financial services firms (such as brokerages) that trade in government securities. If you want to purchase

one of these securities, ask your broker whether they can purchase it for you; if your broker can't help you, they'll direct you to a firm that can.

» **Municipal bonds:** Municipal bonds are debt instruments issued by state and local governments (including issues from Puerto Rico, the District of Columbia, the U.S. Virgin Islands, American Samoa, and Guam) to finance things such as hospitals, higher education, or the construction of roads and sports stadiums. They're only as solid as the governments and agencies issuing them. Here is where you need to begin checking either with Standard & Poor's (http://www.standardandpoors.com) or with Moody's Investors Service (www.moodys.com) regarding the reliability of any particular bond or its issuing body. States and municipalities sometimes have difficulties paying their bills, a situation that reflects negatively on their creditworthiness and rating. While no state has ever defaulted on its loans, many municipalities have. Puerto Rico, whose bonds were once very highly regarded because they were tax-exempt in every state, declared bankruptcy in 2017. In March 2022, Puerto Rico finally closed its books by swapping $22 billion of bonds for $7 billion. In other words, if you were holding Puerto Rico municipal bonds in your portfolio in 2017, every dollar of your initial investment would now be worth only $0.32. That's gotta hurt!

REMEMBER

As ratings drop, interest rates and yields increase. Most interest on municipal bonds is federally tax-free (therefore, not the best investment for your tax-deferred or exempt Coverdell account). However, municipal bonds could make sense for you in some situations.

» **Corporate bonds:** Finally, corporate bonds represent the debt corporations take on to continue doing business. And the quality of that debt corresponds to the financial health of the corporation issuing the bond. A financially healthy company — one that has no problems now or in the foreseeable future — issues investment-grade bonds (above B grade) that pay higher rates of interest than you get from any sort of government bond, whether federal, state, or local, but still not so high that it blows your socks off. The lower that rating drops, though, the higher the interest you'll receive; the company issuing the bond needs to entice investors with inflated rates of return to attract their money.

Taking advantage of dollar cost averaging

Even the pros have difficulty knowing exactly when to buy and figuring out what's really the bottom of the market (on the theory of buy low, sell high). And you're not an investment professional staring at the ticker tape, poised to jump in with your buy or sell order. So what?

TIP

You can use a dollar cost averaging technique to provide almost the same result as those pros are getting, with a lot less effort and time. Simply, dollar cost averaging is when you purchase the same dollar amount of a security at periodic intervals, either over an indefinite term or for a specific number of weeks or months.

Here's how it works: When you set up your account, you outline a portfolio that you want. You tell the account custodian that you want this percentage of your monthly contribution to buy this investment and that percentage to buy the other. Every month when you contribute to the account, and until you give the custodian instructions to stop, you'll be buying these same investments in those percentages. In addition, if you make contributions only once a year, the custodian can divide that money into however many periodic purchases you want to make. You may decide to spread your purchases out over the entire year or maybe just a few months. For as long as you participate in this program by buying, you benefit from all the fluctuations in that particular investment. Although you won't be buying all your shares at the absolute low, neither do you run any danger of buying all of them as they hit their peak.

Doing your research

It's all well and good to read a column and follow someone's advice; the only problem is that the person giving the advice isn't investing their own money in your account. You are, and although advice from the experts may seem like a good thing, you'll never get two experts who completely agree on anything. In the end, *you* will make the decisions regarding your student's account, and your choices will determine how well the account will perform. There's nothing like a little pressure to make you sit up a bit straighter, is there?

WARNING

Don't ever rely on someone's stock tip, whether a friend or stranger; do your own homework and assess the positives and negatives yourself. Every investment has its good points, but it also has bad points. It's up to you to decide whether the upside outweighs the downside. If you can't discover the shortcomings, you'd better run quickly in the opposite direction. There's no such creature as a sure thing, and the person offering advice may have an ulterior motive. That motive may be as mundane as being paid by a newspaper to come up with a column idea or as sinister as trying to artificially crank up the price of a stock to make a personal killing in the market. Never assume that someone is giving you stock market advice for your health.

I'm not saying you should ignore everything written in the newspaper or discussed on television or walk away from the advice of people you know and trust. However, you need to understand the biases of the people giving advice and factor those into your own decision. Many people have their fathers' portfolios because Dad has always told them what to buy. The only problem with that approach is that Dad's investment criteria aren't necessarily your own, and a portfolio that perfectly suits Dad's needs may be completely inappropriate for you.

WARNING

Never rely on investment advice that you receive through unsolicited e-mails or faxes. These are generally scams that you should avoid at all costs. If you follow this type of advice, it'll likely cost you plenty. Remember, what seems too good to be true usually is. Run — don't walk — away from these offers.

Selecting Investments and Placing Buy Orders

After you choose what type of account to open and determine your strategy and rules, you need to sit down and do your research. You may already have devised a reasonable plan to put a certain percentage of your money into stocks and another percentage into bonds. You may even have thought about how much you want to invest in chemical companies and high-tech corporations. Now you must select the actual investments and place your initial buy orders.

Depending on which custodian you're using for your Coverdell account, placing a buy (or sell) order may require contacting the custodian with your instructions (the custodian will actually make the transaction), or you may be able to initiate the transaction online. Many brokerages are valid Coverdell custodians. When your Coverdell account is with one of them, you can usually buy and sell securities within your account just the same as you would in any other brokerage account — by calling your broker or placing the trade online.

Paying Into a Coverdell Education Savings Account

You can put money into your student's account in a variety of ways. Just like with Section 529 plans, you can write a check, make an automatic fund transfer from your bank account, or even have funds deducted through a payroll deduction program. If you use a bank's Coverdell account, you may even have the choice of paying in cash (although this won't work with any brokerage firm or institution that deals primarily through electronic means).

However you choose to fund your student's account, you may not use stocks, bonds, real estate, or built-up value in an insurance policy as a contribution. If the money you plan to put into a Coverdell account is currently in one of those forms, you first need to liquidate your nonqualified investment and then deposit the cash.

You may contribute to a Coverdell account at any point throughout the year. There are no limits on when or how often you may make a deposit, provided, of course, that you don't exceed the limitations on how much you can deposit, which I describe in detail in Chapter 8.

Just like with traditional or Roth IRAs, you can contribute to a Coverdell account for a particular year after the year has ended but before you file your income tax return for that year. Indicate on your deposit slip that you're making a so-called *carryback contribution* and that you want it applied to the preceding calendar year. The ability to contribute for a year just ended in the first part of the following year may provide you with a valuable planning opportunity. Very often, because of year-end bonuses and late-in-the-year stock sales (with capital gains) and distributions from mutual fund companies, you won't know how great your income for a particular year will be until well into January of the following year. If you can defer your bonus (or any other item of income) into the following year, you may not know whether you're even eligible to contribute for a particular year until after December 31.

The absolute deadline for making a Coverdell contribution for a prior year after the end of that tax year is April 15 of the following year or the first business day after April 15 if the 15th falls on a weekend or holiday. While there are some types of accounts for which you can make prior year contributions all the way to the final extended filing deadline, Coverdell accounts aren't in that category. Put the contribution deadline on your calendar and reminders several weeks ahead of that date.

Managing Your Account

You maintain total control over the investments in any Coverdell account you are responsible for. The investment choices you have are amazingly varied and can be quite complex. You can invest through mutual funds and individual investments (known as self-directed accounts). You can limit yourself to Certificates of Deposit and U.S Savings Bonds or leap into the uncharted territory of cybersecurities and cryptocurrency. The extent of available investments in this account may enable you to reap huge rewards if you're savvy. Still, you don't have any safety net to catch you when they fall.

Watching your investments with respect to the overall markets

You rely on outside input to judge your performance in so many ways — from receiving merit increases (and well-deserved pats on the back) at work to cheers from your family for a job well done. Unfortunately, performance measurements on your student's Coverdell account won't come from the outside; you have to provide your own. Whether you choose a self-directed approach to your student's Coverdell account, place your funds in the hands of a mutual fund manager, or hire your own investment advisor to choose investments for you, it's up to you to make sure that your portfolio lives up to the standards of the rest of the market. Although you don't need to perform this sort of assessment every day, you do need to look closely at your investments, at least monthly or quarterly, to make sure that you stay on track and out of trouble.

TIP

Let's say you invest in a more restrictive account — one where your choices are limited to a fixed number of mutual funds or certificates of deposit. Assessing the account's performance against similar investments outside of your account is fairly simple. Remember that making apples-to-oranges comparisons isn't fair — you always need to compare your investments to those roughly the same as what you own. So, if you own an index fund in your Coverdell account, place it against similar index funds and then grade its performance. Likewise, you can compare a foreign fund only to other foreign funds (preferably with the same foreign mix), and you can compare money market funds only to other money market funds.

Individual stocks and bonds are more difficult to compare, as no two are exactly alike. You can, however, get a rough idea of where your choices stand by looking at the various industries you're invested in and seeing how you stack up against the industry average.

Not only do you need to compare the percentage improvement (or devaluation) of your investments against other, similar investments, but you also need to check the overall risk of your investments against other like issues. If you own a particular stock and/or bond that's hopscotching all over the map in price while the rest of that particular industry stays fairly stable, you may want to switch to another company in that overall industry. Likewise, if news sources report that your company is verging on bankruptcy, now may be the time to switch to something that may maintain its value a little better. Yes, you can often make a killing in the market by buying a stock teetering on edge. In your desire to squeeze as much profit out of your investment as possible, you often hold past a stock's high point and then continue holding as the stock plunges off the cliff. You tell yourself that this is merely a minor downturn when, in actuality, the stock's high point was built on a chimera of promise, not on actual fact.

Investing directly in the stock or cryptocurrency market may make you eligible for Gamblers' Anonymous. If you find that you're receiving a rush when the value of your stock rises, crushed when the value falls, and double-down in order to recoup your losses, you may want to turn to a professional advisor to help you invest this Coverdell money. We tend not to think of investing in the stock market in the same way we think about playing slot machines or hitting the blackjack table. Still, there are many similarities, including the house almost always wins if you're not incredibly focused and committed to those investing principles you set up earlier in this chapter.

REMEMBER

Even though you don't need to check your entire portfolio every day, if you're self-directing the investments in your student's Coverdell account, you do need to stay current on your riskier investments (and that does mean checking those stocks every day). The Internet is a good place to start — you can easily create your portfolio on a personalized search engine page and then monitor your individual investments. Especially in the case of companies that may be poised for a breakthrough that suddenly doesn't happen, keeping on top of the breaking news regarding that stock can give you a quick heads-up to sell something before the price sinks to nothing. Remember that the object is to earn money overall in your account; losses are allowed, but do your best to limit their size.

Making the most of investment flexibility

You fully control your strategy and specific investments when you're responsible for a Coverdell account. You may change them at any time without penalty as long as you stay within the boundaries of that particular account. You may buy and sell stocks, bonds, mutual funds, and most other sorts of investments. You can play it safe and keep all the money in a money market fund, or you may choose to crank up the risk and invest in high-growth stocks, high-yield bonds, and even cryptocurrency.

TIP

Not every bank, savings and loan company, or other qualified financial institution offers you various investment options. If you're interested in a more variable approach to investing your student's funds, you may want to search out a custodian or trustee who will. Many banks now have wholly-owned subsidiary investment divisions that can provide you with some or all of the same financial products as a mutual fund company or a brokerage.

REMEMBER

When setting up a Coverdell ESA, you also need to keep in mind that although you can roll over your account to a new custodian, you must complete the rollover within 60 days of the withdrawal from the old account. You may not roll over an account more than once in a 12-month period (see Chapter 8). You can avoid this problem by making sure the account you initially choose gives you a wide variety of investment options and that any account you move to does the same. You have infinite opportunities to change your investments within an account; you're only limited when moving from account to account.

Timing your contributions and withdrawals to gain maximum benefit

Many people liken investing to gambling; one similarity is that both have winners and losers. Although your chances of winning depend to a certain extent on factors beyond your control, you can do some things to increase the odds in your favor. Remember, in this particular game, timing is key; two people who make all the same investments with exactly the same amount of money may still achieve very different results based on timing issues alone. Here are some ways to improve your odds in the investing game:

» **Start saving early.** The sooner you begin to put money inside a Coverdell ESA, the more you'll be able to save overall. You also extend the period of time your investments have to ride through the ups and downs of the investment markets. Remember that unless your designated beneficiary is a special-needs student, you'll have to stop making contributions when they turn 18.

» **Make your contributions as soon as you can instead of waiting until the last minute.** If you're sure you'll be contributing to your student's Coverdell account in any given year, make that contribution as early in the year as you can. Remember, the longer the money stays inside the account, the longer it has to earn tax-free or tax-deferred income. If you think you may be prohibited from contributing in a particular year because you earn too much, gift that money to someone who can contribute it, and then make sure that person puts the money into your student's account.

» **When you sell investments to make distributions, don't limit yourself to selling one or two specific investments.** When you have highly appreciated stocks in your Coverdell account, pare down your positions gradually instead of selling them all at once. If your stock continues to climb after that initial sale, you've then ensured that you'll reap even more profits from that particular company. At the same time, if you need to raise cash in order to make a distribution and have one or two losers sitting in your account, now may be the time to bite the bullet and get rid of your underperformers.

» **Keep an eye on your proportional investment strategy.** If you decide to keep a certain percentage of your account in various market areas, you need to keep an eye on how each investment is doing — one or two companies whose stock either soars or sours will throw off your entire strategy. You may need to periodically buy and sell in your portfolio to achieve the proportional mix you want.

>> **Don't wait until the last minute to sell investments in order to have the cash to make a distribution.** Everyone else who has students waiting for tuition and other payments is also selling at these times; historically, the stock market dips, and prices for securities fall when everyone needs cash in a hurry. Check your portfolio and your student's anticipated expenses, and then sell when you can realize a reasonable profit. Remember, no one can absolutely tell you when a particular stock or bond has reached its absolute top price.

Making Distributions

Your account is now in place, and you've been contributing to it for a while. You've made some great investment decisions, and even though you may have much more money sitting in your student's Section 529 plan, their Coverdell account isn't looking too shabby either. As a matter of fact, as you prepare to make distributions from it to pay for qualified educational expenses, you're feeling pretty good about managing to save so much money.

REMEMBER

As you request checks from your student's Coverdell ESA, keep in mind just how much you actually need. You're responsible for keeping track of what is and isn't a qualified expense (see Chapter 8). Your trustee or custodian doesn't care and can't be bothered. If you request a check for more than your qualified expenses, your student will bear the burden of income tax on the earnings portion of any excess distribution, plus the 10 percent penalty.

Keeping track of distributions and qualified expenses

Whenever your student takes a distribution from their Coverdell account, they'll receive a Form 1099-Q from the custodian/trustee of the account, showing the total distribution, the amount of the distribution that is attributable to contributions (remember, you've already paid the tax on this piece, so your beneficiary doesn't have to pay again), and the balance of the distribution, which represents earnings on your contributions. The earnings piece has never been taxed, and if you use the entire contribution to pay qualifying expenses, the earnings portion will not be taxed.

REMEMBER

You and your student — not the school they attend or your Coverdell custodian — decide how much of their expenses qualify. Your student's school may provide you with a form at the end of the year showing all money that you (or your student) paid. However, this is only one piece of the qualified educational expense pie.

It's up to you to decide if all, or only part of those payments, qualify. (Remember, things like health insurance don't.) Keep track of all receipts for qualifying educational expenses as you receive them. The occasional book or notebook may not seem like a big-ticket item (that is, until you have to buy the latest chemistry or economics text, both of which may have you wondering if someone managed to hide a new car between the covers of the book). Still, over the course of a year, such items can add up to a substantial amount.

At the end of the year, none of the earnings shown on the Form 1099-Q will be taxed to your student if

>> The amount of your student's Coverdell distribution is equal to or less than the total amount of qualified educational expenses

>> Your student didn't receive any money from either a Section 529 plan, a scholarship, a grant, or any other tax-free distribution

>> You've decided you're not going to use either the American Opportunity or Lifetime Learning Credit discussed in Chapter 17

TIP

Computer equipment is a qualified expense only for primary and secondary students, not for post-secondary students, unless the post-secondary educational institution requires that computer. Of course, in these days of online lectures, there aren't too many post-secondary schools that don't require a computer. Keep in mind, though, that the first year of college is also the last year of secondary school, and expenses that might be questionable for a college freshman won't be suspicious for a high school senior. Do your buying before high school graduation, and you should be home-free.

Using distributions for nonqualified expenses

A Coverdell account doesn't provide a completely tax-free ride for all the expenses your student will incur over the course of their education, although it does cover a whole lot of them. Sometimes, there's just no way around it, and your student needs to access money for expenses that don't qualify for tax-free treatment under Section 530. Face it, the kid may need to put gas in the car or pay bus fare, and if they are living off-campus or are less than a half-time student, all or part of their food and rent may not qualify (not to mention utilities). And did I mention clothes, vacations, and health insurance? They may be necessary for the health and well-being of your child, but they don't make the list of qualified educational expenses.

If you're making distributions to your student and you suspect that some of the money being handed over to them may be taxable to them, collecting receipts becomes even more important. Chapter 8 tells you exactly what expenses qualify. You want to be able to exclude as much as possible from the tax man, but you need to substantiate your numbers in case you're asked.

Determining income for tax purposes

Clearly, when your student takes a distribution from their Coverdell account and uses it to buy a car, they will have to pay income tax on the earnings portion of that distribution. Likewise, if they reach their 30th birthday and a balance remains in their account, they receive the balance and pay income tax on the earnings.

The situation becomes a bit more complicated when only a part of your student's distribution pays for nonqualified expenses. When trying to figure out how much of an annual distribution qualifies for tax exemption and how much is taxable, the rules for Coverdell accounts are exactly the same as they are for Section 529 plans. Both the contribution piece and the deferred earnings piece of all distributions are allocated between qualifying and nonqualifying distributions. The earnings on the qualifying piece will not be taxed to the student; the earnings on the nonqualifying piece will.

Chapter 6 shows how to calculate the taxable piece of a combination qualifying/nonqualifying distribution for a Section 529 plan; you do the calculation in exactly the same manner for a Coverdell distribution.

If your student is the designated beneficiary on both a Coverdell account and a Section 529 plan and plans on paying for qualified educational expenses by using money from these plans, they may take distributions from both plans in a year. If the total amount of both distributions exceeds their qualifying educational expenses, a portion of both distributions (Coverdell and Section 529) will be taxable to them based on the proportion of nonqualifying distributions to total distributions and the proportion of each plan distribution to the total annual distribution. The IRS suggests that you can use any reasonable method to determine the proportion of taxable earnings from both accounts; however, in Publication 970, Tax Benefits for Education, the IRS highlights the method illustrated in Figure 9-1.

Keep in mind that distributions qualifying for tax-exempt treatment from both Coverdell accounts and Section 529 plans are reduced by any tuition scholarships or grants that your student may receive.

For example, Lydia attends college, and her annual qualifying expenses were $20,000 for the tax year just ended, although her actual expenses were $25,000. She received a partial tuition scholarship of $5,000. She used a $15,000 distribution from her Section 529 plan (of which $5,000 is accumulated earnings) and $5,000 from her Coverdell account (of which $2,000 represents earnings) to pay the balance of her expenses. In January, she received a 1099-Q from both plans. Check out Figure 9-1 to see Lydia's calculation to determine the taxable amounts from her Coverdell account and from her Section 529 plan.

As you can clearly see from Figure 9-1, even though Lydia's annual education cost is really $25,000, only $20,000 of it is considered qualifying educational expenses on which both Section 529 and Section 530 are built. Although she receives a scholarship to fill the gap, it first reduces the amount of her qualifying educational expenses, leaving poor Lydia in a bind. She needs the full $20,000 distribution from her plans, but now she has to pay tax on a portion of the earnings.

Adding insult to injury: The 10 percent penalty

Fortunately for Lydia, as Figure 9-1 shows, the gap between her actual costs and her total qualified educational expenses was made up by a scholarship. If Lydia had to take distributions from her Coverdell and/or Section 529 plan for the full $25,000, she would have had to pay not only the tax, calculated as shown in the example, but also an additional 10 percent penalty on the income portion only of the nonqualified distribution. Because the $5,000 shortfall between the amount of total expenses and qualified expenses is made up with a scholarship, it falls under one of the allowable exceptions to the penalty rules described in Chapter 5.

Lydia's total qualifying expenses	$20,000	
SUBTRACT: Lydia's partial tuition scholarship	− 5,000	
Lydia's net qualifying expenses	$15,000	
	FROM COVERDELL	*FROM SECTION 529*
Total plan distributions	$5,000	$15,000
SUBTRACT: Net qualifying expenses (allocated between both plans)	− $3,750	− $11,250
Total nonqualifying distribution (allocated proportionately between both plans)	$1,250	$3,750
Ratio of nonqualifying to total distribution	$1,250/$5,000 = 25%	$3,750/$15,000 = 25%
Calculation of nonqualifying earnings portion of distribution	$2,000 × 25% = $500	$5,000 × 25% = $1,250

FIGURE 9-1: Calculating the tax on multiple plan withdrawals.

DEALING WITH DEATH AND TAXES

When you open a Coverdell ESA for your student, you're clearly focusing on the day when they complete their education and join the world of productive adults. And that's as it should be — planning for your children's future is a focal point of many people's lives. Still, sometimes the unforeseen happens, and either you or your student doesn't live to that magic day. And although your first thoughts probably won't be centered on what happens to your Coverdell account, you need to know the consequences.

When you first set up your account, the initial form may have a place for you to insert the name, address, and Social Security number of a successor responsible adult, a topic that I discuss in the section "Meeting the initial requirements (besides money)," earlier in this chapter. If you completed that section at that time and none of the information has changed, great! If you die, your named successor assumes control as the responsible adult, and that person is now in charge of making all the investment and withdrawal decisions. If your designated beneficiary is still under 18, the new responsible adult can even continue contributing to this account, provided their income falls under the phaseout amounts.

The death of a designated beneficiary triggers two sorts of tax events — income and estate. You have to deal with these taxes in completely different ways, and you can't ignore either one. Cover all the bases in both areas; failure to do so will only cause you further grief.

When you first set up a Coverdell ESA for your student, you name one or more additional people who'll receive the proceeds from that account if the named designated beneficiary dies. After you complete that task, you probably think that you're done dealing with that matter — if the truly awful happens, your death designations will take effect, and the account will do whatever the account is supposed to do.

Well, nothing to do with finance and taxes is ever quite as simple as that. By naming death beneficiaries, all you're doing is assuming that your student, should they die, will die without a last will and testament (if they're a minor, that's a safe bet), and all you're doing is determining who you want to receive the money. Still, there are definite tax consequences when the named beneficiary of a Coverdell account dies. Keep the following in mind:

The total value of a Coverdell account is included in the estate of the deceased designated beneficiary.

- If you've named a successor-designated beneficiary who qualifies under the family relationship rules in Chapter 8 and they're under 30 years old when they succeed to

(continued)

(continued)

the account, you may make an income-tax-free rollover from the existing account into a new Coverdell account for the new beneficiary.

- If your successor-designated beneficiary is over age 30, you have to completely distribute the account to that person within 30 days after the death of the original beneficiary.

- If you fail to name a successor beneficiary and the account remains in the original beneficiary's estate, it must be completely distributed to their estate within 30 days after the beneficiary's death.

Because nothing to do with death and taxes is ever as straightforward as you'd like (which is to say you'd like to have nothing at all to do with either), if your designated beneficiary should die, you should not attempt to tackle these tax issues on your own. Seek the advice of a competent attorney who specializes in estates to help you prepare the necessary filings. When looking for professional advice, ask for referrals from friends and family or check with your local bar association. If you're unsure about how to find your local bar association, you can also visit www.findlegalhelp.org, the American Bar Association's guide for people looking for legal advice.

Chapter **10**

Figuring the Pluses and Minuses of Coverdell Accounts

Almost everyone agrees (which is unusual) that education is a good thing and that more education is usually better than less education if you want your children to get the best start in their adult lives. And in a rare instance of unanimity, almost everyone agrees that you should save something to pay those eventual education costs. Where perfect agreement falls apart is when people discuss their "perfect" savings plan.

The truth is that there's no one perfect savings plan. What works for one person may be totally wrong for another, and rules governing one type of account may fit perfectly into one person's saving strategy while strangling another's attempts. Coverdell Education Savings Accounts (CESAs) are a perfect example. Although they may be real players in your strategy to save for your student's education, they're not the perfect solution for everyone. To use a Coverdell account effectively, you need to understand your financial situation and consider where you think you'll be in the future to see if and how a Coverdell plan makes sense for you and your family.

In this chapter, you explore what's really great — and what's really not — about Coverdell ESAs. You also find out how to magnify what's good about Coverdell while minimizing what's bad.

Knowing the Pluses of Coverdells

Before you bog down in the minutiae of all the rules and regulations that go along with Coverdell accounts, take a couple of minutes to reflect on why they can potentially be really good for you and your family.

Having total control

One of the great advantages of Coverdell ESAs (and the one that most banks and financial institutions spend a great deal of time telling you about) is that you, the responsible adult listed on the account, have total control over how the money is invested. If you want to be socially responsible and not buy into tobacco companies or companies that do business in countries with repressive regimes, you can do that. If you only want to buy bonds, you can do that, too. You can also completely change your investment strategy on a dime. When the investments markets start to soar upward — or conversely, begin to plunge — if you're paying attention, you can move your investments to take advantage of a perceived benefit or limit an impending loss faster than any institutional investor can.

Keep in mind, though, that with you in control, you not only take full credit for your successes, but you also bear the responsibility for your failures. And as anyone who's spent any time at all studying the stock and bond markets knows, some of the overall market failures have been spectacular.

TIP

To exercise that control to your best advantage, educate yourself about investing and read Chapters 8 and 9 to find out how Coverdell accounts work and what you need to do to make your student's account a viable entity.

COMPARING COVERDELL TAX SAVINGS TO 529 PLANS

Although the tax-deferred/tax-exempt provisions of Coverdell Education Savings Accounts are almost identical to those of Section 529 plans, the total tax savings in a Coverdell account may not be as great for two reasons:

- No current income tax deduction: Depending on where you live, you may receive a current state income tax deduction or tax credit for contributions into a Section 529 plan; these don't exist for contributions into Coverdell accounts.

- Less time for money to grow: Coverdell accounts usually exist for a much shorter period of time and have less time to earn money. Remember, there is no federally mandated final distribution date for a Section 529 plan, although individual states and plans may impose one. However, Coverdell accounts must be fully distributed by the designated beneficiary's 30th birthday. Thirty days after that date, the money is distributed to that person, regardless of whether they have any expenses for which to use that money.

Still, despite the limitations present in Coverdell accounts, your money can grow faster there than in an ordinary savings or investment account. Because all taxes are deferred until distribution, this gives you a consistently larger pot of money to use in your investment strategy, which should increase your overall return on your initial investment, all other things being equal.

Benefiting from tax-deferred and tax-exempt growth

One great benefit of any tax-deferred account is that the money in it grows every time you receive the following on your investments:

>> Interest.

>> Dividends (generally corporate profits distributed to shareholders, usually in cash, but sometimes in additional shares).

>> Capital gains (when you sell an investment for a higher price than you purchased it). The difference between those two amounts is your *capital gain*) on your investments.

No tax issues arise until the money is taken out.

In a Coverdell ESA, if the money comes out and pays for a qualified educational expense, you pay no income tax on the earnings included in that distribution. On the other hand, if you use the money to pay a nonqualified expense, your designated beneficiary must pay income tax on the earnings portion of the distribution (using the formula shown in Chapter 6). Then, depending on the circumstances of the distribution (see Chapter 5), an additional 10 percent penalty may be tacked on to your beneficiary's tax bill.

Paying for primary and secondary school expenses

You may have absolutely no intention of sending your child to private or parochial school, and certainly, many fine public school systems out there can provide your child with the very best education your tax dollars can buy. (You can pay for private and parochial school fees, uniforms, extra tutoring, and a variety of other costs by using distributions from your child's Coverdell account.) But still, there are always those extra expenses, the little things that come up year after year, such as tutoring, after-school programs, school busing costs (which are becoming more and more prevalent around the country), student athletic fees, and so on. The list seems endless, and as school budgets become tighter and tighter, this list will only continue to grow.

REMEMBER

Any of these big and little primary and secondary school expenses (including school uniforms, computers and peripherals, and any software for which you could conceivably find an educational purpose) can be paid by using tax-free distributions from your child's Coverdell ESA, even if your child is not attending a private school.

Dealing with Coverdell Snags

Now that you've looked at what's really, really good about Coverdell ESAs, you also need to be aware of stuff that may make you think twice about investing here. Coverdell accounts don't make sense for a lot of parents because of these negatives. Conversely, you may decide that a Coverdell account makes sense — but only in a very limited way — if you keep the amounts invested small or use them only for the short term.

Consider three scenarios. 1) Your overall savings come up short, and you need to apply for financial aid; 2) your student wins some outright scholarship, and you have more money in your child's Coverdell account than you need; or 3) your child decides against any education beyond high school while you've been saving for college and beyond. In all these instances, you need to stay on top of how having a Coverdell account for that child will play into these scenarios and figure out ways to minimize any negative consequences.

Minimizing a Coverdell account's impact on financial aid awards

Hopefully, you won't even need to read this part because you've been successful in your savings ventures, and you have all the money you and your student need to see them through college or any other post-secondary educational endeavor. However, you need to pay attention if your savings are a little short and you're not earning quite enough to make up the gap every year. Coverdell accounts can become a negative in this type of scenario. You need to carefully monitor your particular situation to avoid the minefield.

WARNING

If you are both the designated beneficiary and the owner of the account, and if you are no longer your parent(s)' dependent, having a Coverdell account that is insufficient to pay all your expenses may be a big negative for you. That's because with you as both the owner and the designated beneficiary and independent of your parents, the federal financial aid formula will count 20 percent of the account's total value on the day you file your FAFSA as available to pay for education costs. In other words, your expected family contribution (EFC) will rise by 20 percent of the account's value. Adding the account to your EFC calculation may remove you from Pell Grant eligibility or reduce or even eliminate your ability to qualify for subsidized federal student loans.

There is a bit of good news, though. If your parent is still the owner of the account, or if you are still your parent's dependent — even if you are now the account owner — only 5.64 percent of the account's value on the day you file your FAFSA application will be included in your EFC. For this reason alone, it may be worth it to remain your parent(s)' dependent.

TIP

In an even better scenario, if you are the designated beneficiary of a Coverdell account owned by your grandparent, or an aunt or uncle, you won't be required to report the account's value on your FAFSA. You may, however, be required to report any qualifying distributions you receive as income to you on your FAFSA. Still, it's unlikely that this will impact your financial aid award too badly.

If you have a small Coverdell account for your student, the asset and income inclusions probably won't impact their financial aid award too adversely. However, if you've been successful in making contributions and even more successful in your investments, the existence of that Coverdell plan may effectively prevent your student from receiving certain forms of financial aid. In addition, they may be saddled with paying back full-cost, unsubsidized Stafford Loans at the end of their college career (see Chapter 18). Of course, if your student isn't likely to ever qualify for need-based financial aid, you don't need to worry about this consideration.

There are, of course, ways around this dilemma. If you choose to save inside one of these accounts for your student and your student still needs additional funds, it doesn't mean that your saving was in vain. You're not a failure even if your student has to take some loans. This problem has some possible solutions, but you need to be aware that you have a problem well before completing that first financial aid application.

Spending down your student's Coverdell account early

First, you may choose to use your student's Coverdell account before they reach college and start applying for financial aid. Remember, you may use Coverdell distributions to pay for all qualifying educational expenses for primary and secondary school and post-secondary school. The rules concerning what qualifies are far laxer for K–12 expenses than for college ones.

TIP

Even if your child doesn't attend private school, many expenses that qualify during their primary and secondary years won't qualify for post-secondary education (see Chapter 8). If you manage to make the final distribution from your Coverdell plan before your child applies for financial aid — perhaps by buying a new computer you know they need for school or by paying for extra tutoring — the fact that a Coverdell account once existed for your child won't make one whit of difference in their aid award.

REMEMBER

Remember that FAFSA is based on your income tax returns from the prior-prior year, but the assets you report will be the current value as of the date you file the FAFSA.

WARNING

And since no good deed ever goes unpunished, beware of making a non-qualifying distribution in the prior-prior year that will be included on the FAFSA. That distribution will show up on the student's Form 1040 for the year being examined and will count as income in that year.

Rolling over your student's Coverdell account into a Section 529 plan

If you can't completely exhaust your student's Coverdell account before they are likely to start applying for financial aid, consider rolling the account over into a 529 plan for them. The rollover is tax-free if you complete it within 60 days of the initial withdrawal from the Coverdell account.

In a rollover to a Section 529 plan, you need to keep in mind the following:

>> **If you take the check you receive as a distribution from your student's Coverdell account and use it to fund the new Section 529 plan, your student (not you) is the plan owner of the Section 529 plan.** And, of course, if your student is now the plan owner, they get to include the total amount of that Section 529 plan as a personal asset; if they are no longer your dependent, that asset will be included in the FAFSA calculation at a generous 20 percent. However, this distribution is not currently includable as taxable income so long as any deferred income inside that distribution is used to pay for qualified higher education expenses or rolled over into a Section 520 plan.

>> **If you distribute the funds from the Coverdell account directly to your student and then contribute that exact amount to a Section 529 plan, you retain control over the new Section 529 account.** The Section 529 plan is counted as your asset (included at only 5.6 percent in the financial aid formula), and you can change the designated beneficiary (according to the relationship test described in Chapter 5).

REMEMBER

If you choose the second option above, you've just made a new gift to your student (the original Coverdell contributions, which you've just distributed, were gifts to that child when you made them; the new Section 529 contribution is a completely new gift). You may have some gift tax consequences here. In a Snakes and Ladders move, you should go back directly to Chapter 3 to see the implications of the gift and Generation-Skipping Transfer Tax.

Transferring the money to another beneficiary

When you made contributions to your student's Coverdell account, they were considered completed gifts at the time they were made. Because you couldn't contribute more than $2,000 (and less if you were income-restricted or someone else also made a contribution), it's unlikely you would have even bothered to file a gift tax return (Form 709) to report the gift and claim the annual exclusion amount. However, be careful if you move the money to a new beneficiary. While there may be no gift tax consequence to this transfer, if the new designated beneficiary is in the next generation, you may have to file a Form 709 to claim the exemption from the Generation-Skipping Transfer Tax.

This is how it works. Khalilah has set up a Coverdell account for her daughter Rashida, who is brilliant, gets a free ride all the way through primary, secondary, post-secondary, and graduate school, and never needs to touch the money in the Coverdell account. Rashida's 30th birthday is now looming, and the Coverdell account has been accumulating for the past almost 30 years. There is a substantial amount in there. If Rashida takes the distribution 30 days after her 30th birthday, she will pay a significant tax. But here's the good news — Rashida has a newborn daughter. Not only can Khalilah roll the account over to the baby, but because the baby is under age 18, she can also start contributing to the account for the baby. There is one fly in this perfect scenario, though. The baby is two generations below Khalilah, not just one. Enter the Generation-Skipping Transfer Tax. Khalilah must now file a gift tax return. While she's not required to report the gift of the account to the new beneficiary, even though it far exceeds the annual exclusion amount, she is required to apply for a Generation-Skipping Transfer Tax Exemption against the value of the transfer on the date of the transfer.

If you find yourself in this situation, please run — don't walk — to a tax accountant or attorney who is well-versed in the fine art of gift tax preparation. While I'm all in favor of do-it-yourself tax return preparation, this is a return that is not for the faint of heart. Most accountants won't touch these, let alone laypeople. There is a time and a place for tax bravery, but this isn't it.

Do not transfer a Coverdell account to your original designated beneficiary's spouse if you want to maximize the financial aid your original student will qualify for; spousal assets are included at the same rate as the student's own assets. Although married students are no longer treated as their parents' dependents for financial aid calculations (so parental information is no longer included in the FAFSA), it doesn't matter whether the assets are owned by your student or your student's spouse. Transferring an account to a spouse gives you more paperwork but doesn't change the final outcome on the student's financial aid application, which will be that 20 percent of the value of the account on the day the FAFSA is filed will be included in the EFC for the new designated beneficiary.

Closing the account and completely distributing the proceeds to your student

Finally, you may close the Coverdell account and hand the distribution check over to your student. Your student will owe income tax on any accumulated income in the account and a 10 percent penalty for receiving a nonqualified distribution. Still, if the amount of income isn't great and your student has little or no other income to report on their tax return, the overall tax burden may be slight, and this option may be your best way out of this particular jam.

When choosing this option, though, you need to be aware of a couple of points:

>> You're handing a chunk of change to a kid who may not have the best money management skills. However, this is what you're hoping for in this scenario because you really want that money to be spent.

>> If your student has wonderful money management skills and promptly stashes that cash away in a savings or investment account, they still have an asset that will be subject to a 5.64 percent inclusion rate on their FAFSA if they decide to return to school, which is what you were trying to avoid in the first place. The only income counted in calculating your student's aid award is the current income earned on that money, not the amount of any withdrawals they take. It's not much relief from the initial Coverdell/ financial aid dilemma, but it's something.

Taking the best strategy if your student receives educational assistance

I was planning on my son receiving a four-year football scholarship (it didn't happen). If that failed, I was certain he'd be a National Merit Scholar (oops, that one didn't work either) and receive a four-year free ride to the college of his choice. So much for my fantasy life — and I have a rich one. In real life, I saved for his education because I figured those tuition bills would roll around eventually, and I'd be on the hook to pay them. When the time came, although he didn't get the free football ride (thank goodness) or win the National Merit Scholarship prize, he did receive a substantial amount of merit-based scholarship money from his college.

TIP

When your student receives any form of tax-free educational assistance — whether through veterans' benefits, employer tuition reimbursement plans, or outright scholarships and grants — any income from a Coverdell withdrawal originally distributed to cover those higher education expenses is taxable to that student. However, no 10 percent penalty is assessed. Be careful, though. The exemption from the penalty exists only in the year(s) in which your student actually receives the tax-free educational assistance and incurs higher education expenses. You can't save up your withdrawals until the account needs to terminate and then tell the IRS that there's still money in this account because your student received all this tax-free aid in prior years. To limit the amount of taxes your student will pay, go ahead and withdraw from the Coverdell account in the years in which they receive aid.

Keep in mind that tax brackets are incremental based on total income and that a student is usually in a lower bracket because they don't have much income. For example, suppose Nathan receives a full scholarship and his parents have established a Coverdell ESA containing $60,000 on his 18th birthday ($36,000 of contributions and $24,000 of accumulated income). In this situation, they may want to consider making an equal distribution of $15,000 for four years so that an equal amount of their original contribution ($9,000 × 4 = $36,000) is paid to him in each of his four years of college.

Because Nathan is receiving all this extra money, he will not have to get a summer job (probably) or do anything else to earn money for these years. If his parents are willing to withdraw from his Coverdell account for nonqualified expenses, Nathan's tax situation will look like Table 10-1 (assuming the money left in the account continues to earn income at the rate of 5 percent per year).

TABLE 10-1   **Nathan's Federal Income Tax Situation**

College Year	Total Annual Coverdell Withdrawal	Coverdell Contribution Amount	Coverdell Accumulated Earnings	Federal Income Tax on Accumulated Earnings @ 10%
Year 1	$15,000.00	$9,000.00	$6,000.00	$600.00
Year 2	$15,750.00	$9,000.00	$6,750.00	$675.00
Year 3	$16,537.50	$9,000.00	$7,537.50	$753.75
Year 4	$17,364.38	$9,000.00	$8,364.38	$836.44
Totals	$64,651.88	$36,000.00	$28,651.88	$2,865.19

Now, suppose that Nathan's parents wait until his 30th birthday to make that distribution (at which point, he is hopefully earning a reasonable sum of money). And let's assume that he hasn't gone to graduate school and completely depleted the account. In this situation, his parents risk increasing the tax percentage he will pay. Remember, the $60,000 in his Coverdell account on his 18th birthday has now increased significantly. (Using the 5 percent per year assumption, the cash in the account has grown to over $107,750.) Also, all that money will be coming out at once in a lump-sum distribution. Of the $107,750 total distribution, $71,750 represents accumulated earnings on which Nathan must pay income tax. If you assume that he's now paying in a 24 percent federal income tax bracket, his income tax on the lump sum distribution at his 30th birthday will be a princely $17,220. Additionally, he'll also pay an additional $7,175 penalty for a total federal tax liability of $24,395, or more than $22,000 more than he would've paid in taxes had his parents made distributions to him in the same tax years that he was receiving his scholarship. Imagine how much worse this scenario is if Nathan earns enough to be in the 32 percent federal tax bracket. This is a gift made with the best of intentions that have just blown up in the beneficiary's face.

If your designated beneficiary also lives in a state with a so-called piggybacked income tax (where your state income tax is calculated by using a percentage of your federal income tax), they will pay a higher percentage of the total accumulated income in his Coverdell account in federal income and his state income taxes. You should note, though, that state income tax numbers are piggybacked only on the actual federal income tax piece; if a penalty is applied, there should be no additional tax on the penalty portion. If you have another kid you'll be sending to college, you can also consider transferring the account to that beneficiary (see Chapter 8).

Limiting the blow if your beneficiary decides against going to college

Despite your high hopes and careful planning, you may be paying into a Coverdell account that your student will never use. What can you do then with all that money?

Probably your best bet is to transfer the account to a new beneficiary (see Chapter 8). But if you have no one who can step up to the plate and replace him as beneficiary, or if you feel like that money belongs to the person, you can just hand it over. The tax consequences of doing so can be fairly dramatic, as shown by Nathan's example when his plan is distributed to him on his 30th birthday in one lump sum, but they don't have to be quite as drastic. Some careful planning and the ability to remove the rose-colored glasses can minimize the tax bite for your designated beneficiary.

TIP

You always minimize a tax bill when you spread it out over a number of years. There are no limitations on the number of years you may make nonqualified distributions from a Coverdell account as long as the designated beneficiary is under age 30. It's as simple as that. When you realize that your beneficiary is not going to further their education, you may want to start making nonqualified withdrawals immediately.

Although putting money into the hands of someone who's failed to live up to your expectations may cause you to grind your teeth, if you don't have another designated beneficiary waiting in the wings, you really don't have a choice. The money in the account belongs to the beneficiary; you can only control when they actually receive it. Remember that the longer you keep it in the account, the more income will accumulate there and the higher the eventual tax bill. The sooner you start paying, and the more payments you make, the lower the total tax bill will be over time.

For example, let's say Nathan doesn't receive that full scholarship but instead attends a three-week ski instructor school (which isn't an eligible educational institution) when he turns 18. That means the money his parents have saved in his Coverdell account will need to be distributed to him at some point either before or immediately after his 30th birthday. If all the other factors in the earlier example remain the same, the damage incurred by the lump sum distribution on his 30th birthday remains the same. However, suppose his parents choose to distribute the account to him beginning when he's 18 and make equal distributions of their contributions over the 12 remaining years the account may remain open. In that situation, Nathan's overall tax liability is decreased, even if he pays federal income tax on the accumulated earnings at a 24 percent marginal rate (remember, Nathan is now a ski instructor and earning reasonable money).

Table 10-2 shows how spreading the account distributions out over time minimizes the income taxes and penalties Nathan will pay.

Because Nathan's parents have chosen to pay down his Coverdell account over the period of time from when they first realize he won't need this money for qualified educational expenses until the time that the account needs to be completely distributed, they help him save almost $10,000 in taxes. Paying tax and penalties on the earnings accumulated in a Coverdell account is never the outcome you dreamed of when you first opened the account. If that does happen, however, careful planning can help you minimize the damage, as Table 10-2 shows.

TABLE 10-2 **Nathan's Federal Income Tax Situation When He Takes Nonqualifying Distributions over 12 Years**

Age	Total Nonqualified Distribution	Contribution Amount	Accumulated Earnings	Federal Income Tax on at Earnings 24%	10% Penalty on Earnings	Total Tax Paid
18	$5,000.00	$3,000.00	$2,000.00	$480.00	$200.00	$680.00
19	$5,250.00	$3,000.00	$2,250.00	$540.00	$225.00	$765.00
20	$5,512.50	$3,000.00	$2,512.50	$603.00	$251.25	$854.25
21	$5,788.13	$3,000.00	$2,788.13	$669.15	$278.81	$947.96
22	$6,077.53	$3,000.00	$3,077.53	$738.61	$307.75	$1,046.36
23	$6,381.41	$3,000.00	$3,381.41	$811.54	$338.14	$1,149.68
24	$6,700.48	$3,000.00	$3,700.48	$888.12	$370.05	$1,258.17
25	$7,035.50	$3,000.00	$4,035.50	$968.52	$403.55	$1,372.07
26	$7,387.28	$3,000.00	$4,387.28	$1,052.95	$438.73	$1,491.68
27	$7,756.64	$3,000.00	$4,756.64	$1,141.59	$475.66	$1,617.25
28	$8,144.47	$3,000.00	$5,144.47	$1,234.67	$514.45	$1,749.12
29	$8,551.70	$3,000.00	$5,551.70	$1,332.41	$555.17	$1,887.58
Totals	$79,585.63	$36,000.00	$43,585.63	$10,460.56	$4,358.56	$14,819.12

INVESTING IN TAX-DEFERRED ACCOUNTS AS TAX RATES DROP

The old saw that nothing in life is sure except for birth, death, and taxes has never been truer. And nothing seems to please Congress more than tinkering with the Internal Revenue Code, which easily giveth and then taketh away. Every time Congress plays with the numbers, it gives job security to investment brokers, accountants, and just about everyone else who works in the investment and money fields.

Since this book's first edition was written almost 20 years ago, annual tax acts have raised and lowered rates, created new deductions while taking away old ones, played with the concept of the personal exemption, and everything else in between. As a result, trying to predict what Congress will do next has become a fool's errand. Just know that tax benefits come, and tax benefits go, and if you're patient, they come back again.

That said, saving for education in a tax-deferred environment may make sense, even though there may be more benefits in one year and less in another. It seems clear, though, that the concept of keeping tax rates lower on qualified dividends and long-term capital gains first introduced in The Jobs and Growth Tax Relief Reconciliation Act of 2003 is here to stay. And that presents something of a conundrum when taking taxable distributions from a tax-deferred account, as taxable distributions from tax-deferred accounts are always treated as ordinary income, taxed at the taxpayer's highest applicable rate. For example, imagine you are a very low-income taxpayer who pays no tax on qualified dividends and long-term capital gains. When you take a non-qualifying distribution from a Coverdell account, you'll be taxed at a 10 percent ordinary income rate (in this example), plus the 10 percent additional tax for taking a nonqualified distribution.

Tax-deferred accounts still have benefits, though. Remember, the longer your money isn't taxed within the account, the longer it has to grow. In addition, you have every reason to believe that the income earned in your Coverdell account or Section 529 plan will eventually be distributed to your student tax-free to pay for qualified educational expenses. And even if your student takes nonqualified distributions from these accounts, the odds are in their favor that they'll be in a lower tax bracket than you are currently (even with the reduced rates on these forms of income).

4

Filling in the Gaps: More Ways to Save for College

Chapter **11**

Saving for College with Qualified U.S. Savings Bonds

When members of Congress first dabbled with the idea of giving taxpayers incentives to save for college expenses, they didn't roll out some fancy new plan or program, creating unnecessary complexity (they saved that for much later). And they also didn't want to target the upper and upper-middle classes — they figured those folks could pay for college expenses on their own. Instead, they looked to the solidly middle class, checked out the ever-dropping savings rate, and built a new savings perk into an already existing savings option that people viewed as generally stodgy and unexciting: U.S. Savings Bonds.

U.S. Savings Bonds, specifically Series EE and Series I bonds, remain both stodgy and unexciting, but dull can be beautiful. This is why you may be surprised to find out that these small pieces of the national debt can often provide you with a great tax-saving option. When you use them to pay for qualified higher education expenses, you're allowed to exclude from your taxable income all the interest you've earned on them over the years.

In this chapter, you take a fresh look at Series EE and Series I savings bonds and find out how they work, what they do, and how you can use them to save for all or a part of what you later will need to pay to cover your own, your spouse's, or your child's post-secondary educational expenses. You see how easy savings bonds are to buy, own, and redeem. You find out how interest rates are set and when interest is posted. And finally, you discover what to do when you redeem your bonds and use them to pay for college expenses.

Choosing Savings Bonds that Work

You may use any sort of U.S. Treasury obligation, from bonds, notes, and T-bills all the way to Series EE, Series H, and Series I savings bonds to pay for anything you'd like, including college expenses. Every one of them is backed by the "full faith and credit" of the U.S. Treasury, and all of them represent safe, if somewhat uninspired, investments. In the general scheme of life, all produce income taxable federally but exempt from state income taxes.

There are two types – Series EE and Series I savings bonds – which can be used to pay post-secondary education costs income tax-free. Once again, a limited number of people will qualify for this type of tax-free college investment, but if you're one of them, you should check this option out.

Series EE savings bonds

Series EE savings bonds are your old-fashioned, garden-variety sort of savings bond, the kind your grandmother used to give you for high school graduation or your wedding. If you meet all the requirements (see the "Rating the Usefulness of Saving Bonds for You" section later in the chapter), you may redeem them to pay for some college expenses without paying any federal income tax. In addition, they have the following features:

>> **They're issued at 100 percent of their face value through TreasuryDirect.gov.** There are still paper bonds in existence that were purchased at 50 percent of face value, but these paper bonds are no longer available to buy.

>> **They're offered in a variety of face amounts.** They range in face value from $25 to $10,000 and can be sold in any denomination between those two amounts. So, if one month, you had $43.58 to save in a Series EE Bond, the face value of the bond would be $43.58

>> **They're guaranteed to reach their face value within 20 years.** For bonds purchased currently, the interest rate is set for the first 20 years on the date you purchase the bond. Between years 21 through 30, the rate will adjust according to the long-term interest rates in effect at that time. Make sure to cash the bonds in before you reach 30 years, and one day — the bonds stop earning interest after their 30th anniversary.

>> **Series EE Bonds are non-marketable securities.** This means that you may not trade them on any bond market — they must be redeemed through TreasuryDirect.

>> **Their issue date is always the first of the month, no matter what day of the month you actually purchase the bond.**

>> **Interest is compounded semiannually and is paid only when the bond is redeemed.** Interest rates are announced every May 1 and November 1 for the following 6-month period.

>> **You may cash the bond at any time, provided it is at least 6 months after the issue date for a bond issued prior to February 1, 2003, or 12 months after the issue date for a bond issued after that date.** If you cash a bond you purchased after April 30, 1997, that you've owned for less than 5 years, you'll also forfeit 3 months' interest. For example, if you hold a bond for 2 years and then cash it in, you'll only receive interest for 21 months. You may cash your bonds held in your TreasuryDirect account electronically with TreasuryDirect. If you are cashing paper bonds, check with the bank where you do your personal banking. Many banks will still cash Series EE bonds; if your bank won't, your banker will likely know of a bank that will. Alternatively, you may send your bond with a completed FS Form 1522 to Treasury Retail Securities Services, P.O. Box 9150, Minneapolis, MN 55480-9150 (toll-free tel. 844-284-2676).

>> **You may not purchase more than $10,000 face value of Series EE bonds in any calendar year.**

WARNING

Not every Series EE bond is eligible for the educational expenses tax exemption. If you purchased any of these bonds before January 1, 1990, you have to pay tax on the interest, even if you and your expenses are qualified in every other respect. Congress didn't grandfather older bonds when it enacted the new rules.

Series I savings bonds

TECHNICAL
STUFF

Series I bonds represent a major departure for the U.S. Treasury in that they offer you some inflation protection. Although Series EE bond interest rates are calculated using a fixed formula (the interest rate is adjusted every six months), the Series I bond interest rate is calculated to give you a fixed rate of return *plus* an inflation adjustment based on the Consumer Price Index. As of the writing of this book, the current interest rate on Series I bonds has become particularly popular during this period of soaring inflation. For most of 2022, Series I bonds paid a lofty 9.62 percent. On November 1, 2022, the Treasury announced that the composite interest rate for Series I bonds issued from November 2022 through April 2023 was 6.89% — still very attractive.

Like Series EE bonds, Series I bonds may be used to pay some college fees if you can meet all the requirements (see the "Rating the Usefulness of Saving Bonds for You" section later in the chapter). Series I and Series EE bonds are very similar in several ways:

>> They follow the same rules regarding issue dates.

>> You must hold them for the same amount of time before cashing them in.

>> The amount of interest you forfeit if you redeem a bond that you've owned for less than five years (three months).

Importantly, however, Series I savings bonds have the following differences:

>> **Series I savings bonds have only ever been offered at face value.** You may purchase them in denominations ranging from $25 to $10,000 electronically or in $50, $100, $200, and $1,000 face values on paper with all or a portion of your IRS refund.

>> **They have no guaranteed return.** The government doesn't guarantee that you'll double your money in 20 years; however, based on the current interest rate, the value of the bond will currently double in under 10 years. On redemption, you receive your original $100 investment *plus* the interest on that $100 — calculated monthly and compounded semiannually — making the value of your bond grow and grow.

>> **Like Series EE savings bonds, Series I savings bonds are not marketable securities.** You may only buy them through the U.S. Treasury and redeem them either through TreasuryDirect.com or your local bank.

>> **You may not purchase more than $10,000 face value electronically + $5,000 through your IRS annual income tax refund (or a total of not more than $15,000) of Series I bonds in any calendar year.**

>> **The only thing you may exchange this bond for is cash.**

Determining Who's Eligible

There are no limitations on who may own a U.S. Savings Bond. These bonds existed long before Congress ever attempted to mold them into a preferred college savings option, and they're far too embedded in the savings psyches of a wide group of people for Congress to ever try to limit who can own them or how many may be owned.

On the other hand, when the regulations surrounding using these bonds as a tax-free way to pay for college were created, Congress was in a position to place limitations on who could use this method of saving and how much could be saved. If you've already read the chapters on Section 529 plans (Part II) and/or Coverdell Education Savings Accounts (Part III), you may find the restrictions surrounding the use of U.S. Savings Bonds to be particularly burdensome. However, remember that without this first foray into the world of tax-exempt saving for college, Section 529 plans and Coverdell accounts probably wouldn't exist today.

Age requirements

To save for college tax-free using either Series EE or Series I savings bonds, the owner needs to be at least 24 years old on the first day of the month when the bond is issued. There are no exceptions here. If you turn 24 on June 18, 2022, and purchase a bond on June 19, 2022, the issue date is regarded as June 1, 2022, when you weren't yet 24 years old. Tough luck, but you'll have to pay tax on the interest that you earn on that particular bond. You should have waited until July.

Ownership

To exclude the income earned from a Series EE or Series I savings bond from your income, you must be the owner of the bond. You may not buy bonds as a gift for someone (perhaps you're 24, and the person you want to buy for is not) and retain the tax benefit for yourself. Additionally, if you buy bonds as gifts for your children or grandchildren who are under 24 at the time the bonds are purchased, they'll have to pay any income tax that is due on the earnings, regardless of how old you were when you purchased the bonds.

TIP

If you want to give these bonds as gifts to be used for your child or grandchild's post-secondary education, register them in your name and Social Security number (for your child) or your child's name and Social Security number (for your grandchild) in order to take full advantage of the tax-exemption for educational provided by these bonds. When the time comes to pay those tuition bills, the person who is redeeming the bond will also be the person who is paying the bill. But don't forget: In order to qualify for this treatment, the person to whom you register the bond must be at least 24 years old in the month before the bond is issued.

Relationship test

REMEMBER

Education savings schemes such as Section 529 plans and Coverdell Education Savings Accounts allow you almost unlimited scope when choosing a potential student to save for. Series EE or Series I savings bonds, however, are much more restrictive. You may pay for qualified educational expenses for only the following students without paying income tax on the interest you've earned:

>> **Yourself:** Provided the bonds were issued after your 24th birthday, you can use them for your own qualified educational expenses and not pay any income tax at all.

>> **Your spouse:** A spouse qualifies if you're filing a joint income tax return.

>> **Your dependents:** Anyone listed as your dependent on your Form 1040 is eligible. Once they cease to be your dependent, they also cease to be eligible recipients of this particular tax break.

WARNING

If you're buying bonds for your grandchildren, be sure to register the name of the owner of the bonds as your child — remember, if you own the bonds, you're not qualified for the tax-exempt treatment of the interest.

Annual income

Congress always intended for this particular tax break to be reserved for people who, despite limited income, were doing their best to see their children through college. Because of that, it seriously restricted who could participate in these tax-free redemptions by putting very strict income requirements in place. Fortunately, these amounts are adjusted annually for inflation. Unfortunately, the amounts were never overly generous to begin with, and they don't improve much, even with the inflation adjustment. Table 11-1 shows the 2021 and 2022 limitations for both married and single taxpayers.

REMEMBER

If you file your tax returns using the "Married filing separately" filing status, you can't redeem any of your bonds tax-free, even if you meet all the other criteria. It just isn't allowed.

If you're planning on using savings bonds to pay for college, you need to know what expenses are qualified for the purpose of redeeming these bonds tax-free. Remember that U.S. Savings Bonds are safe and reliable, but they're not particularly exciting when you look at how much money you can make with them. The current 2.10 percent on the first 20 years of Series EE bonds doesn't exactly blow anyone's skirt up. That said, they become bigger players when you can make that money and not pay any income tax.

TABLE 11-1: **2021 And 2022 Income Phaseouts for Tax-Free Series EE and Series I Savings Bond Redemptions, Based on Modified Adjusted Gross Income (MAGI)**

Year	Single and Head of Household		Married Filing Joint and Qualifying Widow(er) with a Dependent Child		Married filing Separate Returns	
	Beginning Phaseout	Ending Phaseout	Beginning Phaseout	Ending Phaseout	Beginning Phaseout	Ending Phaseout
2021	83,200.00	98,200.00	124,800.00	154,800.00	-	-
2022	85,800.00	100,800.00	128,650.00	158,650.00	-	-

REMEMBER

Compared to the definition of qualified educational expenses for Section 529 plans (Chapter 5) and Coverdell Education Savings Accounts (Chapter 8), the expenses you may pay using tax-free redemptions of Series EE and/or Series I savings bonds are quite restrictive. Only post-secondary expenses qualify, and of those expenses, only the following are allowed:

>> **Tuition and fees to an eligible post-secondary educational institution:** The school's ability to participate in federal financial aid programs administered by the U.S. Department of Education is the test here. Although you're not required to provide anyone with proof of what you include as qualified educational expenses, be sure that you can substantiate your claims. If the IRS comes calling and asks for your records, be certain that you can gently place those canceled checks or receipted tuition bills under the agent's nose.

>> **Payments into Section 529 plans or Coverdell Education Savings Accounts:** You may already have purchased one or two or more Series EE or Series I savings bonds with the idea of using them for educational expenses, but you're watching your salary rise and think you may soon be earning more than is allowed in order to take advantage of tax-free redemptions (see the "Annual income" section later in this chapter). Before this window closes, you may want to redeem those bonds and invest all your redemption funds into a Section 529 plan, a Coverdell account, or both.

You can't pay for room and board, books, supplies, and all the other great things that you're allowed to pay for by using distributions from Section 529 plans or Coverdell accounts with tax-free savings bond redemptions.

Keep in mind, though, that whenever you redeem a bond, even if some of what you use it for is a nonqualified expense, you pay only the federal income tax on the income portion — no state tax or 10 percent penalty for a nonqualified withdrawal. So, even if you don't get the tax exemption, you still get a pretty good deal.

WARNING

You may not double dip. You may claim any qualified expenses you have incurred in only one place. If you make a qualified withdrawal from a Coverdell account or Section 529 plan to pay for certain expenses, you aren't allowed to also have a tax-free savings bond redemption to cover those same charges. You may, however, choose to pay some educational expenses from one savings plan and others from another.

To further complicate matters, if you're planning on taking the American Opportunity Credit or the Lifetime Learning Credit (see Chapter 17), you must pay for the qualified expenses that you assign to these credits with money you've paid tax on. If you're paying for expenses using Series EE or Series I savings bonds, you have to pay the income tax on the interest to be eligible for the credits.

REMEMBER

Just as with Coverdell and Section 529, you must have actually paid these expenses to be able to exempt the income earned on these bonds from tax. If you received scholarships, veteran's educational assistance benefits, or qualified tuition reductions, you need to reduce the otherwise qualifying amounts by the tax-free assistance you receive.

TIP

If you're buying savings bonds with the expectation that you're going to be using the value of those bonds to pay for qualified education expenses, you may want to elect to pay the income tax annually on the Series EE bonds that are earning only 2.10 percent per year, compounded semiannually. It is unlikely that the interest earned will ever amount to much, and it may only raise your income tax bill a little. For example, if you had $100,000 in Series EE bonds less than 20 years old, the annual interest payment would be $2,100. If you are in the 24 percent marginal bracket, that would add $504 to your annual tax bill. If you had $10,000, there would only be $210 of interest and a $50.40 increase in your tax bill. These amounts are so small that it seems a small price to pay to know that, when you cash the bonds, only the current year's income will be taxable, and you no longer have to worry about the income limits, especially as multiple years of untaxed accrued interest may push you over the limit, whereas one year's interest will not.

If, on the other hand, you're purchasing Series I bonds, you may want to not pay the taxes annually, as the interest rate is much, much greater. For purchasers of Series I bonds, it makes much more sense to watch your income carefully and make a well-timed redemption and a 60-day rollover into a 529 plan.

Buying and Redeeming Savings Bonds

You may have decided that Series EE and/or Series I savings bonds sound good to you. You want to start implementing a savings program using them, but you're not quite sure how you go about buying them. Actually, they're quite easy to buy through various means, and they require a lot less paperwork than Section 529 plans or Coverdell accounts. And, after you actually buy a bond, you don't need to do anything further until you redeem it. You don't have to read any statements or make any investment decisions.

TIP

You may purchase Series EE and Series I Savings Bonds in two ways:

>> Online, through TreasuryDirect.gov. You'll need to open an account, and the bonds will exist virtually; you will receive no paper savings bond (for both Series EE and Series I bonds). Remember, you are limited to no more than $10,000 of Series EE and $10,000 of Series I bond purchases per calendar year, for a total of $20,000 of U.S. Savings Bonds.

>> In addition to the $10,000 of Series EE and $10,000 of Series I bonds that you may purchase per year through TreasuryDirect.gov, you may also purchase up to $5,000 in $50 increments of Series I bonds by completing and attaching Form 8888 to your income tax return. Paper bonds will be issued to you, usually within three weeks or so of your return being processed.

When you buy your bonds, you must provide your name, address, and Social Security number to complete the transaction. And that's it. If you buy a bond as a gift for someone else, you need to provide their name, address, and Social Security number.

TIP

If you buy bonds intending to use them to pay for qualified educational expenses, and you're sure that you won't have any difficulty falling under the income phase-outs, don't pay income tax yearly on each year's interest income. You can always pay income tax on U.S. Savings Bond interest each year or wait until you redeem the bond. If you pay as you go and then choose to use the bond redemption to pay educational expenses, you lose the tax benefit that you could have had.

TreasuryDirect.gov will only redeem bonds held in your account at its site. Remember, these bonds are not marketable securities, and you're not allowed to sell them to just anyone. Bonds you physically hold in paper form can be converted into electronic bonds through TreasuryDirect.gov, or you may redeem them. Most commercial banks will still redeem paper bonds, but you'll likely have the best luck going to your own bank and depositing the proceeds into your bank account.

However you make your redemption, you will receive a Form 1099-INT for the unreported interest no later than early February of the following year. (Form 1099-INT must be mailed out no later than January 31 of any year. If January 31 falls on a weekend, it must be mailed the first business day after January 31. If you're receiving your 1099-INT through the mail, it could take several days to reach you after it's been mailed.)

If you use the total amount of the proceeds (the amount you first paid to buy the bond plus all the interest) to pay for qualified expenses, no problem. Using Form 8815 on your income tax return, you'll exclude that interest. Form 8815 also walks you through the calculations if you fall into the income phaseout gray area or if you use only part of the bond proceeds to pay for qualified expenses.

Rating the Usefulness of Saving Bonds for You

On their face, U.S. Series EE and Series I savings bonds may not seem the swiftest way to stash a substantial amount of money away for college. However, they have a lot of good points, especially for the small investor, including the following:

>> **Your money is safe with Uncle Sam.** No ifs, ands, or buts about it — U.S. Treasury issues are the safest investment around. If you're worried about the stock market's ups and downs or just watched yet another bank close its doors, that safety may appeal to you.

>> **You may save in very small amounts.** As in any investment scheme, you must pay a minimum amount to start playing. With U.S. Series EE savings bonds, that amount is a princely $25. If you're concerned about paying the rent but want to put something aside, this may be just the ticket for you.

>> **You'll never pay any initiation or annual fees to maintain a savings bond account.** Even if your bonds exist only on the records of the Bureau of Public Debt (which cuts down on the chances that you may lose the little slips of cardboard that pass for savings bonds these days), it doesn't charge you for the privilege of looking after your money.

>> **Interest rates are competitive and actually exceed most bank and money market interest rates, and you won't ever pay any state income tax on your interest.** The interest rates for Series EE bonds are calculated at between 85 and 90 percent of the current five-year U.S. Treasury Note, depending on the bond's issue date. For Series I bonds, the rate is calculated

by adding a fixed rate of return to an inflation component that is calculated semiannually.

>> **If your student ends up not going to college or another eligible school, you don't have to pay any penalty to get your money out.** When you redeem your bonds, you'll pay the federal income tax on the interest, but you don't have a mandatory deadline for cashing in your bonds.

On the flip side (and there's always a flip side), you won't ever get rich putting all your money into U.S. Savings Bonds. The interest rates on Series EE are still very low and will probably stay that way for quite some time. While the interest rates on Series I bonds are currently high enough to be interesting, as inflation drops, so will the interest rate on this particular bond. Also, interest is compounded only semiannually, lowering your potential earnings. If you're looking to make a lot of money fast, Series EE and Series I savings bonds aren't for you.

However, if you've started saving early and have another college savings plan in place, savings bonds can be a great addition — and an incredibly flexible one.

Chapter **12**

Setting Up Personal Investment Accounts for Yourself and Your Kids

S ection 529 plans and Coverdell Education Savings Accounts are great vehicles to save money for education from kindergarten through a PhD and beyond, and even good old U.S. Savings Bonds can ease the financial burden of putting your student through college. All these methods allow you to put away money for later use, deferring and even exempting income you earn on that money from the income tax monster. And, given that everyone can invest in at least one of these savings plans and reap the tax benefits, why would you even consider putting money into more traditional investment accounts for yourself, your spouse, or your children and/or grandchildren with an eye toward using the cash for future education expenses?

The answer is simple: Funds from tax-advantaged college savings accounts may only be used to pay certain qualified educational expenses. All other college expenses, such as health insurance, transportation costs, and excess living expenses, don't fall into this category. You may be looking at income tax and a penalty if you use funds from your Section 529 plan or Coverdell account to pay for them.

In this chapter, you discover how to save enough to pay for those nonqualified (but necessary) expenses that the other plans just can't cover. You find out how total flexibility and absolute control may sometimes be worth the price of admission (the loss of income tax breaks). You explore the most advantageous ways to register for and invest in personal investment accounts in order to maximize their potential while minimizing your tax burden. You look at how new tax legislation may affect your investment choices. And finally, you see the pitfalls to avoid at all costs.

Pondering Personal Investment Accounts

Basically, a *personal investment account* is any financial account, whether a savings account, a stock or bond account, or a mutual fund account, into which you deposit money and on which you should receive some sort of investment return — either interest, dividends, or capital gains. These accounts are all *taxed currently* (you pay the tax in the year in which you earn the income), and you have absolute freedom to add money, subtract money, or leave the whole thing alone.

REMEMBER

Freedom is what a personal investment account is all about. Other than following the rules that apply to all people dealing with investments (for example, no insider trading is allowed), you have absolutely no limits on what you may, and may not, do with the money going into or out of these accounts.

That's why personal investment accounts can be valuable when planning for a future event that may or may not happen. Also, the flexibility of a personal investment account registered in your name, your spouse's, or jointly allows you to concentrate on your investments rather than trying to allocate resources between your children before determining their needs. If you think you're saving for one child's college education, that's fine; if that child then does not need the money, you're free to use it to pay for another child's expenses, for your retirement, or to buy a sailboat and sail around the world. You have no limits on what you may use the money in the account for.

By lumping the available funds for all your children's excess needs in one place, you minimize fees and can therefore maximize results. And, if it turns out that your children's financial needs aren't exactly equal (one child is happy at a community college; another heads off to a private college and multiple degrees), you can allocate your resources as needed without having to deal with complicated roll-over rules or worrying about tax penalties.

In addition to flexibility, you maintain complete and total control over your money. When you take distributions from an account registered to you, the check is made payable to you, and you get to cash it. You may even register an account in the name of your minor child, which then becomes theirs when they reach the age of majority (either 18 or 21, depending on what state you live in). You direct your investments unless you hire someone like a broker or an investment advisor to give you advice (see the "Choosing to hire an advisor or go it alone" section later in the chapter). You may move from investment to investment or between accounts as often as you like and for any reason.

REMEMBER

You get the benefits of flexibility and freedom for the low, low price of. . .paying taxes on any income earned. As your money grows, so does your annual tax bill. Because income taxes aren't deferred in this type of account, the amount you pay in income tax will probably increase each year. (The larger the account becomes, the more income will likely be earned on those investments.)

Still, when invested appropriately, personal investment accounts can be a valuable addition to your overall college savings program, and it's up to you to know how to make the best choices for your money.

Looking at Your Investment Options

No matter what you're looking for, there's a type of account that will fit you perfectly. You may choose to go the staid and sedate route, sticking with a savings account at your local bank or savings and loan. You could give a broker a call and set up an appointment. You can go online and see what's being offered there. Or you can walk into the local office of your friendly mutual fund company and check out its offerings.

Interest-bearing bank accounts — "Ol' Faithful"

Bank accounts are the most common type of personal investment account, and they may not be something you typically associate with the term *investment*. Still, interest-bearing bank accounts have been around for a long time, representing a very safe, not-too-exciting place to keep your money. Savings and loan companies, commercial banks, and credit unions (which aren't strictly banks but operate so similarly to a savings and loan that the difference for this discussion is moot) offer these accounts.

When you put your money in a savings account (including passbook, regular savings, bank money market, or even certificates of deposit), you give your money to the bank, which in turn lends it to someone else. That person pays interest to the bank on the money they borrow, and the bank pays you interest (lower than the amount it charges the borrower) on your deposit. For handling this transaction, the bank keeps the difference between the amount it charges the borrower and the amount you receive. Everyone's happy — at least while bank interest rates offer a reasonable return on your investment.

TIP

As in everything interesting, timing is always a factor. In the past many years, overall loan interest rates have hovered in the low single digits. As a result, most bank and credit union savings accounts have been offering returns of less than 1 percent; however, as the Federal Reserve raises interest rates with hopes of curbing inflation, the interest being offered in traditional savings accounts is beginning to creep upward. If you shop carefully and check your options, you may find a bank offering savings options that pique your interest. (Remember, you are no longer required to bank in the state where you live. You may choose any bank in the country, both brick-and-mortar institutions and fully digital ones.)

Interest-bearing savings accounts at commercial banks and savings and loan companies are insured by the Federal Deposit Insurance Corporation (FDIC) up to $250,000 for your total deposits inside one particular institution. Credit union accounts are usually federally insured by the National Credit Union Administration for the same amount but check with your credit union.

WARNING

The $250,000 maximum insured amount isn't per account; it's per depositor per institution. If you have several accounts at one bank — all registered the same way (John Jones, for example) — be certain that your combined balance doesn't exceed that figure. If it does and the bank goes bust, you can recover only the $250,000. You lose the rest. If you have multiple accounts at the same bank, but they are registered differently (one is John Jones, for example, and the second is to John Jones and Mary Jones, jointly), each account is insured for the maximum $250,000 in case the bank fails.

Brokerage accounts

The days are long gone when only the rich had stockbrokers and brokerage accounts. In these times of easy access to stocks via discount and Internet brokers, anyone with a minimal amount to stake can play the stock market. And, because you need to have a brokerage account to buy or sell any stocks, bonds, or other types of marketable security, many people find themselves with one or more accounts in their names.

REMEMBER

A *brokerage account* is one of the most flexible investment vehicles: You may buy, sell, and hold stocks and bonds, mutual funds, and any other sort of investment, including cash. If the brokerage lets you, you may borrow against the value of your stocks inside the account (a so-called *margin account*). You can place shares of stocks that you already own into this account. In fact, there's not much that's publicly traded that you can't invest inside a brokerage account.

If you are currently holding stock certificates and you want to transfer them into a so-called "street name" at your brokerage, all you're doing is digitizing those shares. There's no more hassle of signing stock powers and physically delivering shares to the broker when you want to sell something. The broker virtually holds the shares in your name (the broker is acting as your nominee, in case you hear someone throw that term around) and can deliver them to the buyer electronically. Regardless of whether you have physical certificates with your name typed on the front or your shares are registered in the brokerage's nominee name, you remain the owner of the shares. But trust me: nominee shares are much easier to manage, and there's no way I would ever go back to dealing with physical shares.

WARNING

If you hold physical certificates, you may note a blank stock power on the back side of the certificate. Never, ever, ever use that stock power. Instead, use a stock power on a separate piece of paper. If you are mailing stock certificates to your broker, mail the completed stock powers separately. The combination of a stock certificate plus a stock power turns the certificate into something that can be paid out to the bearer or whoever is physically holding those pieces of paper. If you are mailing certificates and powers, please be sure to send them via Certified Mail, Return Receipt Requested to ensure that the recipient signs for the certificates and the powers.

TIP

There are many types of investment accounts, and the services you receive in each vary wildly:

>> **Full-service brokers:** They may charge you a fee to manage your account (but not always). They will either charge you a full fee commission every time they place a trade for you or an annual fee, paid quarterly based on a percentage of the account's market value and sometimes, on a percentage of the income collected from the investments. Only the broker is allowed to place trades; you can never place the trades yourself. Full-service brokers mostly market themselves under the rubric of investment advisors.

>> **Discount brokers:** They offer you no advice but provide you with *statements* showing transactions for the period covered, lists of your securities at the end of the month, and the beginning and ending values in your account. Discount brokers still exist, but they are rapidly disappearing and are being replaced by Internet brokers, who do everything online rather than in person.

>> **Internet brokers:** They operate entirely online. Internet brokers may charge a commission on each sale or, like a full-service broker, charge based on the account's value. They really don't want to talk with you personally unless you have a whole lot of money with them, so they discourage trades placed over

the phone. They very much prefer that you place all trades online through your account.

>> **Commercial banks:** Many of them now own subsidiary brokerages and market themselves as wealth management experts. Like full-service brokers, commercial banks are looking for large accounts to manage. With them, their fee is almost always based on the market value of your portfolio, paid quarterly. If you are banking with a commercial bank, you will always have a person on the other end of the telephone who is familiar with your account and, hopefully, with your needs.

WARNING

Although brokerages have insurance on the securities they hold, that's insurance in case someone in their operation decides to walk off with the contents of the company vault. You're not insured if the investments in your account do poorly or completely lose their value.

For more details on investing, check out *Investing For Dummies*, by Eric Tyson, and *Stock Investing For Dummies*, by Paul Mladenovic (both published by Wiley).

Mutual fund accounts

Last but not least are *mutual fund accounts*, which you open any time you purchase a mutual fund directly from a mutual fund company. These accounts often function more like a bank account than a brokerage account (many accounts offer check-writing privileges and give you deposit tickets to add new money to an existing account), yet the investments inside the account more closely resemble those in the brokerage account.

Mutual fund accounts offer you the ability to hold one or more of a fund company's funds inside the same account. After you purchase a fund, you can redeem it for cash at a later date or transfer it to any of the company's other funds if you decide to change your investment strategy.

Unlike a brokerage account, a mutual fund account typically permits you to invest in the funds of only one particular mutual fund company, and that is its biggest limitation. If you want to change to another company's funds, you have to open an account with that company or purchase that fund through your brokerage account. (Not all fund companies allow you to do this; many only sell their products and don't allow brokers to become involved.)

Mutual fund accounts, like brokerage accounts, aren't insured against market downturns and loss in value. Invest carefully — there are no safety nets.

Some of the larger mutual fund companies allow a hybrid between a traditional mutual fund account and an internet broker and allow you to use your account (or multiple accounts grouped as a family of accounts) to buy and sell mutual funds and traditional stocks and bonds. These companies have, in actuality, become two things: a mutual fund company AND an internet broker, and are giving you the benefit of keeping your different types of investments in the same place.

As with everything in life, there are benefits and downsides to using mutual funds to invest. The biggest benefit is that you can access exposure to a much larger segment of investments using a mutual fund without having a whole lot of money to invest. But the downside is that you're paying a fee to be in that fund, whether it is separately stated or not. No one works for free in the investment world, and mutual fund advisors and managers are certainly creatures of the investment world. By investing in mutual funds, you may be paying a higher fee for the services of that advisor than you would for an advisor you pick yourself, and certainly a much higher fee than if you decided to self-direct your investments. But the tradeoff is twofold: The mutual fund manager has far greater experience in investing than you do and has a staff of people working for them to research where the markets are going. Also, you're getting a much broader scope of investments inside your account than you would by buying individual stocks and bonds.

Registering Your Account

Whether you open a bank account, a brokerage account, or a mutual fund account, you have to provide the financial institution with some bare-bones information about yourself, namely your name, address, and Social Security number. You may also have to provide employment information and your date of birth. With this information, the institution can report your annual taxable earnings to you and the government for income tax purposes.

When you open that account, though, you'll have a variety of options as to how you want that account owned or registered. The two most popular choices are individual ownership and joint tenants with the right of survivorship. You may also choose to register an account in the name of your minor child, either as a custodial account (which may accept only cash), or as an account opened under the Uniform Gift (or Transfer) to Minors Act, discussed below. What you choose may have a staggering difference in what happens to that account down the road.

Owning the account all by yourself

Only your name will appear on the account registration when you open an individual account (and you must be at least 18 years old to do so). You are the sole owner and are responsible for paying income tax on all the taxable earnings from the account.

Whenever you take money out of the account, you don't become subject to income tax on that withdrawal. However, should you take the money and give it to someone else, you may have to deal with Gift Tax and/or Generation-Skipping Transfer Tax issues, depending on the gift amount. Check out Chapter 3 for the Gift and Generation-Skipping Transfer Tax rules.

WARNING

Be prepared with a plan in case you die. With an individual account, if you die without a valid last will and testament, the value in the account is divided according to the laws of intestacy in your state. If you assume that the money will automatically go entirely to your spouse or kids, think again. Living parents or siblings may also get a cut. If you don't have a last will when you die, you may be able to avoid this scenario by setting up a so-called living trust or grantor trust and registering the account in the name of the trust. Alternatively, many companies allow a "transfer on death (TOD)" or "payment on death (POD)" option that permits you to name a beneficiary to whom you would like the account to go in the event of your death.

Sharing ownership

Joint tenants with right of survivorship (JTWRS) is typically what people think of when they refer to *joint ownership,* and for most people who use it, it works well. *Joint tenants with right of survivorship* mean two owners are listed on a particular account; in the event of the death of one of the owners, the other becomes the owner of all the property inside the account.

When you open a JTWRS account, both account holders must supply all the required information. At tax reporting time, you are each responsible for half of the total tax due. If you hold the account jointly with your spouse and you file a joint income tax return, there's no problem. You report the full amount of your taxable income on the return. However, if you hold the account jointly and you each file your own income tax returns, you need to split the income between the two of you so that you each pay tax on your half.

If you make a gift using funds from the account, there is no income tax consequence for you. However, the IRS considers that half of the gift comes from you and the other half from your joint tenant, and you may both be required to file a Form 709, U.S. Gift (and Generation-Skipping Transfer) Tax return, depending on the size of the gift (see Chapter 3).

Finally, if you die, it doesn't matter at all what your last will says — the joint owner inherits your share of the account.

Gifting your money to a minor

REMEMBER

If ever there was a place where good tax planning ran completely counter to parental common sense, gifting money or securities to your minor children qualifies. When you deposit cash into a *custodial bank account* (which may only accept cash), you transfer those funds into your child's name and Social Security number. The taxes earned on income generated by that cash are now your child's responsibility, and when your child turns 18, you no longer even have the nominal control over that account that you had as a parent.

If you want to make a gift of something other than cash, you may opt, instead, to fund an account for your child that is regulated by the Uniform Gifts to Minors Act (UGMA), also sometimes called the Uniform Transfers to Minors Act (UTMA) in some states. Under this provision, you can open an investment account for a minor child (even if it's not your own child), gift it with money or securities, and operate it for the benefit of that child until the kid reaches either 18 or 21, depending on what state you live in and the age of majority. At that point, the account (which has always belonged to the minor child anyway) ceases to be your responsibility. Whatever is in the account on that date reverts to the tender mercies of your formerly minor person.

Tax avoidance

What a great idea! When Congress first came up with the UGMA/UTMA marvel, it was touted as a great tax-planning device. Subsequent legislation has closed up most of this particular loophole, and whatever income tax benefit you (and your child) may still have will largely be eaten up trying to figure out how to calculate your child's income tax. The implementation of the so-called "kiddie tax" takes much of the tax advantage away from these accounts, as only a small amount will be taxed at the child's applicable rate, while larger amounts will be taxed at the parents' highest applicable rate. And, adding insult to injury, this tax doesn't magically disappear when your child turns 18; in a particularly noxious move on Congress' part, they extended the Kiddie Tax to include all children who remain students from their 18th–24th birthdays, provided those children are not providing more than 50 percent of their own support. If you're paying for your child's college tuition and other costs, it will have to be a whopper of a summer job for your child to meet that 50 percent threshold.

When your child reaches majority

WARNING

If UGMA/UTMA and custodial accounts no longer pack much punch as an income tax avoidance scheme, these fare even worse when you think about some of the real-life consequences of gifting large amounts of cash and securities to a child with no real-world experience. When your minor child is no longer a minor, they own the property and may save or spend as they will. If they opt to trek the

Amazon instead of paying tuition, well, they can, and you have no recourse. The same holds true if they become the target of some unscrupulous scum who sees a chicken ripe for the plucking.

Financial aid impact

And then there's the financial aid angle. Actually, with a UGMA, UTMA, or large custodial account in your child's life, there is not much of a financial aid angle, if any. If you can't find all the money to pay your child's full expenses, you'll probably end up taking unsubsidized Stafford Loans and/or PLUS Loans to pay the balance. (See Chapter 18 for more info on Stafford loans and other forms of financial aid.)

When your child files their FAFSA (Free Application for Federal Student Aid), the full value of any account held in your child's name, even if you are still listed as the custodian or trustee, is counted as an asset of the child. Also, 20 percent of the account's value (plus any other assets your child has) will be counted as available to pay college costs for the next year. Your child may have other ideas, though, and between the time you fill out the form in the spring and attend in the fall, they may spend all that money on a car.

Registering and administering a UGMA/UTMA account

Still, if you're absolutely bound and determined to set up one of these accounts for your child, you need to provide the financial institution where you set up the account with your kid's name, address, date of birth, and Social Security number. The registration on the account will actually show your name as custodian for your child under the Uniform Gifts (or Transfers) to Minors Act. Generally speaking, to make sure that you're giving up all right, title, and interest in the property you're gifting, it usually makes sense for one parent (or grandparent) to make the gift, while the other parent acts as the account custodian.

Each state has specific rules under which the account may operate. Regardless of where you live, you're acting only as a *fiduciary* (a person responsible for someone else's assets), so you must act prudently and make every effort to maintain the value of the account. Here's what you can do with the account:

>> Buy and sell securities inside the account

>> Transfer the account from one financial institution to another

>> Make any other reasonable financial decision concerning account assets

You may not transfer a UGMA or UTMA account from one child to another. Once you've made the gift into the account, that gift is a done deal, and no amount of wringing of hands will ever bring it back under your absolute control.

Managing Your Personal Investment Account

After you open a personal investment account, you need to figure out what to do with it. Obviously, you'll have to decide for what purpose you're saving and how much you want to save on a regular basis. And then you need to follow through, making sure that money is deposited in the amounts and with the frequency you've determined.

You clearly have other matters to consider here. You must decide what types of investments you're comfortable with and understand how those investments will help you achieve your goals. (Chapter 9 explains many terms you'll run across as you begin your life as an investor and many of the different sorts of investments available to you.)

Your personal investment accounts and your tax-deferred or tax-exempt accounts differ in two important ways: the level of control you have over your assets and how (and when) the income you earn on your investments is taxed.

Choosing to hire an advisor or go it alone

When you place money into a personal investment account, whether it's a savings account, a mutual fund account, or a brokerage account, you retain absolute control over the money and your investments. You may add or subtract money at any time in the account and completely change investment strategies whenever and wherever you want. You may choose to wing it and invest solely based on your own research, or you can hire someone to do it for you. Literally, all options are open to you.

Because you have almost no limitations, creating an investment strategy is an important step, as outlined in Chapter 10. An investor who flails about and never clearly identifies any sort of direction is a gambler who almost always loses money.

Do-it-yourself research

When I was growing up, my father checked his stocks every morning in the newspaper, crowing when they inched up and turning stony-faced when they lost money. Now, of course, thanks to the Internet, you can go through that exercise as many times in the day as you want. Stock and bond quotes are available, at no cost, on a variety of search engines and Web sites. If you already have an Internet brokerage account, you can research an offering and buy some shares on the spot — all in a matter of a few seconds. Snagging a few shares of some hot stock can be incredibly gratifying, especially if you never have to pick up a phone or talk to another breathing body.

REMEMBER

The ease with which you can trade in the stock and bond markets doesn't mean that making money in these markets is easy. Take advantage of all the literature available on the Internet, through libraries, and in newspapers; find out how to read the detailed quote pages for various types of investments. Before you ever click on the "buy" icon, check out the available earnings reports and ensure that you'll still want to own a piece of this company tomorrow. When you buy on a whim, you generally live to regret it. Do your research first!

Hiring (and firing) an investment advisor

Should you feel uncomfortable investing in anything more exciting than a bank certificate of deposit without first checking with someone else, you may be a prime candidate for the services of a professional investment advisor. An investment advisor can be anyone — your accountant, your lawyer, an insurance agent, a financial planner, or any other person who claims to know how to make money in investments. Remember, however, that people setting themselves up as investment advisors may bring with them a slew of pertinent credentials, or they may have none at all.

It is possible to find a qualified person who can help you choose and manage your investments. Here's how to shop for an advisor:

>> **Check credentials.** Not everyone in the investment world has the same credentials, so find out whether the person has some professional standing, financially speaking. If the advisor is an accountant, tax professional, attorney, Certified Financial Advisor, Certified Financial Planner, or something along those lines, take some comfort in knowing that the person actually has some knowledge of what they're doing.

>> **Check references.** Anyone who wants your business should be willing to provide you with some business and personal references. You want to trust not only your advisor's business acumen but also their personal integrity. You're considering handing control of your money over to a relative stranger; make sure that you trust them.

>> **Find out how they make their money.** An advisor who makes their money selling a financial services product will generally steer you to the benefits of that product instead of looking at all available investments. You're better off paying an hourly rate or a percentage of your asset base as your advisor's fee. Without the need to sell you a specific product, your advisor can then help you select what's truly best for you.

>> **Trust your personal instincts.** If an advisor you're thinking of hiring makes you in the least bit uncomfortable, walk away. They may be a terrific analyst, but if you can't get past your feelings of unease about them personally, they're not the person to handle your money. And if they're promising you guaranteed wealth with no input or money from you, run for the nearest exit.

TIP

After you choose an advisor, you're not honor-bound to stick by them through thick and thin. If you give that person a reasonable amount of time to manage your account and they don't do as well as you'd have liked, or you find someone you think you like better, you can move your account and change your advisor. Even if you sign an agreement with an advisor, it's generally not set in stone, and an escape clause is usually built in. An ethical advisor never wants an unhappy client. Keep in mind, though, that investment advisors are not magicians. The stock and bond markets are sometimes very unhappy places, making it nearly impossible to make money. If you're evaluating the job your advisor is doing, it's best to evaluate it against what the stock and bond markets are doing at the same time. If everyone is losing money in the markets, your judgment should be based on whether you are losing more or less than the average. I know it still hurts to lose money, but periods when the markets are down are a big part of the investment game.

Talking taxes

When you invest in a personal investment account like those described in this chapter, you pay income tax each year on the income your account earns on your investments annually. This means that when you take money out to pay for education expenses, for example, you don't pay any tax at the time you withdraw the money because you've been paying the tax on an as-you-go basis. Because the tax is already paid, you don't need to worry about whether your withdrawal is used to pay for qualified or nonqualified expenses.

The Jobs Growth and Tax Relief Reconciliation Act of 2003 has made investing outside of tax-deferred and tax-exempt savings accounts more attractive. The reduction of income tax rates on *corporate dividends* (the slice of profits that a corporation may choose to pay its shareholders) and *long-term capital gains* (the profit you make when you sell a security that you've owned for longer than one year for more money than you purchased it for) means that, even without the tax deferrals, your money may grow faster and cost you less in income tax than it would within a tax-deferred account. However, all bets are off with a tax-exempt account because paying no tax is always better than paying just a little tax.

While The Job Growth and Tax Relief Reconciliation Act is old news, two of its provisions have become permanent in a slightly modified form:

>> **A top income tax rate on corporate dividends of 20 percent:** If you are a lower-bracket taxpayer, this new tax rate on dividends may be as low as 0 percent. If you are a very high-income taxpayer, you may also be subject to a 3.8 percent Net Investment Income Tax (NIIT), which is a completely different tax than the ordinary income tax. But taxes are taxes, right?

>> **A top income tax rate on long-term capital gains of 20 percent:** You must own an asset for over one year to qualify for this rate. Once again, lower-bracket taxpayers could pay as little as 0 percent if their income tax rate is only 10 or 15 percent, while high-income earners could be subject to a 20 percent tax plus the NIIT.

TIP

To make the best use of these preferential income tax rates, you may want to consider using your investment account to buy securities that pay corporate dividends or have a real chance of appreciation, enabling you to realize a long-term capital gain when you sell. Interest-bearing bonds you own may be better placed in tax-deferred or tax-exempt accounts, such as Section 529 plans or Coverdell ESAs. The interest earned on these securities isn't subject to the preferential rate; instead, it is taxed at ordinary income rates inside your investment account.

INVESTING IN REAL LIFE

Almost everything that is written about investing and investments is tackled from a purely theoretical standpoint — how to achieve the best result given a certain set of circumstances. In real life, your circumstances almost never absolutely conform to the model, so your proper choices may not be the same as those of the so-called experts.

No place is this truer than when looking at tax benefits and ways to avoid tax. Paying tax is, to some extent, inevitable and necessary. And while trying to minimize the amount you pay is natural, using the tax card to trump every other consideration is short-sighted and foolish. You may actually save some tax by gifting securities to your child in a Uniform Gifts to Minors Act account; however, you may have also just given control over a substantial sum of money to someone who, at age 18 or 21, will probably not be equipped to handle it. The amount of money you save in income tax during the time your child is a minor could be far exceeded by the amount your minor could lose when they take possession of the account.

When you invest, first identify your savings goal, whether it's education expenses, retirement money, or just the security of knowing that you have a healthy nest egg stashed away. Then you should arrive at a plan for how you think you'll get there — through careful saving and cautious investing, perhaps, or through a more aggressive investment approach, if you're comfortable with that. Only after you've outlined your plan should you attempt to mold it more by using the various tax considerations.

Remember, an investment plan that makes perfect tax sense but doesn't serve your needs is a plan doomed to failure. Use your common sense.

Chapter **13**

Saving for Education in Trust Accounts

I f you're like most people, you may immediately associate the word *trusts* with a picture of great wealth and privilege. After all, the only people who set up trusts are those who can afford to fund them, and the only people who have trust funds set up for them do things like play polo and wear blazers with little crests on the pockets. Right?

Wrong. Trusts come in all sizes and shapes and may serve your needs. Because of their amazing flexibility, the protections they offer you and your family, and the fact that you determine how the trust will operate, saving for all or a part of future college expenses inside of a trust may suit you better than relying totally on other forms of college saving, including a Section 529 plan or a Coverdell Education Savings Account (ESA). You may also discover that augmenting other savings you have with those in a trust gives you the control and the safeguards you're looking for.

In this chapter, you find out what trusts are and what they can do for you. You see how they can assure you that the money you save today will be used only for purposes you approve down the road. You discover ways to be certain that your children or grandchildren receive the education they deserve (and you want to pay for) even if you're not around to see it happen. And you find out how to structure your trust(s) so that you pay the least tax possible while gaining the greatest advantage.

Getting the Definitive Word on Trusts

A *trust* is a legal entity that can hold one person's assets for the benefit of any other person or people (including the person whose assets the trust holds). Imagine the perfect being that could address every single one of your worries and concerns about a particular family member while you're alive and after your death, an entity that would behave as you would. This is what a well-drafted trust can be.

You may put as much money into a trust as you want. The money is always invested (trustees have rules regarding how much money can sit in an account without working for its keep), and when the time comes, a trustee can make distributions for whatever expenses, educational or otherwise, you want. You have no limitations on contributions if you make over a certain amount of money and no restrictions (other than the ones you impose) on the size of the distributions when they are made. None of the rules that govern what expenses you may pay using tax-free or tax-deferred distributions from Section 529 plans, Coverdell Education Savings Accounts, or Series EE or Series I savings bonds apply to trusts. Depending on the rules contained in the trust instrument (which you create when you create the trust), the trustee may make distributions to the beneficiary — or on the beneficiary's behalf — to pay for any of that beneficiary's expenses, whether directly for educational expenses or for any other purpose.

REMEMBER

In exchange for the freedom a trust offers, you pay a price. The income earned inside a trust is taxed in the year in which it is earned; there are no deferrals.

When you hear people talking about trusts, they generally throw around a lot of terms that sound impressive, but that really only define clear roles and relationships within this legal entity. Here are a few of those terms:

>> **The grantor (or the donor):** This person (or people) actually creates and funds a trust.

>> **The beneficiary:** This is the person (or other being) who is entitled to receive payments from the trust. You're not at all limited here. When you create a trust instrument, you must define who the beneficiary is (either by name or class of people, such as your children or your grandchildren), as well as a whole slew of contingencies if the beneficiary can't or doesn't use up all the money. Your contingent beneficiaries, however, don't have to be related to

the original beneficiary in any way. Not only do you not need to name specific names, but beneficiaries (and contingent beneficiaries) don't even need to be alive yet when you set up your trust. You choose.

» **The trustee (or fiduciary):** This person or institution (accountants, attorneys, banks, and trust companies are very popular choices here) is responsible for the assets in the trust and for making sure that the assets are used in the manner you indicate when you set up the trust.

» **The trust instrument:** This legal document governs how your trust works. Have an attorney who is very knowledgeable about trusts and how they function draft this document for you and be certain you understand its provisions before you sign it.

No two trusts are identical, and there is no one perfect trust that will solve everyone's needs. When creating your trust, be as specific as you can about what you're trying to achieve. Only then will the attorney drafting your trust instrument be certain to include all the provisions you feel are important. You can change it before you sign the document (if it is an irrevocable trust) or at any time during your lifetime (if it is revocable or grantor). If you decide that a provision is missing or the trust rules may be too restrictive, you can change it. You are in the driver's seat and get to make all the rules regarding how this particular vehicle works.

WARNING

Never, never, never use a fill-in-the-blank trust form. Having the right trust can make all the difference in your savings; having the wrong one usually spells disaster. Take the time, pay for good advice, and get it done right the first time. Fixing mistakes after they've happened is far costlier. When engaging an attorney to draft a trust for you, ask for recommendations from people you trust. If you're the first person on your block to explore this option, you may obtain the names and specialties of attorneys in your area by checking with your state's bar association. For an attorney to practice law in any state, they must first pass a rigorous test (the so-called "bar exam") and be admitted to that state's bar. Once admitted to a particular state's bar, the state will keep that attorney's name on its list and usually will provide what areas of law this particular attorney specializes in. You can also access lists of estate & trust attorneys (which includes estate planning) through avvo.com/estate-planning-lawyer.

REMEMBER

Trusts are among the costliest ways to save money. Not only will you pay for an attorney to draft the instrument, but you may also pay yearly trustee and tax preparation fees in addition to the normal investment fees associated with an investment account. However, as in so many things, you get what you pay for: A well-drafted, well-invested trust account *may*, in some circumstances, serve to fill the gaps in your college savings better than personal investment accounts or any other assets that you own outright.

Because the trust is its own entity, it enjoys its own set of legal protections. Depending on what type of trust you create, you may be able to completely separate the affairs of the trust from your own, providing your student with adequate funding for those important college years even if your personal affairs suffer from declines and setbacks. When you look at the initial sticker price to create a trust and the costs associated with running it, think of this as a way to protect your children from the financial fallout of a major family disruption such as death, divorce, or remarriage.

Looking at Types of Trusts and How They Work

No two trusts are alike in every respect. Different grantors, beneficiaries, and fiduciaries make sure this is the case. Individual provisions make the variations even more pronounced. And that doesn't even begin to touch the wide variety of available trusts: living trusts, grantor-type trusts, irrevocable *inter vivos* trusts, testamentary trusts, and so on. The list is lengthy, and each serves a particular purpose. Still, some basic types of trusts may be particularly appropriate for you when saving for your children's college education.

Investigating inter vivos trusts

If you're so fortunate as to remember some of the Latin you learned in school, you know "inter vivos" refers to a period during life. In the case of these trusts, it's during *your* life. *Inter vivos trusts* are created by you (the grantor) to hold assets for another person during your lifetime and after your death. These trusts can be *revocable* (you can change your mind at any time and do away with it, taking back all the assets that you've placed in it) or *irrevocable*.

Living and other grantor-type trusts

A so-called living trust is probably the most talked-about trust variety in the media these days. Everyone and their brother are touting these trusts to avoid probate and even estate taxes, and they're generally being sold as the greatest thing since sliced bread. In reality, a *living trust* is an entity you set up, fund, and then retain total control over during your lifetime. You have the right to revoke the trust at any time as long as you're still alive — once you die, all bets are off. All trusts become irrevocable at the death of the grantor. Because you retain control over the assets, you're personally taxed on any income earned by this trust, just as if you never put it into the trust. Usually, the income from the trust is included on your own Form 1040 without needing a separate trust income tax return.

As a college savings vehicle, a living trust really doesn't make much sense. Here are a few reasons why:

» When the financial aid folks come around counting your assets, whatever is in this trust is counted as your asset, and a maximum of 5.6 percent of the value will be included in the federal formula for the expected family contribution outlined in Chapter 18. You haven't successfully removed it from the mix.

» Even if you make a distribution to your child to pay for their college expenses, you still have to pay the annual income tax bill on the income you've earned in the current year (just like you've been paying every year since you set up the trust).

» If you're the type of parent that wants your child to really understand how much this education is costing, and you hand your child a check and tell them to use it to pay their expenses (fortunately for you, they're a good kid and does what they're told), you've just made a gift to them that may have gift tax consequences (see Chapter 3).

Irrevocable inter vivos trusts

Although many financial planners use the term *inter vivos trust* interchangeably with *living or grantor trust, you can create an irrevocable inter vivos trust*. And with irrevocable trusts, you begin to see some benefits of using trusts to save for future events.

With an inter vivos irrevocable trust, any assets you put into the trust represent a gift to the person for whose benefit you've created the trust, even though that person may not receive any benefit from the money either now or ever. And here begins the tricky legal waltz you'll dance because in order to receive annual exclusion treatment for the gifts you're making (see Chapter 3), you have to make a completed gift of a present interest.

A completed gift of a present interest contains two essential aspects: First, it consists of property over which you've given up all dominion and control, and second, the person to whom you've given the property must receive immediate benefit from that property (a present interest). Because, in the case of a trust, you're not actually putting the money into the beneficiary's hands, most contributions to ordinary irrevocable inter vivos trusts don't qualify as annual exclusion gifts (see Chapter 3) and become subject to gift tax (and Generation-Skipping Transfer Tax for gifts to grandchildren) rules and regulations. Even though your control over the gift is severed, your beneficiary doesn't receive any current benefit from it.

REMEMBER

Although making taxable gifts into an inter vivos irrevocable trust isn't necessarily a bad tax move, if you're in the position to be able to gift money away, you really want to be able to benefit from the annual gift exclusion. Two types of trusts allow you to take advantage of this particular tax break.

Crummey trusts

The name of this particular type of trust isn't a reflection on whether it's a good or a bad trust. It's actually named after the poor soul who invented it who was blessed with an awkward last name.

Crummey trusts are irrevocable and must contain so-called *Crummey powers* or specific instructions regarding what must happen every time you make a contribution to the trust. For the gift to be deemed completed and a present interest, your trustee must notify all the beneficiaries that a gift has been made. The trust must then give them the opportunity to withdraw the value of the gift (within a specific period of time, usually 30 or 45 days from the date the gift is made) from the trust and take the cash or other property. The beneficiary's ability to cash out the gift to the trust is what makes it a gift of a present interest and, therefore, eligible for annual exclusion treatment.

Here's how it works. Aunt Jane sets up a Crummey trust for her nieces and nephew (she has three) and names her sister as trustee. Each year, Aunt Jane makes a gift of $48,000 (3 x $16,000) — the current annual exclusion gift per child) into the trust. After her sister receives the check, she sends letters (certified mail and with return receipts, so she can prove to the Internal Revenue Service (IRS) that the notices went out should they decide to ask) to each of the children (or their parents, in the case of minor children), notifying them that a gift has been made into the trust and that they each have the right to withdraw $16,000 within the next 45 days.

Not surprisingly, no one decides to withdraw their share of the money, and their right to ask for the money expires with all the money still sitting in the trustee's possession. Now the trustee is free to invest the money, and Aunt Jane is perfectly within her rights to show she made three annual exclusion gifts on her gift tax return. Meanwhile, the money remains invested in the trust, growing until that time when the beneficiaries need distributions to pay for education expenses (or to buy that first house, pay for a wedding, or whatever other good reason the beneficiary needs the money for).

Even though Crummey trusts are irrevocable, remember that it's very easy to inadvertently turn them into grantor-type trusts (where the grantor pays all the tax each and every year). To avoid this treatment, don't make yourself or your spouse a beneficiary of the trust, and don't name yourself or your spouse as trustee of the trust because the IRS views a husband and wife as essentially the same person (in case you wondered). To have this trust treated as its own entity, you really need to keep all the roles very distinct.

Section 2053(c) trusts for minors

A minor child can only own securities outright through a Uniform Gift to Minors Act (UGMA) account (see Chapter 12). However, one of the great drawbacks of this account is that, at age 18 (or 21, depending on the state), the no-longer minor child now controls the account and everything in it to use as they determine.

To give parents and grandparents more control over the situation, you may also create trusts under Internal Revenue Code Section 2053(c), which allows you to save for that child until they reach age 21. Unlike the Crummey trust, this trust doesn't require that you maintain the rather elaborate fiction of providing an opportunity for that child to take money out every time you put money in.

Instead, Section 2053(c) trusts to minors allow the grantor to create the premise of making annual exclusion gifts (as described in Chapter 3) by requiring that the trust (all contributions plus all accumulated income) become completely payable to the beneficiary on their 21st birthday.

You may wonder where the benefit lies in creating trusts of this type when you can achieve much the same result by using a UGMA/UTMA account. When drafting the trust instrument, you can include language that allows you to change the trust to a Crummey trust when the beneficiary reaches age 21. Because staying away from grantor-trust rules when dealing with a minor child is especially difficult, formulating the trust as a Section 2053(c) trust during your child's minority and then changing it over after they become an adult allows you to neatly sidestep some unfavorable tax treatments.

Irrevocable inter vivos trusts may be funded during your lifetime, but they can also be funded after your death. In this case, where you want to make sure that money is set aside for children or grandchildren who you deem to be too young to deal with a large influx of cash, you can direct through your last will and testament. After all estate taxes, debts of the estate and decedent, and individual bequests are paid, the remainder of the estate (or some portion of it) can be directed into this trust you created before your death but never fully funded. Many families choose to go this route so that the terms of the trust remain private as an inter vivos trust is not subject to the probate process.

Tackling testamentary trusts

And then there are instances where professional scrutiny is called for, and you may want a neutral third party overseeing everything done in your trust. In this instance, you may choose to use a different type of trust: a testamentary trust or a trust where all the trust's provisions are included in the decedent's last will and testament. Because your last will doesn't become truly effective until you die, a testamentary trust comes into being and is administered after your death. Beyond that, it functions in all ways exactly the same as an irrevocable inter vivos trust does. You may include the same provisions in your testamentary trust as you might in any other, especially regarding how, when, and to whom distributions are made.

TIP

For obvious reasons, funding a testamentary trust has no gift tax consequences; however, you may have estate tax consequences. To ensure that all your desires for your children and/or grandchildren are carried out after your death, make sure that a competent trust and estate attorney draws up your last will.

As with an irrevocable inter vivos trust funded after death, the testamentary trust will only be funded once all debts of the decedent, estate debts, estate taxes, and specific bequests have been paid. At that point, the remainder of the estate — or some portion of it — will be directed into the trust and the terms of the trust governing how those assets will be used take over.

If your priority during life is being sure you have adequate resources for your own needs, and you haven't made lifetime gifts of significant pieces of wealth to your family, a testamentary trust may be the ticket. Rather than making specific bequests of money to your children, grandchildren, or other relatives, the terms of the trust govern how your money will be used, preventing your descendants from frittering away their legacies. Because you define what that money may be used for (education is always a nice choice) before you die, you ensure that your money is actually used for those purposes.

Paying Tax on Your Trust

As you've no doubt figured out by now, putting money into a trust doesn't mean you don't pay any tax on the income. Quite the contrary — all taxable income earned by a trust, in whatever form, is subject to applicable federal, state, and local income taxes. You have to figure out who pays the tax, how much has to be paid, and what you can do to make the taxes as minimal as possible.

Figuring out who foots the bill

What makes trust taxation interesting is figuring out who pays the tax. If the trust is a revocable trust or otherwise falls within the grantor's rules (where the grantor retains at least some of the benefit of the assets inside the trust), the grantor includes the income on their income tax return and pays the tax. In certain situations, the trust may need to file its own income tax return, but in such cases, it shows only that the income will be reported on the grantor's return.

For all other trusts, the rules are more complex. Irrevocable trusts — such as Crummey trusts, Section 2053(c) trusts for minors, and testamentary trusts — must file their own income tax returns. For trusts that make no distributions to beneficiaries, the tax return preparation is roughly the same for an individual. However, certain deductions are allowable in the trust environment that aren't allowed on an individual return and vice versa. For the lowdown on preparing a trust income tax return, you may want to check out *Estate & Trust Administration for Dummies, 2nd Edition.*

However, things change if a trust makes distributions to a beneficiary during the year. A trust is an entity the IRS refers to as *flow-through* or *pass-through.* Just as the income comes into the trust (in the form of interest, dividends, rents, or business earnings) and then flows from the trust to the beneficiary in the same form, the income tax liability traveling with the income flows into the trust and out to the beneficiary, who then has the responsibility to pay the tax. Every year a distribution is made, the trustee must provide the trust beneficiary a copy of Schedule K-1 from the trust's income tax return, which provides the beneficiary with the breakdown of the various types of income they received during the year. The only category of income that won't flow to the beneficiary is income from capital gains, which is trapped at the trust level until the year the trust terminates and final distributions are made.

Running through the trust tax brackets

Although most trust tax laws do follow the individual tax rules very closely, there is one place with a huge discrepancy: where the tax bracket changes occur. Trusts aren't a very popular area with the IRS, and Congress generally considers trusts fair game when trying to balance its checkbook — after all, trusts don't vote.

Accordingly, the amount of income you need to go from the lowest income tax rate to the highest (the *bracket ride*) for non-grantor trusts is short, not-so-sweet, and very much to the point. For example, in 2022, a trust begins to pay income tax at the highest rate with only $13,450 of taxable income (as compared to $539,900 for single individuals and $647,500 for married couples filing jointly). There is some relief, though — the 20 percent preferential qualified dividend and long-term capital gains rates explained in Chapter 12 apply to trusts as well as to individuals. Unfortunately, so does the net investment income tax (NIIT), which tacks an additional 3.8 percent tax on top of all investment income exceeding $13,450 in 2022. As always, the tax bracket numbers and the point at which the NIIT surcharge takes effect are indexed annually for inflation.

TIP

Obviously, when investing the assets in a trust, you want to make the most of the dividends and long-term capital gains tax rates (see Chapter 12) and rely less on other investments that produce income taxed at a higher rate. Municipal bonds are also very popular trust investments due to the tax-exempt nature of the interest. A great trust investment strategy is to buy investments that you expect will appreciate but that don't produce much income. When you finally sell, you'll pay the tax at the lower long-term capital gain tax rate rather than the rate on ordinary investment income.

KIDDIE TAX: MAKING THE CHILDREN PAY

If you fund a trust for a minor child and you determine that they should receive a distribution from the trust, the trust distribution may trigger the kiddie tax if they are under age 18 (or 24 for a full-time student).

The kiddie tax was inaugurated in 1986 to prevent high-income taxpayers from shifting their income to their children, who were presumably in a lower tax bracket. The rules and forms are somewhat complicated, but the net result is this: In any year, a child under age 18 (under age 24 for full-time students) who has investment income exceeding a pathetically low base amount, which is looked at annually and adjusted periodically ($2,300 in 2022) will pay tax on the excess amount at their parents' highest bracket. In other words, if in 2022 you paid in a 24 percent tax bracket, your child also paid at that rate for all investment income over $2,300.

The kiddie tax only applies to unearned income, such as interest, dividends, capital gains, other forms of passive income, and unemployment benefits. So, in 2020, when everyone and their brother was collecting unemployment benefits due to COVID-related layoffs, many a working student who had, and then lost, a part-time job received unemployment benefits. The tax cost of these benefits was massive, as many full-time students who would never have been subject to the kiddie tax were suddenly subject to the kiddie tax. Talk about unintended consequences.

Identifying the Pros and Cons of Trusts in Relation to College Savings

Funding trust accounts has some very real benefits when saving for your kids' future education expenses. Trusts also have a very strong downside. You have to decide whether the balance tips are positive or negative for your own financial and family situation.

REMEMBER

Trusts have these benefits:

>> You have absolute flexibility in funding, choosing beneficiaries, investing, and deciding how much, when, and for what distributions may be made.

>> These accounts keep control out of the hands of your kids but give them the benefit of your savings.

>> A properly drafted trust protects you and your family from personal catastrophes and financial disruptions. Funds segregated in an irrevocable inter vivos trust (and your intentions when you put that money there) will survive your death, divorce (either your own or one of your beneficiaries), or remarriage, to name a few issues.

>> You pay no penalties for failing to use the money for its intended purpose, and you can use what you don't use for education expenses to help purchase that first home, pay for your kid's wedding, or even start funding their retirement. You really have no limitations.

WARNING

On the downside, if you plan to fund a trust for your child's education, depending on the eventual value of the trust, you may want to consider not even filling out the financial aid forms discussed in Chapter 18 (which may be a positive because these forms are bears). In Chapter 18, you'll find a discussion of how to include the trust's value on your FAFSA application.

Chapter **14**

Saving in Your Retirement Plans: The IRA Dilemma

You've saved for college in a 529 plan and/or a Coverdell Education Savings Account. You've purchased your U.S. Savings Bonds and I Bonds. You've convinced all your friends and family to give gifts of college funding rather than another teddy bear for birthdays and holidays. And then you confront that first tuition bill and have to acknowledge that, as hard as you tried (and you tried really, really hard — I've been there), you're still coming up short. If you pay the full amount owed for the first few semesters, there's a very real possibility that you won't have enough to see your child through a four-year undergraduate degree, let alone anything beyond that. And if you don't cough up the full amount due, well, you or your child will have to start applying for loans.

But wait, there is another option: if you've been good about saving for education, you've probably also excelled at saving for retirement. The missing money for that custom education you've always wanted to give your child is just sitting there in one of your retirement accounts. And, after all, education is now; retirement is somewhere in the future. But before you decide to dig into that IRA you've been guarding with your life to pay for Junior's education, you should make sure you have absolutely no other options. Spending retirement savings for something other than retirement may often be necessary, but it should not be your first option.

In this chapter, you find out how to access some of the money in your retirement accounts (if you absolutely, positively must) to pay for qualified educational expenses. You see how best to liberate that money to minimize the tax you'll pay on it. You explore how to strategically move savings around in order to actually take distributions from the most tax-advantageous account. And finally, you take a look at how using these funds will affect your own retirement down the road and why you may want to view using any part of your retirement savings to fill college savings gaps as a last resort.

WARNING

Although using some or all the money in your traditional IRA may make perfect sense when you're still relatively young and retirement seems distant and unreal, you need to remember that while you can borrow for college, you can't borrow for retirement. Use retirement funds of any variety for college expenses only if you're certain you'll have enough for retirement without that money. If you're far from retirement age, you may still be able to increase your contributions to retirement plans. However, if you're paying for college expenses only shortly before you'll need these funds yourself, be certain that you're not condemning yourself to a lifetime of limited opportunities and beans-on-toast dinners. Retirement now lasts longer, on average, than it ever has, and raiding your retirement savings now could sentence you to 20 to 30 years of subsistence living without adequate funds.

Using Your Traditional IRA to Cover College Expenses

If you've been contributing and saving every year in your traditional *Individual Retirement Account* (IRA), you may already have a tidy sum socked away and earmarked for your retirement. That money may beckon to you when the bills for your child's tuition and other educational expenses begin to roll in, and your savings in other areas just aren't enough to cover them all. Clearly, the temptation is great — that money is just sitting there, you don't need any of it yet for retirement purposes, and your only option may be to either take a distribution from your IRA or take a loan to pay for those pesky college expenses.

What's more, you can do it and not pay an early distribution penalty (if you plan things right). The IRS allows you to take penalty-free distributions from your traditional IRA before you turn 59 1/2 years old if that distribution is used to pay qualified educational expenses, although you do, of course, have to pay the income tax on the distribution.

TIP

Before you jump in and cash out your traditional IRA, consider these questions:

>> **How much money will you need in order to retire and maintain your current lifestyle?** Calculators that allow you to make this estimate are available on the Internet and in most money management software packages. In addition, any good financial planner should be able to help you make this calculation.

>> **How much money do you currently have saved in your (and your spouse's) various retirement funds, investment accounts, and so on?**

>> **If you use part, or all, of your current retirement savings to pay for college expenses for your kids, will you still be able to save enough to adequately pay for your retirement after doing so?**

Figuring out qualified expenses

REMEMBER

Maybe you're quite certain that you have more than you'll ever need and that it makes perfect sense for you to pay at least some of your student's expenses from your traditional IRA. If so, here's what you need to know to avoid paying a 10 percent penalty on your distribution:

>> **You may pay only for qualified higher education expenses.** Once again, these expenses include tuition, fees, books, supplies, and equipment required for enrollment at a qualified educational institution (schools qualified to participate in federal financial aid programs administered by the U.S. Department of Education). In addition, if the student attends school at least half-time, room and board paid to the school itself or as determined by the school also qualifies.

>> **You may only pay qualified expenses for yourself, your spouse, your children (and your spouse's children, if they are different), and your and your spouse's grandchildren.**

>> **If your beneficiary is a special-needs student, services incurred by them or for their benefit qualify.** Of course, regulations defining who is a special-needs student and what services are covered by this designation haven't been issued yet — use your best judgment when deciding what you think will be covered.

Calculating the amount of the distribution not subject to the 10 percent penalty

If you're under age 59 1/2 when you take a distribution from your traditional IRA, remember that the general rule is that you will pay income tax on one of the following:

>> The full amount of the distribution if you were able to make pre-tax contributions to the account

>> The income earned in the account over its lifetime if you made after-tax contributions

>> An amount somewhere in the middle if some of your contributions were made pre-tax and others were made after-tax

In addition to the income tax piece, the general rule is that you're also liable for a 10 percent penalty because you've taken an early distribution. However, you meet a valid exception to this rule when you use all or part of that distribution to pay for qualified educational expenses. And if you use a distribution from your traditional IRA to pay for only qualified expenses, the result is clear. You'll need to calculate the portion of your taxable distribution and then pay the income tax on it, but you'll escape the penalty entirely.

REMEMBER

Calculating the income tax and penalties on an early traditional IRA distribution becomes a bit trickier when the distribution pays only a part of your student's qualified expenses. The treatment here is similar to that used for Section 529 plans (see Chapter 5) and for Coverdell Education Savings Accounts (see Chapter 8), with one major difference: While you're allowed to make a reasonable determination of how you want to assign your Coverdell and Section 529 distributions, you may use a distribution from a traditional IRA only to pay for qualified educational expenses left on the table after considering any of the following:

>> Tax-free Coverdell and/or Section 529 withdrawals

>> Tax-free scholarships

>> Tax-free, employer-provided educational assistance

>> Any other tax-free payment (other than a gift or bequest) that your student receives due to enrollment at a particular institution, such as veteran's benefits, AmeriCorps benefits, and the like

In other words, distributions from IRAs come last in the pecking order. If your student receives payments or credits from these sources equal to or in excess of the total amount of their qualifying expenses, all your traditional IRA distribution will be subject to the 10 percent penalty. If the IRA distribution partially exceeds the adjusted qualifying expenses, only that part that is in excess will be assessed the penalty.

For example, Julia's annual qualifying educational expenses at her university are currently $30,000 per year. She expects that the total cost, including all non-qualifying expenses, such as insurance and transportation, will be $35,000. This year, she's been extremely fortunate, and the university has given her a $5,000 scholarship. In addition, her mother's employer gives her a $1,000 scholarship. However, Julia's parents were late in starting a 529 plan for her benefit, so there is only $15,000 left in that account, and her parents distribute the full amount to cover part of her current expenses. Now, she has $21,000 toward the total $30,000 qualifying amount. To make up the funding gap, Julia's father has an old IRA account that doesn't play a huge role in his retirement planning, so he decides to cash it in to come up with the remaining $14,000 Julia will need to pay her expenses — both qualifying and non — for the current year.

Based on these numbers, Julia's family will face the following tax consequences:

>> Julia will pay no tax on the $15,000 Section 529 distribution, as the full amount of the distribution is used to pay for qualifying educational expenses, nor will she pay any tax on the $5,000 university scholarship or the $1,000 scholarship from her mother's employer.

>> Julia's parents will pay income tax only on $9,000 of the total $14,000 IRA distribution since that is the amount left on the table after all other tax-free sources of income were considered.

>> Julia's parents will pay both income tax and a 10 percent penalty on the remaining $5,000 of the IRA distribution since even though that money was used to pay Julia's expenses, those expenses were not qualified educational expenses.

Tapping into Your Roth IRA for College Savings

A Roth IRA can be a valuable tool for funding education. Remember, you fund Roth IRAs with after-tax dollars, and then you pay no tax whatsoever when you take distributions, provided the account has existed for at least five years. Roth IRA contributions are subject to much more stringent income restrictions than are contributions into Traditional IRAs (tax-deductible in the year of contribution, taxes paid on every dollar when distributions are made). However, if you can put money into one of these accounts in at least some years, the opportunity that money has to grow unmolested by taxation is great. Over time, your money will grow as your investments earn interest, dividends, and capital gains. And hopefully, the value of the individual investments will increase along the way. This is not a tax-deferred account containing "qualified money" or money on which taxes will be due at a later date. Instead, by paying taxes before contributing, you guarantee that future withdrawals will be income-tax-free, provided you follow the rules.

Making distributions and avoiding penalties with a Roth IRA

Roth IRAs differ from traditional IRAs in many aspects, especially regarding the distribution rules. There are certain requirements about who may take distributions and when they may take them. Failure to fulfill both of these requirements may result in a 10 percent penalty on the income portion of the distribution:

>> **Your Roth IRA account must be open for a period of five years before you may take any distributions tax-free.** If you fail the five-year holding period test, the income portion will be taxed at your ordinary income tax rates, and you will, most likely, be charged a 10 percent penalty (although certain exceptions apply).

>> **Your distribution must satisfy one of the following conditions:**

- It must be made on or after the date on which you attain the age of 59 1/2.

- It must be made to your estate or your named beneficiary on or after your death.

- It must be attributable to your being disabled.

- Up to $10,000 may be used to pay for qualified first-time homebuyer expenses.

Clearly, if you're an older parent or grandparent (over age 59 1/2) and you've had a Roth IRA sitting in the wings for at least five years, you're free to use it to pay whatever educational expenses you want. Because the distribution will be made to you and it's already designated as a tax-free distribution, you may choose to use that money for whatever purpose your heart desires.

If, on the other hand, you have a Roth IRA and you haven't yet reached that magic age, you're still allowed to take distributions from your Roth IRA to pay for qualified educational expenses. You should note, though, that the income portion of these distributions will be taxable to you, although no 10 percent penalty will be applied on money used to pay qualifying expenses. And here, the qualifying expenses are exactly the same as those for a traditional IRA. In essence, if you use your Roth IRA to pay for college and you're younger than 59 1/2, the net result to you is almost identical as it would be if you used your traditional IRA — you pay the income tax, but you avoid the penalty.

Playing with Roth IRA's flexibility without getting burned

If you're eligible to contribute to a Roth IRA, it's a terrific way to save for the future. And, if you're an older parent, it gives you a great deal of flexibility when you're trying to determine how much to save for college and how much for retirement. With a Roth, you can gain many of the same tax benefits of a Section 529 plan or Coverdell Education Savings Account without limiting the use of your savings to only future educational expenses.

TIP

If you're okay with gifting money to your teenage children, you may want to consider opening a Roth IRA in their name. However, you need to know that for this strategy to work, your children must be earning some money each year that you make a gift into their Roth IRA because only earned income is eligible to be contributed to a Roth account. Creating these accounts when your kids are barely earning allows contributions to be made while paying little or no tax on them, and then the money is free to grow for a longer period of time. Down the road, if your children need to apply for financial aid, this account (and any other retirement accounts, life insurance policies, or prepaid tuition plans that they may own) won't be included in the FAFSA calculation of the *expected family contribution* (EFC) described in Chapter 18.

There are definite downsides to paying higher education expenses with either a traditional or Roth IRA; surprisingly, the cons are not the same for both. In a traditional IRA, you will pay income tax on the full amount of the distribution. Some portion of the distribution may also be subject to the 10 percent additional tax because a portion of the distribution was used for non-qualifying expenses. And since the account owner pays the taxes, their tax rate is likely higher than the student's. On the other hand, a distribution made from a traditional IRA will reduce the account's value, which may come in handy when you reach the age where you're required to begin taking distributions (currently, age 73, but due to reach 75 for those born in 1960 and later). People receiving income from various places in retirement may not need the distributions from their IRA when they reach age 73, but they are required to take them. This additional chunk of income added to your return can make more of your Social Security taxable, may push you into a higher tax bracket, or both. So, in this case, a lower Required Minimum Distribution (RMD) may save you on taxes down the road.

On the other hand, RMDs are not a feature of Roth IRAs; these accounts are allowed to accumulate up to your death without ever being required to take money out of it. Because of this feature of the account, no distributions are required until after you die. Upon your death, your heirs must completely deplete the account within a specified number of years, depending on their relationship to you. Taking distributions from Roth IRAs to pay qualified educational expenses will reduce the account's value today and down the road, leaving less at your death to pass to your heirs.

Making Early Distributions from Other Retirement Accounts

If you're like many people, you may not have a traditional IRA or a Roth IRA. Maybe you have some other form of retirement savings in some sort of retirement account. Not surprisingly, these accounts are intended to be there for you when you retire; however, many are available under limited circumstances to pay for other expenses, including qualified educational expenses.

The following list is by no means all-inclusive, but it does cover many of the major types of self-funded and employer-sponsored retirement plans and what the tax consequences are if you need to take a distribution to pay for college expenses:

>> **401(k) plan:** This plan allows you to make pre-tax contributions to a retirement fund for your benefit. Your employer sets up and administers the plan and may match all or part of your contribution. If you take an early distribution (a so-called *hardship distribution*) from this plan to pay for educational expenses, be prepared to pay a lot of tax on the distribution. You'll pay income tax at your top tax bracket on the full amount (remember, you've never paid tax on any of it), plus a 10 percent penalty. If you absolutely must access money from this account, you're much better off taking a loan from your plan, if your employer allows it, and then making sure to pay it back within five years.

>> **403(b) plan:** This is essentially the same as a 401(k) plan but is offered to public sector and nonprofit organization employees. Once again, early educational expense distributions are taxable and subject to the penalty.

>> **SEP IRA:** A *Simplified Employee Pension* (SEP) is administered in much the same way as a traditional IRA. The biggest difference is that your employer — not you — will make the contributions to this account for your benefit. Because it runs exactly like an IRA in all other respects, it follows the rules for traditional IRAs regarding early distributions to pay for qualified educational expenses. You'll pay the income tax, but there won't be any penalty.

>> **SIMPLE retirement account:** A *Savings Incentive Match Plan for Employees* (SIMPLE) may be set up by your employer to follow either the 401(k) plan or the traditional IRA model. It allows you to make contributions to your retirement fund that your employer matches. Your tax cost, should you take an early distribution to pay for qualified educational expenses, depends on what type of plan you belong to. Beware, though: If you put money in only to take it out within your first two years of participation in the plan, a 25 percent penalty may be tacked on to your tax bill for good measure.

SAVING FOR COLLEGE WITH RETIREMENT ACCOUNTS: GOOD OR BAD IDEA?

So much of financial planning rests on the contents of your crystal ball, and any savings plan is only as focused as what you can see there. This means there is absolutely no clarity whatsoever when you're trying to decide where to save money and how much you need to put away.

Using retirement accounts to save for your retirement makes perfect sense. These accounts are designed to defer income you're earning now and pick it up later in your life. For most people, that means that you'll also be paying income tax on it at a time when your income will be more limited than it is now, thereby reducing the overall amount of income tax you'll pay on that money.

These accounts aren't intended to pay for college expenses, which doesn't mean they can't be used for that purpose. It does mean, though, that you may lose many of the advantages you might have if you keep the money in the account until you hit retirement age.

As you look at all the assets you have available to pay for college expenses (including your retirement accounts), keep the following in mind:

- **Tax deferrals:** Should you take a distribution to pay for college expenses, you'll pick up that income on your current year's tax returns. Many people are in their highest earning years when their children are in college, so you may find that you pay tax on these distributions at an even higher rate than you would have if you'd never put the money into the account.

- **Reduction in available retirement income:** You have no idea how long you'll live or how much money you'll need to see you through the end of your life. Using retirement funds to pay for college expenses may compromise your future standard of living.

(continued)

(continued)

> • **Great flexibility in uncertain family situations:** Face it: You don't know for certain whether your children will attend college or where or exactly how much it will cost. If you don't want to put too much into specific college savings accounts because of your uncertainties, adding a cushion to your retirement accounts may provide you with whatever extra you may need to meet all contingencies.

Rolling Over Retirement Accounts to Obtain Maximum Benefit

Clearly, when you're looking to raid your retirement accounts to pay for educational expenses, not all types of accounts are created equal. And, if you've spent your entire working life with one company, you have only the one retirement plan the company offers and may be out of luck. You aren't allowed to take money out of a retirement plan of the company you're currently working at and switch it to another sort of retirement plan.

On the other hand, if you're like most people, you probably have moved periodically from job to job throughout your career as you looked for that perfect place to put down your working roots. And you may have accumulated one or more retirement accounts along the way. If so, you may be in luck.

TIP

A retirement account with a company for which you no longer work may legitimately be rolled over into a traditional or Roth IRA account. For accounts with a low value, the rollover may be mandatory after you leave that company. For accounts with greater value, you may leave your retirement funds under that company's management for as long as you like; however, you may roll over the funds at any time.

TIP

If you don't already have a traditional IRA or Roth IRA account, open the new account before you request the rollover, and then specify to your old company that you want a *trustee-to-trustee transfer*. When the money is transferred in this way, you have no tax consequence (unless you move the money into a Roth IRA, in which case you'll have to pay income tax on the transaction).

WARNING

If you forget to make a trustee-to-trustee transfer, your original pension manager will withhold 20 percent of the value of the account for income tax, give you a check for 80 percent of the value of the account, and leave it up to you to deposit 100 percent of the old account value into the new account within 60 days after the withdrawal from the first account. You have to wait until you file your income tax returns the following year to recoup the 20 percent that was withheld.

Chapter **15**

Buying, Selling, or Refinancing Real Estate

The college acceptance letters have all arrived, and you and your child have selected one lucky school. Then the first tuition bill arrives, and the theoretical amounts you've been looking at for the past 18 years become actual amounts requiring payment. For many of you, the amount you've managed to stash away in your Section 529 plan (see Part II) or your Coverdell account (see Part III) by scrimping and saving will be painfully inadequate to tackle the size of this bill, and the ones that follow.

Welcome to the reality of paying, rather than saving, for college.

But wait! You may be sitting on a treasure that can be accessed to pay the (tuition) piper — money you may use without paying any additional tax. You may be reading this while sitting in that highly appreciated, mortgaged commodity called your home. Or, you could have a valuable piece of real estate that you use for a vacation home from which you could begin generating income.

Alternatively, you could lower the overall cost of your student's education by purchasing a second home close to the college or university your child is attending. By acquiring a piece of real estate with more than one bedroom, you can provide your child with better living quarters than a tiny room shared with one, two, or more students or rent out additional bedrooms to subsidize the cost of that piece of real estate.

TIP

Although you may not think that your home, or any real estate you own, is something you want to place on the table as a possible way to pay for a college education, in many instances, doing so may make a lot of sense. By doing a little research and taking careful stock of your situation, you may uncover a previously untapped asset or produce a new, income-generating asset — either of which may allow you to provide your child with a loan-free education without unduly burdening you.

Saving for College in Your House

Many of you probably never thought about using your house as a piggy bank for your children's college tuition, but your house could be more than just a place to lay your head for the night; it might actually contain the necessary funds to pay for college costs.

Believe it or not, your house contains many similarities to college savings plans:

>> You put money into it each month.

>> The money you put into it appreciates.

>> You can cash in that value for your child's college education.

When you spend money at the grocery store or on clothes, what you purchase has a value that is quickly consumed. On the other hand, the money you spend on your house often creates value that you keep, the same as money that you put into a bank or college savings account. The following sections explain how the value contained in your house can increase, making your house an asset for your college savings.

Recognizing your house as an asset

REMEMBER

If you're thinking of making your family house a player in the game of educational funding and saving, you first need to look at your house from the correct perspective so that you see it as an asset.

Distinguishing house from home

Your first step to gaining the correct perspective of your house is to recognize what is your *house* and what is your *home.* You own a *house,* not a *home.* The presence of four walls and a roof does not, by definition, create a home — you do. Your efforts turn a building into the warm and inviting nest you use to shelter your family, especially your children. But your money turns that building into a house you can cash in for a college education. So, when you walk through the door, make sure that you can distinguish your home, a place full of memories, from your house, which you may choose to use as an alternative to other forms of college savings plans.

REMEMBER

Discover the economics of house ownership. Whatever memories your home may hold, your house — those walls, floors, and ceilings — have a specific monetary value. Your house is an asset you own, which, over time, should significantly appreciate. Maintaining that value helps you maintain an asset that may be cashed in, just like any other type of college savings plan.

Getting rid of housing debt

TIP

Changing your perspective is the easiest way to rid yourself of housing debt. Don't focus on the amount you owe on your *mortgage loan* (the amount of money you've borrowed against the value of your house). Instead, concentrate on the *net equity* in your house (the current market value less the balance remaining on your mortgage loan).

For example, if you have a $100,000 balance remaining on the mortgage loan you borrowed to buy your house, but your house is actually worth $350,000, you may choose to focus on your debt ($100,000) or on the amount of net equity you have ($250,000). That net equity represents more than enough savings to put at least one child through four years of college — don't ignore it.

Adding to your monthly savings

Regardless of whether you can adequately fund your specific college savings plans, if you own your house and have one or more mortgages on it, you are adding an amount to your overall, nonspecific savings each and every month. While the payment plan for your mortgage loans may seem endless (and they often are), each monthly payment includes a small amount of *principal* or a piece of the original face amount of the loan. The payment of this piece each month decreases the amount you owe, increasing your house's net equity. Remember, you now owe less; therefore, your equity is greater.

If you go back to the $100,000 30-year mortgage loan on the house worth $350,000 from the previous section (with a monthly payment amount of $600 per month), you will pay off $1,475 of the principal balance (leaving a $98,525 balance yet to be paid) in the first year of that loan. Therefore, your net equity in the house increases from $250,000 to $251,475. By the time you get to the fifteenth year of the mortgage (and assuming the value of the house has not increased), the principal you will pay in one year on your mortgage loan will increase to $2,967. You will have paid $32,116 in principal over 15 years, and your total net equity will have increased to $282,116.

Making home improvements

Whether you purchased an already existing house or built one from scratch, every time you add anything to it, you potentially increase that house's value. Over time, your construction/improvement program may substantially alter the value of what you initially bought and add a significant amount to the total you feel you've saved. A new bathroom here, a rehabbed kitchen there, furnace or window upgrades, or a room addition — before you know it, you're talking about real money.

REMEMBER

If you can pay cash for improvements, the net equity — or value — you have in your house increases accordingly and rapidly (although there's not a direct and absolute correlation between the cost of the improvement or repair and the increased value of the house). On the other hand, if you need to take a second mortgage or home equity loan to pay for part or all these changes and repairs, the net value of your house will increase more slowly and in the same way as it does with your first mortgage. Each monthly payment will contain a portion of the principal that reduces the outstanding debt, thereby increasing the net value.

For example, you decide that you can no longer live with avocado appliances, rustic pine cabinets, and a no-wax floor that lost its shine two decades ago and has never found it since. And you discover that achieving the transformation you want will cost you $30,000. Now, despite the $30,000 price tag, your new kitchen adds only $20,000 to the value of your house.

Depending on whether you pay for the change out of current savings or choose to finance the change with a home equity loan, a second mortgage, or a complete refinance of your first mortgage loan, your net equity in your house will shift, as shown in Table 15-1.

If you finance the kitchen improvement, you'll need to factor the additional money you've borrowed into your monthly budget. How much more you'll have to pay each month will depend on the type of loan you choose, current interest rates, and the length of your repayment schedule.

No matter how you find yourself paying for this improvement program, your house's net value and savings will increase over time. As a result, when the day arrives that you need to tap into your house's equity, you may be pleased to find that the exorbitant cost of your new kitchen will also partially fund a college education.

TABLE 15-1   **Calculating Net Equity Changes from Home Updates**

	Paying with Cash	Taking out a Loan
Value of house before the kitchen updates	$350,000	$350,000
Amount of the outstanding loans before the kitchen updates	$70,000	$70,000
Net equity in the house before the kitchen updates	$280,000	$280,000
Value of the house after the kitchen updates	$370,000	$370,000
Amount of outstanding loans after the kitchen updates	$70,000	$100,000
Net equity in the house after the kitchen updates	$300,000	$270,000

Appreciating the appreciation

Finally, your home is increasing in value over time due to appreciation. Like the stock market, real estate values can rise and fall based on a number of factors, such as interest rates, employment rates, and housing stock availability. If you own your house for a long time, chances are great that its value will increase without you doing anything at all to it. (If you do make improvements, however, its value will increase more than if you don't — a house with a 30-year-old kitchen is far less attractive to buyers than one whose kitchen is brand-new.) You need to be aware of trends in your area, though. Real estate markets are, by definition, local, and what may be true in Boston may not be so in Boise.

Using Home Equity

If you've been saving money in your house, then you understand your home increases in value as time passes (*appreciation*). (And by "saving money in your house," I don't mean under your mattress or cellar floor. See the "Saving for College in Your House" section for more information. Your house increases even more in value with all the money, such as mortgage payments or home improvements, that you put into it. And when you take that appreciated value and subtract from it the balance remaining on your mortgage, you have a rough estimate of the *equity* you have in your house. You can cash in that equity for college expenses, much like traditional college savings plans.

Check out the examples throughout this chapter of how you can cash in the equity of your house, but make sure that you review the warnings I include in the "Being cautious when cashing in" section. Be sure that using the equity in your house is a reasonable approach for you financially.

Being cautious when cashing in

WARNING

Although you may find that the benefits of using home equity greatly outweigh the disadvantages, let me be very upfront and in your face about the downsides:

>> If you sell your house to cash in your equity, you need to find somewhere else to live, with its associated, although presumably lower, cost (new mortgage if you buy, otherwise rental expenses). And with mortgage interest rates on the rise, you'll have to find a much less expensive house to lower your monthly housing costs.

>> If you choose to refinance your first mortgage or take a second mortgage on your existing house to cash in your equity, you need to know that you'll be able to pay the increased monthly amount if it increases. Often, if the interest rate at the time you are refinancing is significantly lower than the one on your original loan, you may be able to take money out of your house without increasing your payment at all. Lately, though, interest rates have been rising, and taking equity out of your house to pay for college expenses is going to cost you more right now.

>> Sad to say, but if you choose to refinance, chances are good that you'll lose a portion of your mortgage interest deduction even as the amount of interest you're paying will increase. In 2017, the Tax Cuts and Jobs Act placed some serious limitations on the deduction for interest paid on loans secured by your home. As a result of this legislation, for any new mortgages you take, you are now only allowed to deduct interest on loans of up to $750,000 ($375,000 if you file Married Filing Separately), and of that amount, only on the acquisition indebtedness plus any home improvements and/or additions to that property. The interest you pay on money you borrow against your home to pay for college is no longer deductible. To make matters worse, interest on home equity lines of credit is no longer deductible at all.

Still, if you can handle the costs associated with selling or refinancing your home, you may consider cashing in your home equity that you've saved to pay for college expenses.

Considering the tax benefits

TIP

The first decision you must make is figuring out which approach to use when cashing in the value of your house. Consider the following circumstances to determine which approach works best for your situation:

>> Selling your home makes sense under the following circumstances:

- You no longer need as big a house and were thinking of downsizing anyway.

- Your current mortgage is either all paid (or substantially paid), so your mortgage interest deduction is either all gone or shrinking away.

- You've been in your house a long time, and it's increased in value considerably over what you originally paid.

>> Taking out a second mortgage may work better for you under the following circumstance:

- Interest rates are currently higher than they are on your first mortgage loan, and you want to limit the amount you will be paying back at a higher rate.

>> Refinancing your house may be the best approach under the following circumstances:

- Interest rates have dropped, and you may be able to borrow the amount of money you need and still make substantially the same payment as you currently are.

- You want the income tax deduction that comes with paying mortgage interest. Remember, the portion of the mortgage interest that is attributable to the original acquisition cost of your house, plus the cost of any substantial improvements or additions, will be deductible. Plus, starting over on a new mortgage moves most of each payment to interest, increasing the size of your overall mortgage interest deduction. Add interest rates, which increased substantially in 2022 and are unlikely to recede in the next several years. The combination of these factors may move you from being unable to itemize your deductions to itemizing your deductions. Remember, you may have itemizable medical expenses or charitable contributions that you're currently losing because you cannot itemize. Picking up a mortgage interest deduction may just push you to a place where it's profitable to itemize your deductions.

REMEMBER

Whether you sell or refinance your house in order to access your equity, you have freed up savings that haven't come from a tax-deferred or tax-exempt source, such as a Section 529 or Coverdell plan. Therefore, you're probably not paying any income tax on these amounts when you withdraw them (just like distributions from these plans used to pay qualified education expenses). In addition, you're entitled to claim education tax credits (the American Opportunity Credit and Lifetime Learning Credit) (discussed in Chapter 17 and more thoroughly in *Taxes For Dummies*, written by Eric Tyson, Margaret Atkins Munro, and David J. Silverman and published by Wiley) to the extent allowable. These credits are not insubstantial; at the time of this writing, they're up to $2,500 per year for the American Opportunity Credit and $2,000 per year for the Lifetime Learning Credit. They can be used to offset ordinary income taxes not associated with any sort of college savings scheme. In addition, $1,000 of the American Opportunity Credit is a refundable tax credit, which could generate a tax refund for you.

TIP

Because selling or refinancing your house is never something you undertake lightly (filling out mortgage applications is up there with having my teeth drilled as my favorite thing to do), please be sure to go through this exercise only once. Take out as much equity as you think you'll need to complete your child's education the first time you either sell or refinance, so you don't have to do it again for that same purpose. After you have the cash in hand, safely stash any amounts you don't need to pay current education expenses in an investment account as outlined in Chapter 12.

Selling your home

When you sell your existing residence, you're selling an asset (your house) and may recognize a *capital gain* (the amount over and above your cost, or basis, in your house) on the sale. Federal tax law allows you to exclude up to $250,000 (if you're single) or $500,000 (if you're married) from your total capital gain, provided that you've lived in that residence for at least 2 out of the last 5 years. For most people, this means that you won't pay a penny of federal capital gains tax when you sell your house. Because the federal capital gains tax on $500,000 could be anywhere from $75,000 to $100,000, depending on your other income, this exclusion represents huge tax savings to you when you cash in a valuable asset (your house) and should provide enough cash (after you've arranged other housing) to see at least one or two students through college. If you no longer need the big family home as the youngest children head off to school, the proceeds from the sale of your house can be a bonanza that finances the education of multiple children.

For example, Hector and Grace purchased their house in the suburbs 15 years ago for $100,000, and they have since redone their kitchen and one bathroom for $30,000, so their total *basis* (purchase price plus capital improvements) in their house is $130,000. Their last child is heading off to college in the fall, and they realize they'd rather be living in a condominium in the city, closer to their jobs. They sell the house for $450,000. Their capital gain on the sale is $320,000 ($450,000 − $130,000), on which they'll pay no tax because they're married and have lived in the house for at least two of the previous five years and, therefore, fall within the exclusion amount. (Remember, if they had to pay the federal capital gains tax on that amount, their federal tax liability on the sale alone would be $48,000.) From a tax standpoint, they have just earned $320,000 tax-free; from a cash position, even after they pay off their outstanding mortgage of $65,000, they will still have $385,000 with which to pay for their youngest child's education and buy a new residence, or at least put a down payment on one.

Figure 15-1 shows how Hector and Grace calculate the capital gain they realized when they sold their house.

Sales price of house	$450,000
SUBTRACT: Basis of house	
Purchase price of house – $100,000	
Improvements (additions to basis) – $30,000	
Total basis of house	–$130,000
Capital Gain	320,000
Amount of tax to be paid	NONE

FIGURE 15-1: Calculating capital gains on the sale of a house.

Taking out an additional mortgage

Instead of selling your house, you may choose to take a second mortgage on your property. When you borrow money against the value of your house in the form of an additional mortgage, the amount of cash you receive from the loan isn't taxed. If you itemize your deductions on your income tax return, you can deduct some or all the mortgage interest from your income, depending on the total size of your mortgage and your total income. When you add a mortgage loan to the one you already have, you undoubtedly raise the amount of your combined monthly payments. However, you haven't extended the life of your first mortgage loan. Over time (and depending on interest rates and whether you and your student are eligible for low-cost loans), borrowing money this way may be considerably cheaper than saddling yourself or your student with excessive student loans.

Here's how it works: Using the same set of circumstances as in the previous example (house valued at $450,000 with a current first mortgage value of $65,000), Hector and Grace choose to add a second mortgage of $30,000 to their house rather than sell it. They choose this option for two reasons:

>> The interest rates currently offered for second mortgages in their area are lower than the Parent PLUS loans (see Chapter 18), which are all that they qualify for.

>> The payback period is longer on the mortgage than it would be on the loan, lowering their monthly loan costs.

The interest may be at least partially tax-deductible, depending on their original acquisition cost plus improvements and additions. Their current first mortgage loan principal and interest payment are $421 per month (30-year note with 3 percent interest rate), and they manage to get a second mortgage for 15 years and an 8 percent interest rate. The payment on the second mortgage is $286, bringing their total monthly mortgage payment to $707.

Refinancing your house

Recent increases in mortgage interest rates have made complete refinancing an iffy proposition, but mortgage interest rates may still be lower than Parent PLUS loan rates, so if you need to borrow a large sum for education, a total refinance may still make sense. Just be aware that the low, low, low interest rate you may currently have on your mortgage will be lost to the ages, and it may never come back. Still, sometimes none of your choices are terrific, and you have to choose the least bad one.

You may decide to stay in your current house, but completely *refinancing or* borrowing enough to pay off your existing mortgage loan — plus covering additional education expenses — makes more sense than taking a second mortgage. If your first mortgage is almost paid off (or has a very small balance), you may get a better interest rate on a refinance rather than a cash-out second mortgage. Remember, second mortgages are almost always given at a higher interest rate than the first mortgage because, in the case of a foreclosure, the first mortgagee is paid first, and there may not be enough funds left to pay off the second mortgage holder. Also, you may be able to move from a 30-year mortgage to a 15-year one because your income has increased since you took your first mortgage. This increase in income allows you to support a much higher payment without unduly taxing your family budget. It's important to note that the shorter the mortgage term, the lower the interest rate.

Seong and Leon purchased a house with a $250,000 30-year mortgage 15 years ago, with an interest rate of 3 percent. Today, their house is worth $600,000, they have a remaining balance of about $161,219 on their original mortgage, and their monthly payment of principal and interest is approximately $1,306. Now, their son is ready for college, and they anticipate a $50,000 shortfall between what they've managed to save and what they realistically think sending him through four years of school will cost. They decide to explore the possibility of a complete refinance of their house, checking out their payment if they refinance their house and take a new loan ($50,000) to complete their son's education.

When they actually fill out the necessary paperwork to apply for the new loan, Seong and Leon are facing much higher interest rates (a 30-year mortgage is going to cost them around 7 percent interest, while a 15-year mortgage's rate will be around 5.5 percent), but they're earning reasonable money and opt to lower the rate by choosing the 15-year payback period instead of 30 years. When the loan finally closes (the refinance process generally takes between four and eight weeks from start to finish), the face amount of the new loan is $225,000 ($161,219 balance on the first mortgage plus $50,000 for college expenses and $$13,781 because the house needs a new roof), and their new monthly mortgage payment is now $2,065. By refinancing, Seong and Leon will add $759 a month to their mortgage payment, and they'll still fully pay off the loan at about the same time as they would have had they not refinanced. Plus, of the $225,000 they are borrowing, the interest on $175,000 will be deductible on their income tax; the interest on the amount of the loan used for education expenses is non-deductible.

USING THE EQUITY IN A VACATION HOME OR RENTAL PROPERTY

A little place at the lake or in the mountains is the stuff dreams may be made of — but when it comes time to pay for college, if your college savings are shy of the full amount necessary, they may become the stuff of your children's education. Tapping into, or cashing out, the equity in a second or third residence or a piece of rental property may pay for a lot of tuition, but it may be a costly tax event. The following rules apply to any real estate that's not your primary residence:

- If you find that selling a piece of real estate makes the most sense for you, be aware that the $250,000 (single) or $500,000 (married) exemption amount for capital gains doesn't apply to the sale of anything except your principal residence.

- Mortgage interest paid on a second residence is subject to the same rules as mortgage interest paid on your primary residence. Most, if not all, is tax deductible. (Check with your tax advisor.) If you have a third residence, you're out of luck.

- Mortgage interest (and all other expenses related to the care and feeding of a piece of rental real estate) is deductible on IRS Schedule E, Rental Real Estate, not Schedule A, Itemized Deductions. You may need to consult a tax professional to make sure you take all the deductions you're entitled to, but none of the ones you aren't.

Turning Your Vacation Home into a Short-Term Rental

Many families have that beautiful spot in the country or at the beach where they rest, relax, and recreate for a few weeks each year. Getting away from it all is the name of the game here, and these properties, some of which have been in families for generations, are sacred family spaces where the best memories have been made.

These properties can also be a source of income for your family, one which may produce enough revenue to send Junior to summer camp, off on a trip across Europe or South America (or both), or even pay a tuition bill or two or ten.

Short-term rentals have become increasingly popular with the advent of web-based rental services. You gussy up your property, take lots of pretty pictures (making sure that if you're right on the beach, the waves are lapping 10' away from the living room window, or if you're out in the woods, your local moose is nibbling on the trees in the backyard), submit them to the web-based service, set a daily, weekly and/or monthly rate, and go live. Whether you choose to use `Airbnb`, `HomeToGo`, `extendedstayamerica`, `Craigslist`, or any other service, you'll pay a fee to the service for connecting you with your tenant.

In addition to the service fees, you'll also need to be sure your insurance on the property includes short-term rentals. (Check with your insurance agent and update as necessary.) You'll need to provide a cleaning service to make sure the property is always ready for the next guest. Also, you'll have to be sure to keep good records of any other costs you incur, such as all utility costs, repairs and maintenance, landscaping charges, and the like.

Income benefits of short-stay rentals

When you vacation, the hotel generally charges you a fee per night that exceeds what you'd be willing to pay if you rented that room by the month. Face it, paying $250 per night at an average hotel in a big city would work out to $7,500 per month, and that's for a single room with no kitchen and a private bath. Even in the highest of high-cost places, $7,500 per month for a room would seem excessive.

Now insert yourself into the picture with your own vacation property. Maybe your vacation cottage has two bedrooms, a kitchen, a living room, and a single bathroom. What are other properties with similar amenities charging per night or week in your location? Here's where you'll need to do some research. You need to investigate on all those web-based sites what similar properties are charging, and you'll pretty quickly arrive at a price that you think people will be willing to pay to stay in your little slice of heaven.

This is somewhat of a trial-and-error approach, and not every time of year will have an equal value to every other time of year. If you're in Vermont and you have a cabin in the woods or on a lake, you're looking at prime time during leaf-peeping season. If that same property rests on the slope of a ski resort, you know your property will always be rented during ski season, and you'll learn to embrace every snowstorm like it was your long-lost friend.

You will also not have the certainty of knowing that the property is rented every day or every week. There will be weeks when it is empty. (Guess what? Those are the weeks you get to use the property and perhaps make sure everything is working properly.) But the financial benefit of short-term over long-term rentals will quickly become apparent.

It is important to note that the expenses of a short-term rental are far higher than those of a long-term rental. Many locations now include short-term rentals that are subject to state meals and rooms tax. In addition, you'll have to have the property professionally cleaned at least every time a tenant leaves and before the next one arrives. Often, you will have to arrange for either daily or every-other-day cleaning while someone is in residence. Your property will have to be maintained to the highest standard — no one wants a leaky roof while they're on their romantic getaway, and chipping paint and battered furniture are also on the "not desirable" list. But the overall potential increase in the amount of rental income you can produce from a short-term rental, even considering the additional costs, may make it a money generator. You just might be able to generate enough money to put one, two, or even more students through college.

Tax considerations of short-stay rentals

Short-term rentals are an emerging area of tax law as more and more individuals start renting out vacation properties or even rooms in their homes, so the rules here are evolving. However, as it stands now, there are a few major considerations.

» If you are actively participating in the rental, such as providing daily cleaning services for the tenant or preparing meals, giving your guests tours, and so on, the IRS considers that you are in the business of short-term rentals and requires that you complete Schedule C of Form 1040. Your net income will be taxed for income tax purposes and self-employment tax purposes, which is roughly an additional 15.3 percent tax on your net income. Your net income (gross income less all expenses) is considered active income. If the expenses of the property are greater than the income generated, you're allowed to use that negative number to offset any other type of income on your return.

>> If you hand off the day-to-day management of the property to a third party, such as a management company that takes a fee for the cleaning and maintenance of the property, you will be preparing Schedule E of Form 1040, which is used for passive real estate activity. If the property produces a loss, you may only use that loss against the net income generated from other passive activities. If there is inadequate other passive income to offset the loss, the passive loss is suspended to a future year when you do have passive income or to the year of the sale of the property, whichever comes first.

One major benefit of renting out a property, or even a portion of a property, is that you're now entitled to a depreciation deduction. What is depreciation? The deduction expresses the gradual loss of value of a property over its useful lifetime. How does it work? In the case of residential real estate, the IRS considers that a residence has a useful life of 27.5 years. At the end of that period, as far as the IRS is concerned, that building has no value. Now, most of us realize this is ridiculous. How many of us have drooled over an 18th-century farmhouse or a 19th-century Second Empire mansion? Still, every year for 27 ½ years, you are allowed to deduct 3.636363 percent of the value of the building from the gross income generated by that property. Other types of property have other depreciation periods. Furnishings, for example, are depreciated over 5 years, while a new furnace will be depreciated over 15 years. And, if you add onto your property after that property has already been "put into service" (the term the IRS uses to indicate that this property is being used to generate income), you'll end up with a fresh new 27.5 years on the new addition to the building.

Depreciation can be a tricky area. You may want to seek professional help to assist you in setting up the schedules the first time. There are forms of special depreciation available in some years, bonus depreciation in other years (sometimes both in a single year), and occasionally, neither. The rules are constantly shifting, but the benefit of depreciation to you can be great.

Many people are terrified of depreciating property that should be depreciated, and therefore just ignore that this concept is part of the tax code. Don't be one of those people. As far as the IRS is concerned, if you should be depreciating and you're not, you're still going to be treated as though you were depreciating your property. You'll have lost a huge amount of valid tax deductions over the years and still have to recapture the depreciation you didn't take when the property is sold.

One final note about depreciation: you can't depreciate land. For example, if your property is a farm, you're only going to depreciate the value of the farm buildings, not the land they sit on. Why is this, you ask? Well, land doesn't get used up.

It was there before you purchased the property and will still be there long after that farm has turned to dust. Land is just land.

Avoiding The Dormitory Experience: Buying A Place for Your Student to Live

A 300-square-foot room, 3 students who've never met, and an enormous housing bill: What could possibly go wrong with this equation? And yet, this is the expectation of most students heading off to college for the first time. Will I like my roommate(s)? What happens if I hate my roommate(s)? And then there is the cost. The average cost of a dorm room in the academic year 2019-2020 (pre-COVID) across all universities was around $7,000 (and that's only for roughly 6-7 months of the year). That's for a cramped, sometimes claustrophobic experience, often with shared bathrooms, no control over roommates, and more. The list of possible negatives here is fairly endless.

There are positives, of course. The dorm experience is often one of the most formative times in a person's life, where they learn to get along with others, share with someone other than siblings, and amend lifestyles to accommodate someone else. Lifetime friendships are forged in the dorms, and that is not something to be taken lightly.

But the world of college has changed dramatically since the onset of COVID, and you and your student may not want them to be living in a largely unregulated space where good sanitary practices are often lacking. After all, who wants to live in a space wearing a face mask all the time?

And then there is the cost, which is considerable. If rates don't increase and stay at 2019-2020 levels — and when did that ever happen? — that's $28,000 for 4 years of approximately half-time living. The rest of the year, you're paying rent somewhere else, or they're living at home with you and raiding your refrigerator.

Let me present a different scenario: You purchase a condo for your student with two bedrooms and two bathrooms, a full kitchen, a living room, and possibly other amenities. It's within walking distance of the campus, so there's no need for a car. It's in a secure building and in a reasonably nice area. You pay $250,000 for the unit, pay $50,000 as a down payment, and take a mortgage for $200,000 for 30 years at 7 percent. Property taxes are approximately $3,000 per year, insurance is another $600 yearly, and HOA fees come to $1,200 per year. The total monthly cost is $1,732. You rent out the other bedroom to another student for $1,000 per month. So, now your student is living there for $732 a month.

At the end of 4 years, the condominium has increased in value to $300,000, and you decide to sell it, receiving the full asking price. After paying off the remaining mortgage of $190,982.52, a 6 percent brokerage fee of $18,000, and a capital gains tax of approximately $7,500, you walk away with $83,517.48 in your pocket. Meanwhile, your out-of-pocket costs over the 4 years were only $732 per month, or $35,136 plus the $50,000 down payment, or a total of $85,136. Essentially, your student has lived in a much nicer apartment for the full 4 years at substantially no cost to you instead of 4 years which only consists of 6 months per year, costing you a total of $28,000.

$28,000 versus almost nothing. That's a lot of money for the "dorm experience."

Chapter 16

Funding Education Using Whole Life Insurance

W e've all watched the late-night commercials plug life insurance policies for the elderly, and you may have been solicited to buy a life insurance policy for your baby the day after they were born. If you work for a large corporation, you may even have a life insurance policy as part of your benefits package. Or, if you own your own business, your company may hold a key-person policy on you.

Life insurance is a widely known but vastly misunderstood commodity, one where we assume that we pay the premiums until we die. Then, when we die, our family (or whomever else we choose) will receive a large, lump-sum payment. And for many of us, that money may be just enough to pay for our funeral or perhaps pay off the mortgage on our house if we die. Frankly, for most of us, life insurance has nothing to do with life and everything to do with death, whether our own or someone near and dear to us.

In fact, you might be surprised to find that there are more reasons to hold life insurance policies than just to protect your family against the financial burdens associated with death, that different types of policies cover different situations, and that owning a whole life insurance policy could be a very smart way to save for many of life's biggest expenses, including education. Saving inside a whole life insurance contract comes with very few restrictions attached to 529 Plans and Coverdell Education Savings Plans. There are no income limitations on who can contribute to the policy or how much can go into the policy. In fact, one of the only requirements to obtain the policy is that you may have to pass a physical, but most people can pass, even people with underlying health considerations.

In this chapter, you'll dive into the world of life insurance, especially whole life, and why a good policy can protect your family's dreams both during life and after death.

WARNING

Before getting started on all the ins and outs of life insurance, a word of warning — just as not every financial advisor is a paragon of moral and ethical virtue, the same can be said of insurance agents. Take the time to ask around, get references, and check with the Better Business Bureau or your state's Insurance Commissioner (insurance is entirely regulated by the states, not by the federal government) to be sure the person you've been speaking with is on the up and up. Remember, you are risking the financial viability of your dreams with every investment you make — it's up to you to be certain you have the best possible person giving you all the necessary information to make an informed decision.

Understanding The Difference Between Term, Universal and Whole Life Policies

Life insurance is a contract between you and the insurance company. In exchange for your premiums, the company promises to pay you a death benefit at your death. In addition, the contract may allow for investments to be made inside the policy or may permit cash to accumulate inside the policy, available to either increase the death benefit (that's called paid-up additions), to borrow against, or to take the available cash out of the policy outright.

One thing to note: paid-up additions are a great benefit inside a life insurance policy, but it's not an unlimited one. When the policy is first written, a limit to paid-up additions is established. The insurance company will not allow you to increase the death benefit beyond that limit. In order to increase your coverage once you've hit the paid-up additions limit on your policy, you'll have to apply — and be approved for — an additional policy.

Not all policies are created equal, though. The less expensive the policy, the fewer bells and whistles it will have (which isn't to say inexpensive policies are worthless). The policies you see advertised in the back of magazines or on late-night television do serve the purpose of providing a death benefit at the insured person's death. But these policies aren't going to do much else.

Let's take a look at the different types of policies and what they can and can't do.

Renting life insurance: Term Life

TIP

Term life insurance is affordable insurance, but it comes with one major caveat: if you stop paying the premiums, you lose the coverage. It's that simple. For the period you have the policy, you must pay the monthly, quarterly, or annual premium in order to keep the policy in force. There are no do-overs here — failure to pay a premium means the policy dies, and you'll have to buy a new policy if you still need the coverage.

TIP

All policies have a 30-day grace period between when your payment is due and when the policy will lapse. So, if you miss your premium deadline by 15 days, you're still covered. Generally speaking, even after the policy lapses (you didn't pay the premium and you've gone past the 30-day grace period), you can still have the policy reinstated within a 60-day period provided you pay all the past-due premiums, and you've had no health changes during that period.

Because the policies lapse without payment, most term policies never pay out a death benefit. The policy, which is usually written for a period of time (a term), stays in force for the number of years in that term, whether it's five, ten, twenty or even thirty. After the policy term expires, the policy does one of two things: it ceases to exist, or it can continue, but the premiums will rise as your age rises.

The fact that most term life policies never pay out the death benefit means the insurance company collects the premiums and doesn't have to do much else. They bank those premiums against claims, but there are relatively few claims against the total number of policies. So, the premiums are quite low, at least while you're young, making this sort of policy affordable for most families. This is insurance against a day that will most likely never come during the policy term. And all the premiums you've paid during that term? Why, they end up in the insurance company's hands. What do you get if you've been a good customer during the term period and paid all your premiums when the term ends and the policy lapses? Nothing, so long as you're still alive.

Because term policies don't build any cash value, you can't borrow against them or take cash out of them. This is really a case of just renting a policy in case you need the death benefit during the term.

Most life insurance policies provided by your employer are group term policies, and when you leave that job, your former employer stops paying the premiums and lets your policy lapse.

Sometimes during the term, the insurance company will give you an option to convert some or part of the face value of the policy to a whole life policy. If you can pay a higher premium when this time comes, you may want to consider making the conversion, even if it means lowering the eventual death benefit. As you'll see in the section below concerning whole life policies, there is much more flexibility in a whole life policy than in a term, universal life, or variable life policy.

If you can only afford term life insurance, you may want to purchase a policy that will pay off your major debts and cover your children's education should you die. Because you're looking at a fairly large policy, the premiums won't be insignificant, but they will provide your family with the necessary funds to continue with your life plan if you are no longer here.

Playing the Stock or Bond Market: Universal Life and Variable Life

You may think money you put into a life insurance policy is money that can't go into the stock market, at least until you discover the wonders of universal and variable life insurance. The insurance industry considers universal life policies to be permanent life insurance where cash value can accumulate and be invested in mutual fund–like securities.

WARNING

Don't mistake the meaning of the word "permanent." Universal and variable life insurance policies are far more permanent than term policies, but there is no guarantee that the death benefit you choose when you sign up for the policy will be that high by the time you die or will even be there. Universal life and variable life policies require that the investment side of the policy grows. If it doesn't grow at the rate shown in the sales illustrations, the policies could collapse under their own weight before you die unless you start injecting large amounts of additional premiums into the policy beginning in your retirement years, just when other expenses, such as medical costs, are rising.

Here's generally how universal and variable life works. You set the amount of money you want to put into the policy every month. The insurance company then splits that monthly payment into two buckets. The first bucket contains a term life policy, and the monthly amount you pay first goes to pay the term life premium. The remainder goes into the investment bucket. If your monthly payment is insufficient to pay the premium, then the policy will look to the amount of cash value you've accumulated (hopefully — not guaranteed) and take the remaining portion from the cash value. You can raise or lower your monthly payment at your discretion, but you need to know that the bucket containing your insurance premiums will increase in size every year. Remember, as you age, the cost of term life increases, so if you continue to make the same monthly payment, there may come a time when that payment will be insufficient to fully fund the policy. At that point, and if there is no cash value left in the policy to make up the difference between your payment and the monthly insurance premium cost, the insurer will begin to lower the death benefit so that the payments made now equal the premium on the new death benefit.

The second bucket collects all the money you pay over and above the insurance premium amount. This additional money funds the cash value of the policy, which may then be invested in mutual-fund-like investments, similar to what you might find from the major mutual fund companies. The insurance company will offer you a limited choice of investments, and you select from that list. As with investments in the stock and bond markets, some investments will be riskier than others, which means that when the markets rise, the investments will rise, and when the markets fall, so will your investments.

The primary difference between universal and variable life policies exists in the underlying investments — universal life policies typically invest in bonds, which have a fixed interest rate, while variable life policies invest in the stock indexes (or match already existing stock indexes, even if they don't enter the stock market directly. And, to confuse the issue even more, someone may try to sell you an Index Universal Life policy, which invests directly in the stock market, and will only be sold to you by someone with a securities license, not an insurance license.

A major feature of universal and variable life policies is their flexibility. You can change the monthly amount that goes into the policy, take loans against the policy, and make investments within the policy. And strictly speaking, if you purchase a policy, never make a bad investment, and never take a loan, provided the monthly payment amount you select is sufficient, your beneficiaries will receive the full death benefit when you die.

WARNING

Of course, if this sounds too good to be true, remember that no successful company was ever accused of favoring its customers instead of the company itself. With a universal or variable life policy, if there is any cash value in the policy when you die, the company keeps that and only pays out the death benefit. If your investments within the policy have performed poorly, you may need to increase your monthly payment into the policy to keep the original death benefit. If you are unable to do that, the death benefit will decrease to a level consistent with the monthly amount you are paying (and will continue to decrease as you age and premiums increase). Fees tend to be high in universal and variable life policies, so a large chunk of your monthly payment goes neither to your investments nor to your insurance premium. Instead, those fees land straight in the insurance company's pocket. Finally, if you choose to cash out the policy, you'll be hit with a large surrender charge, no matter how long you've held the policy. And, if your investments have done well within the policy and you cash out, you may be hit with a tax bill for the amount the cash out exceeds the payments you've made over your lifetime.

Universal life policies are marketed as a flexible way to provide yourself with life insurance coverage, but they don't offer many of the same boring assurances that more traditional policies offer: a set premium and a set death benefit. As a way to save for college, they are risky, but if you have one of these policies and you're short a tuition payment or two, the accumulated cash value can be accessed to pay those education expenses. There is no distinction between qualified and unqualified expenses, such as those for distributions made from 529 Plans and Coverdell ESAs, but if this policy is an integral part of your future financial planning, taking a loan to cover education costs has the potential to derail your other priorities. Be very careful when taking loans from universal or variable life policies. The reduction in the policy's cash value could very well collapse the policy or at least have it terminated long before you intended.

Making a Permanent Plan: Whole Life Insurance

When you hear someone discussing permanent life insurance, they're talking about whole life. Whole life insurance policies have the following:

- » **A guaranteed death benefit.** The face amount of the policy is the amount your named beneficiaries will receive when you die, plus any paid-up additions that may have accumulated within the policy.

- » **A fixed premium.** Whether you pay the premium all at once (a single premium policy), pay annually, quarterly, or monthly, the premium amount will be fixed when you buy the policy. The only difference between a monthly and annual premium is usually a few dollars per month for processing the additional payment.

- » **Dividend payments and accumulating cash value.** Like the universal life policy, the premiums paid while you are still young(er) are likely more than is required to purchase the death benefit. The additional money you put into the policy accumulates as cash value. These policies also pay annual dividends; depending on the policy's size and the insurance company's success, these dividends can be quite large and are added to its cash value. As you age and the cost of insuring you goes up, you may start to see the cash value decline.

>> **Options to buy paid-up additions**. You can use the dividends to purchase more insurance than the face value of the policy.

>> **Ability to use the cash value as a savings account**. The accumulated cash value of the account can be used to pay extraordinary expenses you may not have planned for adequately, such as a college tuition bill. If you've paid more in premiums than you take out of the account's cash value, any distribution to you will not be subject to income tax.

>> **Ability to take loans against the cash value**. If you'd rather borrow the money to send your child to school, you can take loans against the cash value, paying interest at the rate the insurance company sets. Usually, interest payments aren't actually paid directly from you; rather, the insurance company will add the annual interest to the loan value.

Given that purchasing a whole life policy will be more expensive than just contributing to your child's 529 Plan, why would anyone go this route? Well, you're paying for flexibility in your life planning. A whole life policy covers a lot of possibilities, while a 529 plan or Coverdell ESA is specifically designed for education — and education only. Let's say your child opts not to pursue an education (or that education is fully funded by someone else) and you have no one else to point the education savings account to. In this case, you're likely facing a tax bill when you close out the account and possibly a tax penalty as well. Even if your child does attend school, many of the costs associated with education come under the category of unqualified education costs, such as transportation costs, medical expenses, and so on. With the insurance policy, money that you've saved inside the account can be used for all your non-qualified costs, as well as for any number of other purposes, such as retirement, medical expenses, or even that round-the-world trip you've always wanted to take.

Using Cash Value in a Whole Life Policy

Purchasing a whole life policy may be one of the most boring investments you can make. However, in terms of assuring yourself that the end results will serve the purpose you've intended them to serve — provided you make the required payments — not much can beat it. You can think of the old fable of the tortoise and the hare, where the stock market is the hare, and whole life insurance is the tortoise — solid, slow, not too exciting, but guaranteed to produce results. In fact, a whole life policy that has been around for a while will rarely lapse due to nonpayment of the premium because there is usually sufficient cash value in the policy to keep it afloat for quite some time.

One of the most frustrating aspects of trying to build a substantial pot of money in the stock market is that, while the market often rises (bringing your hopes and expectations along with it), it also declines. While stocks and bonds have always recovered their value, it usually takes time. If the stock market tanks just as you are ramping up toward needing that money for education, you and your student may be sorely disappointed in the type of education you can now afford.

On the other hand, whole life insurance is just going to plod along, doing what it does and building cash value slowly but never losing value along the way unless you take money out of the policy. Every insurance company pays some interest on the account's cash value, and then there are the dividends paid annually. When you look at your annual insurance statement, you'll see a steady increase in the policy's cash value.

How does that cash value grow?

Every time you make a payment, a portion of the payment will go toward funding the death benefit, just like in a universal life policy. And a portion of the money will go to the insurance company to fund its profits. The final piece of the pie goes right back to you in the form of cash value in the policy. For example, when you first purchase the policy, if you know you want the cash value to fund education and aren't too concerned about the size of the death benefit, you can choose a smaller death benefit but more quickly accumulate cash value. On the other hand, if this policy is primarily used to provide your family with money they'll need should you shuffle off this mortal coil prematurely, you can opt to fund a larger death benefit. In this case, the cash value will accumulate much more slowly.

As your policy's cash value grows, you can use it as a savings account, available for those extra expenses that are too large to come out of your regular income. This is where your boring approach to savings will pay off. That first tuition bill rolls around, and all you need to do is arrange a transfer from the policy to your bank account and then from your bank account to the school. Presto! The bill is paid, no taxes are due, and everyone is happy. And if your student decides not to go to school? No worries — the money stays in the policy, earning interest until you need it down the road for whatever you want to use it for. There are no penalties, there are (hopefully) no taxes, and there is no one standing over you, demanding you terminate the account.

WARNING

The taxes and life insurance rules are convoluted, and you can make yourself crazy trying to wrap your head around them. But it is important to remember one thing — since you pay your premiums with money that you've already paid income tax on, when you withdraw money out of the policy, to the extent it doesn't exceed the total amount you've put in, the money won't be taxed. However, if you start withdrawing money exceeding the amount you've paid into the policy, you have created a taxable situation. You need to keep a close eye on your total payments into the policy to make sure you don't run afoul of this rule. And, if you need to access more cash out of the policy than you've put in, you might want to consider taking a loan against the cash value instead. It's important to consult a tax advisor to ensure you are meeting your tax obligations.

Borrowing Against Cash Value to Pay Education Costs

You purchased a whole life policy when your child was born, and you've been religiously making the monthly payments. Now, eighteen years later, your child is ready to start college, and you've built up quite the nest egg of accumulated cash value inside of that policy. You always planned to use the cash value to pay for your child's education, but now your insurance agent is telling you to reconsider and perhaps take a loan instead against the cash value.

This is a head-scratcher. Why would you take out a loan instead of just withdrawing the money from the account?

As in every life decision, there are pros and cons. Let's first take a look at the pros.

>> **There is no loan application, and you can't be turned down for the loan.** If you have sufficient cash value in the policy to support the loan value, you are essentially making the loan to yourself. While interest is charged on the loan, you aren't required to make payments on it. Also, the loan stays on your side of the ledger as an asset. The outstanding balance is subtracted from the death benefit if the loan remains unpaid when you die. If you choose to repay the loan, you can choose your repayment terms and stretch the loan payments out much further than a bank would permit.

>> **The interest charged will likely be less than a bank or Parent PLUS loan.** Not only will interest rates be lower than those charged by a bank, but since you're lending yourself money, the interest you are charged is offset by the interest earned inside the account, effectively reducing your interest rate to almost nothing.

>> **Dividends continue to be paid based on your policy's full accumulated cash value, including the loan amount.** If you withdrew the money outright, your dividend payments from the insurance company would drop because your policy's cash value dropped.

>> **The insurance premium is excluded from the FAFSA application** and is not counted as income.

>> **Missed payments on the loan do not impact your credit score.** In fact, while it's often preferable to repay the loan taken — thereby putting cash back into the policy — if you cannot make the payments at any point in time, the only one who will know is you.

And now for the cons:

>> **It's a loan.** At some point, it needs to be repaid. It may not be repaid until you die, or you can repay it sooner, but it's a debt you've incurred. Just be aware of that.

>> **The interest on the loan is not deductible.** You can't deduct it from your income tax as student loan interest, and it's certainly not deductible investment interest or mortgage interest.

>> **Interest continues to accrue as long as the loan is unpaid.** If you have no intention of repaying the loan and don't die for decades after the loan is taken, you may end up with no death benefit. You probably won't care (you'll be dead), but your policy beneficiaries won't be pleased.

BUT WAIT — WHAT ABOUT ANNUITIES TO FUND SAVING SHORTFALLS?

If whole life insurance policies can be a great way to pay for educational expenses, especially those pesky non-qualified expenses such as travel and health insurance, what about annuities, whole life's first cousins? In case you missed that presentation in school, an annuity is a life insurance product that focuses on giving you an income stream during your lifetime instead of a death benefit after you've died (though many annuities include a death benefit). In a world where stock markets can fall, bringing the value of your 529 plan or Coverdell ESA crashing down with it, having a flexible something in the wings to make up any shortfall may be a blessing.

There are as many types of annuities as there are stars in the sky, containing all sorts of bells and whistles in addition to the income stream, such as death benefits, guaranteed payouts, guaranteed annual increases, and so on. However, it's important to note that all annuities require a large up-front payment and a point in time — immediate or deferred — when the income stream will be turned on. Some annuities are for a period of years, and others last for your lifetime. Some annuities can be held inside qualified retirement plans; you can add to them monthly or annually if you so choose.

Annuities can protect assets from lawsuits, can shelter some assets from seizure from Medicaid, and generally can take assets off the table when looking at what monies are available to pay certain expenses, such as college expenses.

Like a whole life policy, you can purchase an annuity guaranteed not to lose value due to market forces. Make sure to check with the agent selling you the policy that this is, indeed, true of the policy you are buying; many variable and indexed annuities can drop in value if the securities underlying the annuity drop in value.

Annuities can be extremely flexible in terms of what you can use the money inside the policy for. There can be significant tax benefits to taking money from an annuity you've funded with after-tax dollars (non-qualified money) instead of making up a shortfall from your untaxed retirement account (qualified money). Remember, your retirement accounts have not yet been taxed, so every distribution you take from it will be taxed when you take it. On the other hand, money taken from a non-qualified annuity will only be taxed on the portion of that distribution that represents earnings. If you have funded an annuity with $100,000 that is now worth $200,000, and you need to make up a shortfall in college savings in other places by $10,000 per year, only $5,000 of that distribution will be taxable income to you. If you take that $10,000 from a qualified retirement account, the full $10,000 distribution will be taxable income.

For parents who have children later in life, a deferred annuity can make great sense because your child will be reaching college age right around the same time as you'll be approaching retirement. If you have a large-ish sum of money early in the education planning game, an annuity could be an interesting way to at least partially fund that education. If you don't need the money to pay for education, great! You can use it for any other purpose or leave it unmolested until

- You're either required to begin taking distributions (in the case of an annuity funded with qualified money, which you must start drawing down when you reach age 73, as of 2023, or as late as 75 for annuity owners born in 1960 or later).

- Choose to take it to make up shortfalls in your income (deferred annuities can be a great hedge against inflation because you can turn on the income when the purchasing power of your other sources of income falls).

- You die.

Annuities are very popular methods to deal with unascertainable events, such as inflation or medical costs, providing you with a fresh stream of income when you need it most. But they can also keep you debt free as you put your child(ren) through school, not being in any way encumbered by the age or purpose restrictions that come with 529 plans or Coverdell ESAs. One annuity can be used for multiple children rather than needing a separate account for each child. And you'll never have to roll over any unused

(continued)

(continued)

portion to another potential student. What remains inside the annuity after all the education expenses have been paid is yours to do with as you please.

Annuities, like whole life insurance policies, are for long-term planning. You are meant to put the money into the contract and leave it there to grow. Accordingly, if you fund an annuity and then want your money back, you're going to pay to retrieve that money. There are typically large surrender charges for money that is left in the contract for anything less than 10 years, with the exception of a 10 percent per year free withdrawal amount. This surrender charge is to repay the insurance company for the commission it paid the agent who sold you the policy. While you will never see a charge for that commission ($100,000 put into an annuity starts out as $100,000, not $100,000 less a commission amount), the company recoups it over the time it has control over the money. When you shorten that time by making a more than 10 percent withdrawal, the insurance company is entitled to retrieve the commission on the amount you withdrew. This is called a "surrender charge" and it typically runs at about 10 percent in the early years of the annuity, and gradually reduces to 0 percent over a period of around ten years.

If you have an annuity and plan to use it to pay those additional education expenses that aren't covered by your 529 or Coverdell plan, it's best to take a withdrawal as opposed to turning on the income stream if you are relying on any form of financial aid. This is because the value of deferred annuities is not included on the FAFSA application, while the value of an annuity that has begun making monthly payments must be included as an income-producing asset. You are safe turning on the income stream (if you need to) in your student's last two calendar years of school as those years won't be looked at for financial aid purposes. Beware, though, that there are no other potential students in the pipeline; once the income stream is turned on, you can't turn it off, and with other students yet to come, you still have more financial aid applications in your future.

As with any financial product, not everyone is qualified to sell you an annuity, and not every qualified agent will sell you an annuity that fits your needs. Be aware that there are agents who only sell annuities for one company and independent agents who can sell you annuities from a wide range of companies. Generally speaking, the independent agent will have the broadest knowledge about what's available industry-wide, while the company agent will know everything there is to know about the specific products they are offering. You may want to look for referrals from friends, from your financial advisor (who will probably try to dissuade you from purchasing an annuity because that is less money in their pocket), and from your accountant or tax person, who may have a list of reputable agents to whom they refer their clients. Ask around, ask for references, and don't be afraid to walk away.

Defining What's Taxable and What's Not in a Whole Life Policy

No matter what kind of investment you have, the tax consequences of that investment need to be understood. That's the case if you're investing in stocks and bonds, have a savings account, or are investing in life insurance.

Dividends are not taxed, provide additional death benefits while there, and can be taken systematically to pay for college all without any prying eyes. I think of it as a secret account. And increasing or decreasing the death benefit lets you structure, with some boundaries, the amount of cash value and, therefore, dividends.

The good news is that money from a life insurance policy is very lightly taxed, if at all. Because you've already paid income taxes on the money you put into the insurance policy, any money you take out of the policy first repays you. You will only face taxes after you've exhausted the total pot of money you've put in. And, since most people pay more in premiums than they ever take out, the likelihood of you facing a tax on a cash withdrawal from a whole life insurance policy is fairly slim.

If you are in danger of taking too many withdrawals from your cash value, now is the time to start looking at loans against the cash value rather than outright withdrawals. The loan amount won't count as taxable income to you in any circumstance.

REMEMBER

While the insurance company keeps track of all the premiums you pay, you should maintain your own records, and if the two don't match, figure out why. The insurance company may be calculating your basis (the total amount of money you've put into the policy less any amounts you've withdrawn) differently than you are. They may have categorized a loan you requested as a withdrawal instead or vice versa. Remember, mistakes happen and can be corrected, but those corrections are most easily done when the mistake is first made or discovered. Do not put off contacting the insurance company if your basis records don't agree.

Finally, for most people, the whole point of having a life insurance policy is the death benefit when you die. Here, the news is absolutely terrific! Regarding income tax, death benefits for policies that have been purchased using after-income tax dollars (you've already paid the income tax on the premium payments) are paid out to the policy's beneficiaries income tax-free. That's right — even if you purchased the policy two months before you died and only funded it with a little bit of money, if you die and the policy pays, the lump sum received by your beneficiaries isn't subject to income tax. There may be a small amount of income reported by the insurance company to you for interest paid on the policy after you die but before the policy pays out, but on million-dollar policies, that usually amounts to less than $100.

Depending on the size of your estate when you die, it may be subject to estate transfer taxes, but that's a subject for another day. If you're really interested in finding out about it, check out *Estate and Trust Administration for Dummies*, 2nd *Edition* (Wiley) to find out more about the estate taxability of life insurance death benefits.

Again, these are all complex tax issues. It is always advisable to consult with your tax advisor and/or your financial planner prior to making any sort of cash withdrawal or loan from your whole life policy.

IN THIS CHAPTER

» **Figuring out where the scholarship money is hiding**

» **Trading service for college funds**

» **Considering the tax consequences of scholarship money**

Chapter 17

Accessing Scholarships and Awards

Maybe you've been carefully saving for the day your child begins college, or perhaps you've worked on the assumption that Bruiser will be the starting nose tackle for a Division I school's football team and will receive a full athletic scholarship. No matter which category you fall into, you may find that your planning hasn't produced the desired results as you move closer to that fateful day. Maybe the stock market didn't perform as well as you'd expected, or Bruiser is actually more comfortable ripping the guts out of a computer than a live opponent. As you look at that first tuition bill, you may realize you don't have enough saved and can't possibly make up the full amount of the difference from your current earnings.

Now, you could panic — after all, you've told your child all along that you expect them to attend college, and you'll somehow find a way to pay for it. A better option, however, is to take that same energy and begin researching what available free and not-so-free money is out there in the form of outright grants, scholarships, fellowships, and guaranteed payments for service, just waiting for your child to apply for it.

In this chapter, you discover the different groups and organizations with money available to help you with those college expenses. You also find out what your student needs to do to qualify for that money. And you explore the differences between scholarships and low-cost loans in exchange for service commitments instead of outright grants with no strings attached. Finally, you look at what tax consequences, if any, there are when your student receives scholarship aid.

TIP

You may also want to check out *Free $ For College For Dummies*, by David Rosen and Caryn Mladen (Wiley Publishing, Inc.), for more detailed tips and strategies on seeking out scholarships and grants.

Searching for Scholarships, Fellowships, and Grants

Fortunately, finding sources of free money isn't nearly as difficult as finding the lost ark or the sales receipt for the toaster that blew up the first time you used it. You just need to know the different places to look for the money.

Before you start your search, though, you should be aware that the words *scholarship*, *fellowship*, and *grant* are often used interchangeably by various organizations, but they essentially refer to the same thing: money that the organization provides to your student for higher education expenses without any expectation on the organization's part that they will be repaid. These terms do have some subtle differences, however. Generally speaking, a *scholarship* is paid to undergraduate students, a *fellowship* goes to graduate or postgraduate students (often with a research or teaching requirement attached), and grants are usually associated with need (but scholarships and fellowships may also be need-based). The basic theory is the same, however.

TIP

You may think your child isn't smart enough, talented enough, or poor enough to warrant someone else picking up even a part of their tab at college, but you're probably wrong. Money is available from a wide variety of sources, and it runs the gamut from small stipends to full tuition grants. Many of these aren't based on either ability or need; they merely require you to apply for the funds. Do your research and check all available sources — you may be quite surprised to find out just how much money is out there. Use the info in this section as your guide for searching out the possibilities.

REMEMBER

When conducting your search, keep track of all the different ways that your child may be able to access scholarship money. Scholarships are awarded not only on merit and need but also based on residency, ethnic or religious background, college choice, career path, and whether they are left-handed. Some scholarships are awarded only to incoming freshmen; others don't begin until a student's senior year. Don't assume your child won't qualify; instead, work on the assumption that something out there has their name written on it if you dig hard enough. And, if you fail this year to snag some funding, don't give up — as any good Red Sox fan knows, just wait until next year.

WARNING

Beware of scholarship scams, where for a small (or large) entry fee, your student is guaranteed a scholarship or given access to scholarship information that is supposedly not available for free. Remember, all scholarship information is free for the asking, and you must apply for the scholarship directly (not through an intermediary) for the grant. Anyone who asks for your credit card information or charges you a fee for any scholarship-related service is scamming you. Always keep in mind that scholarships are a classic case of receiving money based on hard work, good looks, talent, or a combination of the three, and nothing else; there should be no need for you to pull out your wallet at any point in the application process.

Looking at your child's prospective college

TIP

Begin your scholarship search at your child's college, both in the admissions and financial aid offices. Every college has a list of scholarships available if a student applies for them. Some are well-known and very prestigious; others are buried in obscurity, and you just have to be proactive enough to look for them and apply. Although the size and seeming abundance of athletic scholarships have become the stuff of legend, your child may also qualify for academic scholarships.

Both athletic and academic scholarships are generally awarded before your student even begins their college career, and they need to be renewed for each subsequent year. Substandard performance may lead to a reduction in, or even total loss of, the scholarship.

Don't forget that smaller scholarships are often awarded to students who have already proven themselves at the college level. The annual history award may not carry much cachet outside the history department, but that's real money they're handing out with it.

Working with your employer

Two of the most worthwhile benefits an employer can offer are scholarship programs for employees' children and tuition assistance programs. These programs provide the company with valuable tax deductions and give huge boosts to the educational plans of their employees and their children.

TIP

Even if your employer doesn't directly offer a scholarship program or some form of tuition assistance for employees, the union may provide some aid if you're a member. Assumptions that your union doesn't have anything like this in place will only hurt you — check with your union representative and find out.

Employer-sponsored scholarship programs

Company-sponsored scholarship programs generally aren't need-based at all but are rather merit-based. What company, after all, wants to admit that it doesn't pay its employees enough to enable them to easily send their children to college? The fact that these scholarships are merit-based doesn't mean that your student needs to be a genius (they are, after all, competing only against other children of people employed by the same company). It does mean, however, they must maintain reasonable grades in high school; also, they may have to complete an application, take a test, or both. And once they're in college, they must maintain the necessary grades for the scholarship to continue for all four years. Sometimes, the only stipulations will be that they must not be on academic probation (they're not doing great in their classes) or have failed outright. In other cases, a minimum grade point average (GPA) must be maintained.

Most of these programs don't provide full tuition assistance; instead, they usually give a nominal amount of financial support. Still, any money you receive will supplement what you've saved and may just bridge the gap between your savings and your student's potential costs.

The existence of a scholarship program may be buried deep inside your employee manual. Check with your human resources department to find out if your company has such a program in place, what the requirements are, and what you and your child must do to apply. Often, a charitable foundation is founded by the same family that founded your employer, and grants may come through the foundation rather than the corporation.

TIP

If you're fortunate enough to work for a college, the most valuable benefit your employment contract contains may be that you, your spouse, and your children can attend that institution tuition-free and tax-free, or at least at a discounted rate. Unlike corporate and union scholarships, these tuition reductions aren't based on merit but rather on your employment.

HELP! WE WON TOO MUCH MONEY!

What if you've saved the necessary amount of money in either a Section 529 plan or a Coverdell Education Savings Account (ESA), and suddenly, a full scholarship lands in your student's lap? Well, first, thank your lucky stars that you're one of the few who get to have this problem, and then consider your options for what to do with the unneeded savings account. You may choose any one of the following courses of action:

- **If your student has dreams of graduate school dancing in their head, keep your college savings safely stashed for that day.** Remember, Section 529 or Coverdell plan funds can be used to pay for all post-secondary qualified educational expenses, not just K-12 and undergraduate school expenses.

- **Distribute the money to your student or yourself after graduation.** Remember, though, if money is left over in either your Section 529 plan or your student's Coverdell ESA after they've completed their education, distributions to either you or them will result in income tax owed on the earnings plus a 10 percent penalty.

- **Make distributions to your student in the years they receive their scholarship.** By making distributions in these years, they'll pay only the income tax but no penalty.

- **Roll the account over to a new beneficiary.** By changing the designated beneficiary (see Chapters 5 and 8 for lists of who qualifies) and then using the money to pay qualified educational expenses for that student, you and your new beneficiary may escape paying any income tax on the distributions.

Employer-sponsored tuition assistance/reimbursement programs

Tuition assistance programs are one of the more highly touted benefits a company may offer, but they're often the most misunderstood. If you're contemplating returning to school to either hone your existing skills or to branch off in an entirely different direction, check with your supervisor and with your personnel or human resources office to see how much, if any, your company's program may cover. You may be pleasantly shocked to find that, even though you're taking a course that seems to be completely unrelated to your job, your company may feel that your new skills add value to the company so that it will cover at least a portion of your expenses.

Check out Chapter 3, which has a part-time and summer jobs section, for ways your student can help out here.

REMEMBER

Be prepared to pay the full cost of any course you take upfront, whether you pay cash or use a credit card. Most companies will reimburse you for your tuition expenses only after you successfully complete the course, not before. Also, remember they usually expect a C grade or higher for reimbursement. Sometimes, in addition to a stated grade, they also expect that you'll stay with the company for a set amount of time after you've completed the course — one year, for example.

Scouting local civic groups

What do the Elks, Moose, Knights of Columbus, Daughters of the American Revolution, and the Chamber of Commerce have in common? They all provide prizes and awards to deserving high school seniors who are nominated for the award either by their teachers or members of the organization who are familiar with the students and their work.

Scholarships may be given for academic excellence, athletic prowess, or community service, depending on the organization. Some of these awards are in the form of books, but others are in cash. The checks are generally made out directly to the student, not to the university that the student will be attending the following fall. These small scholarships may provide your student with the necessary money to buy incidentals that often aren't covered by a university scholarship program but are necessary purchases nonetheless.

Competing for corporate-sponsored awards

You may be familiar with the Miss America and Miss U.S.A. pageants and know that these young women receive scholarships from these organizations to further their educations. You may not realize that other types of corporate competitions (that don't require parading around in a swimsuit in front of a national television audience), open to both genders, offer similar benefits to the winners. These competitions don't require that you work for a particular company or business in order for your child to compete; in fact, if you're an employee, your child may not be eligible (check the entry rules).

Corporate scholarships, such as those offered by Best Buy, Burger King, Coca-Cola, Calgon, and the Discover Card, among others, can be very lucrative if you manage to nab one. The first-place award often is more than enough to cover all the expenses for a single year, but even runner-up prizes can be worth thousands. Awards are usually made for only one year at a time. Some are renewable annually, provided your student keeps up their grades. Others are good only for a single year; if students want further funding from that source, they'll have to apply for it each year they're eligible.

WARNING

Corporate competitions are competitive — don't let foolish errors trip up your student's application. Read the entry requirements carefully, and follow them closely. If the application must be postmarked by October 31, don't mail it on November 1 and hope that officials won't notice — they will.

TIP

You may access lists of what corporations sponsor competitions, what the general requirements are for each, and how much money is at stake through a variety of websites. Plug *scholarship* into any search engine to access a list. Good places to start are www.scholarships.com and www.fastweb.com, although new websites sprout almost daily in this very popular area. Libraries may also have books that give you this information, although the information in the books may not be as current as the Internet info. These search engines will allow you to sift through thousands of colleges by many criteria, such as your state of residence, ethnicity, religion, athletic ability, and type of education. The parameters here are really too numerous to list.

Tracking down charitable foundations

The United States has thousands upon thousands of charitable foundations, and most of them are completely obscure. In fact, many of them, according to the terms of their establishing documents, can't give scholarship money directly to students. Instead, they must set up scholarships through another organization, such as a college or university. Check with your student's financial aid office to obtain a list of these charities.

TIP

Some charitable organizations, however, do provide scholarships and fellowships directly to students to help defray the cost of education. Unfortunately, finding these organizations may be difficult (because many keep a very low profile). Still, you can locate them. Here are some suggestions:

>> **Check with your state's attorney general.** The AG's office in each state usually keeps a list of all organized charities operating within the state. They're obligated to provide annual reports, and this information is available to the public.

>> **Check with regional associations of grantmakers.** Their lists may not be as complete as the one you get from the attorney general because charitable foundations don't have to register with them, but this may be the easiest way to access information from charitable foundations around the nation. Remember, if you can find a local foundation giving away money for schooling, your chances of snagging a scholarship from them may be greater than from a national charity because you're competing against a smaller pool of applicants.

>> **Search the Internet.** Not every charitable foundation has a Web site; in fact, most don't. But you can often find the major charitable foundations that do provide scholarship assistance on the big scholarship search Web sites, such as www.scholarships.com and www.fastweb.com.

Snagging state and municipal scholarships

You might not know that a portion of your tax money is spent on scholarships, but most states and some cities and towns provide scholarship aid to some of their neediest students. Even if you're not sure your child will qualify, there's no harm in accessing the information and making sure.

TIP

If you're unsure how to begin searching for these taxpayer-funded scholarships, the Internet is always a good place to begin. You can plug in your state's (or town's) name and *scholarship* into any search engine and come up with a fairly extensive list of what's available to you from local sources. You should also check with your student's guidance counselor for any smaller grants that may not have Web sites. And it's wise to check with your state and local departments of education to see if they have any pertinent information for you.

Generally, strings are sometimes attached when you receive assistance from the state. For one, your student might have to attend a public institution in that state, whether a community or four-year college.

Acquiring College Funding in Exchange for Service

In these days of the all-volunteer military, you've probably seen recruitment ads on television that tout the benefits of the Montgomery GI Bill. Or, if you live in a major city, you'll surely have noticed the red jackets of AmeriCorps, those primarily college-aged nonstudents who give up a year of their time to community service in communities all over the country in exchange for limited tuition assistance.

While these are two visible examples of college tuition assistance available in exchange for completing a public service commitment, they're not the only two. In this section's examples, the federal or state government pays for all or part of your education while you give a period of service as a payback. Clearly, from the government's position, this is a winning strategy — it gives higher education to people who otherwise might do without and gets services in exchange. But for many people who enroll in these programs, it also helps to solve what otherwise might be an unsolvable problem: how to pay for the education they need in order to begin the career they want.

You and your child should ponder a few points before embarking on this road toward financing your student's education:

>> **Your student may have very little control over what type of service they perform and where they do it.** While the military, Public Health Service, and AmeriCorps try very hard to put people where they want to be, not everyone can play in the Marine Corps Band, fly fighter jets, or be in the Army Corps of Engineers.

>> **Once your student actually begins to receive money, their window to back out of the deal closes quickly.** Although the various branches of the service allow a freshman ROTC scholarship student to cancel their scholarship, once you move beyond that first year, your child has pretty much committed to fulfilling their military service obligation. The same holds true for loans with service obligations from the Public Health Service; although you can buy out of your service period, the cost far exceeds the actual amount you received.

>> **The amount of money your student receives may not be enough to pay for the education they want.** Benefits from the Montgomery GI Bill generally pay for a four-year education at a public college or university, but you may come up short if your child's greatest desire is to attend a private four-year college. Even with additional benefits available, you still won't have enough, and you'll have to make up the difference, either through savings, current earnings, or loans.

If you're still game even after the warning, read on and find out more about your options.

Marching in the military

The military provides one of the best bargains around in educational funding. This is true whether your child enlists in a branch of the military or any state National Guard right out of high school, enrolls in the *Reserve Officer Training Corps* (ROTC) at their college, or is fortunate enough to obtain a nomination to a military service academy (West Point, U.S. Naval Academy, U.S. Coast Guard Academy, U.S. Air Force Academy, or the U.S. Merchant Marine Academy). In exchange for either active or reserve service in one of the four branches of the military or the merchant marine, your child will receive enough funding from the government to provide at least a bare-bones post-secondary education. In many cases, the educations provided by the military are some of the finest available.

Programs for active duty, reserves, and veterans

Several programs are available to military personnel who have completed a period of active duty and/or reserve duty, and other programs are open to veterans or their families. Among these are the following:

» **The Montgomery GI Bill:** This bill provides a cash education incentive to either active duty personnel (after they've served one tour of active duty) or veterans for up to 36 months of post-secondary education, including, but not limited to, two- and four-year colleges, vocational and technical training, correspondence courses, apprenticeships/job training, and flight training. The amount your student receives is pegged to the length of their service and whether that service was active duty or reserve/National Guard duty. In addition, the amounts they are eligible to receive are adjusted annually for increases in the cost of living.

» **Tuition assistance:** Enlisted servicepeople may use this aid to pay for secondary and post-secondary courses during the time they're on active duty (including reserve and National Guard duty). These benefits have an annual limit, but money from the Montgomery GI Bill may supplement them.

» **Army/Navy/Marine Corps College Funds:** This program is supplemental to the Montgomery GI Bill and may increase the amount of money the military will contribute to your child's education. Awards aren't automatic or available to everyone; they're made based on academic merit.

» **Community College of the Air Force:** Open only to active-duty Air Force members, it offers primarily technical and scientific courses leading to an associate's degree. The Air Force pays up to 75 percent of the cost of the courses.

» **Survivors' and Dependents' Educational Assistance Program:** This program provides up to 36 months (45 months if you began using the program prior to August 1, 2018) of educational assistance and/or vocational training to the eligible children and spouse of a veteran who has died or become permanently and totally disabled from a service-related incident, or who died after becoming permanently disabled, or who was either a prisoner of war or is currently missing in action. Benefits are provided to veterans' children only between the ages of 18 and 26 and to the veteran's spouse for between 10 to 20 years from the date that spouse becomes eligible or from the date the veteran dies, depending on whether your spouse died or became permanently and totally disabled or if your spouse died while on active duty. If you think you, or your children, may qualify for this, you should contact your local Veteran's Administration Office for all the details.

ROTC and service academy scholarships

These scholarships are available to college students who attend one of the five service academies or a college with an ROTC program. Upon graduation from either the service academy or the ROTC program, your student is immediately commissioned as an officer in one branch of the military, and they are committed to serving for a specific period of time, depending on the size and duration of the scholarship, and the branch of the military that granted the scholarship. For example, a West Point graduate is committed to at least five years of active duty and three additional years of reserve and/or National Guard duty. Because ROTC programs vary between schools, you should check with the ROTC recruiter at your student's school about the after-graduation commitment for this program.

» **ROTC scholarships:** These scholarships may vary in length from two to four years and in amounts up to 100 percent of the tuition, fees, and expenses of a particular institution. These scholarships are intensely competitive; don't assume that, because your student signs up for ROTC as a freshman, they will automatically receive one of these scholarships. You can find out about the general outlines of the ROTC scholarship programs at www.armyrotc.com or www.military.com. For more specific information about a specific program, you should contact the ROTC recruiter at the particular college your student is interested in.

» **Service academy appointments:** These appointments provide a wonderful education and the assurance of a job at the other end. For that reason, they're few and far between, and they require far more legwork on your, and your student's, part to make it happen (not to mention the nomination of your U.S. representative or senator). In fact, all the service academies recommend that your student begin the application process in the spring of their junior year of high school. If your student is so fortunate as to get one of these appointments, they will receive the cost of full tuition plus a living stipend for the four years it takes to complete that undergraduate degree.

Helping others (and yourself) with AmeriCorps

A part of the Corporation for National & Community Service, AmeriCorps encompasses a network of national service programs and projects in a variety of areas, including health, education, environment, disaster relief, youth mentoring, elder care, and affordable housing. In fact, the list of programs under the umbrella is massive, and chances are good that whatever your, or your student's, interest, you'll probably find something there to suit it.

AmeriCorps can provide services in all these areas by tapping into the better nature of its volunteers. In exchange for an approximate one-year commitment (either full- or part-time), AmeriCorps may provide a volunteer with a modest living allowance plus health insurance, training, and a student loan deferment during that year if that volunteer has existing student loans. Volunteers who successfully complete their commitment become entitled to a modest education award that may be used toward college or graduate school or to pay back existing student loans.

AmeriCorps is open to U.S. citizens, nationals, and lawful residents. Provided the volunteer is over age 17, the program doesn't have any age or education restrictions; you, or your student, may choose to serve at any time.

WARNING

AmeriCorps volunteers' services are, without a doubt, priceless in terms of providing needed services at very low cost. But that fact hasn't prevented AmeriCorps from being caught in the crosshairs of annual budget fights between Congress and the President, who all agree that this is a wonderful program and then proceed to slash its funding. Because it does require appropriations from Congress to fund the programs and pay the volunteer stipends and education awards, you may not want to count on a huge number of available openings in AmeriCorps in the future. Still, if your student is determined to do something worthwhile with a year of their life and pick up some assistance for college — no matter how large or small — they could do a lot worse than spending a year with AmeriCorps.

Getting paid by the Public Health Service

The U.S. Public Health Service provides various sorts of educational assistance — from loans to outright grants — to students who are pursuing careers in health-related fields. These programs are designed to provide access to these professions for underprivileged individuals and to entice students into health-related professions that are currently experiencing shortages.

TIP

Programs that are offered may change to respond to changing needs. Some of the scholarships and low-cost loan programs currently available include the following:

>> **National Health Service Corps Scholarship (NHSC) Program:** Scholarships are available for students pursuing an education in medicine, dentistry, midwifery, or as a nurse practitioner or physician assistant. Students are awarded full tuition, required fees, other reasonable educational costs, and a monthly stipend in exchange for a one-year service requirement in a rural, urban, or tribal community for each year of funding received. Only the monthly stipend constitutes taxable income to the student. There is a

one-year minimum and four-year maximum grant availability. The location of your service is determined by the U.S. Public Health Service in either an NHSC-approved site or a Health Professional Shortage Area (HPSA). To qualify, you must be a U.S. citizen or a U.S. national.

>> **National Health Service Corps (NHSC) Loan Repayment Program:** For students who have accumulated large student loans while becoming health-care professionals, this program may provide a way out from under your debt burden. In exchange for a two-year service obligation, the U.S. Public Health Service will repay qualifying educational loans, up to $25,000 each year, in exchange for serving in either an NHSC-approved site or in an HPSA. You will also receive a competitive salary and some tax relief benefits and help a community suffering from a lack of qualified healthcare professionals. You may extend your contract year-by-year after the initial two-year contract to the extent that you still have unpaid qualifying educational loans and serve at either an NHSC-approved site or an HPSA. Once again, you must be a U.S. citizen or a U.S. national to qualify.

REMEMBER

Depending on your specialty, these programs may be used for undergraduate degrees, but others may be used only for graduate programs. Only certain types of practitioners are included, mainly those focused on primary care, whether for medical, dental, or mental health; if your dream is to be a neurosurgeon, you probably won't qualify. For more information regarding these programs, call your school's financial aid office or visit benefits.gov to get the latest information from the U.S. government.

Looking at Tax Issues Regarding Scholarships, Fellowships, and Grants

Whenever your student receives any money in the form of a scholarship, fellow-ship, or outright grant, you need to determine whether some or all that money is subject to income tax payable by the student. If the student receives money in the form of a loan, there are no up-front tax consequences. However, as the loan is being repaid, some interest may be tax-deductible.

TIP

Financial aid officers are generally a pretty savvy group of people who have a great knowledge of tax issues surrounding students, but they may not have much idea of your personal circumstances. If your student receives a financial aid award that creates tax problems for you or your student, don't hesitate to contact the finan-cial aid office and try to reformulate the award's terms to minimize or eliminate the tax implications. Although it's best to make any changes before any money changes hands, you may still be able to change the terms of the award as long as payments remain to be made.

Figuring out what's taxable and what's not

According to the IRS, the following requirements must be met for the scholarship money not to be taxed:

>> The student must be a degree candidate at an educational institution that maintains a regular faculty and curriculum and has a regularly enrolled student body in a place where it carries on its activities. In other words, your student may attend a primary, secondary, or post-secondary school, and whether they ever receive their degree, they must be working toward one. Scholarships for continuing education courses that don't lead to a degree won't qualify here; neither will fees that you pay to audit a course.

>> The scholarship or fellowship payment may not be considered as payment for services performed. Money received for a research or teaching assistantship generally is taxable, but the money received as tuition reduction is not.

>> The money has to go toward tuition and/or required fees and expenses. The student must pay tax on all other funds used to pay for room and board and other living expenses. The fact that the organization granting the scholarship may not make this breakdown for you doesn't mean that you don't have to — you do. You are responsible for keeping track of your expenses and the resources used to pay for them.

Table 17-1, based on IRS Publication 520, shows how the IRS breaks down what's taxable and what isn't:

REMEMBER

Amounts received to cover tuition, fees, books, supplies, and equipment are non-taxable only if those expenses are required of all students in that course. For example, suppose your student chooses to buy a computer that isn't required but that makes their life easier and allows them to achieve better results than they would have without the computer. Even if your student receives an A when they might otherwise have received a B, they still have to declare the funds used to buy the computer on their income tax returns and pay any tax due.

TIP

As you know, all rules have exceptions. Most scholarships and fellowships can be broken down into their taxable and nontaxable components fairly easily by using Table 17-1, but here are some special situations:

TABLE 17-1 **Tax Treatment of Scholarship and Fellowship Payments**

Payment for	Degree Candidate	Non-degree Candidate
Tuition	Tax-free	Taxable
Fees	Tax-free	Taxable
Books	Tax-free	Taxable
Supplies	Tax-free	Taxable
Equipment	Tax-free	Taxable
Room	Taxable	Taxable
Board	Taxable	Taxable
Travel	Taxable	Taxable
Teaching	Taxable	Taxable
Research services	Taxable	Taxable
Other services	Taxable	Taxable

» Veterans' benefits are tax-free, including any money you receive through laws administered by the Department of Veterans Affairs, regardless of whether that money is used to pay for required tuition and fees or living expenses.

» All amounts received under the National Health Service Corps Scholarship Program (except for the designated living stipend) and the Armed Forces Health Professions Scholarship and Financial Assistance Program are tax-free, even if you use a portion of that money to pay living expenses.

» Qualified tuition reduction programs for graduate students that are provided in exchange for teaching or research are tax-free if the value of the fellowship is used to offset tuition charges. In other words, the student is teaching or researching in exchange for tuition, not a living-expense stipend.

Dealing with self-employment income from fellowships

Even if your student needs to report a portion of their scholarship or fellowship to the IRS, chances are good that any income tax liability on that money will be minimal; after all, students are not famous for being high-bracket taxpayers.

WARNING

Unfortunately, if your student receives a fellowship or stipend in the form of payment in exchange for research or teaching exceeding $400 (as opposed to tuition reduction), and if that student is not treated as an employee of the organization paying the money, they're also subject to self-employment tax. This tax is paid by any individual for Social Security and Medicare *plus* the matching amount that an employer would be required to contribute if you were employed by someone else.

And this tax really hurts — it's a flat 15.3 percent (the 7.65 percent you always pay for Social Security and Medicare *plus* the matching 7.65 percent your employer would normally pay) of 92.35 percent (your full self-employment income less the 7.65 percent employer match that you now have to pay) of your self-employment income. No itemized deductions or exemptions are allowed (although valid expenses incurred when earning this money can be deducted). The self-employment tax isn't graduated to be kinder to lower-income individuals, and you aren't allowed to apply any credits against it. So, a graduate student who receives a $500 stipend in exchange for creating the index for a professor's book may not pay any income tax on that money but would have to cough up $70.65 to the IRS in self-employment tax. Your starving student will undoubtedly appreciate that 45 years down the road, they'll be entitled to receive Social Security and Medicare because they've now made this payment.

Claiming the American Opportunity Credit and Lifetime Learning Credit

If your student has to pay tax on a scholarship, fellowship, or grant, they may also be eligible to take advantage of the American Opportunity Credit or Lifetime Learning Credit.

The precise rules of who may (or may not) use these credits and the expenses offset by them are somewhat complex. However, the general point of both is to give some tax relief to parents and/or students (depending on who is actually paying the education expenses) for the taxable income they're using to pay tuition and required fees at a qualified college. You aren't allowed to use expenses for room, board, books, supplies, and living expenses to qualify for the credit. Income limitations exist for both — if the person trying to claim the relief is making too much money, the credit will be limited or eliminated altogether.

The basic outlines of these credits are as follows:

>> **American Opportunity Credit:** This is a $2,500 credit against qualified tuition paid per student in the first four years of post-secondary education leading to a degree. (40 percent this credit is refundable and shows up in the payment section of your Form 1040. The remaining 60 percent is nonrefundable, is

used to offset existing tax liability, and will appear on Schedule 3 of Form 1040.) You may claim this credit for only four years for each student. You may not also claim a Lifetime Learning Credit for the same student in the year you claim the American Opportunity Credit.

>> **Lifetime Learning Credit:** This is a credit of up to $2,000 against the cost of qualified tuition payments at a rate of 20 percent (you need $10,000 worth of tuition expenses to claim the full credit). You may claim this for as many years as you have qualified expenses, but the credit is per tax return, not per student. The Lifetime Learning Credit is a nonrefundable credit, meaning it must be used to offset income tax; if you have no income tax liability, it will be worthless to you. Unused credits do not carry forward to a subsequent year's tax return.

Just as you do with almost every other tax provision, be careful not to double dip and use the same expenses to try to qualify for both an American Opportunity or Lifetime Learning Credit for the same student in the same year. On the other hand, many people pay tuition expenses for multiple students, and each student may qualify for an American Opportunity Credit or a Lifetime Learning Credit. For example, if you have two students in your family who both qualify for the American Opportunity Credit, your total credit in a single year could be as much as $5,000, of which $2,000 is refundable and $3,000 is nonrefundable.

If you think your educational expenses qualify for these credits or deductions, check out the latest edition of *Taxes For Dummies* by Eric Tyson, Margaret Atkins Munro, and David J. Silverman (Wiley Publishing, Inc.) for the precise details for claiming these amounts. Importantly, it is always advisable to check with a tax professional.

Chapter **18**

Turning On the Financial Aid Faucet

I n bygone times, if you didn't have the cash upfront to pay for your child's education, your child did without or waited until you did have enough. And, once the flow of money slowed down to a trickle, so did that kid's educational opportunities. It was a pay-as-you-go world, and those who could pay went to college; those who couldn't didn't. Today, however, federal and private programs are available to help you out, so even though college or private primary or secondary schools may be a financial burden, they don't have to be an impossible dream.

In this chapter, I let you know what sorts of grants, loans, and other programs are available to help you finance your child's education. Also, I explain how to apply for them; and to whom you have to apply. And I discuss how the money you've saved can impact your financial aid eligibility and how you can maximize the amount of aid flowing out to you.

TIP

This chapter contains the bare essentials of financial aid, which is certainly enough to get you on your way. But if you want in-depth info on how to get that much-needed financial aid money flowing in, check out *Free $ For College For Dummies* by David Rosen and Caryn Mladen (Wiley Publishing, Inc.).

Financial Aid 101

People tend to use the term *financial aid* to refer to any sort of outside money that your student may receive to help pay for their education. However, as I discuss in Chapter 17, aid may come to your student based on merit, as in the case of many scholarships, or because they and you lack sufficient resources to pay the full amount when the payment is due.

And it is this second category, the need-based one, that best fits the definition of true financial aid or assistance that you and your child receive to help pay for higher education costs. If you're fortunate, some or all of that assistance may come to you in the form of outright grants or money that carries only the string of satisfactory academic achievement from your student rather than any work obligation or repayment plan. However, most money is not given outright but through work-study and student loan programs.

REMEMBER

Only 11 percent of college students pay the listed tuition price at their college or university; the vast majority receive some sort of aid, whether it's tuition reduction from the university, merit or need-based grants, loans, or work-study. So, while the listed prices for many of these institutions are staggering, relatively few students pay the list price.

Knowing where the money comes from

REMEMBER

Loans, work-study money, and need-based grants are available from a variety of sources. Among these are the following:

>> **United States government:** Uncle Sam provides outright grant money (through Pell Grants and Federal Supplemental Educational Opportunity Grants) and federal work-study funds. It also offers access to and guarantees for other types of loans, such as subsidized and unsubsidized Stafford Loans and Parent PLUS loans.

>> **State governments:** Depending on the state where you live, tuition grants may be available for your in-state student and, occasionally, for a state resident attending an out-of-state school.

>> **Colleges and other post-secondary educational institutions:** Very often, schools have money to help offset their students' costs. These funds are typically awarded based on need, merit, or some combination of the two. The funds available and the basis for awarding the funds vary significantly among colleges. Not common among undergraduate students, but very common among graduate students, especially in purely academic fields or esoteric ones, are tuition waivers made by the institution. For example, as someone

heading into a career as an art historian, you should be treated as a junior professional and not have to pay to obtain the advanced degrees necessary to work at the highest levels of your profession.

>> **Private lenders, such as commercial banks, savings and loan associations, and credit unions:** These institutions lend money directly to you or to your student through a variety of loan programs, some of which the federal government guarantees, and even pays the interest accrued between the date of the loan and the date you must begin repayment, usually a certain period of time after you've either graduated or left school.

While no federal financial aid is available for primary and secondary school students, aid is available from individual schools. Sometimes, that aid comes in the form of tuition reductions or waivers. Other times during your employment, certain private schools may educate your children for free or reduced tuition. This is often true of the clergy whose children attend faith-based schools such as Christian schools or Jewish day schools. In addition, if you have more than one child attending a particular school, there is often a tuition discount for multiple children from the same family.

TIP

When you don't ask, you don't get. You should never hesitate to directly contact a school's financial aid office to explain your situation. If everyone, both applicant and grantor, could rely completely on the formulae contained in the standardized aid applications, there would be no need for financial aid officers. Schools often grant financial aid offices a great deal of discretion regarding awards. It never hurts to ask — the worst that can happen is that someone will say "no."

Finding out what's available

You can choose from a wide variety of financial aid programs, but be aware that they come with an even broader expanse of qualifying rules and regulations. Although I can't possibly cover every program and every requirement, the following subsections highlight the most common forms of financial aid available.

Grants

A grant is free money that doesn't have to be paid back and is often one of the components of a financial aid award. This money may come from the federal government in the form of Pell Grants or Federal Supplemental Educational Opportunity Grants (FSEOGs) awarded solely on need. Grant money may also come from the schools themselves (see Chapter 17), which may choose to award money based on need, merit, or a combination of the two.

>> **Pell Grants:** These need-based, outright grants — given by the federal government — currently are available in amounts up to $6,895 for the 2022-2023 academic year (adjusted annually as a result of federal appropriations — and not always upward). They're generally only for undergraduate students who haven't yet received a bachelor's or professional degree. If your child qualifies for a Pell Grant in any year, they will receive it. These grants aren't subject to any work requirements or loan repayments, and they may be used to pay for any portion of the college's established cost of attendance, including room and board, books, transportation, and so on.

>> **Federal Supplemental Educational Opportunity Grant (FSEOG):** The federal government awards this grant to undergraduate students with exceptional financial need. (The need requirements here are even stricter than for Pell Grants.) These grants, which presently range from $100 to $4,000, don't need to be paid back, nor is there any work requirement.

Generally, students who qualify for an FSEOG also receive a Pell Grant; however, even if your student qualifies for an FSEOG, they may not receive any money from this program. Funds are extremely limited and are awarded to the schools, which determine which students will receive the available money and in what amounts.

Loans

As college costs soar and grant amounts remain fairly constant, loans have become the meat-and-potatoes measure that parents and students use to plug funding gaps. Some of these loans come directly from the federal government. Others come from private sources but carry federal guarantees, so the lender isn't left holding the bag if the borrower doesn't pay the amount due. Still, others come from private sources and carry no guarantees (for which you'll pay a higher interest rate) but may provide you with some added flexibility.

TIP

If you need to borrow some money to pay for college costs, here are a few types of loans you should be familiar with before you begin:

>> **Subsidized Stafford Loans and Unsubsidized Stafford Loans:** Need is one of the criteria for subsidized Stafford Loans, as is filing a FAFSA, discussed in the section "Applying for Aid (Yes, the Dreaded FAFSA)" later in this chapter. But all students may borrow under the Stafford Loan program. These relatively low-cost loans are available for both undergraduate and graduate education. Yearly and lifetime loan ceilings vary, depending on whether a student is a graduate or undergraduate student and whether they are financially independent of their parents.

Interest accrues on the loan amounts over the life of the loan. Loan payments may be made while a student is in school, but you're not required to do so.

However, the unpaid interest continues to accrue and add to the principal amount borrowed.

The major difference between a subsidized and an unsubsidized Stafford Loan is that the federal government pays the interest on a subsidized loan while a student is still enrolled in school and for a six-month deferral period after the student has left school. The U.S. government has directly funded all Stafford loans through the Federal Direct Student Loan Program (FDSLP) since 2010.

>> **Federal Parent Loan for Undergraduate Students (PLUS):** You may use these loans to plug the gaps between what you have saved, your student's actual financial aid award, and the real dollar cost of attending a particular school. These loans carry with them a higher interest rate than Stafford loans, repayment begins 60 days after the loan proceeds are disbursed, and the repayment term is 10 years. Unlike Stafford loans, these loans are the parents' responsibility, not the student's. Loan amounts may be as great as the full cost of attendance at a particular school, and the loans are obtained directly through the FDSLP (from the government).

>> **Private loans:** These loans are available to parents from private lenders based on the lender's own criteria. Because these loans have no federal guarantees, they generally carry higher interest rates (similar to car loans or other consumer debt). They may be used to pay for any expenses you haven't already covered through other forms of funding, such as savings, student loans, or PLUS loans. Because these loans aren't part of any federal program, repayment terms may be more liberal than for the federal loan programs, including the ability to defer payments until after your student has graduated, although interest begins to accrue on the amount borrowed as soon as you receive the money.

Work-study

If your student can juggle their schoolwork with employment and has demonstrated financial need, the federal Work-Study Program may be the answer to your prayers. This program provides part-time employment for eligible undergraduate and graduate students through their university or in public service work in the community. These jobs generally pay at least the minimum wage, and earnings are subject to federal and state income taxes; however, Social Security and Medicare taxes (FICA) are not withheld. Although the federal government provides the funds for this program, they're allocated directly by the individual schools based on the need of a particular student and the number of students who can demonstrate need.

Applying for Aid (Yes, the Dreaded FAFSA)

In the world of financial aid, equitable allocation of available resources is the name of the game. This allocation can be made only when comparing apples to apples, assets to assets, and income to income. The financial aid powers that be make this comparison by using financial aid applications. You and your student have to apply for financial aid every year that your student needs assistance. And your child's need is determined based on the information you provide regarding the year before the year just past — otherwise known as the *base year*. In other words, if your student begins college in the fall of 2023 for the academic 2023-2024 year, you need to fill out a financial aid application using base year information for 2021. On this application, you must provide information about your child's income and assets and your own (unless your child is an independent student, in which case they'll be completing their own application without any parental information). Every academic year your child is in school will have its own base year; a four-year college course will have four corresponding base years and four sets of financial aid forms.

Depending on where your child intends to attend school, you may have to complete more than one financial aid application. Although individual schools and many states have their own forms that they require you to complete, here are the two most common and the information you must provide:

>> **Free Application for Federal Student Aid (FAFSA):** As long and seemingly complicated as the FAFSA is, everyone needs to fill one out each academic year if they need or want aid from any of the federal grant or loan programs. These applications are free (as the name suggests). You may complete the form online or use the more-traditional paper form beginning October 1 of the year before the year for which you're requesting aid, using base year income figures and current asset information for both you and your student. You can take most of the required information directly from your and your student's base-year income tax returns; the rest comes from current bank and investment account statements and your business's balance sheet (if you own part or all of a business). The amount of debt you have, including mortgages, car loans, and credit card debt, isn't included on the FAFSA.

TIP

You can get detailed info on the FAFSA and complete the online application form by visiting www.fafsa.ed.gov.

>> **CSS PROFILE:** Administered by the College Scholarship Service, many private colleges and universities require this form in place of or, in most cases, in addition to the FAFSA. The CSS PROFILE contains much of the same data you put on your FAFSA. However, the information it requests is far more detailed and includes the amount of your net home equity (the value of your primary

residence less any outstanding mortgage loans). You may complete the CSS PROFILE in the fall of the base year. Also, unlike the FAFSA, this isn't a free service; you pay a nominal application fee plus an additional fee for every school you request your application be forwarded to.

For more info, see http://profileonline.collegeboard.com.

These and other financial aid applications help the federal government and your student's school determine your family's need for outside funding sources and your ability to repay loans. Federal financial aid eligibility is determined by a strict formula known as the Federal Methodology based on FAFSA information. Although CSS PROFILE information is far more specific, it impacts only institutional aid (not federal grants, loans, and work-study). Individual financial aid officers can exercise great latitude in determining financial need based on the CSS PROFILE and any other information you may provide. If you believe your financial circumstances are not accurately reflected in the information provided on these forms, talk with the financial aid officer at your prospective colleges about your circumstances and the possibility of a "professional judgment." A professional judgment allows the financial aid officer to make an aid award based on all the factors you present, not just the ones contained in your financial aid applications.

Don't lie on a financial aid application or even try to bend the truth a little. Although copies of your income tax returns and bank statements are not required attachments, you may be asked to provide them later for verification purposes. Lying on your FAFSA application is a felony, subject to up to 5 years in prison and up to a $20,000 fine. In addition, you'll have to repay any grant or loan money your child receives, and chances are very high that your child will be kicked out of school, as lying on any school-related document contravenes most school honesty codes. And if you think you're unlikely to be found out, think again; one out of three FAFSA applications is tagged for verification. The odds of being caught are definitely not in your favor.

Squeezing Out Every Drop of Available Money

After you begin to suspect that your savings and amounts available from current earnings will fall short of your child's anticipated educational costs, some forward planning may increase the number of outright grants and very low-cost loans your student may qualify for.

Hoping to hit the lottery or hiding your head in the sand are both very common responses to savings shortfalls. They won't help you when you're trying to sort out how to make that dream education happen for your student. Be alert, be pro-active, and plan ahead. All is not lost if you fail to save enough, but failing to recognize early in the process that you won't have enough may cost you more in the long run. By not planning for this eventuality earlier, you may be forced to take more loans with higher interest rates than you would have done otherwise.

If you apply for financial aid, you join a group of other parents whose savings are also falling short. Funds are limited and supposed to be distributed as equitably as possible. The following strategies aren't intended to somehow skew the system in your favor. Instead, they are designed to make sure your child receives a fair and reasonable award. Be honest in your assessment of what you can afford; don't make yourself out to be more destitute than you really are.

Timing the receipt of taxable and tax-exempt income

Many a financial aid application has been turned down because the applicant sold something in a base year that produced a large *capital gain* (the amount of money you receive on a sale exceeding what that particular piece of property cost you), received a large year-end bonus, exercised some stock options, took an unplanned distribution from a pension plan, or rolled over a traditional IRA to a Roth IRA.

If you know when your child is due to begin college, do your best to schedule large infusions of income and cash three years or more before they are due to start; the financial aid folks won't care about what's on your income tax return in any years other than your base years. So, if you need to sell an investment, do it sooner rather than later. If you're going to receive a year-end bonus, try to defer it to a non-base year, if possible. If you're an older parent closing in on retirement, don't start collecting your Social Security until you're through all your base years (though you need to start taking it by age 70). And definitely don't start taking retirement account distributions unless you must. (Beginning in 2023, at 73, you're required to start taking your required minimum distributions. If you were born in 1960 or later, your RMDs wouldn't begin until you turn 75.

If you can't avoid large amounts of extra income in one of your base years, try to take that income earlier in the year rather than later to give yourself the best part of a year to find ways to offset at least some of it. For example, you may want to give more to charity, take capital losses, or make extra mortgage payments — all of which should reduce the amount of income you show on your return as well as the amount of cash you have in your account on the day you complete your FAFSA application. And, if you need to access money from a pension plan, try to borrow the money rather than take a distribution; although the borrowed funds may show up as cash in your account, they won't show up on any tax return, but the full amount of any distribution will.

TIP

If you absolutely must raise cash in one of your base years, try to raise it to increase your cash flow but not your taxable or tax-exempt income. For example, if you must sell stocks, try to offset any capital gains with capital losses. This allows you to realize some of the appreciation in your great stock picks while also getting rid of some dogs.

Paying down debt

You know, of course, that debt is bad, but in the case of financial aid, it's horrible! Not only do you have those debt payments to make each and every month, but you don't even get any credit for them on your financial aid application. All the application is concerned with is how much you have in income and assets, not how much you owe.

TIP

To minimize the value of assets you show on your aid application, get rid of your debt. Sell some assets, if necessary, to pay off your car loan, make extra mortgage payments, and bring your credit card balances to zero. Complete all these transactions before you fill in your aid applications; the FAFSA folks are concerned only with your assets' value on the day you complete the application — not the day before and not the day after. Your good intentions will be worth less than nothing if you raise the cash but fail to pay off your debt before filing your application.

Making sure assets are not in your child's name

The financial aid people realize that you may have something other than college to spend at least some of your money on, but they assume that anything your child owns is fair game when they try to assess how much your family can afford to contribute toward the cost of a college education. Accordingly, they include at most 5.6 percent of parents' includable assets in their calculation of *expected family contribution* (EFC), the amount that the U.S. Department of Education figures you should be able to cough up for one child's educational costs in any given year. They expect your child to kick in a whopping 20 percent of their assets as a part of the same EFC for one year.

If you want to minimize the amount of your EFC, keep assets in your name alone, joint with your spouse, or in the name of another relative outside the household. If your child has accumulated assets since birth — for example, in a Coverdell Education Savings Account (Chapter 8) or Uniform Gifts to Minors Act/Uniform Transfers to Minors (UGMA/UTMA) account (Chapter 12) — spend down these assets first. You may not qualify at all for financial aid in the first year or so of college while you're depleting these accounts, but you'll be better off down the road once only you have assets to be counted — not your child. Of course, spending down your assets may not work for some families; if your income is too high, it won't make any difference in your assets' value. The EFC calculation will still place your family outside of the need-based range, depending on what college your child will be attending.

Beware of using your dependent child's money to buy items you expect, as their parent, to provide for them. Your money must be used to supply food, clothing, and shelter, but your child's funds may legitimately purchase computers, trips, a car, life insurance, or anything else extra you feel may benefit them but isn't essential to their health and well-being.

Anticipating your expenses

No one is suggesting that you run out and buy that new Mercedes or sink your money into a new boat, but most people have large expenses that they tend to defer, such as replacing a car, roof, or dental work (my personal favorite). When facing these expenses at the same time as the first college tuition bill, the natural tendency is to postpone these expenditures as long as possible, hopefully until your student completes college.

A certain amount of self-deprivation is normal for parents, but indulging yourself a little may actually help your student's overall financial aid picture. Replace that old rust bucket that's been held together with duct tape for the last three years (but remember, pay cash — don't finance it unless you absolutely must), and repair the roof. Paying for these items will deplete your cash and asset balances, which you must report accurately on the FAFSA. Because the value of the new car and the house repairs isn't included on your aid application, and no one will ever ask you how much your dental implants cost, you can successfully convert reportable assets into nonreportable assets and also take care of some necessary expenses in the process.

Spreading your available assets across multiple students

You may have more than one child who dreams of attending college. If your children are relatively close in age, your dreams may more closely resemble nightmares, thinking of how you will pay for their education.

You may be surprised to find out that while each of your children will have to file their own FAFSA application, your EFC will not be the same for each student. The portion of the EFC calculated based on your income will be divided by the number of students you currently have in college. The student's portion (based on their income and assets) will then be added to each application, arriving at the EFC for each student. The more members of your family who attend a post-secondary school at any given time, the greater the potential financial aid award for each student. Although the total you'll be expected to pay will likely be greater for multiple students than if you just had one in school, the per-student cost should be less (unless your income and/or asset value is very large).

REMEMBER

Your family consists of your children *and* you and your spouse. If either you or your spouse has any plans to return to school, the best time to do it may be when your children are also in school. That all-important EFC also applies to educational expenses that you and your spouse incur.

Postponing gifts

You may be fortunate enough to have other family members or friends who want to contribute money toward your child's education. If those additional funds aren't enough to pay the full amount, even with your contribution, you may want to encourage them to postpone making gifts in any base year and instead wait until after your child finishes school.

WARNING

Any money that is gifted directly to your child into a Coverdell ESA or UGMA/UTMA account or paid directly to your child's college as tuition is included in the EFC at a rate of 20 percent. Your child's benefactor may be working from the noblest of intentions, but the effect of that gift during those all-important base years may be harmful to your attempts at receiving outright grants and low-cost loans.

Student loans have become a boogeyman in the closet, preventing students with high loan balances from ever marrying, buying a house, or starting a business. Enter the world of student loans with the understanding that, while they may help you in the short term to access an education you might not have been able to achieve otherwise, they can bite you on the repayment side, preventing you from achieving any of your other goals.

FINANCIAL FOOD FOR THOUGHT

Face it: Without federal financial aid programs, state aid, corporate sponsorship, and university support, many people who have attended post-secondary schools would not have been able to. The fact that money is available to anyone who wants to attend has leveled the playing field, making college now accessible to anyone who wants to go. And given the opportunity, who wouldn't want to go? From a statistical standpoint, the earnings potential of someone with any post-secondary education is far superior to someone who stopped school after high school. The more education you have, the more your income should increase. As investments go, college is one of the best.

But there has to be a price, and it's constantly growing. With tuition costs rising much faster than the inflation rate, you may have to borrow a substantial portion — or even all — of the money to purchase your child's education. As a result, you may saddle yourself and your child with huge debt just as they begin their first, lowest-paying job and as you head into retirement. As scenarios go, this one isn't great, yet far too many people face this situation without adequate savings upfront.

Still, if you feel that student loans are an inevitable part of your and your child's future, you may want to think about a few points:

- Knowing upfront that they will have to pay a large bill at the other end may vest your child more fully in their education and may help them select a college that works financially for the family. The value of anything is much easier to ascertain when someone places a price tag on it. When your student knows just how much it will cost them down the road, they may study harder to ensure they get the biggest bang for their buck.

- The high cost of borrowing money may limit your student's options. An expensive undergraduate education may not be better than a less-pricey option. By borrowing the money to pay for an education, you might encourage your student to be more efficient in their use of resources to limit the amount of future payback. However, borrowing money may discourage your child from pursuing costlier dreams. Graduate or professional schools may appear out of reach for a student with hefty college loans to pay back.

- You can consolidate the debt and extend payment schedules when facing large monthly payments because of large student loans. Depending on the total amount of federal loans you and/or your student take, repayment schedules may extend to as many as 30 years by consolidating multiple loan balances into one promissory note. Doing so will increase the total amount of interest you'll pay on your loans, but your monthly payment should drop considerably, giving your too-tight monthly budget some relief. However, remember that the current rules only allow you to do this once, so make sure to do it when interest rates are low and after you're reasonably certain you've completed your education.

- While it can extend loan payments far beyond the loan's initial term, if your student isn't earning enough to make the payments required to retire the loan in 10 years, they may elect to use an income-based repayment plan. However, be very wary of using this approach because many students now owe two or three times the amount they initially borrowed because their payments aren't even covering the interest on the loans, let alone paying off any of the principal.

5
The Part of Tens

Chapter **19**

Ten Musts for Successful Savings

This book is entirely about saving money, albeit about a certain type of saving with a specific purpose and end in mind. But saving money is, at its very heart, only saving money. Without good strategies, techniques, and know-how in place, any savings plan is only as good as the mattress you stash the money under.

No savings plan is foolproof; there are way too many variables, some of which rest on your side of the table (such as how much, when, and where you save), and others over which you have absolutely no control (for example, federal monetary policy, which generally defies any sort of reasonable explanation). What you do manage, however, is how you respond to these variables; after all, you know (or hopefully have some idea of) how much you need to have saved by a specific date.

No matter how little you understand about why interest rates are so low and mutual fund fees are so high, you ultimately bear the responsibility for your savings program's success or failure. This chapter highlights some main strategies that may enable you to save enough to see one or more children through college without resorting to loans.

Paying Into Your Savings Plans First and Regularly

Putting money into your savings before you pay anything else and doing so on a regular schedule may seem like obvious advice. Every financial advisor will tell you to do this, but it's not as easy as it sounds. Your savings programs stand the best chance of succeeding if you provide them with more, rather than less, raw material: money.

To successfully save any money anywhere, you really must impose some discipline on yourself and your budget. There's just no getting around that fact. If you find that you're unable to put money away regularly (once a year probably won't cut it here unless you know your Christmas bonus will be really huge), now is the time to accept some help in making sure that you really save money.

If you already have deductions taken from your paycheck for a retirement plan, you know how easy it is not to spend money you never receive. And you probably also get some real satisfaction from seeing the size of that account grow. See whether you can make the same sort of paycheck deduction into either a Section 529 plan or U.S. Series EE or Series I savings bonds. Although both these deductions are made using after-tax dollars (unlike your retirement account contributions), the paycheck you receive will already have these amounts taken out. And you'll know that whatever money you receive from that paycheck will be yours to spend on your monthly bills.

TIP

If your payroll office can't (or won't) make these deductions for you, talk to your bank. Set up automatic monthly withdrawals from your account into your Section 529 or Coverdell accounts. Just make sure that you subtract the money from your balance before paying your monthly bills so that you aren't in any danger of bouncing checks.

Alternatively, with most employers, even teeny-tiny ones like me, offering direct deposit of paychecks, you can elect to have some set amount from each paycheck deposited into another account. If possible, have it deposited into an account at another bank or credit union than the one where you do your regular banking. It's much more difficult to spend money at another bank than in a different account in the same bank.

Be as generous as you can in funding your savings accounts. You'll soon find that you adjust your spending accordingly once you know that a certain amount of money is leaving your account every month for this new savings venture.

Understanding Your Investments

Don't ever let yourself be talked into putting money into an investment that you just don't understand. If you read a *prospectus* (the document any company must provide investors and prospective investors that explain what the investment is and how it works) and you just don't get it, or you think it's not for you, trust your instincts and stay away. If, on the other hand, you can see how the wheels in a certain investment turn and they seem reasonably well-oiled and connected, by all means, consider that particular investment on its merits.

Don't ever be afraid to seek advice, but know that accepting advice doesn't absolve you of responsibility. Pick the brain of someone who knows and understands an investment to help *you* understand the investment. Don't simply accept an outright recommendation to either buy — or not buy — a particular issue.

REMEMBER

If something looks fishy, sounds fishy, and smells fishy, chances are good you're not buying a plum. Beware of scams — scams succeed because the rationale behind them sounds plausible enough that you believe them. Even the most seasoned investors have been taken in by scams, so don't beat yourself up unnecessarily if you get caught. Learn from your mistake, however, and be sure it doesn't happen again.

Changing Investments When Necessary

Everyone miscalculates, and so will you. Don't assume that, because an investment's value is dropping, it will recover and go on to achieve fame and fortune. That type of wooly thinking is what keeps lotteries profitable and casinos in business.

When you keep current with what's happening in your accounts, you can get rid of investments that aren't performing up to your expectations (remembering to keep your expectations realistic at all times). The value of your investment is only one indicator, but it is an important warning sign. If it begins to fall for no reason, it may mean that bad news is looming that you aren't yet privy to. Likewise, unwarranted and rapid gains may be a sign that the stock is becoming speculative, and you may want to get out now. Do your research first and decide only after you're sure you're acting from a position of knowledge rather than fear.

TIP

Keep careful track of any mutual funds you own as compared to other similar mutual funds. (Check out Morningstar's mutual fund lists for lists of comparable funds at www.morningstar.com.) If your fund is performing well below comparable funds, change to one of the other funds. Not every fund manager is equal, and you want your money to be invested by someone who clearly understands the current market, not last year's.

Waiting for a failing investment to recover is a fool's game. So is waiting until you're sure that an investment has peaked. Keep your expectations reasonable and your losses to a minimum, and know that changing underperforming assets is key to successful investing.

Staying Current on Tax Law Changes

REMEMBER

You may think that ongoing changes to the tax code don't really affect your tax-deferred or tax-exempt college savings accounts. You're wrong. Even though you may not begin tapping into these accounts for many years, the current changes may well impact how you choose to save.

For example, the lower tax rates on long-term capital gains and qualified dividends may make you decide to put your non-tax-deferred or exempt savings into either individual stocks or stock-based mutual funds instead of keeping them in savings accounts, bonds, or real estate. Of course, Congress may someday wake up and reinstitute higher taxes on these types of income. If that happens, you'll also want to be ready to readjust how and where your money is invested so you obtain maximum benefit from your savings and any tax deferrals or exemptions you may be entitled to.

Being Realistic about Investment Returns

You may have earned 20 percent, 30 percent, or even 100 percent per year on your investments in the past several years, which probably felt pretty good. If your 16 children were ready for college at the height of the stock market, and you cashed all your college savings at that point, give yourself a big pat on the back and recognize that most of that was luck, not your brilliant investing technique. With those rates of returns, you had to save only relatively small amounts out of your current earnings to achieve Harvard for each of your kids and a fully-paid retirement in Monte Carlo.

If, on the other hand, you've lost 30 percent or 40 percent of your portfolio in the recent stock market downturn, you're not alone. Of course, it's humbling to see your rising high school senior look at the cost of their dream school and realize that it's no longer affordable for them to attend.

Stocks, bonds, commodities, currency, and cybercurrency all rise and fall. And their heights and depths usually have nothing to do with their actual value but have much more to do with how someone important is feeling on a particular day, or whether the Federal Reserve Board is feeling bullish or bearish, or whether there are two "XX"s in the name of the month. Supply chains can be damaged, wars break out, pandemics hit, and inflation runs rampant, and we, individually, have no power to stop any of these. When losses are challenging you, it's time for you to think creatively and perhaps explore other options for funding college.

The reality of investing is that it's a slow and steady race, not a sprint to the finish. Count on average rates of return of between 4 percent and 8 percent. Some years, your portfolio will increase more; other years, it may decline. The important concept to remember is that, with those average rates of returns, you will need constant out-of-pocket cash infusions to reach your goals. If Harvard and Monte Carlo are the pinnacles you're striving for, you'll need to do more than wait for the stock markets to expand exponentially to achieve them.

Not Counting on Great-Aunt Neela's Inheritance

WARNING

Reality dictates that while Great-Aunt Neela can't take it with her, she's probably going to spend most of it before she goes, and no matter what she's told you, whatever's left may be going to help save the North Atlantic salmon.

Funding Your Account Now — Not Later

Yes, you may win the lottery and suddenly have the money you need to see your children through college. And your salary may suddenly triple, so you'll have what you need when you need it. And all of this may well happen on a Wednesday in August, just before the first tuition bill comes due.

It's far more likely that none of these things will happen, all except that the first tuition bill will surely roll in on schedule, and probably for far more money than you currently expect.

You need to be saving now when your future need for the money is still in the future, and you need to be saving as much as you possibly can all the way along the road. Statistically, you're far more likely to encounter periods of less income — rather than more — along the way. You'll also probably face times when you'll have to reduce the amounts you can save. Take full advantage of every opportunity to save for college now, while you can, to have enough when you need it.

Feeding Your Retirement Plan

With the future of Social Security always uncertain and company pension plans continuing to bite the dust, you may be just a bit shortsighted if you fund your children's college savings plans without just as actively saving for your own retirement. Retirement will come hard on the heels of your children's college years — especially for parents who began their families in their 30s. Further, you're not going to have a lot of time to make up for deficiencies in your retirement savings.

REMEMBER

You can borrow for college, but you can't borrow for retirement. As you save for college, always keep sight of your future retirement needs, and make sure that you don't shortchange yourself.

Asking Questions of the Experts

No one can possibly know and understand every type of investment and every effect of every tax code provision on your savings. That's okay. No one expects you to be an expert in every area of your life.

What's not okay is pretending to understand when you just don't get it. Find someone reliable — a professional, family member, or friend — who does get it, and pick that person's brain. Stop the person when the answers get too technical. Make the person back up and go over the information repeatedly until you understand it. Don't accept the assumption that you should know what someone else is talking about, and don't ever feel like you're an idiot because you just don't get it.

Whoever said that ignorance was bliss was mistaken. Ignorance in any of your finances may well lead to disaster.

Learning from Your Mistakes

Making mistakes is what makes people human, and you're no exception. You will screw up in your savings programs, especially at the beginning, and you can't escape that reality. And that's all right — don't apologize to yourself or to anyone else.

At the same time, don't make the same mistake twice. If you lose money on an investment and might have limited the losses by selling sooner, learn from that. If you're not saving as regularly or as much as you should, change your ways. If you miss the timing on a tax code change and pay more tax than you would have had you been more attentive, that's okay. Once. Any of these errors can happen to anyone, but the success of your savings program depends on your making them only once and then doing better the next time.

Crying over lost opportunities and lost money only creates an ocean of tears; fixing what went wrong may help repair the damage.

Chapter **20**

Ten Ways to Dodge the Tax Code Minefield

Almost everything in life carries with it some tax consequences. Some are unavoidable, such as paying a sales tax every time you purchase a roll of toilet tissue. You may choose others voluntarily, such as contributing more tax to the total pot when you begin earning a higher salary. The government tries to discourage certain behaviors by highly taxing products related to those behaviors (such as tobacco and alcohol). Not every consequence makes sense, though: Married couples sometimes pay a higher tax for the privilege of being married. Frankly, if you try to make sense of the social policies that are entwined with taxes, you may go nuts. Suffice it to say that tax policies touch your life in myriad ways.

For the most part, because taxes are such a part of your life, you live it without paying much attention to the number of ways in which you're taxed. If you're like most people, you tend to focus only on newsworthy items, which are generally the ones that affect you the least: things like the drop in capital gains and qualified dividends tax rates, the estate tax, and so on. Although you may realize a small amount of tax relief from these reductions, you'd be far better off if the government magically halved the gasoline tax — a tax that really hits you in your pocket.

So, it will come as no surprise to you that tax implications figure hugely in any discussion about savings and that you may positively impact your savings program by focusing on the various rules and regulations surrounding college savings accounts. This chapter points out several areas where you may want to pay careful attention to maximize your savings and minimize the amount you hand over to the government.

Knowing Who's Giving and How Much

Anonymous benefactors belong in fiction, not in your life. If someone other than you is making gifts to your children in Coverdell Education Savings Accounts (ESAs) or any other type of account, you need to know about it. Coverdell's regulations are especially strict. No more than a total of $2,000 may be given per child per year without triggering excess contribution rules and penalties. Still, anything gifted to your child needs to be on your financial radar. You need to know about any assets your child accumulates that may impact their financial need. Also, should some well-meaning but potentially misguided person be making contributions to a Uniform Gifts to Minors Act or Uniform Transfers to Minors Act (UGMA/UTMA) account, you need to crank up the level of money management skills your child will have by the time they reach majority (age 18 or 21, depending on what state your child lives in). On that date, they will be in charge of a reasonably large sum of money and need to know how to use it wisely.

Being Aware of Your Income and Phaseout Amounts

REMEMBER

If you're using a Coverdell ESA or U.S. Series EE or Series I savings bonds to save for your child's education, you need to know how much your annual income is and how that number slots into the phaseout rules for these savings schemes. Unfortunately, claiming ignorance won't help you here, and a certain amount of both short- and long-term crystal ball reading is required.

Coverdell accounts limit and/or prohibit the amount higher-income taxpayers are allowed to contribute, but the phaseout amounts are always subject to change, as is your income. If you are trying to fund a Coverdell account and feel that your income may begin touching the limitation amounts, you may want to wait until after the end of the year before making your contribution. You have until your tax filing deadline to contribute for a prior year. Remember, contributions from taxpayers who fail to meet the income requirements are considered excess contributions and subject to an excise tax until the excess amount (including all income earned on it) is removed from the account and paid to the beneficiary.

On the other hand, if you're buying Series EE or Series I savings bonds now and intend to use them later, tax-free, to pay for your child's educational expenses, you don't need to be concerned with your income when you purchase the bonds. However, if your income increases to and beyond the phaseout range in the years you need to redeem the bonds, you might pay income tax on the interest you've earned in the interim period.

TIP

You may think that you'll have to wait until the very end of the year to determine whether or not you're going to meet the income limitations, but the IRS understands that many people are planners, and they try to accommodate that behavior as much as possible. All income and contribution amounts, such as gift tax annual exclusions and income limitation amounts for Coverdell contributions or to qualify to use U.S. Savings Bonds, are published annually, usually in September or October of the prior year for the upcoming year. If you know the targets you must fall under, you can plan gifts, increase/decrease income (where possible), or increase/decrease deductions to hit the targets.

Keeping Track of Your Contributions

Only qualified distributions from Section 529 plans and Coverdell ESAs receive tax-exempt treatment, and many accounts will have at least one nonqualified distribution to close out the account at the end of your child's education. For those reasons, you need to know how much money you contributed to the account and how much income was earned on that money in order to accurately calculate any tax and penalties.

REMEMBER

You've already paid federal income tax on your contributions, and you don't want to have to pay tax again on that money simply because you've kept poor records. Keep an ongoing tally of what you give, and make sure that your plan manager, custodian, or trustee agrees with your number. If they don't, investigate and fix the problem. When making distributions, the IRS relies on the financial institution's records, not yours, to determine any taxable amounts.

TIP

IRS Form 1099-Q, Payments from Qualified Education Programs, lists the following amounts:

>> **Box 1, Gross Distribution:** This is the full amount taken from the account during the tax year.

- >> **Box 2, Earnings:** This number represents the proportionate share of earnings that is contained within the Gross Distribution.

- >> **Box 3, Contributions:** As its name suggests, this is the proportionate share of your contributions based on the Gross Distribution.

As you might expect, Box 2 + Box 3 = Box 1. If it doesn't, you should contact your plan administrator.

Avoiding the Penalties for Overfunding an Account

True, you don't know how much sending your child to college will cost, making it difficult to calculate just how much you should save in a Section 529 plan or a Coverdell account. Still, given the penalties you'll pay if you save more than you need in either type of account, you're probably better off saving slightly less than you think you'll need rather than more.

WARNING

Savings shortfalls in these accounts may be made up from other nonexempt savings accounts that you have or even from current earnings. Overfunding accounts, on the other hand, will cost you in the long run.

Knowing Your Effective Tax Rate

If you read articles about college savings plans, you're probably convinced that there are only two tax brackets: the highest (yours, of course) and the lowest (your child's). When you're using these extremes, the examples in these articles always show how beneficial it is to push income to your child, who pays taxes at a lower rate.

The reality is that the gap between your tax bracket and your child's is usually not as great as the illustrations show. The vast majority of taxpayers pay tax at one of the three lowest levels, so the benefit of paying tax at the student's level rather than at the parents' level is generally not all that great.

Plus, there is the "Kiddie Tax" to consider. If you thought it was a great idea to push some of your investments into the hands of your children to capture a lower tax rate, you might have just created more work for yourself and cost yourself a bundle of money in tax preparation fees. In order to prevent this very strategy, only a small amount of investment income in the hands of a child will qualify for their tax rate; the rest of it will be charged at your highest applicable rate.

TIP

When looking at the best way to save, look at your situation, not someone else's. You may be surprised that something highly touted as providing huge tax savings to you may really offer you only very limited tax benefits. Of course, that same financial product may provide you with other advantages that are equally valuable.

Staying Aware of Tax Laws in Your State

Although federal tax regulations for college savings plans are the same for everyone, state laws vary, and no two states are exactly alike. Be sure you understand how your college savings plans are taxed in your state before you begin funding any plan. Before you open any account, check carefully into available income tax deductions for current contributions, the tax-exempt status of qualified distributions, and how other states' plans are treated in your state if you're considering a 529 plan.

Of course, knowing the laws when you create a plan is one thing; keeping track of any changes is something else altogether. If you move, don't assume that you must change your plan — you may not need to. Likewise, don't think that current state laws are set in stone. College savings plans represent a huge amount of currently untapped tax revenues for many states, and currently advantageous laws are always subject to change, particularly in tough economic times.

Keeping Track of Your Qualified Education Expenses

The tax-exempt nature of qualified distributions from Coverdell accounts, Section 529 plans, and tax-exempt redemptions from Series EE and Series I savings bonds are powerful incentives for saving in these vehicles. Keep in mind, though, that anything so attractive is also ripe for abuse, and the IRS may be very vigilant in policing these tax-exempt distributions and redemptions.

Keep copies of paid tuition bills and other qualified educational expenses together with your tax returns and destroy them only after you're certain you're well past the date for audit from the IRS or your state tax department. If one of these agencies calls you for proof of your expenses, your honest face and forthright manner won't hold much water, but receipted bills will.

Staying Informed about Changes in Current Laws

As a tax professional, I love to see Congress change tax laws frequently — that's what keeps me in demand. However, as a taxpayer, I find that trying to keep track of the current law seems to be an exercise in futility. As soon as I think I've got it, Congress changes it.

And this is especially true of Congress's tinkering with any sort of tax-deferred or tax-exempt savings plan, including Section 529 plans and Coverdell accounts. Since their inception, Congress has made myriad changes in the rules and regulations governing these accounts, from who may participate to how much may be contributed to what expenses you may pay for using distributions from these accounts. Because all of these plans and accounts are governed by the Internal Revenue Code, as the code changes, chances are good that the rules governing these accounts will change, too.

Being Honest about Your Child's College Plans

When you look at your newborn for the first time, you do not doubt they are headed for an Ivy League school. With that vision in mind, you open a college savings account. However, as the years go by, that child isn't exactly thriving in school, begins to live inside your car's engine, and comes up for air only long enough to raid your refrigerator.

The lesson here is to be honest with yourself about what your dreams and aspirations are — and what theirs are. Funding a college savings account only for the sake of keeping *your* dreams alive is expensive in the long run. If you're not sure how much money, if any, your child will use for post-secondary qualified expenses, save money in ways that allow you more latitude, such as in personal investment accounts or a trust for that child's benefit. The tax savings may not be as great while you're actually putting money away in these types of accounts because there are no tax deferrals on the income earned, and you'll annually pay the income tax due on that year's earnings. Still, if your child ends up not needing your savings for college expenses, your overall results may be as good as, or even better than, saving the same amount of money entirely in a Section 529 plan or a Coverdell account. Unlike nonqualified distributions from Section 529 or Coverdell accounts, any distribution your child takes from a personal investment or trust account is only taxed to the extent they receive current, untaxed income as part of that distribution. Any amounts previously taxed won't be taxed again to them, and a nonqualified distribution penalty is never imposed.

Getting Answers by Asking Questions

Some tax considerations are complicated. New and different tax provisions crop up frequently, and old provisions are reinterpreted. Consequently, you may find yourself in the position of not being exactly sure what you should do in a given situation. If so, join the crowd. Although college savings accounts are actively marketed as do-it-yourself vehicles, they're do-it-yourself in the same way that bicycle construction instructions are so simple that a 4-year-old could build it.

REMEMBER

Don't hesitate to ask for advice when you are wavering between two or more options and unsure of where the true benefit to yourself and your family lies. Don't rely solely on what you read or on what "everyone else" seems to be doing. Take your particulars to someone you trust, such as your accountant or attorney, ask your questions, and listen carefully to the answers. There is no one-size-fits-all answer here — your situation will dictate your best choice. And don't ever make your decisions based only on tax consequences; by doing so, you may do your family a disservice.

Appendix

Section 529 Plans, State by State

G o ahead. Pick a state, any state. What you see before you is a brief outline of the Section 529 plans offered by each state. I've stuck a bunch of letters in the first column, so you'll need a handy navigation guide. A word of warning, though: States can change any plan's rules, regulations, and who's running the show anytime. Check out the particular plan you're interested in before you invest. With that in mind, here it is:

>> **A:** Plan Name

>> **B:** What Is Covered

>> **C:** Plan Manager

>> **D:** Types of Investments

>> **E:** Investment Return

>> **F:** Participating Colleges

>> **G:** Enrollment Period

>> **H:** Taxability of Investments

>> **I:** Who May Invest

>> **J:** Is a State-Sponsored ABLE (529-type plan available for qualified disabled individuals) Plan Available, and who administers it.

Alabama

	Savings Plan	Prepaid Plan
A	**College Counts 529 Plan** (invest directly with the state). CollegeCounts 529 Advisor Plan (invest through a financial advisor).	**Prepaid Affordable Tuition Plan (PACT)** (invest directly with the state) *Plan is closed to new investors as of 2010; however, participants already invested in the plan as of date may continue investing.
B	Qualified educational expenses for primary, secondary, and post-secondary education; interest and/or principal on qualified education loans up to $10,000 lifetime.	Tuition and mandatory fees for post-secondary education only.
C	Union Bank and Trust Company.	Alabama State Treasurer's Office (PACT Trust Fund)
D	Choice of age-based, static, and individual fund portfolio options using mutual funds available through a variety of mutual fund companies.	Combination of equities and fixed-income securities and money market funds.
E	Variable — depends on market conditions and chosen funds.	Contracts purchased are now guaranteed to pay full tuition and fees at Alabama public schools. Benefits for out-of-state and private schools not to exceed the weighted average tuition and mandatory fees at Alabama public schools.
F	Any U.S. 2- and 4-year college and university, post-secondary trade and vocational school, and graduate and professional school that is eligible for federal financial aid and up to $10,000 lifetime cap on payments of principal and/or interest on qualified education loans.	Any U.S. 2- and 4-year college and university, post-secondary trade and vocational school, graduate and professional school eligible for federal financial aid.
G	Open enrollment; join anytime.	
H	Distributions used for qualifying educational expenses are state and federally tax exempt. Up to $5,000 contribution ($10,000 for married filing joint taxpayers) may be deducted yearly from state income taxes.	Distributions used for qualifying educational expenses are state and federally tax exempt. Up to $5,000 contribution ($10,000 for married filing joint taxpayers) may be deducted yearly from state income taxes.
I	Available to both residents and non-residents of Alabama.	
J	AlabamaABLE plan is available and permits a beneficiary of an ABLE account established under the plan to make tax-free withdrawals to covered qualified disability expenses.	

Alaska

	Savings Plan
A	Alaska 529 (invest directly with state and special benefits to University of Alaska students).
	John Hancock Freedom 529 (invest through financial advisors only).
	T. Rowe Price College Savings (invest directly with the state).
B	Qualified educational expenses for primary, secondary, and post-secondary education; interest and/or principal on qualified education loans up to $10,000 lifetime.
C	T. Rowe Price Associates, Inc.
D	Choice of age-based and static professionally managed investment funds.
E	Variable — depends on market conditions and funds chosen.
F	Any U.S. 2- and 4-year college and university, post-secondary trade and vocational school, and graduate and professional school that is eligible for federal financial aid and up to $10,000 lifetime cap on payments of principal and/or interest on qualified education loans.
G	Open enrollment; join anytime.
H	Distributions used for qualifying educational expenses are federally tax-exempt. No state income tax benefit because Alaska has no state income tax.
I	Both residents and nonresidents.
J	Alaska ABLE Plan is offered through the National ABLE Alliance. Administered by the Alaska Department of Revenue.

Arizona

	Savings Plan
A	AZ529, Arizona's Education Savings Plan (invest directly with the state).
	AZ529, Arizona's Education Savings Plan – Bank Plan (invest directly with the state).
	The Goldman Sachs 529 Plan (invest through Goldman Sachs or financial advisors only).
B	Qualified educational expenses for primary, secondary, and post-secondary education; interest and/or principal on qualified education loans up to $10,000 lifetime.

	Savings Plan
C	AZ529, Arizona's Education Savings Plan: Fidelity Investments. AZ529, Arizona's Education Savings Plan – Bank Plan: College Savings Bank. The Goldman Sachs 529 Plan: AscensusCollege Savings Recordkeeping Services, LLC.
D	AZ529 and The Goldman Sachs 529 Plan offer static professionally managed investment funds, target-risk funds, and individual fund portfolios. AZ529 also offers an interest-bearing deposit account.
E	Variable — depends on market conditions and funds chosen.
F	Any U.S. 2- and 4-year college and university, post-secondary trade and vocational school, and graduate and professional school that is eligible for federal financial aid and up to $10,000 lifetime cap on payments of principal and/or interest on qualified education loans.
G	Open enrollment; join anytime.
H	Distributions used for qualifying educational expenses are state and federally tax exempt. Contributions are tax-deductible in Arizona, up to $2,000/beneficiary ($4,000 for married filing joint taxpayers). Principal portion of nonqualified withdrawals are recaptured in Arizona income to the extent deductions were taken.
I	Both residents and nonresidents.
J	AZABLE is offered by the Arizona Department of Economic Security and is administered by the State of Ohio.

Arkansas

	Savings Plan
A	Arkansas Brighter Future Direct Plan (invest directly with the state). Brighter Future Advisor Plan (invest directly with a financial advisor).
B	Qualified educational expenses for primary, secondary, and post-secondary education; interest and/or principal on qualified education loans up to $10,000 lifetime.
C	Arkansas Brighter Future Direct Plan: The Vanguard Group and Ascensus College Savings. Brighter Future Advisor Plan: Ascensus Broker Dealer Services, Inc.

	Savings Plan
D	Arkansas Brighter Future Direct Plan: Choice of age-based and static professionally managed Vanguard mutual funds and an FDIC savings option. Brighter Future Advisor Plan: comprised solely of iShares ETFs. Offers age-based, static professionally managed, and individual investment portfolios.
E	Variable — depends on market conditions and funds chosen.
F	Any U.S. 2- and 4-year college and university, post-secondary trade and vocational school, and graduate and professional school that is eligible for federal financial aid and up to a $10,000 lifetime cap on payments of principal and/or interest on qualified education loans.
G	Open enrollment; join anytime.
H	Distributions used for qualifying educational expenses are state and federally tax exempt.
	Up to $5,000 contribution ($10,000 for married filing joint taxpayers) may be deducted yearly from state income taxes. Arkansas also gives a deduction for up to $3,000 contribution to an out-of-state 529 plan ($6,000 for married filing joint taxpayers).
I	Both residents and nonresidents.
J	AR ABLE is offered through the National ABLE Alliance and is administered by the Office of the Arkansas State Treasurer.

California

	Savings Plan
A	**ScholarShare 529** (invest directly with the state).
B	Qualified educational expenses for post-secondary education only. TIAA-CREF Tuition Financing, Inc.
D	Choice of age-based and static professionally managed investment funds.
E	Variable — depends on market conditions and funds chosen.
F	Any U.S. 2- and 4-year college and university, post-secondary trade and vocational school, and graduate and professional school that is eligible for federal financial aid.
G	Open enrollment; join anytime.

	Savings Plan
H	Distributions used for qualifying educational expenses are state and federally tax exempt. California 2.5 percent penalty assessed to earnings from non-qualified distributions that are also subject to the 10 percent federal penalty on non-qualified distributions.
I	Both residents and nonresidents
J	CalABLE is offered by The California Achieving a Better Life Experience (ABLE) Act Board and is administered by the CalABLE ABLE Program Trust.

Colorado

	Savings Plan
A	**Direct Portfolio College Savings Plan** (invest directly with the state). **Stable Value Plus College Savings Program** (invest directly with the state). **Smart Choice College Savings Plan** (invest directly with the state). **Scholars Choice Education Savings Plan** (invest with a financial advisor).
B	Qualified educational expenses for post-secondary education only.
C	Direct Portfolio College Savings Plan: Ascensus Broker Dealer Services and The Vanguard Group. Stable Value Plus College Savings Program: Nationwide Mutual Insurance Company. Smart Choice College Savings Plan: First Bank Holding Company. Scholars Choice Education Savings Plan: TIAA-CREF Tuition Financing, Inc.
D	Direct Portfolio College Savings Plan offers a choice of age-based and static professional managed investments using Vanguard funds. Stable Value Plus College Savings Program offers a funding agreement with Nationwide Mutual Insurance Company. The interest rate is declared annually. Smart Choice College Savings Plan offers a one-year time savings account and a money market savings account. Both accounts are fully FDIC-insured. Scholars Choice Education Savings Plan offers age-based, static professional managed, and individual portfolio investments from a wide range of mutual fund and insurance companies.
E	Variable — depends on market conditions, funds chosen, and current interest rates.
F	Any U.S. 2- and 4-year college and university, post-secondary trade and vocational school, and graduate and professional school that is eligible for federal financial aid.

	Savings Plan
G	Open enrollment; join anytime.
H	Distributions used for qualifying educational expenses are state and federally tax exempt. Contributions (other than rollovers, which are subject to state income recapture) are deductible from Colorado resident income tax returns, up to $20,000/beneficiary per year ($30,000 for married filing joint taxpayers).
I	Both residents and nonresidents.
J	Colorado ABLE is offered through the National ABLE Alliance and is administered by CollegeInvest, a not-for-profit division inside the Colorado Department of Higher Education.

Connecticut

	Savings Plan
A	**Connecticut Higher Education Trust (CHET)** (invest directly with the state). CHET Advisor 529 College Savings Program (invest through a financial advisor).
B	Qualified educational expenses for primary, secondary, and post-secondary education; interest and/or principal on qualified education loans up to $10,000 lifetime.
C	Fidelity Investments.
D	Choice of age-based and static professionally managed investment funds.
E	Variable — depends on market conditions and funds chosen.
F	Any U.S. 2- and 4-year college and university, post-secondary trade and vocational school, and graduate and professional school that is eligible for federal financial aid and up to a $10,000 lifetime cap on payments of principal and/or interest on qualified education loans.
G	Open enrollment; join anytime.
H	Distributions used for qualifying educational expenses are state and federally tax exempt. Up to $5,000 contribution ($10,000 for married filing joint taxpayers) may be deducted from state income taxes per year. Rollover contributions are not deductible.
I	Both residents and nonresidents.
J	ABLE CT is offered through the National ABLE Alliance and is administered by the Office of the Connecticut State Treasurer.

Delaware

	Savings Plan
A	**DE529 Education Savings Plan** (invest directly with the state).
B	Qualified educational expenses for primary, secondary, and post-secondary education; interest and/or principal on qualified education loans up to $10,000 lifetime.
C	Fidelity Investments.
D	Choice of age-based and static professionally managed investment funds.
E	Variable — depends on market conditions and funds chosen.
F	Any U.S. 2- and 4-year college and university, post-secondary trade and vocational school, and graduate and professional school that is eligible for federal financial aid and up to a $10,000 lifetime cap on payments of principal and/or interest on qualified education loans.
G	Open enrollment; join anytime.
H	Distributions used for qualifying educational expenses are state and federally tax exempt. Up to $1,000 contribution ($2,000 for married filing joint taxpayers) may be deducted annually from state income taxes. Income limitations apply.
I	Both residents and nonresidents.
J	DEPENDABLE is offered through the National ABLE Alliance, and is administered by the Delaware Plans Management Board.

District of Columbia

	Savings Plan
A	**DC 529 College Savings Program** (invest directly with the state).
B	Qualified educational expenses for primary, secondary, and post-secondary education; interest and/or principal on qualified education loans up to $10,000 lifetime.
C	Ascensus College Savings.
D	Choice of age-based and static professionally managed investment funds.
E	Variable — depends on market conditions and funds chosen.
F	Any U.S. 2- and 4-year college and university, post-secondary trade and vocational school, and graduate and professional school that is eligible for federal financial aid and up to a $10,000 lifetime cap on payments of principal and/or interest on qualified education loans.

Savings Plan	
G	Open enrollment; join anytime.
H	Distributions used for qualifying educational expenses are state and federally tax exempt. Annual contributions up to $4,000 ($8,000 for married filing joint taxpayers) may be deducted from D.C. resident income tax returns. Excess contributions may be carried over and deducted for up to five years.
I	Both residents and nonresidents.
J	DC ABLE is offered through the National ABLE Alliance and is administered by the Government of the District of Columbia, Office of Finance and Treasury.

Florida

	Savings Plan	Prepaid Plan
A	**Florida 529 Savings Plan** (invest directly with the state).	**Stanley G. Tate Florida Prepaid College Plan** (invest directly with the state).
B	Qualified educational expenses for primary, secondary, and post-secondary education; interest and/or principal on qualified education loans up to $10,000 lifetime.	Depending on the type of contract purchased, it will cover tuition and mandatory fees but also may include dormitory fees at any Florida public college or university. The plan value may be used at any qualified educational institution nationwide.
C	Florida Prepaid College Board.	Florida Prepaid College Board.
D	Choice of age-based, static, or professionally managed investment funds and individual fund options.	Fixed investment plan as determined by the Florida Prepaid College Board.
E	Variable — depends on market conditions and funds chosen.	Guaranteed to equal the increase in the rate of tuition, mandatory fees, and dormitory housing (where applicable), based on costs at Florida public community colleges, colleges, and universities.
F	Any U.S. 2- and 4-year college and university, post-secondary trade and vocational school, and graduate and professional school that is eligible for federal financial aid, and up to $10,000 lifetime cap on payments of principal and/or interest on qualified education loans.	Any U.S. 2- and 4-year college and university, post-secondary trade and vocational school, and graduate and professional school that is eligible for federal financial aid.

	Savings Plan	Prepaid Plan
G	Open enrollment; join anytime.	Open enrollment is from 2/1 – 4/30 of every year, but you may enroll anytime. If you enroll outside of the open enrollment period, you will receive pricing information at the next open enrollment period.
H	Distributions used for qualifying educational expenses are federally tax exempt. Florida has no state income tax, and the account is not subject to Florida Intangibles Tax.	Distributions used for qualifying educational expenses are federally tax exempt. Florida has no state income tax, and the account is not subject to Florida Intangibles Tax.
I	Beginning 9/22, the plan beneficiary must be a Florida resident.	Only available to Florida resident beneficiaries. Beneficiary age restrictions apply.
J	ABLE United is offered and administered by the Florida Prepaid College Board.	

Georgia

	Savings Plan
A	**Path2College 529 Plan** (invest directly with the state).
B	Qualified educational expenses for primary, secondary, and post-secondary education; interest and/or principal on qualified education loans up to $10,000 lifetime.
C	TIAA-CREF Tuition Financing, Inc.
D	Choice of age-based and static professionally managed investment funds.
E	Variable — depends on market conditions and funds chosen.
F	Any U.S. 2- and 4-year college and university, post-secondary trade and vocational school, and graduate and professional school that is eligible for federal financial aid and up to a $10,000 lifetime cap on payments of principal and/or interest on qualified education loans.
G	Open enrollment; join anytime.
H	Distributions used for qualifying educational expenses are state and federally tax exempt. Contributions up to $4,000 ($8,000 to married filing joint taxpayers) are deductible from Georgia resident income tax returns. The principal portion of rollovers and nonqualified withdrawals are subject to Georgia income tax to the extent that a deduction was taken for those principal contributions at the time the contribution was made.
I	Both residents and nonresidents.

	Savings Plan
J	Georgia STABLE is offered by the Georgia ABLE Program Corporation ("GPAC"), Office of the Georgia State Treasurer, and is administered by the Ohio Treasurer's Office.

Hawaii

	Savings Plan
A	**Hawaii's College Savings Program** (invest directly with the state or with a financial advisor).
B	Qualified educational expenses for post-secondary education.
C	Ascensus College Savings.
D	Choice of age-based and static Vanguard investment funds.
E	Variable — depends on market conditions and funds chosen.
F	Any U.S. 2- and 4-year college and university, post-secondary trade and vocational school, and graduate and professional school that is eligible for federal financial aid.
G	Open enrollment; join anytime.
H	Distributions used for qualifying educational expenses are state and federally tax exempt.
I	Both residents and nonresidents.
J	Hawai'i ABLE is offered by the Hawai'i Department of Budget and Finance – Director of Finance and is administered by the National Program ABLE for ALL Savings Plan.

Idaho

	Savings Plan
A	**Idaho College Savings Program (IDeal)** (invest directly with the state).
B	Qualified educational expenses for primary, secondary, and post-secondary education; interest and/or principal on qualified education loans up to $10,000 lifetime.
C	Ascensus College Savings.

	Savings Plan
D	Choice of age-based and static professionally managed investment funds.
E	Variable — depends on market conditions and funds chosen.
F	Any U.S. 2- and 4-year college and university, post-secondary trade and vocational school, and graduate and professional school that is eligible for federal financial aid and up to a $10,000 lifetime cap on payments of principal and/or interest on qualified education loans.
G	Open enrollment; join anytime.
H	Distributions used for qualifying educational expenses are state and federally tax exempt. Up to $6,000 of contributions ($12,000 for married filing joint taxpayers) may be deducted annually from Idaho resident income tax returns; however, Idaho taxpayers must include $100 of non-qualifying distributions on Idaho income tax return regardless of whether they deducted their contribution. Outbound rollovers must be included on Idaho income tax return ONLY to the extent of contributions deducted in either the current year or the prior year.
I	Both residents and nonresidents.
J	Idaho currently offers no ABLE program. Idaho residents with qualifying disabilities may enroll in out-of-state programs in states that offer ABLE programs to out-of-state residents.

Illinois

	Savings Plan	Prepaid Plan
A	**Bright Start College Savings Program** (invest directly with the state). **Bright Directions Advisor-Guided 529 College Savings Program** (invest with a financial advisor).	**College Illinois! 529 Prepaid Tuition Program** (invest directly with the state).
B	Qualified educational expenses for post-secondary education.	Tuition and mandatory fees only for post-secondary education, based on fees charged by Illinois public institutions.
C	Union Bank & Trust Company	Illinois Student Assistance Commission
D	Choice of age-based and static professionally managed investment funds.	Fixed investment plan as determined by plan manager and professional investment advisors.

	Savings Plan	Prepaid Plan
E	Variable — depends on market conditions and funds chosen.	Guaranteed to provide number of prepaid semesters at Illinois public community colleges and universities; will provide average mean-weighted credit hour value of public in-state costs at private and out-of-state schools.
F	Any U.S. 2- and 4-year college and and university, post-secondary trade and vocational school, and graduate and professional school that is eligible for federal financial aid.	Any U.S. 2- and 4-year college and university, post-secondary trade and vocational school, and graduate and professional school that is eligible for federal financial aid.
G	Open enrollment; join anytime.	Enrollment is currently closed.
H	Distributions used for qualifying educational expenses are state and federally tax exempt.	Distributions used for qualifying educational expenses are state and federally tax exempt.
	Contributions up to a $10,000 ($20,000 for married filing joint taxpayers) are deductible from Illinois resident income tax returns. Rollovers from this plan to an out-of-state plan and non-qualified distributions are included in Illinois income to the extent that prior Illinois deductions for income tax contributions were taken.	Contributions up to a $10,000 ($20,000 for married filing joint taxpayers) are deductible from Illinois resident income tax returns. Rollovers from this plan to an out-of-state plan and non-qualified distributions are included in Illinois income to the extent that prior Illinois deductions for contributions were taken.
I	Both residents and nonresidents.	Account owner or designated beneficiary must be an Illinois resident for at least one year prior to enrollment. Beneficiary age restrictions apply.
J	Illinois ABLE is offered through the National ABLE Alliance, and is administered through the Office of the Illinois State Treasurer.	

Indiana

	Savings Plan
A	**CollegeChoice 529 Direct Savings Plan** (invest directly with the state). **CollegeChoice CD 529 Savings Plan** (invest directly with the state). **CollegeChoice Advisor 529 Savings Plan** (invest with a financial advisor).
B	Qualified educational expenses for primary, secondary, and post-secondary education.

	Savings Plan
C	Ascensus College Savings for CollegeChoice 529 Direct Savings Plan and for College-Choice Advisor 529 Savings Plan; College Savings Bank for CollegeChoice CD 529 Savings Plan.
D	Choice of age-based or static professionally managed investment funds. College-Choice CD 529 Savings Plan invests solely in either fixed-rate CDs or in an Honors Savings Account with a variable interest rate.
E	Variable — depends on market conditions and funds chosen.
F	Any U.S. 2- and 4-year college and university, post-secondary trade and vocational school, and graduate and professional school that is eligible for federal financial aid, plus $10,000 per year tuition only benefit for primary and secondary schools.
G	Open enrollment; join anytime.
H	Distributions used for qualifying educational expenses are state and federally tax exempt. Indiana offers a 20 percent tax credit on up to $5,000 ($10,000 for married filing joint taxpayers). Non-qualified distributions, rollovers to out-of-state plans, distributions to make payment of up to a $10,000 education loans, and distributions used to pay K-12 tuition for schools outside of Indiana are subject to credit recapture.
I	Both residents and nonresidents.
J	INvestABLE Indiana is offered through the National ABLE Alliance and is administered by The Indiana Achieving a Better Life Experience Authority.

Iowa

	Savings Plan
A	**College Savings Iowa** (invest directly with the state). **IAdvisor 529 Plan** (invest with a financial advisor).
B	Qualified educational expenses for primary, secondary (in-state schools only, and accredited under Iowa Code Section 256.11 and adheres to the provisions of the federal Civil Rights Act of 1964 and Iowa Code Chapter 216) and post-secondary education; interest and/or principal on qualified education loans up to a $10,000 lifetime.
C	State Treasurer of Iowa, Ascensus College Savings and the Vanguard Group.
D	Choice of age-based and static professionally managed investment funds.
E	Variable — depends on market conditions and funds chosen.

Savings Plan	
F	Any U.S. 2- and 4-year college and university, post-secondary trade and vocational school, and graduate and professional school that is eligible for federal financial aid, and up to a $10,000 lifetime cap on payments of principal and/or interest on qualified education loans.
G	Open enrollment; join anytime.
H	Distributions used for qualifying educational expenses are state and federally tax-exempt. Contributions of up to $3,522/beneficiary/year ($7,044 for married filing joint taxpayers) are deducted from Iowa resident income tax returns. Non-qualified distributions and rollovers to out-of-state plans are subject to Iowa state income recapture rules.
I	Both residents and nonresidents.
J	IAble Plan is offered through the National ABLE Alliance and is administered by the Treasurer of the State of Iowa.

Kansas

Savings Plan	
A	**Learning Quest 529 Education Savings Program** (invest directly with the state). **Schwab 529 College Savings Plan** (invest through Charles Schwab). **Learning Quest Advisor** (invest through a financial advisor).
B	Qualified educational expenses for primary, secondary, and post-secondary education; interest and/or principal on qualified education loans up to a $10,000 lifetime.
C	American Century Investment Management Inc.
D	Choice of age-based or static investment professionally managed funds.
E	Variable — depends on market conditions and funds chosen.
F	Any U.S. 2- and 4-year college and university, post-secondary trade and vocational school, and graduate and professional school that is eligible for federal financial aid and up to a $10,000 lifetime cap on payments of principal and/or interest on qualified education loans.
G	Open enrollment; join anytime.
H	Distributions used for qualifying educational expenses are state and federally tax exempt. Up to $3,000/beneficiary/year of contributions to any state plan ($6,000 for married filing joint taxpayers) may be deducted annually from Kentucky resident income tax returns. Non-qualified distributions and rollovers to out-of-state plans are subject to Kansas state income recapture rules.

	Savings Plan
I	Both residents and nonresidents.
J	Kansas ABLE Savings Plan is offered through the National ABLE Alliance and is administered by the Kansas State Treasurer.

Kentucky

	Savings Plan
A	**KY Saves 529** (invest directly with the state).
B	Qualified educational expenses for primary, secondary, and post-secondary education; interest and/or principal on qualified education loans up to a $10,000 lifetime.
C	Ascensus College Savings.
D	Choice of age-based and static professionally managed investment funds.
E	Variable — depends on market conditions and funds chosen.
F	Any U.S. 2- and 4-year college and university, post-secondary trade and vocational school, and graduate and professional school that is eligible for federal financial aid and up to a $10,000 lifetime cap on payments of principal and/or interest on qualified education loans.
G	Open enrollment; join anytime.
H	Distributions used for qualifying educational expenses are state and federally tax exempt.
I	Both residents and nonresidents.
J	STABLE Kentucky offers the STABLE Account Plan to qualifying disabled Kentucky residents. The plan is administered by the Kentucky State Treasurer.

Louisiana

	Savings Plan
A	**START Saving Program** (invest directly with the state).
	Louisiana Student Tuition Assistance and Revenue Trust Kindergarten Through Grade Twelve Program (START K12) (invest directly with the state).

	Savings Plan
B	START Savings Program -- Qualified educational expenses for post-secondary education.
	START K12 – Qualified tuition expenses for primary and secondary education.
C	Louisiana Tuition Trust Authority (LATTA).
D	Choice of age-based and static professionally managed investment funds.
E	Variable — depends on market conditions and funds chosen.
F	START Saving Program – Any U.S. 2- and 4-year college and university, post-secondary trade and vocational school, and graduate and professional school that is eligible for federal financial aid.
	START K-12 – $10,000 tuition-only benefit for primary and secondary school tuition.
G	Open enrollment; join anytime.
H	Distributions used for qualifying educational expenses are state and federally tax exempt. Up to $2,400/beneficiary/year of contributions ($4,800/year for married filing joint taxpayers) may be deducted from Louisiana resident income tax returns for START Savings Program only; START K-12 contributions are not tax deductible. START Savings Program contributions in excess of the annual limits for tax deductibility may be carried over to future tax years.
	The principal portion of non-qualifying distributions are included in Louisiana income to the extent that there was a prior deduction on a Louisiana income tax return. Rollovers are not subject to recapture rules.
I	Account owner or account beneficiary must be a Louisiana resident at time of enrollment.
J	LA ABLE is offered and administered by the Louisiana Tuition Trust Authority (LATTA).

Maine

	Savings Plan
A	**NextGen 529 — Client Direct Series** (invest directly with the state).
	NextGen 529 — Client Select Series (invest with Vestwell State Savings Administration, LLC or through a financial advisor).
B	Qualified educational expenses for primary, secondary, and post-secondary education; interest and/or principal on qualified education loans up to $10,000 lifetime.

	Savings Plan
C	Vestwell State Savings, LLC.
D	Choice of age-based and static professionally managed investment funds.
E	Variable — depends on market conditions and funds chosen.
F	Any U.S. 2- and 4-year college and university, post-secondary trade and vocational school, and graduate and professional school that is eligible for federal financial aid and up to a $10,000 lifetime cap on payments of principal and/or interest on qualified education loans.
G	Open enrollment; join anytime.
H	Distributions used for qualifying educational expenses are state and federally tax exempt.
I	Both residents and nonresidents.
J	ABLE ME is offered by the Maine State Treasurer and is administered by the Bangor Savings Bank.

Maryland

	Savings Plan	Prepaid Plan
A	Maryland 529 – Maryland Senator Edward J. Kasemeyer College Investment Plan.	Maryland 529 – Maryland Senator Edward Kasemeyer Prepaid College Trust.
B	Qualified educational expenses for primary, secondary, and post-secondary education; interest and/or principal on qualified education loans up to a $10,000 lifetime.	Tuition and mandatory fees only for post-secondary education.
C	T. Rowe Price Associates, Inc. Investment Board.	Intuition College Savings Solutions.
D	Choice of age-based and static professionally managed investment funds.	Assets invested in a group of pre-determined no-load mutual funds.
E	Variable — depends on the market.	Guaranteed to pay full in-state tuition and mandatory fees at public Maryland institutions. Will pay an amount equal to the weighted average tuition and mandatory fees of Maryland public instituions for any private post-secondary educational institution.

	Savings Plan	Prepaid Plan
F	Any U.S. 2- and 4-year college and university, post-secondary trade and vocational school, and graduate and professional school that is eligible for federal financial aid and up to a $10,000 lifetime cap on payments of principal and/or interest on qualified education loans.	A variety of options, ranging from one semester to four years at a Maryland public 4-year university, one or two years at a Maryland community college, or two years at each of a Maryland community college and a public 4-year university (4 years total). For a beneficiary attending an out-of-state public or private institution, the plan pays the actual tuition up to either the weighted average tuition in the Prepaid College Trust plan purchased or the minimum benefit, whichever is greater.
G	Open enrollment; join anytime.	December 1 – June 30 of each year.
H	Distributions used for qualifying educational expenses are state and federally tax exempt. Up to $2,500/beneficiary ($5,000 for married filing joint taxpayers) of contributions may be deducted annually from Maryland resident income tax returns; contributions in excess of the annual maximum may be carried forward to, and deducted from income, for up to 10 subsequent tax years. The principal portion of non-qualifying distributions must be recaptured as Maryland taxable income to the extent of prior tax deductions for contributions.	Distributions used for qualifying educational expenses are state and federally tax exempt. Up to $2,500/ beneficiary ($5,000 for married filing joint taxpayers) of contributions may be deducted annually from Maryland resident income tax returns; contributions in excess of the annual maximum may be carried forward to, and deducted from income, for up to 10 subsequent tax years. The principal portion of non-qualifying distributions must be recaptured as Maryland taxable income to the extent of prior tax deductions for contributions.
I	Both residents and nonresidents.	The plan owner or beneficiary must be either a resident of Maryland or the District of Columbia at the time of enrollment. Beneficiary age restrictions apply.
J	Maryland ABLE is offered and administered by the Maryland 529 Board.	

Massachusetts

	Savings Plan	Prepaid Plan
A	**U.Fund College Investing Plan** (invest directly with the state).	**U.Plan Prepaid Tuition Program** (not under Section 529) (invest directly with the state).
B	Qualified educational expenses for primary, secondary, and post-secondary education; interest and/or principal on qualified education loans up to a $10,000 lifetime.	Tuition and mandatory fees only for post-secondary education.
C	Fidelity Investments.	Massachusetts Educational Financing. Authority (MEFA).

	Savings Plan	Prepaid Plan
D	Choice of age-based and static professionally managed investment funds.	Special Massachusetts Bonds.
E	Variable — depends on market conditions and funds chosen.	Guaranteed to equal increase in rate of tuition and mandatory fees at participating institutions in Massachusetts. For non-participating schools (including out-of-state schools), you may cash out the fund and receive back the amount you put in plus interest on the investment compounded annually at the rate of the Consumer Price Index.
F	Any U.S. 2- and 4-year college and university, post-secondary trade and vocational school, and graduate and professional school that is eligible for federal financial aid and up to a $10,000 lifetime cap on payments of principal and/or interest on qualified education loans.	Participating public and private community colleges, colleges, and universities in Massachusetts are covered by the plan. You may also cash out the fund and use the money to pay for education costs at non-participating and out-of-state educational institutions.
G	Open enrollment; join anytime.	Tuition certificates are purchased on July 15 of each year. Contributions made on or after August 2 of each year begin accumulating for the next purchase of tuition certificates on the following July 15.
H	Distributions used for qualifying educational expenses are state and federally tax exempt.	Federally and Massachusetts tax-exempt.
I	Both residents and nonresidents.	Both residents and nonresidents.
J	Attainable Savings Plan is offered and administered by the Massachusetts Educational Financing Authority, and managed by Fidelity Investments.	

Michigan

	Savings Plan	Prepaid Plan
A	**Michigan Education Savings Program (MESP)** (invest directly with the state). **MI 529 Advisor Plan** (invest with a financial advisor).	**Michigan Education Trust (MET)** (invest directly with the state). Contributions are irrevocable.
B	Qualified educational expenses for post-secondary education.	Tuition and mandatory fees only for post-secondary education.

	Savings Plan	Prepaid Plan
C	TIAA-CREF Tuition Financing, Inc.	Michigan Education Trust Board of Directors and Department of Treasury.
D	Choice of age-based and static professionally managed investment funds.	Fixed investment plan as determined by plan manager and professional investment advisors.
E	Variable — depends on market conditions and funds chosen.	Depending on the type of program purchased, the return is guaranteed to equal the increase in the rate of in-state tuition and mandatory fees at Michigan public community colleges, colleges, and universities.
F	Any U.S. 2- and 4-year college and university, post-secondary trade and vocational school, and graduate and professional school that is eligible for federal financial aid.	A variety of plans may be purchased for Michigan public community colleges, colleges, and universities. For beneficiaries attending either private or out-of-state public institutions, the plan will pay weighted average public tuition for in-state private institutions and the average public tuition if used out-of-state.
G	Open enrollment; join anytime.	Check with plan manager for current and future enrollment periods.
H	Distributions used for qualifying educational expenses are state and federally tax exempt. Annual contributions of up to $5,000 ($10,000 for married filing joint taxpayers) are deductible from Michigan resident income tax returns. Rollovers are non-deductible. Non-qualifying distributions are subject to income recapture on Michigan income tax returns to the extent that deductions for contributions were taken.	Distributions used for qualifying educational expenses are state and federally tax exempt. Annual contributions of up to $5,000 ($10,000 for married filing joint taxpayers) are deductible from Michigan resident income tax returns. Rollovers are non-deductible. Non-qualifying distributions are subject to income recapture on Michigan income tax returns to the extent that deductions for contributions were taken.
I	Both residents and nonresidents.	Beneficiary must be a Michigan resident at time of enrollment. Beneficiary age restrictions apply.
J	MiABLE is offered and administered by the Michigan Department of Treasury's Student Financial Services Bureau.	

Minnesota

	Savings Plan
A	**Minnesota College Savings Plan** (invest directly with the state).
B	Qualified educational expenses for post-secondary education.
C	TIAA-CREF Tuition Financing, Inc.
D	Choice of age-based and static professionally managed investment funds.
E	Variable — depends on market conditions and funds chosen.
F	Any U.S. 2- and 4-year college and university, post-secondary trade and vocational school, and graduate and professional school that is eligible for federal financial aid.
G	Open enrollment; join anytime.
H	Distributions used for qualifying educational expenses are state and federally tax exempt. Annual contributions of up to $1,500 ($3,000 for married filing joint taxpayers) are deductible from Minnesota resident income tax returns. Alternatively, there is a tax credit of up to $500 which is income-limited. Rollovers are non-deductible. Non-qualifying distributions are subject to income recapture on Minnesota income tax returns to the extent that deductions for contributions were taken.
I	Both residents and nonresidents.
J	Minnesota ABLE Plan is offered through the National ABLE Alliance and is administered by the Minnesota Department of Human Services.

Mississippi

	Savings Plan	Prepaid Plan
A	**Mississippi Affordable College Savings (MACS) Program** (invest directly with the state).	**Mississippi Prepaid Affordable College Tuition (MPACT) Program** (invest directly with the state).
B	Qualified educational expenses primary, secondary, and post-secondary education.	Tuition and mandatory fees only for post-secondary education.
C	Intuition College Savings Solutions, LLC	Mississippi Treasury Department.
D	Choice of age-based and static professionally managed investmenet funds.	Invested in a managed, balanced investment portfolio identical to that of the Mississippi State Public Employees Retirement System.

Savings Plan	Prepaid Plan
E	Variable — depends on market conditions and funds chosen.	Return is guaranteed to equal increase in rate of in-state tuition and mandatory fees at Mississippi public community colleges, colleges, and universities.
F	Any U.S. 2- and 4-year college and university, post-secondary trade and vocational school, and graduate and professional school that is eligible for federal financial aid, plus $10,000 per year tuition only benefit for primary and secondary schools.	Different plans that cover tuition and mandatory fees for either Mississippi public university, college, or community college. Weighted average tuition and mandatory fees at Mississippi public institutions for private or out-of-state public institutions, not to exceed their actual tuition and mandatory fees.
G	Open enrollment; join anytime.	September 1 to May 31.
H	Distributions used for qualifying educational expenses are state and federally tax exempt. Annual contributions of up to a $10,000 ($20,000 for married filing joint taxpayers) are deductible from Mississippi resident income tax returns. Rollovers are not subject to income recapture. Non-qualifying distributions are subject to income recapture on Mississippi income tax returns to the extent that deductions for contributions were taken.	Distributions used for qualifying educational expenses are state and federally tax exempt. Annual contributions of up to a $10,000 ($20,000 for married filing joint taxpayers) are deductible from Mississippi resident income tax returns. Rollovers are not subject to income recapture. Non-qualifying distributions are subject to income recapture on Mississippi income tax returns to the extent that deductions for contributions were taken.
I	Both residents and nonresidents.	The account owner must be a Mississippi resident and either the parent, grandparent, or legal guardian of the beneficiary or the designated beneficiary when the contract was first purchased. Beneficiary age restrictions apply.
J	Mississippi ABLE is offered through the National ABLE Alliance and is administered by the Mississippi ABLE Board.	

Missouri

Savings Plan	
A	**MOST – Missouri's 529 Education Plan** (invest directly with the state).
B	Qualified educational expenses for primary, secondary, and post-secondary education; interest and/or principal on qualified education loans up to a $10,000 lifetime cap.
C	Ascensus College Savings.
D	Choice of age-based and static professionally managed investment funds.

Savings Plan

E	Variable — depends on market conditions and funds chosen.
F	Any U.S. 2- and 4-year college and university, post-secondary trade and vocational school, and graduate and professional school that is eligible for federal financial aid, plus a $10,000 per year tuition-only benefit for primary and secondary schools and up to a $10,000 lifetime cap on payments of principal and/or interest on qualified education loans.
G	Open enrollment; join anytime.
H	Distributions used for qualifying educational expenses are state and federally tax exempt. Annual contributions of up to $8,000 ($16,000 for married filing joint taxpayers) are deductible from Missouri resident income tax returns. Rollovers are not deductible. Non-qualifying distributions are subject to income recapture on Missouri income tax returns to the extent that deductions for contributions were taken.
I	Both residents and nonresidents.
J	MO ABLE is offered through the STABLE Account Plan, which is administered by the Missouri Treasurer's Office.

Montana

Savings Plan

A	**Achieve Montana** (invest directly with the state).
B	Qualified educational expenses for primary, secondary, and post-secondary education; interest and/or principal on qualified education loans up to a $10,000 lifetime cap.
C	Ascensus College Savings.
D	Choice of age-based and static professionally managed investment funds.
E	Variable — depends on the market conditions and funds chosen.
F	Any U.S. 2- and 4-year college and university, post-secondary trade and vocational school, and graduate and professional school that is eligible for federal financial aid, plus $10,000 per year tuition-only benefit for primary and secondary schools and up to a $10,000 lifetime cap on payments of principal and/or interest on qualified education loans.
G	Open enrollment; join anytime.

	Savings Plan
H	Distributions used for qualifying educational expenses are state and federally tax exempt. Annual contributions of up to $3,000 ($6,000 for married filing joint taxpayers) are deductible from Montana resident income tax returns. Rollovers and non-qualifying distributions are subject to income recapture on Montana income tax returns to the extent that deductions for contributions were taken.
I	Both residents and non-residents. Some length-of-investment requirements apply.
J	Montana ABLE is offered through the National ABLE Alliance and is administered by the Montana Department of Public Health and Human Services.

Nebraska

	Savings Plan
A	**Nebraska Education Savings Trust – Direct College Savings Plan** (invest directly with the state. **Bloomwell 529 Education Savings Plan** (invest directly with the state). **Nebraska Education Savings Trust** – Advisor College Savings Plan (invest with a financial advisor only). **State Farm College Savings Plan** (invest with a financial advisor only).
B	Qualified educational expenses for post-secondary education; interest and/or principal on qualified education loans up to a $10,000 lifetime cap.
C	Union Bank & Trust Company.
D	Choice of age-based and static professionally managed investment funds.
E	Variable — depends on market conditions and funds chosen.
F	Any U.S. 2- and 4-year college and university, post-secondary trade and vocational school, and graduate and professional school that is eligible for federal financial aid and up to a $10,000 lifetime cap on payments of principal and/or interest on qualified education loans.
G	Open enrollment; join anytime.
H	Distributions used for qualifying educational expenses are state and federally tax exempt. Annual contributions of up to a $10,000 ($10,000 for married filing joint taxpayers) are deductible from Nebraska resident income tax returns. Rollovers and non-qualifying distributions are subject to income recapture on Nebraska income tax returns to the extent that deductions for contributions were taken.
I	Both residents and nonresidents.
J	Enable Savings Plan is issued by The Nebraska Achieving a Better Life Experience Program Trust and administered by the Nebraska State Treasurer.

Nevada

	Savings Plan	Prepaid Plan
A	**SSGA Upromise 529 Plan** (invest directly with the state or link to Upromise rewards service). **The Vanguard 529 College Savings Plan** (invest directly with the state). **USAA 529 College Savings Plan** (invest directly with the state or link to Upromise rewards service). **Putnam 529 for America** (invest through financial advisors only). **Wealthfront 529 College Savings Plan** (invest through financial advisors only).	**Nevada Prepaid Tuition Program.**
B	Qualified educational expenses for primary, secondary, and post-secondary education; interest and/or principal on qualified education loans up to a $10,000 lifetime cap.	Tuition and mandatory fees only for post-secondary education.
C	Putnam 529 for America Plan: Putnam Investment Management, LLC. All others: Ascensus College Savings.	Board of Trustees of the College Savings Plans of Nevada and the State Treasurer's Office.
D	Choice of age-based and static professionally-managed investment funds.	Fixed investment plan as determined by the Board of Trustees of the Nevada Higher Education Tuition Trust Fund and professional investment advisors.
E	Variable — depends on market conditions and funds chosen.	Plan purchased will provide 100% and mandatory fees at public community colleges, universities, or a combination of the two. Value of the contract may also be used at public out-of-state, and private post-secondary educational institutions.
F	Any U.S. 2- and 4-year college and university, post-secondary trade and vocational school, and graduate and professional school that is eligible for federal financial aid, plus $10,000 per year tuition only benefit for primary and secondary schools, and up to a $10,000 lifetime cap on payments of principal and/or interest on qualified education loans.	Nevada public institution packages include four-year, two-year and one-year university plans, a two-year community college plan, or a combination plan. Weighted average tuition at in-state Nevada private institutions for both in-state Nevada private institutions and out-of-state institutions.

Savings Plan	Prepaid Plan
G	Open enrollment; join anytime.	Check with plan manager for current and future enrollment periods.
H	Distributions used for qualifying educational expenses are federally tax exempt. Nevada has no state income tax.	Distributions used for qualifying educational expenses are federally tax exempt. Nevada has no state income tax.
I	Both residents and nonresidents.	Account owner or designated beneficiary must be a Nevada resident or an alumnus/a of a Nevada college or university. Beneficiary age restrictions apply.
J	ABLE Nevada is offered throught the National ABLE Alliance and is administered by the Office of the Nevada Sate Treasurer.	

New Hampshire

	Savings Plan
A	**Fidelity Advisor 529 Plan** (invest with a financial advisor only). **UNIQUE College Investing Plan** (invest directly with the state).
B	Qualified educational expenses for primary, secondary, and post-secondary education; interest and/or principal on qualified education loans up to $10,000 lifetime.
C	Fidelity Investments.
D	Choice of age-based and static professionally managed investment funds.
E	Variable — depends on market conditions and funds chosen.
F	Any U.S. 2- and 4-year college and university, post-secondary trade and vocational school, and graduate and professional school that is eligible for federal financial aid, plus $10,000 per year tuition only benefit for primary and secondary schools and up to a $10,000 lifetime cap on payments of principal and/or interest on qualified education loans.
G	Open enrollment; join anytime.
H	Distributions used for qualifying educational expenses are federally income tax-exempt, and qualify for exemption from New Hampshire dividends and interest tax. New Hampshire doesn't have an income tax.
I	Both residents and nonresidents.
J	STABLE NH is offered by the STABLE Account Plan and administered by the New Hampshire State Treasurer and the New Hampshire Executive Director of the Governor's Commission on Disability.

New Jersey

	Savings Plan
A	**New Jersey 529 College Savings Plan** (invest directly with the state). **Franklin Templeton 529 College Savings Plan** (invest with a financial advisor).
B	Qualified educational expenses for primary, secondary, and post-secondary education; interest and/or principal on qualified education loans up to $10,000 lifetime.
C	Franklin Templeton Distributors, Inc.
D	Choice of age-based and static professionally managed investment funds.
E	Variable — depends on market conditions and funds chosen.
F	Any U.S. 2- and 4-year college and university, post-secondary trade and vocational school, and graduate and professional school that is eligible for federal financial aid, plus $10,000 per year tuition only benefit for primary and secondary schools and up to a $10,000 lifetime cap on payments of principal and/or interest on qualified education loans.
G	Open enrollment; join anytime.
H	Distributions used for qualifying educational expenses are state and federally tax exempt. Annual contributions of up to $10,000 ($10,000 for married filing joint taxpayers) are deductible from New Jersey resident income tax returns. Non-qualifying distributions are subject to income recapture on New Jersey income tax returns to the extent that deductions for contributions were taken.
I	Both residents and nonresidents may invest in the Franklin Templeton 529 College Savings Plan; the New Jersey 529 College Savings Plan may only be purchased by a New Jersey resident account owner or on behalf of a New Jersey resident designated beneficiary.
J	NJ ABLE is offered through the National ABLE Alliance and is administered by the New Jersey Department of the Treasury.

New Mexico

	Savings Plan	Prepaid Plan
A	**The Education Plan's College Savings Program** (invest directly with the state). **Scholar'sEdge** (invest through financial advisors only).	

Savings Plan	Prepaid Plan
B Qualified educational expenses for post-secondary education.	Tuition and mandatory fees only for post-secondary education.
C Ascensus College Savings Recordkeeping Services LLC.	
D Choice of age-based and static professionally managed investment funds.	
E Variable — depends on market conditions and funds chosen.	
F Any U.S. 2- and 4-year college and university, post-secondary trade and vocational school, and graduate and professional school that is eligible for federal financial aid, and up to a $10,000 lifetime cap on payments of principal and/or interest on qualified education loans.	
G Open enrollment; join anytime.	
H Distributions used for qualifying educational expenses are state and federally tax exempt. New Mexico gives residents an unlimited deduction against state income for annual contributions. Rollovers and non-qualifying distributions are subject to income recapture on New Mexico income tax returns to the extent that deductions for contributions were taken.	
I Both residents and nonresidents.	
J ABLE New Mexico is offered through the STABLE Account Plan and is administered by the Office of New Mexico State Treasurer.	

New York

Savings Plan
A **New York's 529 College Savings Program – Direct Plan** (invest directly with the state). **New York's 529 Advisor-Guided College Savings Plan** (invest with a financial advisor).
B Qualified educational expenses for post-secondary education.
C Ascensus Broker Dealer Services, Inc.
D Choice of age-based and static professionally managed investment funds.
E Variable — depends on market conditions and funds chosen.

	Savings Plan
F	Any U.S. 2- and 4-year college and university, post-secondary trade and vocational school, and graduate and professional school that is eligible for federal financial aid.
G	Open enrollment; join anytime.
H	Distributions used for qualifying educational expenses are state and federally tax exempt. Annual contributions of up to $5,000 ($10,000 for married filing joint tax-payers) are deductible from New York State (including New York City) resident income tax returns. Principal portion of rollovers and nonqualified distributions are subject to income recapture to the extent that a deduction was received for the contribution in a prior year. Trustee-to-trustee transfers between two New York 529 plans are exempt from income recapture provisions.
I	Both residents and nonresidents.
J	NY ABLE is issued by the New York Achieving a Better Life Experience (ABLE) Savings Account Program and is administered by the Office of the Comptroller of the State of New York.

North Carolina

	Savings Plan
A	**NC 529 Plan** (invest directly with the state). **Morgan Stanley National Advisory 529 Plan** (invest with a financial advisor).
B	Qualified educational expenses for primary, secondary, and post-secondary educa-tion; interest and/or principal on qualified education loans up to $10,000 lifetime.
C	The NC 529 Plan: College Foundation, Inc. Morgan Stanley National Advisory 529 Plan: Morgan Stanley Smith Barney LLC.
D	The NC 529 Plan has a choice of age-based and static Vanguard investment funds as well as a federally insured option offered by the State Employees' Credit Union. Morgan Stanley National Advisory 529 Plan offers 13 investment models represent-ing a variety of different risk levels ranging from conservative to all equity aggres-sive allocations.
E	Variable — depends on market conditions and funds chosen.
F	Any U.S. 2- and 4-year college and university, post-secondary trade and vocational school, and graduate and professional school that is eligible for federal financial aid, plus $10,000 per year tuition only benefit for primary and secondary schools, and up to a $10,000 lifetime cap on payments of principal and/or interest on qualified education loans.

Savings Plan	
G	Open enrollment; join anytime.
H	Distributions used for qualifying educational expenses are state and federally tax exempt.
I	Both residents and nonresidents.
J	NC ABLE is offered through the National ABLE Alliance and is administered by the North Carolina Department of State Treasurer.

North Dakota

Savings Plan	
A	**College SAVE** (invest directly with the state or with a financial advisor).
B	Qualified educational expenses for primary, secondary, and post-secondary education; interest and/or principal on qualified education loans up to a $10,000 lifetime.
C	Ascensus College Savings.
D	Choice of age-based and static professionally managed investment portfolios.
E	Variable — depends on market conditions and funds chosen.
F	Any U.S. 2- and 4-year college and university, post-secondary trade and vocational school, and graduate and professional school that is eligible for federal financial aid, plus $10,000 per year tuition only benefit for primary and secondary schools and up to a $10,000 lifetime cap on payments of principal and/or interest on qualified education loans.
G	Open enrollment; join anytime.
H	Distributions used for qualifying educational expenses are state and federally tax exempt. Annual contributions of up to $5,000 ($10,000 for married filing joint taxpayers) are deductible from North Dakota resident income tax returns. Principal portion nonqualified distributions are subject to income recapture to the extent that a deduction was received for the contribution in a prior year.
I	Both residents and nonresidents.
J	North Dakota has adopted laws related to the ABLE Act, but does not currently offer any state-sponsored plan. It encourages people who qualify for these accounts to open an ABLE account in another state.

Ohio

	Savings Plan
A	**Ohio's 529 Plan, CollegeAdvantage** (invest directly with the state). **BlackRock College Advantage Advisor 529 Savings Plan** (invest with a financial advisor).
B	Qualified educational expenses for primary, secondary, and post-secondary education; interest and/or principal on qualified education loans up to a $10,000 lifetime.
C	Ohio's 529 Plan, College Advantage: Ohio Tuition Trust Authority. BlackRock College Advantage Advisor 529 Savings Plan: BlackRock Advisors, LLC.
D	Choice of age-based and static professionally managed investment portfolios.
E	Variable — depends on market conditions and funds chosen.
F	Any U.S. 2- and 4-year college and university, post-secondary trade and vocational school, and graduate and professional school that is eligible for federal financial aid, plus $10,000 per year tuition only benefit for primary and secondary schools and up to a $10,000 lifetime cap on payments of principal and/or interest on qualified education loans.
G	Open enrollment; join anytime.
H	Distributions used for qualifying educational expenses are state and federally tax exempt. Ohio residents may deduct up to $4,000/beneficiary annually ($4,000 for married filing joint taxpayers). There is an unlimited carryover period for excess contributions. The principal portion of nonqualifying distributions are subject to Ohio income recapture provisions to the extent that income tax deductions were taken for contributions. Nonqualifying distributions made on account of death, disability or scholarship receipt are exempt from income recapture for Ohio income tax purposes.
I	Both residents and nonresidents.
J	STABLE Account is offered and administered by the Office of the Ohio State Treasurer.

Oklahoma

	Savings Plan
A	**Oklahoma 529** (invest directly with the state). **Oklahoma Dream 529 Plan** (invest with a financial advisor).
B	Qualified educational expenses for primary, secondary, and post-secondary education.

	Savings Plan
C	Oklahoma 529: TIAA-CREF Tuition Financing, Inc.
	Oklahoma Dream 529 Plan: Fidelity Investments.
D	Choice of age-based and static professionally managed investment funds.
E	Variable — depends on market conditions and funds chosen.
F	Any U.S. 2- and 4-year college and university, post-secondary trade and vocational school, and graduate and professional school that is eligible for federal financial aid, plus $10,000 per year tuition only benefit for primary and secondary schools.
G	Open enrollment; join anytime.
H	Distributions used for qualifying educational expenses are state and federally tax exempt. Annual contributions of up to a $10,000 ($20,000 for married filing joint taxpayers) are deductible from Oklahoma resident income tax returns, with a 5-year carryover period for excess contributions. Principal portion nonqualified distributions (other than for death, disability, or receipt of scholarship) and rollovers made within one year of the date of contribution are subject to income recapture to the extent that a deduction was received for the contribution in a prior year.
I	Both residents and nonresidents.
J	Oklahoma STABLE is offered by the Oklahoma State Treasurer and administered by the Ohio Treasurer's Office.

Oregon

	Savings Plan
A	**Oregon College Savings Plan** (invest directly with state).
	MFS 529 Savings Plan (invest through financial advisors only).
B	Qualified educational expenses for post-secondary education.
C	Sumday Administration, LLC.
D	Choice of age-based and static professionally managed investment funds.
E	Variable — depends on market conditions and funds chosen.
F	Any U.S. 2- and 4-year college and university, post-secondary trade and vocational school, and graduate and professional school that is eligible for federal financial aid.
G	Open enrollment; join anytime.

	Savings Plan
H	Distributions used for qualifying educational expenses are state and federally tax exempt. Annual contributions made by Oregon taxpayers are eligible for up to a $150 tax credit ($300 for married filing joint taxpayers). Principal portion of non qualified withdrawals are subject to income recapture on Oregon income tax returns to the extent prior deductions were taken for contributions. There is no recapture provision for rollovers.
I	Both residents and nonresidents.
J	Oregon ABLE Savings Plan is offered and administered by The Oregon 529 Savings Board and is only available to Oregon residents. The ABLE for All plan is also offered and administered by The Oregon 529 Savings Board and is available to Both residents and nonresidents.

Pennsylvania

	Savings Plan	Prepaid Unit/Guaranteed
A	**Pennsylvania 529 Investment Plan** (invest directly with the state).	**Pennsylvania 529 Guaranteed Savings Plan** (invest directly with the state).
B	Qualified educational expenses for primary, secondary, and post-secondary education.	Qualified educational expenses for post-secondary education.
C	Pennsylvania Treasury Department with Ascensus College Savings as recordkeeper and servicing agent.	Delaware Investments.
D	Choice of age-based and static professionally managed investment funds.	Pennsylvania residents acquire units that increase in value over time to track average tuition increases in one of several school categories as selected by the participant. Participant can switch categories to fit expected needs.
E	Variable — depends on market conditions and funds chosen.	Depends on tuition rate of inflation in category chosen by participant.
F	Any U.S. 2- and 4-year college and university, post-secondary trade and vocational school, and graduate and professional school that is eligible for federal financial aid, plus $10,000 per year tuition only benefit for primary and secondary schools.	Any U.S. 2- and 4-year college and university, post-secondary trade and vocational school, and graduate and professional school that is eligible for federal financial aid.
G	Open enrollment; join anytime.	Open enrollment; join anytime. New prices for different categories are set each year on September 1.

Savings Plan	Prepaid Unit/Guaranteed
H Distributions used for qualifying educational expenses are state and federally tax exempt. Annual contributions of up to the 2022 annual federal gift tax exclusion of $16,000/beneficiary ($32,000 for married filing joint taxpayers) are deductible from Pennsylvania resident income tax returns. Pennsylvania per beneficiary deduction will adjust in concert with increases to annual federal gift tax exclusion. Principal portion of non-qualified distributions (other than for death, disability, or receipt of scholarship) are subject to income recapture to the extent that a deduction was received for the contribution in a prior year. Rollovers are not eligible for Pennsylvania income tax deduction.	Distributions used for qualifying educational expenses are state and federally tax exempt. Annual contributions of up to the 2022 annual federal gift tax exclusion of $16,000/beneficiary ($32,000 for married filing joint taxpayers) are deductible from Pennsylvania resident income tax returns. Pennsylvania per beneficiary deduction will adjust in concert with increases to annual federal gift tax exclusion. Principal portion of nonqualified distributions (other than for death, disability, or receipt of scholarship) are subject to income recapture to the extent that a deduction was received for the contribution in a prior year. Rollovers are not eligible for Pennsylvania income tax deduction.
I Both residents and nonresidents.	Account owner or designated beneficiary must be Pennsylvania resident at time of enrollment in account. Age restrictions apply.
J PA ABLE is offered by the Commonwealth of Pennsylvania and administered by the Pennsylvania Treasurer.	

Private, non state-specific prepaid plan

	Prepaid Plan
A	**Private College 529 Plan** (invest directly with the state).
B	Qualified tuition and mandatory fees for up to five years of undergraduate study.
C	Intuition College Savings Solutions, LLC.
D	Investments are made in tuition certificates eligible for redemption against tuition and mandatory fees at each participating institution.
E	Variable — depends on market conditions and funds chosen.
F	Any participating college or university (there are currently hundreds, and new ones are constantly being recruited). Institution does not need to be identified at the point of purchase of tuition certificates. If designated beneficiary chooses to go to a nonparticipating institution, the plan may be rolled over to a different designated beneficiary or a full or partial refund may be requested.
G	Open enrollment; join anytime.

Prepaid Plan	
H	Distributions used for qualifying educational expenses are state and federally tax exempt. State tax deductions may be available if your state offers a tax deduction for contributions into any plan.
I	No residency requirements. Significant time restrictions apply.

Rhode Island

Savings Plan	
A	**CollegeBound Saver** (invest directly with the state). **CollegeBound 529** (invest with a financial advisor).
B	Qualified educational expenses for primary, secondary, and post-secondary education; interest and/or principal on qualified education loans up to a $10,000 lifetime.
C	Ascencus College Savings.
D	Choice of age-based and static professionally managed investment funds.
E	Variable — depends on market conditions and funds chosen.
F	Any U.S. 2- and 4-year college and university, post-secondary trade and vocational school, and graduate and professional school that is eligible for federal financial aid, plus $10,000 per year tuition only benefit for primary and secondary schools and up to a $10,000 lifetime cap on payments of principal and/or interest on qualified education loans.
G	Open enrollment; join anytime.
H	Distributions used for qualifying educational expenses are state and federally tax exempt. Annual contributions of up to $500 ($1,000 for married filing joint taxpayers) may be deducted from Rhode Island resident income tax returns; excess contributions may be carried forward indefinitely. The principal portion of rollovers of nonqualified distributions are subject to income recapture of the prior two years deductions.
I	Both residents and nonresidents.
J	RI's ABLE is offered by the Executive Office of Health and Human Services and is administered by the State Investment Commission.

South Carolina

	Savings Plan
A	**Future Scholar 529 College Savings Plan** (invest directly with the state or with a financial advisor).
B	Qualified educational expenses for primary, secondary, and post-secondary education; interest and/or principal on qualified education loans up to a $10,000 lifetime.
C	Columbia Management Advisors, LLC.
D	Choice of age-based and static professionally managed investment funds.
E	Variable — depends on market conditions and funds chosen.
F	Any U.S. 2- and 4-year college and university, post-secondary trade and vocational school, and graduate and professional school that is eligible for federal financial aid, plus $10,000 per year tuition only benefit for primary and secondary schools and up to a $10,000 lifetime cap on payments of principal and/or interest on qualified education loans.
G	Open enrollment; join anytime.
H	Distributions used for qualifying educational expenses are state and federally tax exempt. All contributions (including rollovers) into plan are deductible from South Carolina resident income tax returns. The principal portion of nonqualifying distributions are subject to income recapture to the extent of prior South Carolina tax deductions. Rollovers do not need to be recaptured.
I	May only invest directly if account owner or designated beneficiary is a South Carolina resident or a state employee at the time of enrollment. Nonresidents may only invest through a financial advisor.
J	Palmetto ABLE Savings Program is offered by the Office of the South Carolina Treasurer and is administered by the Ohio Treasurer's Office.

South Dakota

	Savings Plan
A	**CollegeAccess 529** (invest directly with the state or with a financial advisor).
B	Qualified educational expenses for primary, secondary, and post-secondary education; interest and/or principal on qualified education loans up to a $10,000 lifetime.
C	VP Distributors LLC.
D	Choice of age-based and static professionally managed investment funds.

	Savings Plan
E	Variable — depends on market conditions and funds chosen.
F	Any U.S. 2- and 4-year college and university, post-secondary trade and vocational school, and graduate and professional school that is eligible for federal financial aid, plus $10,000 per year tuition only benefit for primary and secondary schools and up to a $10,000 lifetime cap on payments of principal and/or interest on qualified education loans.
G	Open enrollment; join anytime.
H	Distributions used for qualifying educational expenses are federally tax exempt. South Dakota has no state income tax.
I	May only invest directly in CollegeAccess 529 if account owner or designated beneficiary is a South Dakota resident at the time of enrollment. Nonresidents may only invest with a financial advisor.
J	South Dakota has not passed ABLE legislation and currently offers no state-sponsored ABLE plan. The South Dakota Investment Council suggests qualified individuals open an ABLE account in another state.

Tennessee

	Savings Plan
A	**TNStars College Savings 529 Plan** (invest directly with the state).
B	Qualified educational expenses for primary, secondary, and post-secondary education; interest and/or principal on qualified education loans up to a $10,000 lifetime.
C	State of Tennessee Department of Treasury.
D	Choice of age-based and static professionally managed investment funds.
E	Variable — depends on market conditions and funds chosen.
F	Any U.S. 2- and 4-year college and university, post-secondary trade and vocational school, and graduate and professional school that is eligible for federal financial aid, plus $10,000 per year tuition only benefit for primary and secondary schools and up to a $10,000 lifetime cap on payments of principal and/or interest on qualified education loans.
G	Open enrollment; join anytime.
H	Distributions used for qualifying educational expenses are state and federally tax exempt. There is no income tax deduction available to Tennessee residents on Tennessee income tax returns.

Savings Plan	
I	Both residents and nonresidents.
J	ABLE TN is offered and administered by the Tennessee Department of Treasury.

Texas

	Savings Plan	Prepaid Plan
A	**Texas College Savings Plan** (invest directly with the state). **LoneStar 529 Plan** (invest directly with a financial advisor).	**Texas Tuition Promise Fund** (invest directly with the state).
B	Qualified educational expenses for primary, secondary, and post-secondary education; interest and/or principal on qualified education loans up to a $10,000 lifetime.	Unit-based plan prepays future tuition and mandatory fees at Texas public institutions.
C	Orion Advisor Solutions, Inc.	Orion Advisor Solutions, Inc.
D	Choice of age-based and static professionally managed investment funds.	
E	Variable — depends on market conditions and funds chosen.	Guaranteed to pay in-state public institutions tuition and mandatory fees based on the number of units required by the institution, and the number of units purchased.
F	Any U.S. 2- and 4-year college and university, post-secondary trade and vocational school, and graduate and professional school that is eligible for federal financial aid, plus $10,000 per year tuition only benefit for primary and secondary schools, and up to a $10,000 lifetime cap on payments of principal and/or interest on qualified education loans.	Any Texas public 2- and 4-year college or university, excluding medical and dental faculties. For private institutions or out-of-state public institutions, a transfer value of your units may be applied toward tuition and mandatory costs.
G	Open enrollment; join anytime.	Enrollments for new participants can be made anytime between September 1 and February 28/29. Enrollments for children under age 1 extends through July 31.
H	Distributions used for qualifying educational expenses are federally tax exempt. Texas has no state income tax.	Distributions used for qualifying educational expenses are federally tax exempt. Texas has no state income tax.

	Savings Plan	Prepaid Plan
I	Both residents and nonresidents.	Beneficiary must be a Texas resident at the time of enrollment, or must have a parent who is a Texas resident and the named purchaser at the time of enrollment.
		Beneficiary may not use tuition units within three years of the units' purchase. Tuition units must be used within ten years after the projected date of high school graduation, excluding any periods of active military service.
J	Texas ABLE is offered and administered by the Texas Prepaid Higher Education Tuition Board.	

Utah

	Savings Plan
A	**my529** (invest directly with the state).
B	Qualified educational expenses for primary, secondary and post-secondary education; interest and/or principal on qualified education loans up to a $10,000 lifetime.
C	Utah Higher Education Assistance Authority.
D	Choice of age-based and static professionally managed investment funds.
E	Variable — depends on market conditions and funds chosen.
F	Any U.S. 2- and 4-year college and university, post-secondary trade and vocational school, and graduate and professional school that is eligible for federal financial aid, plus $10,000 per year tuition only benefit for primary and secondary schools, and up to a $10,000 lifetime cap on payments of principal and/or interest on qualified education loans.
G	Open enrollment; join anytime.
H	Distributions used for qualifying educational expenses are state and federally tax exempt. Utah offers a 4.95 percent tax credit on the first $2,130/beneficiary ($4,260/beneficiary for married filing joint taxpayers) in 2022. The credit is adjusted annually for inflation. Principal portion of rollovers and nonqualified withdrawals from the plan is included in Utah income to the extent of prior Utah deductions and/or tax credits.
I	Both residents and nonresidents.
J	ABLE Utah is offered by the Utah Department of Workforce Services and Utah State Treasurer's Office, and is administered by the State of Ohio.

Vermont

	Savings Plan
A	**Vermont Higher Education Investment Plan** (invest directly with the state).
B	Qualified educational expenses for primary, secondary, and post-secondary education; interest and/or principal on qualified education loans up to a $10,000 lifetime.
C	Intuition College Savings Solutions, LLC.
D	Choice of age-based and static professionally managed investment funds.
E	Variable — depends on market conditions and funds chosen.
F	Any U.S. 2- and 4-year college and university, post-secondary trade and vocational school, and graduate and professional school that is eligible for federal financial aid, plus $10,000 per year tuition only benefit for primary and secondary schools and up to a $10,000 lifetime cap on payments of principal and/or interest on qualified education loans.
G	Open enrollment; join anytime.
H	Distributions used for qualifying educational expenses are state and federally tax exempt. Vermont residents may claim a non-refundable tax credit of up to $250/beneficiary ($500/beneficiary for married filing joint taxpayers) for accounts owned by the taxpayer as well as for gift contributions made to accounts owned by others. The principal portion of nonqualified withdrawals is subject to income recapture. Outbound rollovers are exempt from income recapture.
I	Both residents and nonresidents.
J	Vermont ABLE is offered and administered by the Vermont State Treasurer.

Virginia

	Savings Plan
A	**Invest529** (invest directly with the state). **CollegeAmerica** (invest through financial advisors only).
B	Qualified educational expenses for primary, secondary, and post-secondary education; interest and/or principal on qualified education loans up to a $10,000 lifetime.
C	Invest529: Virginia 529 Board and its CEO. CollegeAmerica: American Funds Service Company, American Funds Distributors, and Capital Research and Management Company.

	Savings Plan
D	Choice of age-based and static professional managed investment funds.
E	Variable — depends on market conditions and funds chosen.
F	Any U.S. 2- and 4-year college and university, post-secondary trade and vocational school, and graduate and professional school that is eligible for federal financial aid, plus $10,000 per year tuition only benefit for primary and secondary schools, and up to a $10,000 lifetime cap on payments of principal and/or interest on qualified education loans.
G	Open enrollment; join anytime.
H	Distributions used for qualifying educational expenses are state and federally tax exempt. Virginia offers a $4,000/beneficiary ($4,000 for married filing joint taxpayers) income tax deduction, with an unlimited carryforward of excess contributions. Contributions from a non-account holder are deductible by the account holder, not the contributor. Principal portion of rollovers and nonqualified distributions are recaptured for Virginia income tax purposes to the extent of prior deductions. Nonqualifying distributions made on the basis of death, disability, or receipt of a scholarship are not subject to income recapture.
I	Both residents and nonresidents. Some age and time requirements apply.
J	ABLEnow is offered and administered by the Virginia College Savings Plan. ABLEAmerica is the first ABLE plan available through financial advisors. It is offered and administered through Virginia529, with American Funds as its investment manager.

Washington

	Savings Plan	Prepaid Plan
A	**DreamAhead College Investment Plan** (invest directly with the state).	**Guaranteed Education Tuition (GET)** (invest directly with the state).
B	Qualified educational expenses for primary, secondary, and post-secondary education; interest and/or principal on qualified education loans up to $10,000 lifetime.	Tuition and mandatory fees for post-secondary education; to the extent a program has been funded with excess units, the excess units may be used to pay for other qualified post-secondary educational expenses. The value of each unit may also be used to pay tuition and mandatory fees at private colleges or public out-of-state institutions. Also, GET units may be used to pay interest and/or principal on qualified education loans up to a $10,000.
C	Vestwell State Savings, LLC.	Committee on Advanced Tuition Payment and College Savings (WA529 Committee).

Savings Plan	Prepaid Plan
D	Choice of age-based and static professional managed investment funds.	Fixed investment plan as determined by Washington State.
E	Variable — depends on market conditions and funds chosen.	Each 100 units purchased is guaranteed to pay one year of tuition and mandatory fees at the highest cost Washington State public university. Return is guaranteed by Washington State.
F	Any U.S. 2- and 4-year college and university, post-secondary trade and vocational school, and graduate and professional school that is eligible for federal financial aid, plus $10,000 per year tuition only benefit for primary and secondary schools, and up to a $10,000 lifetime cap on payments of principal and/or interest on qualified education loans.	Any U.S. 2- and 4-year college and university, post-secondary trade and vocational school, and graduate and professional school that is eligible for federal financial aid, and up to a $10,000 lifetime cap on payments of principal and/or interest on qualified education loans.
G	Open enrollment – join anytime.	November 1 – May 31 annually. Units can be purchased at annual unit price through June 25 each year.
H	Distributions used for qualifying educational expenses are federally tax exempt. Washington State has no state income tax.	Distributions used for qualifying educational expenses are federally tax exempt. Washington State has no state income tax.
I	Both residents and nonresidents.	Designated beneficiary or account owner of plan must be a resident of Washington State at time of enrollment. Some age restrictions apply.
J	Washington State ABLE Plan is offered and administered by the Governing Board of the Washington Achieving a Better Life Experience Program.	

West Virginia

Savings Plan	
A	**SMART529 WV Direct College Savings Plan** (invest directly with the state). **SMART529 Select** (invest directly with the state). **The Hartford SMART529** (invest with a financial advisor).
B	Qualified educational expenses for primary, secondary, and post-secondary education; interest and/or principal on qualified education loans up to a $10,000 lifetime.
C	Hartford Funds Management Company, LLC.
D	Choice of age-based and static professionally managed investment funds.

	Savings Plan
E	Variable — depends on market conditions and funds chosen.
F	Any U.S. 2- and 4-year college and university, post-secondary trade and vocational school, and graduate and professional school that is eligible for federal financial aid, plus $10,000 per year tuition only benefit for primary and secondary schools, and up to a $10,000 lifetime cap on payments of principal and/or interest on qualified education loans.
G	Open enrollment; join anytime.
H	Distributions used for qualifying educational expenses are state and federally tax exempt. All contributions into plan are deductible from West Virginia resident income tax returns. Principal portion of nonqualifying distributions are recaptured into West Virginia income to the extent prior deductions were taken.
I	SMART529 WV Direct College Savings Plan: account owner or designated beneficiary must have a West Virginia mailing address or be a West Virginia resident on active duty in the US Military. Smart529 Select and The Hartford 529 are open to Both residents and nonresidents.
J	WVABLE is offered by the West Virginia State Treasurer's Office and is administered by the State of Ohio.

Wisconsin

	Savings Plan
A	**EdVest** (invest directly with the state or with a financial advisor). **Tomorrow's Scholar 529 Plan** (invest only through financial advisors).
B	Qualified educational expenses for primary, secondary, and post-secondary education; interest and/or principal on qualified education loans up to $10,000 lifetime.
C	TIAA-CREF Tuition Financing, Inc.
D	Choice of age-based and static professionally managed investment funds.
E	Variable — depends on market conditions and funds chosen.
F	Any U.S. 2- and 4-year college and university, post-secondary trade and vocational school, and graduate and professional school that is eligible for federal financial aid, plus $10,000 per year tuition-only benefit for primary and secondary schools and up to a $10,000 lifetime cap on payments of principal and/or interest on qualified education loans.

	Savings Plan
G	Open enrollment; join anytime.
H	Distributions used for qualifying educational expenses are state and federally tax exempt. Annual contributions of up to $3,560/beneficiary ($3,560/beneficiary for married filing joint taxpayers) are deductible from Wisconsin resident income tax returns. Per beneficiary income tax deductions are adjusted annually for inflation. Contributions in excess of the maximum deductible may be carried forward indefinitely. The principal portion of nonqualifying distributions is subject to income recapture to the extent that prior deductions were taken. Nonqualifying distributions made due to death, disability, or scholarship receipt are exempt from income recapture.
I	Both residents and nonresidents.
J	Wisconsin passed, and then repealed, ABLE legislation and currently offers no state-sponsored ABLE plan. Wisconsin suggests qualified individuals open an ABLE account in another state.

Wyoming

	Savings Plan
A	Wyoming offers no 529 plan. Wyoming residents looking to invest in a 529 plan should investigate the plans offered in other states.
J	WYABLE is offered by the Governor's Council on Developmental Disabilities of the State of Wyoming and is administered by the State of Ohio.

Index

A

automatically scheduled bank withdrawals, for funding Section 529 plans, 100–102

awards and scholarships

about, 108, 283–284

American Opportunity Credit, 77–78, 108, 259–260, 298–299

AmeriCorps, 293–294

assessing from employers, 37

charitable foundations, 289–290

corporate-sponsored, 288–289

from employer, 285–286

employer-sponsored programs, 286

employer-sponsored tuition assistance/ reimbursement programs, 287–288

in exchange for service, 290–295

Lifetime Learning Credit, 77–78, 108, 298–299

local civic groups, 288

military, 291–293

municipal, 290

from prospective college, 285

Public Health Service, 294–295

ROTC, 293

searching for, 284–290

self-employment income from fellowships, 297–298

service academy, 293

state, 290

as a student resource, 47

taxes and, 295–299

unneeded, 287

B

Backer.com, 61

bad debt, 62–63

beneficiaries

changing

about, 127–128, 133

for Coverdell accounts, 156–159

maximum age of successor, 157–158

transferring to others with Coverdell accounts, 193–194

trust accounts and, 232–233

Best Buy, 288

birth, saving from, 64–65

bond options, 173–174

books

costs for, 23–24

as qualified education expenses, 144, 145

borrowing

against cash value in whole life policies, 277–278

money, 16

bracket ride, 239

brokerage accounts, as an investment option, 218–220

Burger King, 288

business schools, sample yearly tuition costs for, 32

buy orders, placing, 176

buying

student housing, 267–268

U.S. Savings Bonds, 211–212

C

calculating

costs, 10

distributions for traditional IRAs, 246–247

taxes on unused funds, 134–135

Calgon, 288

California

sample yearly tuition costs in, 27, 28

Section 529 plans in, 337–338

career training schools, costs for, 25

cash value

in homes, 37

in whole life insurance policies, 15, 274–278

CESAs (Coverdell Education Savings Accounts)

about, 12–13, 139–140, 142, 161–162, 187–188

account owner, 142

changing account beneficiaries, 156–159

cons of, 190–199

contribution limits, 149–151

contributions to, 39, 148–154

creating investment strategies for, 167–176

E

F

About the Author

Margaret Atkins Munro, EA (who answers to Peggy and is still trying to figure out why her parents named her Margaret) is a tax consultant/advisor/writer/lecturer with over 40 years of experience in various areas of finance and taxation. She is an enrolled agent licensed by the federal government to represent clients in the areas of tax and tax-related issues. She currently operates a widely diverse private practice specializing in the financial concerns of families with school-age children, a group near and dear to her heart.

In addition to counseling her clients with young families on the advisability of college savings plans, Peggy has great personal experience in the area of paying for college. She began receiving grants and loans in 1977, helped pay for her husband's education, and has hopefully finished paying her son's loans, 45 years after she began accumulating her own college debt.

Peggy is a graduate of The Johns Hopkins University and has also attended University College Cork and the Pontifical Institute of Mediaeval Studies in Toronto. She lives with her husband, Colin, on the back of an active volcano in Costa Rica, together with their three golden retrievers and two cats of dubious heritage.

Dedication

To my family, both two- and four-footed, who are my everything.

Author's Acknowledgments

Where does anyone begin with a project of this size and depth? To everyone who ever commented on my writing, my teachers who taught me when and when not to dangle a participle, my legal and tax mentors over decades of working with clients to plan the best outcomes for them and their families, and my clients, who put up with my constant "on the other hand, you could do this." This book has been written on the back of vast experience, both good and bad, and I could not have done it without everyone already mentioned and those not mentioned at all.

I would like to give a special shout-out to my good friend Kirk Shamberger and his encyclopedic knowledge of life insurance in all its shapes, sizes, and colors. His assistance was invaluable.

Finally, special thanks to my editors at Wiley, who have once again done a sterling job keeping me on task and making sure that I've formatted everything correctly.

Publisher's Acknowledgments

Acquisitions Editor: Tracy Boggier
Project Manager: Rick Kughen
Development Editor: Rick Kughen
Technical Editor: Mark Friedlich

Production Editor: Tamilmani Varadharaj
Cover Image: © porcorex/Getty Images